Sannyasa Darshan

With kind regards, ॐ and prem

Swami Niranjan

Sannyasa Darshan

A Treatise on Traditional and Contemporary Sannyasa

Swami Niranjanananda Saraswati

*Lectures given during the one year Sannyasa Training
Course held at Ganga Darshan, Munger, in 1991*

Yoga Publications Trust, Munger, Bihar, India

Published by Sri Panchdashnam Paramahamsa Alakh Bara
    First edition 1993

Published by Yoga Publications Trust
    Reprinted with corrections 2005

ISBN: 81-85787-72-7

Publisher and distributor: Yoga Publications Trust, Ganga Darshan, Munger, Bihar, India.

Printed at Thomson Press (India) Limited, New Delhi, 110001

SWAMI SIVANANDA SARASWATI

Swami Sivananda was born at Pattamadai, Tamil Nadu, in 1887. After serving as a medical doctor in Malaya, he renounced his practice, went to Rishikesh and was initiated into Dashnami sannyasa in 1924 by Swami Vishwananda Saraswati. He toured extensively throughout India, inspiring people to practise yoga and lead a divine life. He founded the Divine Life Society at Rishikesh in 1936, the Sivananda Ayurvedic Pharmacy in 1945, the Yoga Vedanta Forest Academy in 1948 and the Sivananda Eye Hospital in 1957. During his lifetime Swami Sivananda guided thousands of disciples and aspirants all over the world and authored over 200 books.

SWAMI SATYANANDA SARASWATI

Swami Satyananda was born at Almora, Uttar Pradesh, in 1923. In 1943 he met Swami Sivananda in Rishikesh and adopted the Dashnami sannyasa way of life. In 1955 he left his guru's ashram to live as a wandering mendicant and later founded the International Yoga Fellowship in 1956 and the Bihar School of Yoga in 1963. Over the next 20 years Swami Satyananda toured internationally and authored over 80 books. In 1987 he founded Sivananda Math, a charitable institution for aiding rural development, and the Yoga Research Foundation. In 1988 he renounced his mission, adopting kshetra sannyasa, and now lives as a paramahamsa sannyasin.

SWAMI NIRANJANANANDA SARASWATI

Swami Niranjanananda was born in Madhya Pradesh in 1960. At the age of four he joined the Bihar School of Yoga and was initiated into Dashnami sannyasa at the age of ten. From 1971 he travelled overseas and toured many countries for the next 11 years. In 1983 he was recalled to India and appointed President of Bihar School of Yoga. Since then he has guided the development of Ganga Darshan, Sivananda Math, Yoga Publications Trust and the Yoga Research Foundation. In 1990 he was initiated as a paramahamsa and in 1993 anointed preceptor in succession to Swami Satyananda. Bihar Yoga Bharati was founded under his direction in 1994. He has authored over 20 books and guides national and international yoga programs.

SWAMI SATYASANGANANDA SARASWATI

Swami Satyasangananda (Satsangi) was born on 24th March 1953, in Chandorenagore, West Bengal. From the age of 22 she experienced a series of inner awakenings which led her to her guru, Swami Satyananda. From 1981 she travelled ceaselessly with her guru in India and overseas and developed into a scholar with deep insight into the yogic and tantric traditions as well as modern sciences and philosophies. She is an efficient channel for the transmission of her guru's teachings. The establishment of Sivananda Math in Rikhia is her creation and mission, and she guides all its activities there, working tirelessly to uplift the weaker and underprivileged areas. She embodies compassion with clear reason and is the foundation of her guru's vision.

Message to New Sannyasins

Sannyasa is not merely an order.
It is a complete spiritual life,
Both exoteric and esoteric.
Manifestation of unqualified consciousness takes place
And the light of atman shines.

Why sadhana for a sannyasin?
Let him stand as a witness.
Let him stand as a non-doer.

Various yoga practices
Constitute gross practices for a sannyasin,
For these practices do not eradicate
The dross of inner life,
Nor do they bring the knowledge
Of the true spirit.

A sannyasin should enter into ashram life
And stay there for quite a long period,
In a life of spirit and service,
And thus render himself
Humble and egoless.

For a sannyasin
There is nothing as sadhana,
And nothing as an ultimate.
Even the state of turiya
Is non-existent for a sannyasin,
Because sannyasa is to attain total equilibrium.

The spiritual state is eternal,
It is always there.
This a sannyasin has to know.
Renounce the sacred thread and chop the tuft

And renounce the association
With the previous relations,
Together with caste, tribe, sect.
All these constitute the gross man.

Gradually the stages of sannyasa will manifest,
The spirit of service will unfold
Various stages of sannyasa.
Guru is the master key for a sannyasin.

Do not go the wrong way
When you are convalescing.
Do not ignore the rules of sannyasa.
Live by yourself,
Free from attachment.
Do not attend marriage ceremonies,
Burial ceremonies, ancestral worship.
Very few can see why.

When sannyasa blooms
And knowledge dawns
And power unfolds,
It sanctifies history and posterity.
One single sannyasin
Can be the creator of an epoch,
A seer of intuition
And a mastermind of tradition.

Keeping this ablaze in your mind,
Step into sannyasa.

Swami Satyananda Saraswati

Sannyasa Mala

Sannyasa life is a training in dedication;
This was the vision of Swami Sivanandaji,
Which was fulfilled by Swami Satyanandaji.
This was the first vision of India;
Awakened men should walk the planet.

Only those can quench the spiritual thirst of society
Who live away from the physical attractions
and the world,
And through dedication, service, study and sadhana
Can lead an untainted life, like a lotus in water.

Sannyasa is not renunciation;
It is sacrifice.
Sacrifice is not death;
It is life dedicated to service.

One does not colour life
By wearing geru robes.
When one forgets about the colours and clothes,
Then life itself is coloured.

Sannyasa is not achieved
By keeping matted locks or shaven head.
One who is dedicated to service
Cannot think about his hair and body.

There is madness in sannyasa
Towards commitment and guru,
Towards the world, humanity and God.

Swami Niranjanananda Saraswati

Contents

Introduction	1
Sannyasa Parampara	
1. Origin of Sannyasa	7
2. The Ashrama System	12
3. Rishis and Munis	17
4. Caste system	22
5. Sannyasa tradition	27
6. Renunciation Rites	33
7. Stages of Sannyasa	38
8. Traditional Rules and Requirements	43
9. Shaiva Sampradaya	47
10. Advent of Shankara	51
11. Dashnama Sannyasa Order	56
12. Dashnami Akhara and Alaka Bara	60
13. Vaishnava Sampradaya	66
Sannyasa Today	
14. Song of the Sannyasin	73
15. Sannyasa in Modern Times	77
16. Who is Eligible for Sannyasa?	83
17. Code of Conduct	91
18. Qualities of a Sannyasin	103
19. Role of the Guru	112
20. Food for Sannyasins	121
21. Sublimation and Sannyasa	128
22. Suppression and Control	135
23. Keeping a Spiritual Diary	140
24. Women and Sannyasa	145
25. Women Saints and Sannyasins of India	150

Sannyasa Lineage
26. Dattatreya   169
27. Shankaracharya   231
28. Swami Sivananda   256
29. Swami Satyananda   279

Sannyasa Upanishads
30. Nirvanopanishad   345
31. Kundikopanishad   398
32. Bhikshukopanishad   411
33. Avadhootopanishad   415
34. Paramahamsa Parivrajaka Upanishad   430

Glossary   446
Index   465

Introduction

The sannyasa tradition should not be confused with any form of organized religion. The concept and aim of sannyasa predates every kind of religion in existence in the world today. Sannyasa is not just an Indian tradition, but a universal tradition which represents the original spiritual thoughts of humanity. Prior to the advent and organization of religions such as Christianity, Islam and Buddhism, people had their views about spiritual life. In every culture there have been people who had spiritual experiences and who have thought about spiritual life and values, and along with these thoughts, different systems of understanding spirituality arose.

From the beginning, man has believed in the existence of the soul, and so the question has arisen as to what happens after death. This question has led people to investigate many areas of thought and belief, and thus the different cultures have devised their own ways for the attainment of realization. Despite the diversities in each culture, certain common ideas about spirituality are found which have linked the spiritual thoughts together. The common ideas are contemplation, introspection, faith, prayer, devotion and self-study. These concepts and ideas gave birth to different meditative techniques, which suited the people of each culture.

In order to follow a life of contemplation, meditation, self-study and analysis, people had to disassociate themselves

1

from external distractions and go and live in the seclusion of forests or jungles, where they were free to follow their own pursuits. In the course of time, groups of such people became known by many different names. One common name was 'mystic'. We find the same link in the Essene, Celtic, Taoist and other traditions of the past. So, the pursuit of spiritual experience is the basic desire of humanity. The discovery of the Self, the experience of the divine power and the awakening of the dormant potential of the personality are ideas which have always attracted people.

Powerful people like Christ, Mohammed and Buddha were able to translate the age-old tradition into the current languages of those days, with the idea of increasing spiritual awareness within the social framework. Their thoughts and interpretation of spiritual experience according to the social context gave birth to many new philosophies. Later on, their ideas were given the structure of a religion by their followers. In order not to deviate from the spiritual tradition, religion was further divided into two groups, one which could be followed by ordinary people and another which could be followed, preserved and propagated by a select group of monks. That is the form of religion which we find today.

The sannyasa tradition, however, has always remained very aloof from and opposed to such kinds of religious influence. There have been many saints and sages who, with their experience, understanding and exposition, could have created new philosophies and religions, but did not wish to alienate themselves from the mainstream of spiritual thought. Such examples are found in the Indian tradition of spirituality. The Vedas, Upanishads and other systems of Indian thought, such as Samkhya, Nyaya, Mimamsa and Tantra, reflect the depth of understanding of such seers and saints. At the end of their spiritual quest they have all voiced the same opinion and have insisted, "Let our ideas not become a religion, rather let them be incorporated in the spiritual thought of humanity." Therefore, when we

2

speak of the sannyasa tradition, we are not talking about an order which adheres to one particular system of thought, but which has maintained and transmitted a collection of many experiences and teachings which have come down through the ages. Today this collection has come to be known as Hinduism, but in actual truth there is no such thing as Hinduism.

The word 'Hindu' was coined by the invaders of this country to identify the people who lived beyond the river Indus. It is similar to today's concept of East and West. Those who live in the East are known as Easterners and those who live in the West are known as Westerners. This is a very inadequate description for a culture which has developed its spiritual thought to such a vast extent. The real name by which this culture was known is *Sanatan*, which means 'eternal', and followers of Sanatan precepts were known as *Sanatani*, which means 'follower of eternal life'. This name represents a culture which has given deep reflective thought to eternal life and has searched for ways of experiencing it.

The sannyasa tradition, which has always upheld these eternal principles and values, is a system or a way of life which can be used as a means to discover the potential inherent within. This tradition was reorganized by Shankaracharya, who was a very great thinker and philosopher. He laid down certain rules which are the basic precepts for every sannyasin. These rules represent the yamas and niyamas. By following the yamas and niyamas, one is able to transform the limitations of life and experience the full growth of human potential. This ultimately relieves one from the bondage of pain and pleasure, the limitations of likes and dislikes, and infuses one with a sense of commitment.

Previously sannyasins were known as mystics or hermits, those who led secluded lives in order to delve into the higher dimensions of consciousness. The whole concept of sannyasa is represented in the word *swami*, which means 'master of the self'. A sannyasin must attain that mastery. For those who sincerely follow the sannyasa system, it is a very tough life. There is a saying from the *Katha Upanishad* that the life of a sannyasin is like walking on a razor's edge, one false step and you fall and cut yourself. This Upanishadic idea points out the necessity of a very disciplined, harmonious and integrated lifestyle within the framework of sannyasa.

The later religions have retained a connection with the sannyasa tradition, and this is reflected in their teachings on continence, prayer, compassion and leading a secluded, reflective life. Of course, the actual system according to each line of thought and religion is different, but you will find the basic principles of sannyasa in every religion and culture.

Sannyasa Parampara

1

Origin of Sannyasa

Most of the ancient spiritual traditions which were once flourishing and influential have become extinct. Thus the traditions of Greece, Italy and Egypt, so celebrated in ancient days, have completely disappeared. So have the religions of the Celtic, Teutonic and Slavic races, as well as those of Syria and Asia Minor. In India, however, the system of vedic thought, which is known as Sanatan Dharma, has shown more stability. Not only does it stand amongst the world's most ancient spiritual cultures, but it is perhaps the only one to have survived, and even today it is still an integral part of Indian life.

Why did the Sanatan culture survive when other ancient cultures did not? In the history of humanity, the last one to two thousand years have been a very dark period full of wars, accessions and natural calamities. When a country was plundered, its culture was also destroyed or weakened. When this dark period was setting in, the wise seers of India decided that in order to preserve the culture from marauders and inclement times, a group of people should live apart from society and dedicate themselves totally to the preservation and transmission of the spiritual tradition. These people were to live simply so that their needs could be supplied by society and, in turn, they would be able to return the teachings to society when the times were auspicious.

Those people who chose to live apart from society in order to preserve the spiritual heritage became known as sannyasins. They were very tough and independent people with no tribal, caste or political identities. When the times became inclement due to invasion, despotic rulers, flood or famine, they would disappear into the remote areas where no one could find or hear of them. There they continued their lives in solitude and seclusion, maintaining the tradition, sometimes adding their experiences or thoughts to it, and then passing it down to a few trustworthy disciples whom they deemed capable of preserving it and passing it down to the next generation. This method of transmission became known as the sannyasa parampara. In this way the Sanatan culture was preserved and protected even during times of total political upheaval and social disintegration, whereas in other lands the ancient cultures all disappeared.

What is the sannyasa parampara? From what philosophical base did it develop? How did it differ from the rishi parampara of ancient days? To understand these and other related questions, we will first have to look at the prevailing philosophy and culture of ancient India.

Vedic culture

The vedic period was pervaded by the smoke of sacrifice and the incense of ritual. The principle aim of these practices was to please the deities invoked in order to receive their blessings, thus ensuring a happy, healthy and prosperous life. Daily and periodical sacrifices such as the morning and evening offerings, the new and full moon sacrifices, and the four monthly or seasonal sacrifices were generally performed by the householders themselves and were accompanied by appropriate prayers. As one's status and prosperity increased, the sacrifices took the shape of elaborate rituals, requiring a formidable array of priests, sacrificial articles and great wealth for distribution. This was an age of spiritual materialism. Through such practices the people strove to maintain a balance between the material and spiritual dimensions.

Later philosophers of the Upanishads, who were actually highly realized sages and teachers, made a deep enquiry into the ultimate truth that lies behind the world of matter and creation. They expressed their findings in terms of Brahman, the highest reality, which could be experienced through the union of *paramatma*, the cosmic soul, with *jivatma*, the individual soul. This union was termed as *moksha*, or liberation from the bondage of samsara.

According to Indian philosophy, human destiny is controlled by *karma* (cause and effect). Whatever good or bad actions you do in life, follow you in the next life, and there is a prospect of rebirth again and again, for both the pious and the wicked. This beginningless and endless cycle of birth and death, which is called *samsara*, must be transcended in order to experience moksha or liberation. The karmas are in turn controlled by the five *kleshas* or afflictions, namely, ignorance, 'I' feeling, attraction, repulsion and fear of death. The cycle begins with ignorance, which leads to identification with the ego. This in turn leads to desire and its fulfilment from which the vicious circle of karma and samsara ensues. The only way out of this entanglement is through the cultivation of dissociation, detachment and renunciation. This is possible through the process of discrimination, which leads one to higher knowledge and ultimately to freedom from bondage, which is known as moksha or liberation.

Path of liberation

The path leading to moksha, liberation or knowledge of the absolute, is very long and arduous. It is full of pitfalls, obstacles and uncertainties. Sincere seekers have traversed this path life after life without reaching the goal. They found that while being engaged in family and social duties, it was very difficult to progress on the spiritual path.

Therefore, the more aspiring seekers decided they would live apart from society in jungles and forests along with their families, in order to perfect their spiritual practices in peace and solitude. This became known as the rishi tradition, and it dates back to very ancient times. From the *Ramayana* and *Mahabharata* we can understand the significance of this tradition, for in those days the kings and political leaders were always guided by such rishis and their sons were educated by them. Even today, in South India family genealogies are connected with the lineage of one of the great rishis. Sometimes it also happened that a king would renounce his kingdom and go to live in the forest in order to perfect his spiritual practices, thereby becoming a *raja rishi*.

The rishis belonged to the brahman or priest caste, which was the highest level of vedic society. They lived strictly in accordance with the principles of vedic dharma, and one of these was the obligation of every individual to produce offspring. This was the reason why even though they chose to lead a spiritual life in solitude, they had to marry and live with their families. However, they spent their time in spiritual practice, penance and conducting various vedic rituals for the benefit of themselves and others. They were able to reach a very high level of spiritual evolution, as is evident in the Upanishads and other teachings which they left behind.

However, at a certain point, the rishis began to feel that their family attachments were holding them back from achieving the final spiritual goal. So, those who were inclined towards a life of total renunciation in order to fulfil their aspirations began to opt for the sannyasa path. These were not the first sannyasins. There had always been renunciates living in solitude and roaming from place to place, but they were not organized. Each one managed for himself, or sometimes they formed small groups which were disbanded after a short time. However, as more of the rishis opted for a life of total renunciation, the sannyasa parampara took on a definite shape and the rishi parampara slowly receded into the background.

While the rishi parampara was bound by social, family and religious obligations, the sannyasa parampara was not.

The sannyasins believed that not by rituals, not by begetting children, not by wealth, but by renunciation alone can one attain liberation. For them, renunciation meant the severance of the individual from all bonds of the phenomenal world: no family ties, no social ties, no caste, no creed, no religion, no political identity. It was a virtual rebirth, and once one entered upon this path there was no going back. Thus the sannyasa parampara was conceived to be the direct path to moksha, while the rishi parampara was an indirect path.

While discussing the rishi and sannyasa traditions, it is important to keep in mind the fact that sannyasa did not develop out of the vedic culture as the rishi tradition did. Sannyasa is rooted in the depths of prehistory. It is commonly believed that the sannyasa tradition started with the four Kumaras who were the mental sons of Brahma, the creator. They possessed absolute renunciation. However, sannyasa also owes its origin to the Dravidian ascetics, known as *yatis*, of the tantric culture, which existed in India long before the advent of vedic or rishi culture. Later on, the Aryans absorbed these ascetics into the fourth ashrama, namely the sannyasa ashrama, as sannyasins, bhikshus or parivrajakas.

2

The Ashrama System

The rishis of ancient India formulated the four divisions of life called the ashrama system, which was designed to harmonize a person's life from birth to death. It was a progressive system whereby each person could fulfil his or her ambitions and role in life without regret. It was devised so that each person could eventually attain moksha (self-realization) as a natural course of events, without suppressing their natural desires or rejecting the responsibilities of the world. It combined worldly and spiritual life.

It is interesting to note that in the beginning there were only three ashramas: *brahmacharya* (childhood and student life), *grihastha* or *garhasthya* (married life) and *vanaprastha* or *aranyaka* (retirement in the forest with one's husband or wife). The fourth ashrama, sannyasa ashrama, was added later, in the same way as the *Atharva Veda* was added to the first three Vedas, *Rig Veda*, *Yajur Veda* and *Sama Veda*.

Purusharthas

The rishis believed that one is born in this world to attain moksha, liberation from the cycle of birth and death. They saw that this could be achieved through the expansion of consciousness. For this purpose, there are two paths which can be followed. One is *pravritti marga*, the path of extroversion, which involves attachment to the objects of the world. The other is *nivritti marga*, the path of introversion,

12

for realization of the Self. After leading a full life and fulfilling one's commitments to society, family and oneself, which corresponds to the pravritti marga, and also to the brahmacharya and grihastha ashramas, one was permitted to renounce family and society for the sake of spiritual unfoldment, which corresponds to the nivritti marga, and to the vanaprastha and sannyasa ashramas. Everyone has the same possibility of self-realization when life follows this order. It was for this reason that the ashrama system was devised. The rishis further divided the needs of human life into four basic groups called the *purusharthas*, i.e. effort, labour or exertion. For the development of consciousness the purusharthas are essential, and they are closely interwoven with the ashrama system. The four purusharthas are: kama, artha, dharma and moksha. *Kama* implies fulfilment of one's desires, not only the sexual desire, but all desires. *Artha* means one should be accomplished and attain in all spheres. *Dharma* implies fulfilling one's role in life, according to the dictates of one's nature. *Moksha* means liberation or self-realization.

If life is to be lived perfectly from beginning to end, then all these purusharthas must be fulfilled. Suppression of the first three leads to neurosis and away from moksha. Natural expression and fulfilment of the first three needs: kama, artha and dharma, eventually leads to fulfilment of the ultimate need, moksha. Overindulgence in the first three leads to delusion and away from moksha. Careful guidance of one's life and fulfilment of the first three purusharthas through the ashrama system eventually leads to moksha. It is a smooth path to self-realization which all people can tread.

The ashramas

The ashrama system was utilized long before the present day orders of sannyasa were founded. According to the ashrama system, sannyasa involved total renunciation, a natural consequence of having followed the first three stages of life, and fulfilled all the basic desires and needs. It is a

13

logical system which brings order and purpose to life. No longer is the aim of life restricted to the satisfaction of material desires and ambitions, but includes spiritual emancipation as the culmination. The highlight of life is self-realization. For those people who followed the dictates of the ashrama system, sannyasa would have been adopted in old age. The implications are that as one progresses through the ashramas or stages of life, one naturally becomes more attuned to the deeper aspects of one's being. Now, let us briefly outline the patterns of life under the ashrama system.

Brahamacharya ashrama (studentship – up to twenty-five years): According to tradition, one was sent during childhood and early adulthood to live with a guru in order to receive an education. Living in the family of the guru from an early age gave one a deeper understanding and basis for living life on harmonious lines. This is considered to be the first stage in the fulfilment of one's desires. During this period one receives an education and the knowledge of a profession for the fulfilment of one's future desires, needs and attainments. One is committed to the maintenance of chastity in thought, word and deed, and this is brahmacharya. A chaste brain has tremendous energy and willpower. In this stage of life, apart from spiritual and secular studies, the greatest stress is laid upon total development of the personality and character, namely through the cultivation of self-control, truthfulness and self-surrender.

Grihastha ashrama (householder – twenty-five to fifty years): At a suitable age, the brahmachari was sent home. He married, had children and became an active and contributing member of society. Here he put into use the knowledge, skill, ability and moral training, gained during his student days, for the betterment of society and the nation. He repaid the debt to his parents by looking after their needs. According to Manu, the law giver, this ashrama is considered to be the basis and the support of the other three ashramas.

Vanaprastha ashrama (forest dweller – fifty to seventy-five years): A person living in conformity with the sacred laws and traditions should retire to the forest when his family commitments come to an end. Manu says that a man should retire from active life when his hair turns grey, his skin becomes wrinkled and he becomes a grandfather. All the while he prepares himself for this ashrama, his sacred aim being renunciation and God-realization. He is supposed to live in the forest, and his wife may accompany him, subjecting herself to the same rigorous life. Renouncing pleasures, they live frugally on fruits and roots, and spend most of their time in sadhana, prayer and study of the scriptures. Self-realization becomes the urgent mission of life. The body is gradually attuned and trained to the life of austerity and penance, and they develop internal consciousness.

Sannyasa ashrama (total renunciation – seventy-five years and over): In this ashrama the sannyasin is obliged to lead a solitary life and to renounce all previous achievements and attachments, including wife or husband. He frees himself from duality by fixing his mind steadily in meditation. Book VI of the *Laws of Manu* directs him to wander about as a bhikshu or parivrajaka. He lives without fire, habitation or support. He takes alms once a day, keeps mouna and avoids doing injury to anyone. In short, he totally abandons all worldly attachments. He has no more duty or obligation to society. His life becomes a continual search to discover the relationship between the individual self (jivatman) and the supreme self (paramatman).

The ashrama system was such an integral part of life that rishis even assigned specific sections of the Vedas for each ashrama: Samhitas for brahmacharya ashrama, Brahmanas for grihastha ashrama, Aranyakas for vanaprastha ashrama and the Upanishads for sannyasa ashrama. They also associated the four states of consciousness with each of the ashramas: *jagrat* (waking) with brahmacharya ashrama, *swapna* (dreaming) with grihastha ashrama, *sushupti* (deep sleep) with vanaprastha ashrama, and *turiya* (superconsciousness) with sannyasa ashrama. For a complete explanation of these states of consciousness, refer to the *Mandukya Upanishad*.

Although the ashrama system was an important part of the vedic tradition, one was not bound to follow the exact rules of the ashrama. This is explained in the *Jabala Upanishad* (v.4) as follows: Once Janaka, the king of Videha, approached the sage Yajnavalkya and said, "Venerable sir, teach me about renunciation." Yajnavalkya replied, "After completing the life of a student (brahmacharya), let one become a householder (grihastha). After completing the life of a householder, one should become a forest dweller (vana-prastha). After this, one should renounce (sannyasa). Also, if a suitable occasion arises, one can even renounce from the stage of student or householder or forest hermit. Let one who is ready, renounce on that day when one has a deep feeling of renunciation." In this way, although having rules, the ashrama system was also flexible.

3

Rishis and Munis

The word rishi comes from the Sanskrit root *rish* meaning 'to go inward' or 'to flow'. Thus *rishi* means one who contemplates or meditates for self-realization; one whose consciousness is not stagnant but flowing. The rishis were those through whom the vedic hymns were revealed. They were the authors of sacred hymns, poets, saints and sages of ancient India. It is believed that the rishi tradition or parampara started from Lord Narayana. He imparted this knowledge to Lord Brahma. Brahma transmitted it to his *manas putra* (mentally born son) Vashishtha. Vashishtha transmitted it to his son Sakti, Sakti to his son Parasara, Parasara to his son Vyasa, Vyasa to his son Sukhadev, and so it was passed on to many others down the line.

The rishis had three characteristics: positivity, universality and divinity. They believed that one who has self-control makes the hermitage one's home. Through the medium of sadhana they made their consciousness subtle. They practised *gurucharya*, teaching principles and infusing disciples with spiritual energy. The Indian culture is what it is today because of rishis who reached a high point of spiritual attunement and contributed their might for the upliftment of society.

Originally this land was not known as India; the rishis had named it Bharat. In Sanskrit the word *Bharat* is composed of two roots: *bha*, meaning 'light', and *rat*, meaning 'engulfed'.

17

Hence Bharat was perceived by the rishis as a land which was engulfed in light.

Glory of the rishis

The rishi culture is considered great because of its humanitarian aspect. The rishis were always ready to reconcile public good with their own. After fulfilling their responsibilities towards their kith and kin, they engaged themselves in writing books, propagation of vedic knowledge, performing and encouraging dharmic activities, protection of the downtrodden, and work connected with the welfare of society. It is due to these characteristics that the rishi culture could become everlasting and distinctive. They were visionary seers of vedic hymns, and performers of sacrifice and penance in various forms.

On the basis of their special inclination, some were householders while others were not; some were hermitage dwellers and some continuous wanderers; some imparted sacred knowledge to disciples and some taught the use of weapons; some practised ordinary austerity while others adopted severe penances. No rishi could be without self-respect, strong willpower, straightforwardness, truthfulness, kindness, readiness to offer shelter to the distressed, forgiveness and control over greed. Being ascetics, the rishis were normally so lean that their arteries could be seen distinctly. Their hair was matted, coiled and tied on top of the head in what is called *jata mandala*. They were bearded and their dress was very simple, generally made of kusha grass, the bark of trees and the skin of antelopes.

Lifestyle

The ashrams and hermitages of the rishis were located throughout India. The rishis particularly liked to dwell in the mountains, on the sea coast, on river banks and lake shores, and at *tirthasthanas* (holy places). Parashurama, Vashishtha and Vyasa had their ashrams in the North, Bhrigu and Angiras in the East, Agastya and Kapila in the

South, and Durvasa and Kasyapa in the West. The Himalayas were used for austerities. The ashrams were inhabited by many animals, like antelope and cows. Most of the rishis had special cows called *homa dhenus*, whose milk was used specifically for offerings to the sacred fire. Nandini, the beloved cow of Vashishtha, was supposed to have possessed divine powers.

The ashrams of the rishis had certain characteristics by which they could be recognized at once, such as a grove of trees near the entrance, special doors, sadhana fires *(homa dhunis)* and places for instructing disciples and giving religious discourses. Usually entry to the ashram was not restricted for visitors. Some of the rishis subsisted on fruits and roots found in the forest, while others lived on alms from the householders. Most of the rishis were fruit eaters, but some existed on water or air only. They drank the intoxicating juice of the soma plant at sacrifices. Eating of flesh was very rare but not prohibited.

During vedic times it was commonly believed that there were only three ways to obtain the highest state after death. These were penance, religious conduct and the production of offspring *(Mahabharata,* Adiparva 13:21). Some of the rishis, having studied the Vedas, engaged themselves in austerities and religious conduct while others married in order to procreate sons, for example, Astavakra and Suprabha, Agastya and Lopamudra, Drona and Kripi, Kasyapa and Aditi. They believed that by producing a son, the departed ancestors would be propitiated and the lineage would not die out. The *rishi patnis*, wives of the rishis, also practised austerities and observed religious rites.

Academic and religious life

The rishis devoted much of their time to study and composition of various literary works. The entire vedic literature: Samhitas, Brahmanas, Aranyakas, Kalpasutras, Upanishads, Khilas (addenda to the Vedas) and Vedangas (grammar, metrics, astronomy and astrology, etc.) was

19

composed by rishis. They were the authors of philosophical literature: Vaisheshika by Uluka (also known as Kanada), Nyaya by Gotama, Samkhya by Kapila, Yoga Sutras by Patanjali, Mimamsa by Jaimini, Vedanta by Badarayana. They collected, collated and wrote down the Agama literature, the Puranas and other historical and poetical works. Many works relating to theology, diplomacy, political science and economics are also attributed to them. They were authors of books on medicine, music and military science. Baudhyana was the first great geometer; Gargya was the first enumerator of constellations; Sushruta was the father of surgery; Astharvana was the first discoverer of fire, and Kanada was the first expounder of the atomic theory.

Some of the rishis were educated under one guru and preceptor, while others underwent training under various gurus. In vedic times, girls were also educated along with boys. While living in the gurukul, they engaged themselves in learning as well as in the service of their guru.

The religious life of the rishis differed from their academic life. They performed certain daily rites such as sandhya and japa, sacrifices, adoration of the gods, fire rituals *(agnihotra)* and so on. They drank soma during the performance of sacrifices. They never missed performing rites like tarpana and shraaddha for the souls of departed ancestors. They often went on pilgrimage and performed yajnas at shrines. The rishis also lived in solitude, practising austerities as well as long meditations on Shiva, Vishnu, Brahma and other deities. Through these practices they were able to obtain many supernatural powers. While engaged in austerities, many of the rishis did not eat any food, sustaining themselves on water and air, and sometimes on prana alone.

Humanitarian aspects

It is an established fact that the rishis were engaged in self-realization most of their lives. However, it is also true that they were always ready to relinquish their own self-interest for the welfare of society. They were always ready to assist the downtrodden and those who were dependent on them, and to destroy the wicked. They were well versed in the use of weapons for the sake of defence or for suppressing arrogant, high-handed persons. They often went on excursions for observing social activities like *swayamvara* (selection of husband in public ceremony) and coronation of a new king. The rishis were greatly venerated by the kings, and those rishis who were highly learned and realized were venerated by the other rishis.

Munis

The word muni comes from the Sanskrit *man*, meaning 'to think'. Thus *muni* implies one who contemplates or who has conquered the mind. The term muni was used for highly spiritual persons. In Sanskrit it also means sage, seer, ascetic and hermit. One of Lord Buddha's titles was Sakyamuni, muni of the Sakyas.

The munis wore saffron cloth, renounced the sacred fire and lived alone in the forest. They avoided food cooked on fire, practised celibacy and underwent severe penance. They refrained from killing any living being and followed strict truth. Generally they shaved their heads. They totally abstained from taking flesh and practised non-violence. They observed *mouna* (silence) and engaged themselves in yoga practices. By means of contemplation, they aimed at achieving union with the universal soul, and many obtained supernatural powers. It is the munis who were eventually assimilated by the Aryan culture as the fourth stage of life, the sannyasa ashrama.

4

Caste system

The elaborate institution known as the caste system or *varnashrama*, wherein society has been formally divided into four castes: brahmana, kshatriya, vaishya and shudra, may be said to be without a parallel in the world. However, there is hardly any country where some classes or grades of social distinction are not made. The Vedas view society as an organism which naturally produces groups of individuals with different aptitudes and abilities, so that each group can function like a specialized organ for the well-being of the whole.

The Sanskrit term *varna* means 'colour'. This word is used in the *Rig Veda* to denote the colour of the first three castes, which were Aryan and hence fair in colour, as compared with the fourth caste or *dasya varna*, which was comprised of Dravidians who were dark in colour. Originally it appears that the Aryans had only the first three castes. Many scholars are of the opinion that the fourth caste was added during the latter part of the *Rig Veda*.

The division of the castes was based on an individual's aptitude for a particular occupation or profession, which in turn was influenced by his internal state of consciousness and predominant *guna* (attribute or quality). According to vedic philosophy, *tamoguna* clouds the consciousness and creates lethargy, cruelty and ill temper; *rajoguna* makes one dynamic, restless and anxious; and *sattoguna* creates calmness,

22

alertness and equanimity, assisting in the expansion of consciousness.

Division of castes

In the vedic tradition, the brahmana represented the highest embodiment of all virtues and qualities. Hence he had the special prerogative of studying the Vedas and other scriptures. The second position in the hierarchy was held by the kshatriya, whose main function in the social scheme was to protect the other three varnas and to maintain law and order for the progress of dharma. This caste was composed of kings, warriors and other chiefs of petty states. The third position was held by the vaishya who were engaged in trade, commerce, keeping cattle and agricultural affairs. They were responsible for maintaining the economic stability of the society. Finally came the shudra, whose main duty was to serve the other three varnas and to provide a workforce.

According to vedic philosophy, a man should study, learn and develop. The harmonious growth of the individual and his traits or the predominant guna under the influence of which he performs his karmas was envisaged in the fourfold division of vedic society. Initially the caste system was not rigid and there was no prohibition of interdining and intermarriage; there was no determination of merit by hereditary descent.

There are many speculations about how the caste system became rigid and intolerant. One speculation is echoed in the famous *Purusha Sukta*, a hymn of the *Rig Veda*. This explains how the brahmanas, kshatriyas, vaishyas and shudras were created from the head, arms, thighs and feet respectively, of the supreme *Purusha* (consciousness). This passage led the first three classes to believe that they were superior and the shudras were inferior. Thus vedic society gradually developed into privileged classes and 'untouchables'.

The shudras, comprising nearly all the indigenous, tribal people, were gradually isolated from the mainstream of vedic society, and at times were forced to live outside the limits of a village or town. They were denied entry into temples and the privilege of taking sannyasa. The shudra marriage took place without the recitation of mantras by a brahmana. In the *Dharma Sutras* of Vashishtha and Gautama, we find the idea of impurity communicated through the touch or contact of a person belonging to an inferior caste.

It is interesting to note that even among numerous subcastes of shudras, interdining and inter-subcaste marriages are still not allowed, thus showing how deep the varna of caste system has penetrated into Hindu society. This was all due to the power play of people motivated by self-interest, based on the hypocrisy prevalent in the social way of living and thinking. Thus by altering the basic human values down through the centuries, occupation and social status became hereditary, depending upon one's caste.

Realistic interpretation
A view which refutes the interpretation of such passages referred to in the preceding section endeavours to explain its meaning through the medium of Sanskrit grammar. The brahmana did not come out of the head or mouth of the creator, nor for that matter did the shudra spring from his feet. According to Sanskrit grammar, the word brahmana originated from the root *brinh*, meaning 'to expand', 'to grow'. Thus the word *brahmana* means one who constantly endeavours to better himself and society. According to this interpretation, a brahmana may be from any caste provided he fulfils the above qualification.

The word kshatriya originates from the root *kshat*, meaning 'to injure' and *tra*, meaning 'to protect'. Thus the *kshatriya* is one who protects others from injuries. Similarly, the word vaishya comes from the root, *vish*, meaning 'to take responsibility'. The *vaishya* is one who undertakes the responsibility of caring for society. The word shudra comes from the root *shuch*, which means 'to weep', 'to mourn'. Thus the *shudra* is a person whose consciousness is least

24

developed due to which he remains in a state of *avidya* (ignorance) or *dukha* (suffering), causing him to weep or mourn.

The four varnas or castes can also be understood as an integral part of the life process of each individual. Before conception, the soul is one with the cosmic consciousness; it is pure spirit. After conception, the soul gradually takes on a human form, still maintaining its divinity. However, when the foetus enters the birth canal and is propelled into the world, it becomes subject to suffering as it enters the cycle of birth and death. Hence as soon as the child is born, the first thing it does is cry. This cry represents the child's break or separation from the source, cosmic consciousness, and its entry into the world of duality or individuality. After its first cry, the child is immersed in *avidya* (ignorance). Then slowly, in the process of growing up, the child studies and learns about life in order to develop the consciousness, the *vidya* (higher knowledge), and to come out of the shudra varna.

As the child comes of age, he enters into the vaishya varna where he takes up the responsibilities of grihastha life and performs useful work within society. Here he is primarily occupied with producing progeny and acquiring property and wealth. As his family and assets increase, it becomes necessary to take some protective measures to ensure their safety and growth. At this time the kshatriya varna becomes dominant as the individual exerts himself for the protection of his family, property and wealth. Finally the individual realizes the temporal nature of all things, and the urge develops in him to return to the source, to know the truth. Hence, he begins to walk the spiritual path, to develop his consciousness in order to experience the higher self from which he has become separated at the time of his birth. At this point he enters into the brahmana varna, whereby he raises his own consciousness and helps to elevate society.

From the point of view of consciousness, it can be surmised that the brahmana is the most highly developed, and the shudra the least developed, the kshatriya and vaishya falling in between. Again, seen from the point of view of the gunas, it can be said that the brahmana has sattoguna predominant, the kshatriya rajoguna, the vaishya rajoguna and tamoguna, and the shudra tamoguna. When the interpretation of the four castes is made from the above criteria, then the caste to which a man belongs is not decided on the basis of birth, but on his merit and ability. This was first envisioned by emperor Bharat (son of Shakuntala) who nominated a commoner's son to succeed him instead of his own son.

Caste system and sannyasa

Both the traditional and modern approach to sannyasa are closely linked with the caste system. It influenced the behaviour pattern of sannyasins until they reached the stage of *avadhoota*, absolute renunciation. Until the stage of avadhoota, the sannyasin thought in terms of touchable and untouchable and would not even tolerate an untouchable's shadow falling on him. Even Shankara was an example of such thinking and behaviour when a *chandala* (outcaste) crossed his path at the Gana Ghat in Varanasi.

During the twentieth century, the evils of the caste system have been reduced to a great extent by the efforts of Mahatma Gandhi and others. However, in modern society, sannyasins have a great responsibility to ameliorate the suffering of the downtrodden, which is service to God in the human form. A present-day example of such revolutionary sannyasins is Swami Sivananda Saraswati, who dedicated his life to removing the social barriers and uplifting the neglected and downtrodden. He even established a leper colony, called Brahmapuri, at Rishikesh for service to the extreme untouchables.

5

Sannyasa tradition

The Sanskrit word *samnyasa* is made up of two roots: *sam*, meaning 'perfect' or 'complete', and *nyasa*, meaning 'renunciation'. Thus, the literal meaning of sannyasa is complete renunciation. The word nyasa also implies 'dedication' or 'donation'. Therefore, sannyasa may be understood as the complete dedication or donation of one's faculties for the upliftment of mankind. In a nutshell we can say that sannyasa is *atmano mokshartham jagat hittaya cha*, meaning for the good of the world and for the liberation of the soul.

The sannyasin considers himself or herself to be beyond both knowledge and ignorance. By exercising complete control over the mind and discarding all worldly affairs in thought, word and deed, the sannyasin becomes liberated from worldly bondage through deep meditation on the Self. For this purpose the sannyasin meditates on the dictums *Tat Twam Asi*, Thou art That; *Aham Brahma Asmi*, I am Brahma; and on the pranava, which is the mantra Aum.

It has been said that the whole world is maintained by the glory of sannyasa. A sannyasin renounces the desire for progeny, wealth, name and fame, in fact all that which is transitory in nature, in order to identify and absorb himself in that which is eternal. Hence in the *Kathopanishad* we find the following description: "Like the sharp edge of a razor is that path, difficult to cross and hard to tread." On account

27

of its sublime philosophy, sannyasa came to be regarded as a path of utmost purity and sanctity. Those renunciates who followed this path were considered to be the most blessed amongst men.

The sannyasin is bliss incarnate. His life is one of spiritual endeavour and achievement, along with renunciation. Moreover, the sannyasin is not bound by any religion or dogmas, rather he stands for those eternal principles and values which he has cultivated in his life. He lives in the universal dimension which transcends all boundaries of tribe, caste nation and sect. He is concerned with spiritual upliftment and therefore he says, "I do not care for you and your society. I think for myself and you should not think for me."

Vairagya or detachment

Vairagya has always been emphasized as the foundation of sannyasa life, and without it there cannot be any real spiritual progress. In the *Yoga Sutras* of Patanjali (1:15) it says, "When an individual becomes free of craving for the sense objects which he has experienced as well as for those of which he has heard, that state of consciousness is *vairagya*." There are three stages of vairagya. The first stage is characterized by the struggle to overcome the effects of likes and dislikes. In the second stage, some of the likes and dislikes are under control and some are not. In the third stage, likes and dislikes are completely controlled, although their roots may still be there.

This is the lower form of vairagya, then there is the higher form or *paravairagya*, which involves not only giving up enjoyment, but even the deep-rooted taste for enjoyment. Paravairagya is characterized by the absence of desire in all its forms. There is no desire for pleasure, enjoyment, knowledge, or even sleep. This higher form of vairagya comes through awareness of the nature of pure con-sciousness, which is the result of higher meditative practice. Through this awareness, the mind is freed from the three gunas or the qualities of nature, which bind one to the world of matter or manifestation.

Tyaga or renunciation only arises through the cultivation of vairagya, detachment. The sannyasin tries to become as detached as possible from the pleasures of the world, so that they do not prevent him or her from treading the spiritual path. In the beginning he may transfer his desire for worldly pleasures to desire for spiritual experiences, but eventually he must become detached from these also, as these experiences accentuate the power of the ego, especially when there is continual expectation. First one should be detached from all worldly pleasures, then from spiritual pleasure. This is the path of a sannyasin.

Types of sannyasins
According to the level of vairagya, there are different kinds of renunciation and calibre of sannyasins. Perfect renunciation (*paravairagya*) is very rare and this type only arises with self-realization. For most sannyasins vairagya develops slowly in step with one's individual level of aspiration and understanding. There are sannyasins of a high order who achieve almost total renunciation, rejecting all material things apart from food and a loin cloth. In some cases, even the loin cloth is discarded, as with avadhootas or digambaras. Other sannyasins live in ashrams or maths, performing duties, teaching, training disciples, as well as offering spiritual guidance to all who seek it. In this way vairagya develops slowly, and when the desires are completely exhausted, the sannyasin will then be able to move into a higher order of renunciation without experiencing difficulties or falling back.

Several of the Upanishads give descriptions of the various types of sannyasins and the way of life they should adopt. The *Sannyasa Upanishad* lists four types: vairagya sannyasa, jnana sannyasa, jnana-vairagya sannyasa and karma-vairagya sannyasa. Later on, Adi Shankara added two more types: vividisha sannyasa and vidvat sannyasa. These classifications of sannyasa are explained as follows:

Vairagya sannyasa (renunciation due to dispassion): These are people who feel intense detachment and absence of

29

craving from an early age. Their very nature is detached due to the influence of *sanchit karmas*, actions done in previous lives. A good example is Ramana Maharshi.

Jnana sannyasa (renunciation due to knowledge): These are people who experience the world, study the scriptures, and then become disciples of a guru. Knowledge arises through contact with the guru and the reading of spiritual texts. Swami Dayananda Saraswati is an example. He received knowledge of the scriptures by being near his guru.

Jnana-vairagya sannyasa (renunciation due to knowledge and dispassion): These are people in whom detachment arises through deeper knowledge and understanding. This type of sannyasa is ahead of jnana sannyasa. It begins after one has studied the scriptural texts and experienced the world. With the aim of attaining moksha, one retires from active life and resorts to deep meditation on the Self. To facilitate this endeavour, one becomes an ascetic, leading a life of almost total renunciation. Paramahamsa Satyananda is a good example of this. After leading a fully active sannyasa life, serving his guru, writing books, founding a mission and guiding thousands of disciples, he renounced all and, donning the loin cloth, went into seclusion, where he engaged himself in higher spiritual practice for the attainment of liberation.

Karma-vairagya sannyasa (renunciation due to dispassion arising from worldly activities): These are people who develop vairagya after passing through the other stages of life, i.e. brahmacharya, grihastha and vanaprastha, associated with the ashrama system. In this case, sannyasa is the last of the ashramas. In the *Sannyasa Upanishad* it is recommended that all people should renounce worldly activities and adopt this way of life after seventy-five years of age, even if they do not possess knowledge or dispassion. Most people who reach old age fall into this category. It is a process of natural selection.

Vividisha sannyasa (renunciation while living in the world): These people practise internal renunciation for the purpose of attaining moksha while living in the world. They gain knowledge and dispassion from their experiences in life. Society is greatly benefited and uplifted by their example. This was the renunciation practised by Sri Rama and Sri Krishna and their lives remain an inspiration for everyone to this day. Bhakta saints such as Mira Bai, Eknath, Tukaram and others are also good examples of vividisha sannyasins.

Vidvat sannyasa (renunciation due to paravairagya): These are people who have totally exhausted all their desires, both material and spiritual, including the desire for self-realization. This is the highest order of sannyasa. Avadhootas such as Dattatreya are examples of vidvat sannyasins.

Atura sannyasa (renunciation due to the imminence of death): This type of sannyasa is recommended by the shastras for those people who develop vairagya in the face of death. This is an emergency procedure, requiring simply the recitation of a particular mantra. If the person recovers, he should embrace sannyasa in the prescribed manner. If not, he dies with the highest of vows on his lips, and merit will accrue to him in his next birth. Adi Shankara is an example of this kind of sannyasa.

Traditional views on eligibility for sannyasa

One who has fulfilled the basic desires for family, wealth and progeny, and who has discarded attachment for and pride in the body, is eligible for sannyasa. As and when dispassion for worldly life arises in one's mind, one may take sannyasa without any previous conditions being laid down.

A brahmachari can renounce worldly life and become a sannyasin of a higher order, i.e. paramahamsa. It is not necessary to proceed from the first order, as these early stages are intended for renunciates whose vairagya is not perfected.

According to the traditional view, those who do not qualify for sannyasa life are as follows: (i) a eunuch, (ii) a deformed person, (iii) a woman, (iv) one who is deaf, dumb or blind, (v) a heretic, (vi) a man without prepuce, (vii) a child, (viii) a religious student, (ix) a vaikhanasa, (x) a haradvija (kapalika), (xi) an emperor, (xii) one who does not maintain the sacred fire, (xiii) one guilty of crime, (xiv) one who is always seeking the help of another, (xv) a hired teacher, and (xvi) a hired kshatriya.

A hired kshatriya and others who are not entitled to renunciation may seek liberation in the path of the brave who court death on the battlefield, fast unto death, enter into water to rise no more, enter fire to be burnt to ashes, or undertake a great journey on which they collapse (*Jabalopanishad* 5:2).

6

Renunciation Rites

During the traditional sannyasa initiation, certain rituals were followed. The act of renunciation being their ritual death, the customary *shraaddhas* (commemorative religious rites) were not performed after the death of sannyasins, as was done in the case of persons who are not sannyasins. At the time of taking initiation, the aspirant had to undergo a symbolic cremation, as cremation is the last samskara of the human body. Henceforth, the sannyasin, who is considered to be dead, is not permitted to perform sacrifices or any other samskara, or even to participate in any rituals either in life or in death. For this reason, the initiation ceremony for one entering the sannyasa order was ordained. After making the decision to take sannyasa, the aspirant distributed his property among his family members.

Purification rites
Before being initiated into sannyasa, the aspirant performed purification rites, known as the four penances or the *prajapatya* penance, in order to expiate all his sins. These penances consisted of consuming hot milk, hot ghee and hot water, and inhaling hot air for three days each.

Another variation of the prajapatya penance lasts for twelve days. It consists of taking one meal a day in the morning for three days, eating one meal a day in the evening

33

for the next three days, eating what is received unasked for the following three days and fasting during the final three days.

Performance of eight shraaddhas

After undergoing the purification rites as mentioned above, the aspirant for sannyasa next performed the eight shraaddhas. The shraaddhas have a cosmic dimension. According to Hindu cosmology, the divinities to which the shraaddhas are offered inhabit the universe. It is appropriate that the last shraaddha offered by a man in search of the absolute is offered to all beings. It is a conviction amongst Hindus that renunciation constitutes the ritual death of the renouncer and the shraaddhas constitute his funeral.

The eight shraaddhas are propitiation of the following:
1. Gods, i.e. Brahma, Vishnu, Mahesh
2. Sages of yore, i.e. Narada, Janaka
3. Other divine beings, i.e. Rudras, Adityas, Vasus
4. Man (the four sons of Brahma), i.e. Sanatkumara, Sanaka, Sanandana and Sanatana
5. Five elements, i.e. earth, water, fire, air and ether
6. Manes, i.e. grandfather, great-grandfather up to seven generations
7. Father and mother, and the seven future generations
8. Oneself.

The above shraaddhas are performed in eight days, i.e. one shraaddha per day or in one day as per the ritual offering of riceballs (*pindadan*) to the souls of departed ancestors *(manes)*.

Preparation for renunciation rites

After dividing one's property and performing the purification rites and shraaddhas, preparation for the renunciation rites are made. All of these preparatory rites are accompanied by the chanting of mantras. Some of the important rites are as follows:

34

1. Shaving the head, beard and body; paring of nails and bathing
2. Repetition of Gayatri mantra one thousand times
3. Kindling the *aupasana* (sacred fire)
4. Eating barley meals three times a day
5. Listening to the Puranas at night
6. Bathing at the end of the fourth watch of the night
7. Offering of rice oblations
8. Repetition of *Purusha Sukta* sixteen times
9. Performing the viraja ritual so as to free oneself from all sins
10. Recitation of mantras invoking fire, maruts, etc., and meditation upon them
11. Worshipping the dawn
12. Repetition of Gayatri mantra one thousand times while sitting in water
13. Abandoning the sacred thread.

Renunciation ceremony
After repetition of the Gayatri mantra one thousand times while sitting in water, the sannyasa initiation mantra is repeated three times as follows:

Aum Bhu Sannyastam Maya
I renounce everything in this earthly world.
Aum Bhuvah Sannyastam Maya
I renounce everything in the astral plane.
Aum Svaha Sannyastam Maya
I renounce everything in the heavenly plane.
Aum Bhu Bhuvah Svaha Sannyastam Maya
I renounce everything in these three planes,
earthly, astral and heavenly.

Then the sannyasa initiate discards the clothing which he is wearing in the water. He comes out of the water and is invested by the guru with geru cloth, staff, loin cloth and water vessel. He has become a sannyasin now.

Significance of the name

The name given to the sannyasin at the time of initiation is full of meaning. It is chosen intuitively by the guru to awaken the dormant potential of the initiate. When the aspirant comes before the guru with the idea of renouncing, he comes endowed with faith, the feeling of surrender and love for the master. The guru utilizes these aspects to enter the psyche of the aspirant to understand the predominant inner, positive trait which is the basic quality of the aspirant. This enables the guru to endow the disciple with a sankalpa for his emancipation and growth in his inner life, in the form of the name.

After sannyasa initiation, the combination of ananda with the name of the sannyasin is also very significant. *Ananda* means ecstasy or bliss. A sannyasin is always in ecstasy and bliss as a result of having renounced the kleshas or afflictions of worldly life. The addition of ananda to the name further strengthens the aim of the sannyasin, enabling him to discover the source of beatitude and integrated harmony in the structure of his conflict-free, inner personality.

The surname of the sannyasin indicates the particular branch of the order to which he or she belongs. When Shankaracharya restructured the sannyasa order, he divided it into ten groups which were called the *Dashnami sampradaya*. These ten traditional groups were then assigned to four *maths* or headquarters. For example, Saraswati, Bharati and Puri are under the southern math of Sringeri. Tirtha and Ashrama are under the western math at Dwarka. Giri, Parvat and Sagar are under the northern math at Badrinath. Vanam and Aranyan are under the eastern math in Puri.

Each of the ten groups represents different spiritual qualities, tendencies or aspects. According to tradition, Saraswati is the goddess of wisdom, learning and speech. This means that those sannyasins with the surname Saraswati tend to be learned and wise, and gifted in speech. Similarly, those sannyasins who dwelled in holy places were called

Tirtha, those who dwelled in the mountains were called Parvat, those who dwelled by the sea were called Sagar, those who dwelled in the forests and jungles were called Vanam and Aranya, and so on.

7

Stages of Sannyasa

There are six stages of renunciation in the life of a sannyasin. These start with kutichak, bahudak and hamsa, gradually becoming more and more difficult to follow as one aspires towards the higher stages of paramahamsa, turiyatita and avadhoota. We find these six stages described in the different Upanishads which deal with sannyasa. As each stage of sannyasa is dealt with one by one, the pattern of spiritual evolution in the life of a sannyasin emerges.

Kutichak (hut dweller)
This is the first rung on the traditional six rung ladder. Here the rules of traditional and orthodox sannyasa have been simplified so that the initiate can adjust to the life of a renunciate. A *brahmachari* (celibate) or *grihasthi* (householder) can become a kutichak. He is allowed to wear the tuft, although the rest of the head is shaved, and the sacred thread, along with ochre-coloured clothes. He renounces the family but is still devoted to the service of parents and preceptor. He also renounces the ritual fires.

Kutichak is comparable to the gurukul period, where the sannyasin lives with and serves his guru in order to purify and prepare himself for the further stages of sannyasa. Here he studies the scriptures, learns the use of mantras, meditation and other sadhanas, and how to live an ascetic life, scrupulously maintaining the *yamas* and *niyamas* (rules and restraints for self-regulation). The traditional period to be spent in the hut or gurukul was twelve years. Only after completing this period of training was the initiate considered competent to undertake the life of sannyasa independently, becoming a wandering ascetic without any fixed dwelling place.

Bahudak (supported by many)

The sannyasin becomes a bahudak after completing the initial twelve years of training in the gurukul, or he can enter the bahudak stage directly from grihastha or vana-prastha (forest dweller) ashrama after renouncing his family and the sacred fire. His head is shaven, although he may retain the tuft, and he carries a staff.

Now, he journeys alone as a wandering ascetic for eight months of the year, and during the *chaturmas* period, the rainy season, he stays in one place, devoting his time solely to sadhana and self-study. According to tradition, he moves from place to place, without attracting any attention to himself. He subsists on alms and sleeps on the ground. He carries only his staff and water vessel and wears the barest minimum of clothing. He roams freely, visiting places of pilgrimage, but is not permitted to remain in any one place for more than a few days.

Bahudak is a stage in which the sannyasin gets plenty of opportunities to put into practice what he had imbibed during the kutichak period, and also to further the mission entrusted to him by his preceptor towards propagation of the dharma. During his journey from village to village, he is faced with all sorts of situations, providing a wonderful testing ground for his vairagya or dispassion. Brahmacharya, or sexual continence, is strictly practised. He abstains totally from the eight forms of contact with women, namely: looking at, touching, sporting with, talking about, entering into secret dialogue, imagining, thinking about, and physical enjoyment. This is why sannyasins traditionally shunned women.

As a bahudak, the sannyasin practices the yamas and niyamas, as prescribed in kutichak. He ponders over the Vedantic texts and meditates on Brahman. In this way he develops inner renunciation, gradually shedding the duality of good and bad, virtue and vice, pleasure and pain, etc. Thus he develops equanimity and cultivates no evil propensities towards others. He tries to free himself from pride and ego, to purify his mind and gain knowledge of the Self, leading to moksha and higher stages of sannyasa.

Hamsa (swan)

In this stage the sannyasin does not keep the tuft, but either keeps matted hair or shaves fully. Nor does he wear the sacred thread. He remains alone, not mixing with company. He discards clothing and wears only a loin cloth or a deer skin. He sustains himself in the manner of a bee, by collecting alms from eight predetermined houses per day.

The hamsa sannyasin does not recite mantras aloud nor does he give instructions to others. He meditates on the anta pranava of eight matras, consisting of the vowels 'A', 'U' and the consonant 'M', the *ardhamatra* (half syllable), the nada, the bindu, the kala and the sakti (*Narada Parivrajaka Upanishad*, 8:2). He abandons passions, anger, greed, pride and delusion, and dwells in Brahman.

In the stage of hamsa, the sannyasin develops the following characteristics:
- He becomes tongueless (in relishing food and speech)
- He becomes a eunuch (in sexual affairs)
- He becomes lame (going only for alms and calls of nature)
- He becomes blind (in seeing sensory objects)
- He becomes deaf (in hearing praises or curses)
- He becomes innocent (like a child).

Paramahamsa (supreme swan)

The paramahamsa remains either unclad or wears a single loincloth, and smears ashes all over his body. He collects alms from only five houses per day. He sleeps on the ground, usually in temple compounds, and in winter he may use a woollen blanket. He does not bother his body with too much comfort or pain. Generally he does not shave, and if he does, then only once in six months at the time of solstice. The paramahamsa lives in solitude and becomes established in Brahman. Having abandoned all attachment and freed himself from the influence of duality, worldly affairs can no longer bind him. He has the ability to see and to control the gunas, and to separate purusha and prakriti, consciousness and energy. He transcends prakriti and enters the fourth dimension of consciousness called turiya or samadhi.

Turiyatita (beyond the fetters of nature)

The turiyatita has gone beyond the states of waking, dreaming and sleep. He is established in the turiya or transcendental state of consciousness. He remains in a state of perpetual union with the One which is beyond all attributes. This is the stage of total inner renunciation. However, even in this state, a very thin cord of attachment still persists, which holds the sannyasin in the world. From time to time the consciousness fluctuates from the state of turiya towards the *samsaric pravrittis* (worldly tendencies) and then back again to turiya.

In this stage the sannyasin remains unclad in all seasons and keeps his body just alive. He takes food without solicitation, his sustenance depending solely on the will of others. He takes food without using his hands, like a cow, hence the turiyatita is also known as 'cow faced'. Usually he subsists on fruits. If at all he takes cooked food, he obtains it from only three houses. He smears his body with ashes. He does not put any mark on his forehead.

Avadhoota (total transcendence)

The avadhoota represents the pinnacle of spiritual evolution; none is superior to him. *Avadhoota* means 'one who is immortal' *(akshara)*, and who has totally discarded worldly ties. He is verily Brahman himself. He realizes himself to be pure intelligence. He is unmindful of the six infirmities of human birth, namely: sorrow, delusion, old age, death, hunger and thirst. He has shaken off all bondage of the experiential world, and moves about freely like a child, a madman or one possessed by spirits.

He may be with or without clothes. He does not wear any distinct emblem of any order. He has no desire to sleep, beg or bathe. He views his body as a corpse and subsists on food which comes to him from all classes. He does not interpret the shastras or the Vedas. For him nothing is righteous or unrighteous, holy or unholy.

He is free of karma. The karmas of this life and past lives are all burnt away, and due to the absence of *kartritva* (doership) and *bhoktritva* (desire for enjoyment), no future karmas are created. Only the *prarabdha* (unalterable) karmas which have already begun to operate will affect his body, helping to sustain it, but his mind will remain unaffected. He will live in this world until the prarabdha karmas are worked out, after which his body will fall off. Then he is said to attain *videhamukti* (state beyond body consciousness). Such a liberated soul never returns to the embodied state. He is not born again; he is immortal. He has achieved the final aim of taking birth in this world.

8

Traditional Rules
and Requirements

Since ancient times the sannyasa order had been a closed and compact organization with strict rules of conduct clearly laid down for all sannyasins. Each sannyasin was expected to follow the rules of conduct meticulously, not only to uphold the lofty standard of the tradition, but also to ensure that he did not deviate from the way. After he has renounced all worldly ties, it is quite possible to lose his direction or fall back in moments of weakness. Therefore, certain rules of conduct were framed by the sannyasins of early times, who understood the pitfalls, obstacles and difficulties on the path of renunciation very well.

The sannyasins realized that true dispassion was an integral part of their quest, and that detachment from the world was directly proportionate to detachment from the body and mind. Thus, they reasoned that the sannyasin must be capable of complete severance from all worldly affairs. For this reason, the sannyasin renounced the three primary desires for wife, wealth and progeny. In order that this would actually be put into practice, rules of conduct were formulated, such as sannyasins should not associate with women, they should not possess more than the barest essentials, they should not stay in towns for more than three days at a time, and so on.

Although such rules may appear extreme by our present standards, they were imposed on the sannyasin in order to ensure the success of his spiritual endeavour, and also to protect and maintain a high standard within the order. Those who failed to follow the code of conduct were considered 'fallen' and were ostracized to the extent that the son of such a sannyasin was not entitled to renounce. The following are some of the general rules which sannyasins of all orders have adhered to from early periods until now. They must be examined in the light of the above discussion, in order to evolve a code which will be in keeping with modern times, while maintaining the lofty standards of those who have walked this path for thousands of years before us.

Activities to be avoided

Sannyasins should not engage in the following pursuits:
- Watching dancers perform
- Gambling
- Associating with lady friends of former days
- Becoming intoxicated with spirits or drugs
- Climbing trees for fruit
- Staying for two nights in the same village
- Travelling at night, between dusk and dawn
- Buying and selling
- Swimming across a river
- Travelling in a carriage
- Fasting too often
- Going to a place of pilgrimage frequently
- Pursuing a means of livelihood
- Having a following of disciples for material gain
- Attending receptions, shraaddha ceremonies, sacrifices, religious processions and festivities
- Consuming ghee
- Taking oil baths
- Indulging in useless talk
- Disclosing his family name, lineage, place of birth, age, conduct and vows observed by him
- Returning anger for anger

- Entering a house for alms when the door is closed
- Living in pairs or in groups
- Bowing to anyone except the preceptor.

Requisites for sannyasa

The regulations for taking sannyasa differ from sect to sect. Ancient texts laying down the procedures are not much in evidence, as most of the knowledge was passed down by word of mouth from guru to disciple. Still, we can find adequate references to present the system prevalent in the vedic and post-vedic eras.

General requirements for taking sannyasa: The aspirant should be equipped with the four disciplines which are essential prior to the study of Brahmavidya. These are:

1. Discrimination between permanent and transitory things, meaning that a person must always subject the nature of things to a rigid analysis by discrimination between what is permanent and what is transitory, what is true and what is false.
2. Absence of desire for enjoying the fruits of action here and hereafter, in order to reduce the accumulation and influence of karmas.
3. Cultivation of mental peace and self-control through patience, faith and surrender.
4. Desire for moksha, liberation from worldly life *(mumukshutva)*.

Additional requirements for aspirants coming to sannyasa from brahmacharya ashrama included:
- Perfect control over the tongue, genitals, stomach and hands.
- Dedication to service and surrender to God and guru.

Additional requirements for aspirants coming to sannyasa from grihastha ashrama:
- Before renouncing worldly life, the householder should have discharged his three debts: (i) to the sages by studying the Vedas, (ii) to the gods by performing sacrifices, and (iii) to the ancestors by begetting a son.

Additional requirements for aspirants coming to sannyasa from vanaprastha ashrama:
- They should have undergone purification through forty sacred rites. These are samskaras beginning with the consummation of the marriage of their parents.
- They should have the ten virtues characterizing right conduct: contentment, forgiveness, self-control, non-stealing, purity, control of the senses, humility, scriptural learning, truthfulness and an even temper.

Search for the preceptor

After taking the decision to renounce the world, the aspirant must search for a guru or preceptor who will initiate him into the sannyasa order. It is only a guru who can perform the homa and pooja, who can whisper the sacred mantra in one,s ear. It is the guru who gives the initiate the necessary instructions of the order. Unless one has been initiated by a guru, one cannot become a sannyasin of a traditional sannyasa order. Unlike the Dashnama order organized by Shankaracharya, in which the gurus reside in maths, the gurus in ancient India were dispersed throughout the country. Therefore, the aspirant had to first make the decision to take sannyasa, and then search for the nearest available guru, who embodied the qualities required for imparting sannyasa initiation.

Not all sannyasins are qualified to give initiation. The following qualities are laid down for a guru of the traditional sannyasa order:
- One who maintains the sannyasa tradition
- Whose lineage remains unbroken
- Who has faith in vedic lore
- Who is born of a good family
- Who is well versed in the Vedas
- Who has love for the shastras
- Who is virtuous and free from devious ways.

9

Shaiva Sampradaya

Until the twelfth century AD, most sannyasins were designated as Shaivas. Shaivism is the oldest sampradaya, sect or denomination of India. The Dravidians, who were the original inhabitants, worshipped Shiva as their chief deity. A section of Shaivites later began to worship his consort, Parvati, and gradually developed certain tantric systems. These worshippers of female energy, although closely affiliated to the Shaiva sampradaya, came to form a distinct sect of their own, called Shakta.

The Shaivite schools base their knowledge on the Agama or Tantra shastras, which contain the direct revelation from Shiva for all classes, even women and shudras. Those who venerate Shiva in the form of the linga are called Lingayats. They are found mostly in southern India. Those who follow the system taught by Lakuli in the first century AD, which aims at the union of the soul with Shiva through the practice of yoga, are known as Lakulis Pashupatas. The Shaiva Siddhanta school of Tamil Nadu, which is dualistic in approach, and the Pratyabhijna school of Kashmir, which is monistic in approach, both grew out of the school of Lakulis Pashupatas.

The sectarian mark of the Shaivas consists of three horizontal lines with or without a dot below or above the middle line or on the middle line, and with or without an oval or half oval, a triangle, a cone or any other pointed or

47

arched figure, having its apex upward. The figure of a crescent moon or that of a trident is also used by some Shaiva ascetics. These marks are made by hand or by metallic stamps with ashes collected from sacrificial fires or from burnt cow dung or sandalwood paste. The ashes are said to represent Lord Shiva. There are several sub-sects belonging to the Shaiva sampradaya. Some of the more important ones are described below:

1. *Dashnami Sampradaya*: In the eighth century Shankaracharya established this important sect. Dashnamis are also known as vedic Shaivas. Before the establishment of the Dashnami sampradaya, tantric Shaivas such as Kanphatas, Aghoris, Kalamukhis and Kapalikas, dominated the Shaiva scene. Shankaracharya included ten categories of sannyasins, hence ten names, in his order, and he established four monastic headquarters in the north, south, east and west of India to propagate his spiritual teaching.

The Dashnami sannyasins are divided into two broad categories: staffholders and non-staffholders. The staffholders are known as dandadharis and the non-staffholders are called paramahamsas. Of the ten sub-sects of the Dashnami order, only the sannyasins of the Tirtha, Ashrama and Saraswati sects are allowed to hold the staff, and the rest are not allowed to do so. The three Dandi sub-sects initiate only brahmanas into sannyasa, but in the others, persons from kshatriya and vaishya castes may also be initiated.

2. *Kanphata or Gorakh Panth*: This is a sub-sect of tantric Shaivism. Kanphatas pierce their ears and insert large earrings in them. This sect was founded by Adinath, or Lord Shiva. The next guru was Matsyendranath, and the third was Gorakhnath, who is regarded as the reorganizer of this sect. The Kanphatas regard Shiva as the supreme reality; salvation lies in union with Shiva. The chief scripture of this sect is the *Hatha Yoga Pradipika*. In the Nath sampradaya, hatha yoga and tantra are recommended as the best means of salvation. No caste prejudices are observed in this sect.

Kanphatas are also called yogis and their sannyasin name is given with the suffix *nath*, meaning Lord.

3. *Aghori Panth*: This sect was founded by Brahmagiri, a disciple of Gorakhnath. The epithet Aghor is usually used for Shiva, hence Aghoris are sannyasins who worship Shiva. These sannyasins move about all year round and are found all over India. No food is prohibited them. They can even eat decomposed corpses. The Aghori smears himself with ashes from the funeral pyre. He wears a rudraksha mala and a necklace of bones.

4. *Vir Shaiva or Lingayat Sampradaya*: The name of this sect was derived from the word linga. The Lingayat wears a small silver box on his body containing a stone linga which is a symbol of his faith, the loss of which means his spiritual death. It is worn by both male and female members of this sect. Lingayats are against the caste system. All wearers of the linga are proclaimed equal in the eyes of God. Vir Shaivas deny the supremacy of brahmanas. This sect was founded by the saint Basava in the twelfth century.

5. *Karalingi Sampradaya*: Karalingis are roaming Shiva sannyasins. They roam in groups, wearing ochre cloth and sometimes naked, with matted hair. To mark their triumph over sexual desire they affix an iron ring and chain to their male organ, which they also mutilate.

6. *Kapalik Panth*: This sect was prominent in ancient India. Kapaliks are pure tantric sadhus. They wear a bone mala and eat their food from a human skull. They live naked near the burning ghats. Their tutelary deity is Kal Bhairav. Today these sannyasins are few, but they are found all over India.

Shakta sampradaya

Followers of the Shakta sampradaya regard Shakti as the supreme reality. Brahma, Vishnu and Shiva do their work of creation, preservation and destruction through the medium of Shakti. Shakti is the embodiment of power, the universal mother, manifesting in the forms of Durga, Kali, Bhagavati,

Chandi, Chamundi, Tripura Sundari, Parvati, Sita, Radha and so forth. One who worships Shakti, or the Divine Mother, is known as a Shakta. Shaktism involves the systematic practices of kundalini yoga and tantra. There are several radical sects of the Shakta sampradaya, such as Muni Samaj which opposes the practice of celibacy on the basis that the spirit of the cosmic sound Om cannot be fully comprehended by celibates, and the Kumbhi Patia sect which opposes Hinduism and many of its basic tenets.

10

Advent of Shankara

The sannyasins were consolidated into orders as a corollary to the adoption of the four ashramas, in accordance with the vedic code. Before this there had been a tendency amongst sannyasins to form themselves into small groups or bands according to their schools or doctrine. The rishis and munis were spread all over the country in small ashrams or hermitages, and the sannyasins roamed about continuously. With the passage of time, however, some great spiritual leaders arose with new insights and modes of applying the dharmic principles, making them more accessible to the masses.

Buddhism arose as a protest against the supremacy of the brahmin caste and the prodigious sacrificial rites. Buddha preached purity of heart, right conduct and attainment of moksha through adherence to the eightfold path. Buddhist monks practised congregational living in monastic centres called *viharas*, which eventually gave rise to such institutions of learning as Nalanda, the Buddhist University in Bihar, which once housed over ten thousand monks.

In addition, the Buddhist monks were ordained to preach and bring religion to the doors of the people, whereas sannyasins, being renunciate ascetics, had no fixed rules requiring them to instruct others in spiritual precepts and practice. Buddha also accepted aspirants from the lower castes and even women into his order, thus further defying the brahmanic tradition. For these reasons Buddhism grew very quickly and became popular amongst the masses, while the vedic religion and culture began to decline.

Kumarilla Bhatta: doctrine of karma

Just before the advent of Shankara, Kumarilla Bhatta and his disciple, Mandan Mishra, set about to revive the vedic teachings. In some biographies of Shankara, it is said that all the gods went to Parameshwara and complained that dharma had declined in the world. In order to resuscitate the eternal truth, dharma incarnated as Shankara, and of the other gods, Brahma became Mandan Mishra, Saraswati the wife of Mandan Mishra, and Subramanya became Kumarilla Bhatta.

During the time of Kumarilla Bhatta, the Buddhists were very powerful. They had no use for recitation of the Vedas, upanayana (sacred thread ceremony) and yajna. They criticized the Vedas and converted people to the path of atheism. In order to understand the tenets of Buddhism thoroughly, Kumarilla Bhatta attired himself in the garb of a Buddhist monk and became a student of Buddhist teachers. Had these teachers known that he was a brahmin, they would not have accepted him as their student.

While living in the vihara, Kumarilla Bhatta performed vedic rituals without the knowledge of the others. Simultaneously, he attended his lessons with the Buddhists teachers in which the Vedas and vedic rituals were criticized. Finally the Buddhists found out that Kumarilla Bhatta was not a monk like themselves, but a brahmin in disguise, and he was asked to leave the vihara.

After this, Kumarilla Bhatta commenced his mission of spreading the Purva Mimamsa view, according to which the doctrine of karma or ritual is the main path for achieving moksha, as expounded in the Vedas. He said that, "Karma (ritual) will itself yield its fruits, and all accomplishments are obtained through karma (ritual) only."

Before the advent of Shankara, the prevalent view was that karma or ritual is absolutely essential for spiritual attainment and welfare. However, Shankara wanted to establish the Vedantic view that, "Karma alone cannot bring the highest attainment. Eternal good can only come through the grace of God. One should not stop with following the karmakanda, as its fruits are to be found only in the jnanakanda."

Shankara wanted to argue with Kumarilla Bhatta on these points, knowing fully well that once Kumarilla Bhatta was convinced, everyone would be ready to listen to his view. However, by the time Shankara met him, Kumarilla Bhatta was about to immolate himself in expiation for the sin he had committed against his Buddhist guru, when he appeared before him in disguise. However, he directed Shankara to another Mimamsaka, Mandan Mishra, who was absolutely devoted to the path of ritual, to hold a debate on the subject.

Shankara versus Mandan Mishra

Mandan Mishra was a champion of the cause of vedic ritual. He preached against Buddhism and was able to establish the Mimamsa view. According to Purva Mimamsa, relinquishing karma is a great defeat. Therefore, they rejected the sannyasa ashrama on the grounds that voluntarily giving up karma and taking sannyasa was like a brahmin becoming a shudra. They said that, according to the *Ishavasya Upanishad*, one must desire to live for a hundred years doing karma. The *Taittireya Brahmana* declares that by extinguishing the agnihotra fire, one incurs the sin of killing a hero. Performing evil karma is sin; omitting to perform *nitya karma* (daily rituals such as sandhya, vandana or early morning prayer) is also a sin.

Refraining from performance of karma is wrong, so becoming a sannyasin is also wrong. The sannyasin is a transgressor; therefore, if one happens to even see him one must perform the appropriate expiatory ceremony. Sin will accrue to one who sees a sinner, who talks with him, who touches him or eats with him. Hence one should not see a sannyasin. Such were the views held by Mandan Mishra when Shankara went to hold a debate with him on the doctrine of karma and on the true meaning of the Vedas.

Shankara knew the tremendous impact his victory over the irreconcilable Mandan Mishra would have on his mission. Keeping this in view, Shankara imposed the condition that, if Mandan Mishra was defeated in the debate then he would become a sannyasin, and if Shankara was defeated then he would give up sannyasa.

Shankara considered that a Mimamsaka with the above views could not gain eternal bliss. Mimamsakas longed for transitory happiness and believed in repeated births. He wanted them to realize that their beliefs were wrong. All karmas should be offered to Parameshwara. Remaining without karma is the supreme truth and unsurpassable bliss. When this is realized, there will be no more births. The entire *karmakanda* (ritual) of the Vedas must be construed as auxiliary to *jnanakanda* (knowledge), and only then will karmakanda become useful. These views were diametrically opposed to the philosophy of Mandan Mishra, which maintained that the vedic texts were not intended to describe the nature of the supreme Self. Their truth was in the performance of karma or ritual.

During the debate Shankara was successful in establishing his views over those of Mandan Mishra. It took eighteen days of debate to subdue Mandan Mishra, who was capable of receiving the mighty, intellectual punches of Shankara. At the end of the debate, Mandan Mishra was forced to accept defeat, and he became a disciple of Shankara by taking sannyasa diksha from him. He was given the name Sureshwara.

With his victory over Mandan Mishra, Shankara was hailed as the undisputed spiritual leader of India. At that time there were seventy-two schools existing in the country, such as Buddhist, Samkhya, Vaisheshika, etc. Shankara rejected all of them. During his visits to important centres of learning, Shankara met with the great scholars of his period. After understanding their different views, he debated with them and convinced them that their doctrines were contradicting the Vedas.

Restructuring the sannyasa order

While debating with the various scholars, Shankara circumambulated the country three times. During these journeys he established four monastic institutions called *maths*, in order to unify the various and diverse groups of sannyasins which were scattered throughout the country and bring them all under one banner of vedic dharma. The establishment of the maths virtually amounted to the restructuring of the entire sannyasa order and brought about the spiritual renaissance of India.

These four maths were founded as the headquarters for the sannyasins of different traditions and were located at the four corners of the country, with the idea that the spiritual heritage should spread uniformly throughout the land. They were also meant to facilitate the *parivrajaka* or wandering sannyasins who were to reside in one place during the four months of chaturmas, the rainy season. These four maths which Shankara founded about one thousand two hundred years ago still continue to convey his eternal message of the synthesis of all religions, culminating in *Adwaita*, the monistic vision of reality.

11

Dashnama Sannyasa Order

In the four maths founded by Shankara, a new vision of sannyasa life was introduced in order to spread adwaitic philosophy among the people. Whereas previously sannyasins had been total renunciates, having no duty or mission in the world, in the new order the sannyasins were inspired to propagate and uphold the vedic dharma, and to guide and uplift society through their teachings. Sannyasins, who had previously been clothed in space and communed with God only, were encouraged to wear the geru cloth as a symbol of renunciation, and to communicate with the people through *satsang* and *upadesh*, spiritual gatherings and discourses. In return society would support the maths, so that each sannyasin could be provided with the basic requirements.

In the four maths Shankara advocated a system of devotion. He installed a devi and devata in each math, the purpose being, not idol worship, but to teach a path for the realization of Shiva and Shakti as one. The devi and devata were installed as follows:

Math	Devi	Devata
Sharda (Dwarka)	Bhadrikali	Siddhesvara
Sringeri (Sringeri)	Saraswati	Adi Varaha
Jyotir (Badrinath)	Punyagiri	Narayana
Govardhan (Jagannath Puri)	Vimla	Jagannath

The four maths can be regarded as the nuclei of the Dashnami sannyasa order. After the establishment of these maths and the ten orders, there began a gradual development in both the numbers and activities of the Dashnami sannyasins. The maths and the reformed sannyasa order made a vital contribution towards the upliftment of the spiritual, social and political atmosphere of India. The heads of the four maths became the direct representatives of Shankara, and to this day they are still called shankaracharyas. Shankara chose the first four heads from amongst his closest and most capable disciples. They were as follows:

1. Padmapadacharya, Govardhan Math (Puri)
2. Hastamalakacharya, Sharda Math (Dwarka)
3. Sureshwaracharya, Sringeri Math (Sringeri)
4. Trotakacharya, Jyotir Math (Badrinath).

As the symbols of their philosophical quintessence, each math was assigned one of the four Vedas and one of the four mahavakyas. These are given as follows:

Math	Veda	Mahavakya
Govardhan	Rik	Prajnanam Brahma (Knowledge is Brahma)
Sringeri	Yajur	Aham Brahmasmi (I am Brahma)
Sharda	Sama	Tat Twam Asi (Thou art That)
Jyotir	Atharva	Ayam Atma Brahma (Soul is Brahma)

Each math has its own brahmacharyas for training, its own *kshetra* (sacred place), its own *tirtha* (sacred waters), and its own *gotra* (spiritual lineage). Similarly each math has its own *sampradaya* or sect. The exact rationale is not provided by the significance attached to each, but is based on the different ascetic qualities of each group.

Math	Sampradaya	
Sringeri	Bhurivara	(who have given up wealth and pleasure)
Sharda	Kitavara	(who have compassion for all living beings)
Jyotir	Anandavara	(who have freedom from desire for sensual pleasures)
Govardhan	Bhogavara	(who have freedom from desire for enjoyments)

Shankara divided all the sannyasins of India into ten main groups which are collectively known as the Dashnama Sannyasa Order. Each group was given a special name according to the habitat or lineage of those sannyasins. These names are as follows:

1. *Giri* – one who lives on a hill
2. *Parvata* – one who lives on mountain tops
3. *Sagara* – one who lives near the sea
4. *Vanam* – one who lives in the forest
5. *Aranya* – one who lives in the jungle
6. *Ashrama* – one who lives in a hermitage
7. *Saraswati* – one who is well-versed in knowledge
8. *Tirtha* – one who lives near sacred waters
9. *Puri* – one who dwells in a town
10. *Bharati* – one without bondage, an adept in Brahma-vidya.

Each sannyasin must bear one of the above distinctive titles after their sannyasa name. These titles do not in any way indicate one's superiority or inferiority to another. The Dashnami sannyasins have played a more active role in propagating the institution of sannyasa. Shankara allocated the ten groups of sannyasins to the four maths. This allocation is only a nominal one, which means that this math is the headquarters of their sampradaya. However, the sannyasins are not required to receive sannyasa initiation from these maths or to follow any direction or control from them. Their allocation to the different maths is as follows:

Math	Dashnami sannyasins
Sringeri (Rameshwara)	Saraswati, Bharati, Puri
Sharda (Dwarka)	Tirtha, Ashrama
Jyotir (Badrinath)	Giri, Parvata, Sagara
Govardhan (Puri)	Vanam, Aranyam

Each of the Dashnamis was assigned a particular Upanishad for study, although they are encouraged to study the other Upanishads as well. The Upanishads were assigned as follows:

Dashnami sannyasin	Upanishad to be studied
1. Saraswati	Brihadaranyaka
2. Bharati	Taittiriya
3. Puri	Katha
4. Tirtha	Kena
5. Ashrama	Chandogya
6. Giri	Mundaka
7. Parvata	Prashna
8. Sagara	Mandukya
9. Vanam	Aitareya
10. Aranya	Kausitaki

Some of the main contributions of Shankara towards restructuring the sannyasa order are enumerated below:
1. Sannyasins were freed from all ritualistic sacrifices.
2. They became engaged in vedantic disciplines connected with the Upanishadic texts.
3. Renunciation or vairagya was completely internalized.
4. The fourfold practice of *viveka* (discrimination), *vairagya* (detachment), *sat-sampatti* (moral codes like endurance, faith etc.) and *moksha* (liberation) was stressed.
5. Parivrajaka or mendicancy, except during the four months of the rainy season, was advocated.
6. Emphasis was laid on renunciation of all worldly connections as a prerequisite to moksha.
7. An authentic guru parampara or tradition was created.

12

Dashnami Akhara
and Alaka Bara

Dashnami sannyasins are divided into two categories: *astradharis* (weapon holders) and *shastradharis* (scripture holders). The former are militant ascetics and the latter are learned ascetics. The militant sannyasins are recruited from all ten orders and are known as *naga* sannyasins. Nagas generally remain unclothed all year round. Traditionally only those who are unmarried, widowers or who have no family obligations are recruited. Their initiation ceremony takes place during the Kumbha Mela and their initiation rites are different from the shastradhari sannyasins.

Akhara

The naga headquarters are known as akhara. The literal meaning of the word *akhara* is 'a place for training in arms'. Formerly the aim of these akharas was to protect the traditional culture. The sannyasins took up arms when Hindu pilgrims were tortured during the Pathan, Mogul and British periods. The nagas live a communal life and enjoy such rights and privileges as the marhi sanctions. In the akhara all property belongs to the community. Their organization is purely military and they undergo hard physical training and training in the use of weapons.

The nagas may either shave their heads or have long matted hair which is coiled in the jata on top of the head. Every akhara has its own distinct custom of wearing the jata, so that on seeing a naga one can at once recognize the akhara to which he belongs. For example, the members of Nirvani akhara bind their hair on the right side of the head, the members of Juna on the left and the members of Niranjani in the middle. The nagas worship their *bhallas*, or spears. These have been given different names in each akhara: Surya Prakash, Bhairav Prakash, etc. Sometimes these names are engraved on the spears in gold and silver. In the Kumbha Mela, these spears are carried in procession and are bathed first.

Reliable information about the origin and history of the akharas is not available today. However, on the basis of records and reports, the origins of the main akharas are given below.

Name of Akhara	Place	Vikram Samvata	Anno Domini
Ananda	Unknown	912	856 AD
Niranjani	Kachcha Mandivi	960	904 AD
Juna or Bhairon	Karna Prayag	1202	1106 AD
Avahan	Kasi	1603	1547 AD
Atal	Gondwana	1704	1648 AD
Mahanirvani	Baidyanath Dham	1805	1749 AD

Atal, Avahan and Ananda are affiliated to Mahanirvani, Juna and Niranjani akharas respectively. It is well known that during the nineteenth century sannyasins of Ananda akhara played a leading role in India's struggle for freedom. Juna akhara also fought against the British, although on the side of the Portuguese.

Organization of the akhara

The organization of the akhara is based on a democratic tradition, although most of the decisions are made by consensus, in case there are divergent views. Akharas are

61

divided into eight *dava* or divisions, where training is imparted, and fifty-two *marhi*, which are the recruiting centres. The marhi form the nucleus of the akhara and are headed by *mahants*, great souls. Formerly, the mahants were rich persons who acted as guardians of the sannyasins. The mahants are assisted by *karobaris*, or administrators, who help in the execution of managerial duties. *Thanapatis*, or supervisors, supervise the area of eight mahants, *mandalacharyas* control eight to twelve thanapatis, *mahamandalacharyas* control eight to twelve mandalacharyas, and at the head is the *acharya*, or preceptor, who exercises control over the eight to twelve mahamandalacharyas. He is maintained as Parameshwara.

Sri Panch, which literally means a body of five persons, controls virtually everything in the akhara. The Sri Panch represents Brahma, Vishnu, Shiva, Shakti and Ganesha. Parameshwara is Shiva. Apart from this, each akhara has its own tutelary deity. Selection of the Sri Panch is made during the Kumbha Mela. These five persons hold office for four years. Sri Panch is the working committee (*karya samiti*) of the akhara. They also form a wandering committee known as *ramta panch*, which visits and inspects establishments under their jurisdiction and solves the problems of the sannyasins. Thus, the organizational structure of the akhara is sannyasin, ramta panch, Sri Panch and acharya.

Agni akhara

The brahmacharis of Agni akhara organized themselves into a separate akhara of their own. These brahmacharis are all brahmanas and agnihotras; they offer oblations to the sacrificial fire. In the other akhara they could not perform this rite as sannyasins are supposed to have renounced all sacrificial rites. This akhara was founded in 1482 AD. The Agni akhara does not have any marhi, or recruitment centre, as its nucleus, but it has established over three hundred large and small maths all over India. The Devi of this akhara is Gayatri. The brahmacharis perform homa (sacrificial fire ceremonies), study the shastras (scriptures) and lead a life of celibacy.

Alakh Bara

As the headquarters of astradhari (weapon holder) or naga sannyasins was the akhara, so the shastradhari (scripture holder) sannyasins lived outside society in the alakh bara. *Alakh bara* means 'invisible boundary'. Before the astradhari sannyasins were established in the different akhara, it was the duty of the shastradhari sannyasins to protect and pass down the scriptural knowledge. Whenever they felt any impending threat, and there were many in ancient times due to invasions, political upheavals and natural calamities, these sannyasins immediately disappeared into the high mountain vastnesses and deep, uncharted forests and jungles where they remained alone or with small bands of disciples.

In the alakh bara or 'invisible boundary' they remained for long periods of time, unknown or unseen by the members of the society from which they had come. They lived on roots and herbs, practising austerities and deep meditation, untroubled by social holocausts. In peaceful times, when they felt the need to return the spiritual knowledge to the people, they would come down from the alakh bara and again move amongst society. At such times they lived in a different type of establishment, which was known as an ashram and later as a math.

Gradually, with the need for more spiritual protection as the threat of foreign invasions increased, the militant sannyasin sects arose. As the akharas grew more powerful, they assumed the responsibility for protecting the scriptures and the dharma. Therefore, there was no need for the shastradharis to live in isolated, unknown hermitages as they had previously and so the concept of alakh bara was slowly forgotten. The shastradharis founded, or were affiliated with, one of the ashrams or maths and these ashrams and maths were again protected by the akhara.

Sri Panch Dashnam Paramahamsa Alakh Bara

In 1990, Paramahamsa Satyananda commenced his sadhana at Rikhia, Deoghar, in the state of Bihar (now Jharkhand), under the inspiration of his ishta devata. At that time, the concept of the alakh bara slowly evolved around him. This alakh bara within the sannyasa tradition came as a means of fulfilling the higher stages of sannyasa, starting from the stage of paramahamsa. A sannyasin who has exhausted all his or her karmas could live there in total isolation from society and practise sadhanas and austerities undisturbed by the hustle and bustle of external social life.

This alakh bara became known as Sri Panch Dashnam Paramahamsa Alakh Bara and is structured to uphold the highest traditions of sannyasa, namely *vairagya* (dispassion), *tyaga* (renunciation) and *tapasya* (austerity). The alakh bara propounds the tapovan style of living adopted by the rishis and munis of the vedic era and is intended only for paramahamsa sannyasins.

The guidelines for Sri Panch Dashnam Paramahamsa Alakh Bara are based on the vedic tradition of sadhana, tapasya, *swadhyaya* (self-study) and *atma chintan* (introspection), emphasizing the need of each sannyasin to develop and cultivate the sublime spiritual qualities within. The alakh bara does not preach any religion or religious precepts.

The tutelary deities of the Sri Panch Dashnam Paramahamsa Alakh Bara are Adi Guru Shankaracharya and Swami Sivananda Saraswati. The Sri Panch are Brahma, Vishnu, Shiva, Shakti and Ganesha. The insignia is the dakshinmukhi conch or *shankha*. The flag is an orange-coloured triangle on which the symbol of the dakshinmukhi conch is printed. The yantra is a combination of various symbols representing the Sri Panch. Devi is represented by Sri Yantra, Brahma by a *kalash* (copper vessel), Vishnu by a conch, Shiva by a trident, and Ganesha by Ganapati yantra.

The colour of dress of the initiates of Sri Panch Dashnam Paramahamsa Alakh Bara is black. Black represents *avyakta prakriti*, or the unmanifest nature. The colour of *vyakta prakriki*, or the manifest nature, is white in which all colours, shapes, forms and ideas become visible. The black colour of avyakta prakriti is the colour of Kali, the dark-hued one, where all forms, shapes, colours and identities are merged into shoonya, the void.

The name of the dhuni where fire is constantly burning is Mahakal Chitta Dhuni.

Other establishments related with the Sri Panch Dashnam Paramahamsa Alakh Bara are as follows:

- *Sukhman (or Sushumna) Marhi Amarwa*, the sadhana place of Paramahamsa Atmananda, the first sannyasin disciple of Paramahamsa Satyananda. This marhi is located opposite the Alakh Bara at Rikhia.
- *Hamsa Marhi*, Munger, is the sadhana place of Paramahamsa Niranjanananda.

A sannyasin of the Dashnami order who has reached a higher state of consciousness is admitted to the Alakh Bara to lead the life of a recluse. Such recluses are called avadhootas. The word *avadhoota* means 'one who is destroyed'. An avadhoota sannyasin has renounced *samsara*, worldly bondage, and has destroyed his desires for sensual pleasures from the roots. The avadhoota resides at the Alakh Bara. The meaning of alakh is 'invisible', bara means 'boundary'. Invisible boundary means it is not a public place; it is a place of sadhana and tapasya. Entrance to the Alakh Bara and the other marhis is strictly controlled, so that the sadhana of serious-minded spiritual aspirants is not disturbed.

13

Vaishnava Sampradaya

India is an amalgam of different peoples, with different cultures and religious traditions. Two of the most ancient cultures are the vedic which advocated the worship of Vishnu, and the tantric which advocated the worship of Shiva and Shakti. Gradually a synthesis of the two sampradayas was brought about by the efforts of various reformers, poets and saints. This synthesis is what is now broadly termed as Hinduism, wherein both Shiva and Vishnu command equal respect.

Vaishnavism refers to the sect of Vishnu, who is considered to be the protector and maintainer of the universe. Vaishnava sannyasins worship Vishnu and his different incarnations such as Rama and Krishna, as well as their consorts, Sita and Radha. These sannyasins usually draw U-like marks on the body, known as *khara tilak*. They also mark their bodies with the emblems of Vishnu such as the *chakra* (discus), *shankha* (conch), *gada* (mace) and *padma* (lotus). The Vaishnava marks are red, yellow, black or white in colour and are made from gopi chandan, clay brought from sacred places or centres of pilgrimage, or from sandalwood paste.

The sects and sub-sects of the Vaishnava sampradaya are generally divided into two categories, orthodox and reformist. In the eleventh century, Ramanuja refuted Shankara's views and gave a new interpretation of the Brahma Sutras. Later, Nimbarka, Madhavacharya and Vallabhacharya established other schools of Vaishnavism. These four schools are known as the *Chatuh sampradaya* (the four denominations). The underlying unity of these philosophical schools is recognition of some form of Vishnu, although in daily worship the various aspects recognized as tutelary deities were significantly different.

The Vaishnava sects also had their own guru parampara, like the Shaivas. Until the advent of the vairagi sects, the monastic ideal was more or less based on jnana, knowledge or intellectual pursuits. The vairagis, called Akhadamalla, are equivalent to the naga sannyasins of the Dashnami sampradaya. Ramanuja, Chaitanya and Ramananda all established bhakti movements. Neither Chaitanya nor Ramananda favoured discrimination in matters of caste or sex. The main Vaishnava sects are as follows:

1. *Sri sampradaya*: This is the largest and oldest of the orthodox sects. This sampradaya is called Sri because Lakshmi or Sri, who is the consort of Vishnu, was its legendary founder. Ramanuja, the expounder of the Vishishtadwaita philosophy, is the historical founder. *Vishishtadwaita* is the philosophy of qualified monism which refutes Shankara's philosophy of Adwaita or monism. The sannyasins of this sampradaya fall into two groups, Badgal and Tangal. The Badgal follow the *markat nyaya* (monkey theory) which emphasizes the concomitancy of the human will in the wake of salvation, and represents the soul that envisions God as a young monkey which clings to its mother. The Tengal maintains the theory of divine grace and the utter helplessness of the soul until it is seized and carried off like a kitten in the mouth of its mother. This doctrine is called *marjara nyaya* (kitten theory).

The sannyasins of this sect are known as Ramanuji. They lead very rigorous and regulated lives. They are usually great scholars in Sanskrit and theology. They repeat the Ashtakshara mantra, Om Namo Narayana.

2. *Namawat sampradaya*: The Namawat sannyasins follow the philosophy of *Dwaitadwaita*, dualistic monism, expounded by Nimbarkacharya. He held that the relation of God to

67

the soul is one of identity in difference. The soul and the world are different from God because they are endowed with qualities different from those found in God. At the same time, they are not different from God, because he is omnipresent and all beings depend entirely upon him.

The Namawat sannyasins carry a tulsi mala and a *tribanda* (three bamboo sticks tied together). Most of them are parivrajaka, roaming throughout the year.

3. *Brahma sampradaya*: This order is so called because its key principles were originally transmitted by Vishnu to Brahma, who revealed them to the world through Vayu, the lord of the wind. Madhavacharya is regarded as the incarnation of Vayu, who came into this world to counter the teachings of Shankara. According to this sect, Kumarila Bhatta explains the true principles of dharma in his commentary on Purva Mimamsa; all else is untruth. The teachings of Kumarila Bhatta were revived by Madhav-acharya. He developed the system of dualism or Dwaita philosophy, as opposed to Shankara's philosophy of monism or Adwaita. The Madhavachari sannyasins lead a life of continuous fasting. The chief math of this sect is situated at Udupi in Karnataka.

4. *Madhavagauriya sampradaya*: The founder of this sect was Chaitanya Mahaprabhu, who was born in Bengal in 1486. He recruited his disciples from all castes and creeds. Gradually the Chaitanya sampradaya came to be affiliated with the Madhava sampradaya. Madhavacharya expounded the philosophy of Dwaita, or dualism, while Chaitanya expounded the philosophy of *Achintyabhedabheda*, or inconceivable unity in diversity. After the affiliation, the Chaitanya sampradaya became known as the Madhava-gauriya sampradaya.

Madhavagauriya sannyasins regard Vishnu as the ultimate reality. They worship all the incarnations of Vishnu, but regard Lord Krishna as the most complete incarnation of God. They believe that samkirtan, the singing of God's name, is the most important practice for this age. They practise non-violence in thought, action and speech. These sannyasins are generally found in eastern India. Nowadays they are divided into two sects: one upholds the caste system and the other denounces it.

5. *Vallabhachari sampradaya*: The philosophy expounded by Vallabhacharya is called *Shuddhadwaita*, or pure monism. He said that the whole world of matter and soul is real and that it is a settled form of God. Those who bring in maya for the explanation of the world, such as Shankara, are not pure adwaitins, because they admit a second to Brahman. Brahman can create the world without any help from any principle, such as maya. Vallabhacharya advocated worship of Vishnu in the form of Krishna, whom he regarded as the highest Brahman.Vallabhachari sannyasins believe that a sound mind lives in a sound body. Therefore, they do not practise fasting and other forms of extreme tapasya.

6. *Ramanandi Sampradaya*: This sect was founded by Saint Ramananda who was regarded as one of the most revolutionary Indian sannyasins. Ramananda stood for the emotional integration of the entire Hindu society. He opened the gates of bhakti for all, high and low. He accepted all aspirants irrespective of religion, caste or sex. He even accepted Kabir, a Muslim, and Ravidas, a shudra, as his disciples. Prior to him, all religious and sectarian books had been written in Sanskrit, so as not to be intelligible to the common folk. Ramananda was the first to start writing religious books in common, national dialect which could be read and understood by all.

The sannyasins of this sect are called vairagi. One who renounces worldly ties for the pursuit of spiritual bliss is called a vairagi. Vairagis worship Vishnu along with Rama and Krishna. Vairagis are also called avadhootas because they smear their bodies with ashes collected from places of worship. Vairagis have long matted hair. They carry *chimta* (tongs) and deerskin. The colour of their dress is white, although some move about practically naked. They sleep on the ground or on wooden planks, but never on beds. Vairagis live mostly in Ayodhya, the birthplace of Rama. Today the Ramanandi sampradaya is the largest order of Vaishnava sannyasins.

These are the main orthodox Vaishnava sampradaya, but there are other smaller sects and also a number of reformed sects such as Kabir Panth, Dadu Panth, Nirmala Panth, Radha Soami sect, Bhagat Panth, and so on. The Vaishnava, like the Dashnami, also have their own naga sannyasins. They are organized into *ani* (companies) and akharas, which were started around 1700 AD. There are seven major akharas and some minor akharas. They are organized along the same lines as the Dashnami akhara.

Sannyasa Today

14

Song of the Sannyasin

*The immortal call to sannyasa composed
by Swami Vivekananda in 1895.*

Wake up the note! the song that had its birth
Far off, where worldly taint could never reach,
In mountain caves and glades of forest deep,
Whose calm no sigh for lust or wealth or fame
Could ever dare to break; where rolled the stream
Of knowledge, truth and bliss that follows both.
Sing high that note, Sannyasin bold! Say –

"Om tat sat, Om!"

Strike off thy fetters! bonds that bind thee down,
Of shining gold or darker, baser ore;
Love, hate; good, bad; and all the dual throng,
Know, slave is slave, caressed or whipped, not free;
For fetters, though of gold, are not less strong to bind;
Then off with them, Sannyasin bold! Say –

"Om tat sat, Om!"

Let darkness go! the will-o'-the-wisp that leads
With blinking light to pile more gloom on gloom.
This thirst for life, forever quench; it drags
From birth to death, and death to birth, the soul.
He conquers all who conquers self. Know this
And never yield, Sannyasin bold! Say –

"Om tat sat, Om!"

"Who sows must reap," they say, "and cause must bring
The sure effect; good, good; bad, bad; and none
Escape the law. But who so wears a form
Must wear the chain." Too true; but far beyond
Both name and form is Atman, ever free.
Know thou art That, Sannyasin bold! Say –

"Om tat sat, Om!"

They know not truth who dream such vacant dreams
As father, mother, children, wife and friend.
The sexless Self! Whose father He? Whose child?
Whose friend, whose foe is He who is but One?
The Self is all in all, none else exists;
And thou are That, Sannyasin bold! Say –

"Om tat sat, Om!"

There is but One – The Free – The Knower – Self!
Without a name, without a form or stain.
In him is Maya, dreaming all this dream.
The Witness, He appears as nature, soul.
Know thou art That, Sannyasin bold! Say –

"Om tat sat, Om!"

Where seekest thou? That freedom, friend, this world
Nor that can give. In books and temples vain
Thy search. Thine only is the hand that holds
The rope that drags thee on. Then cease lament,
Let go thy hold, Sannyasin bold! Say –

"Om tat sat, Om!"

Say, "Peace to all: From me no danger be
To aught that lives. In those that dwell on high,
In those that lowly creep, I am the Self in all!
All life both here and there, do I renounce,

74

All heavens and earths and hells, all hopes and fears."
Thus cut thy bonds, Sannyasin bold! Say–

"Om tat sat, Om!"

Heed then no more how body lives or goes,
Its task is done, let Karma float it down;
Let one put garlands on, another kick this frame;
Say naught. No praise or blame can be
Where praiser praised, and blamer blamed are one.
Thus be thou calm, Sannyasin bold! Say –

"Om tat sat, Om!"

Truth never comes where lust and fame and greed
Of gain reside. No man who thinks of woman
As his wife can ever perfect be;
Nor he who owns the least of things, nor he
Whom anger chains, can ever pass thro' Maya's gates.
So give these up, Sannyasin bold! Say –

"Om tat sat, Om!"

Have thou no home – what home can hold thee, friend?
The sky thy roof, the grass thy bed; and food
What chance may bring, well cooked or ill, judge not.
No food or drink can taint the noble Self
Which knows itself. Like rolling river free
Thou ever be, Sannyasin bold! Say –

"Om tat sat, Om!"

Few only know the truth. The rest will hate
And laugh at thee, great one; but pay no heed.
Go thou, the free, from place to place
And help them out of darkness, Maya's veil.
Without the fear of pain or search for pleasure,
Go beyond them both, Sannyasin bold! Say –

"Om tat sat, Om!"

Thus, day by day, till Karma's power is spent
Release the soul forever. No more is birth,
No I, nor thou, nor God, nor man. The 'I'
Has All become, the All is 'I' and Bliss.
Know thou art That, Sannyasin bold! Say –

"Om tat sat, Om!"

15

Sannyasa in Modern Times

During the vedic era, asceticism was influenced by the preponderance of *karmakanda*, or ritual, with the underlying quest for Brahman, the ultimate truth. It seems that the rishi parampara was the accepted form of vedic asceticism and not sannyasa, which evolved at a later date. In the Upanishadic period, doubts were expressed as to whether karmakanda could by itself lead to moksha. Such questioning eventually resulted in a greater emphasis on *viveka* and *vairagya*, discrimination and detachment, for final liberation from worldly bondage.

In the eighth century, Shankara established the first Shaiva monastic headquarters, wherein knowledge was considered supreme to the exclusion of karma (ritual). Later, Ramananda and other Vaishnava sannyasins added an element of bhakti into the tradition. From the sixteenth to the nineteenth centuries, however, the sannyasa orders passed through a difficult period due to foreign invasions and political upheavals. Further, under the materialistic influence of Western culture the sannyasa tradition was considered as an anachronism by the educated intellectuals of the century.

With the advent of Ramakrishna Paramahamsa, Swami Dayananda, Swami Vivekananda, Swami Rama Tirtha, Swami Sivananda Saraswati, Paramahamsa Yogananda Giri, Paramahamsa Satyananda and other spiritual luminaries of the nineteenth and twentieth centuries, the sannyasa tradition was again elevated to a position of respect and reverence in the minds of the people. Although many of the sannyasa traditions and values have been modified to suit the changing social, religious and political views, still the essence of the sannyasa ideal remains the same.

New interpretation of ancient traditions

The three fundamental principles of sannyasa: yajna, viraja and parivrajna, depict the sannyasin's attitude towards himself, society and the cosmos.

Yajna (sacrifice): The ancient rishis performed sacrifices in order to maintain a relationship with the cosmos. Today, due to social and economic factors, these ritualistic sacrifices are no longer being performed. However, the sannyasin is now expected to perform the sacrifice, making himself an oblation. His whole life is regarded as a part of the cosmic ritual. The exoteric sacrifices prevalent in vedic times became esoteric as they were integrated into sannyasa life. This demands a spirit of utter dedication to the guru and to the precepts of sannyasa.

Viraja homa (purification or death rite): An oblation in the cosmic sacrifice must be pure and free from blemish. Hence a sannyasin must be purified before offering himself as an oblation. Purity cannot be attained without renunciation. Renunciation of all worldly attachments is the foundation on which sannyasa is built. Viraja homa is the symbolic death rite which the aspirant undergoes at the time of sannyasa initiation, as an act of renunciation. Performance of the viraja homa signifies that the initiate has died to his previous life and associations and is born again into sannyasa. Being new and pure, he is fit for oblation into the cosmic sacrifice, and henceforth he undertakes to lead a life of dedication and renunciation.

Parivrajna (wandering): The aim of undertaking parivrajna by a sannyasin is to put the ideal of renunciation into practice, and thereby to test one's purity. The parivrajaka sannyasin gets plenty of opportunities to give up passion, anger, delusion, possessiveness, egotism and duality, while wandering. In modern times, parivrajna is undertaken by those sannyasins who move about continuously, spreading the guru's teachings and mission. In this way parivrajaka sannyasins are able to elevate society while moving from place to place. They are no longer looked down upon as beggars and parasites as they are able to offer something worthwhile to the people. Instead of begging, they receive the food and shelter which is offered, as well as guru dakshina and the fare to their next destination.

Modern views on sannyasa

During the twentieth century the sannyasa lifestyle underwent many changes, and a new concept of sannyasa is developing in order to balance spiritual aspiration with the increasing influence of the modern technological society. Today, for example, most sannyasins are not only educated in spiritual matters, but many are degree holders in various areas of philosophy, literature, science and medicine. Whereas previously young and illiterate sannyasins were allowed to live in the gurukul and then roam about outside without doing any useful work, now they must complete their education before receiving initiation. After initiation, their spiritual education begins. This means that the sannyasins of today are fully educated in all matters, practical as well as spiritual, and so they are better able to deal with the maintenance, management and propagation of the mission.

The age of idle sannyasins is over. Now aspirants who are not ready, able or willing to work are not considered eligible for sannyasa. Sannyasins are expected to work ceaselessly for the mission, to obey the guru implicitly and to follow strict discipline in the ashram as well as outside. Today's society will no longer support those sannyasins who roam about and beg without giving anything substantial to the people in return. Such stray sannyasins are like a canker on society. Neither do they develop themselves, nor do they help others to develop. So why should the people have to feed them? The same question is being asked regarding the missions. Unless they are able to elevate society and help to remove human suffering, why should they be maintained? They are living off the benefits of an ancient ideal, but not up to its standards, and this creates a kind of rot within the social structure.

In order to stem this rot and revive the sannyasa tradition and values in view of the changes taking place within the Indian culture, it was necessary to introduce the element of *karma yoga*, or selfless service, into sannyasa life. This is one of the basic differences between the traditional and modern concepts of sannyasa. The vedic religion had looked down upon karma as an expendable preliminary for the attainment of moksha. However, the truth is that karma is unavoidable for all living beings. So, why not spiritualize it and help to create a better world? Through karma yoga, work is raised to the level of worship. Work is regarded as a means of manifesting the potential divinity of the sannyasin. It helps to maintain a good relationship with society and enhances the dignity of the sannyasins. Those sannyasins who spend their time in useful works, along with self-study and meditation, are able to inspire and elevate people; others are not.

Open door policy
During the second half of the twentieth century, the gulf between sannyasins following the traditional lifestyle and those advocating changes has increased. Many sannyasins have concluded that certain views and rules of conduct are neither feasible nor practical in the modern age. Some of these are given as follows:
• Sannyasins should shun karma in order to achieve moksha.
• All contact with women is to be avoided to the extent that even looking at, thinking about or talking about women is taboo.

80

- Eligibility for sannyasa is restricted to those who are born in the brahmin caste.
- Women are prohibited from entering the order.

For several decades now, many of the leading sannyasins of our time worked to bring sannyasa out of this straitjacket approach. They have opened it to all, irrespective of religion, caste, creed, nationality or sex. They have spread sannyasa dharma throughout the world and given it a new meaning. The following points outline the new concept of sannyasa:

- The aim of sannyasa is to discover one's self and to establish one's own independence in life.
- Sannyasa is a way of life which promotes physical, emotional, mental, psychic and spiritual well-being.
- Sannyasa is not confined to any religious or socio-political identity.
- Sannyasa life is total involvement in ceaseless, selfless service, relinquishing all the fruits of action.
- Sannyasa does not mean expecting to be maintained by society without making a worthwhile contribution in return, which amounts to living on an allowance provided for the unemployed.
- By devotion to service, meditation and study, the sannyasin becomes a model and inspiration for others within society.
- By establishing viveka (discrimination) and vairagya (detachment), the sannyasin cultivates tyaga (renunciation), internally as well as externally.
- Without depending on dogmas or doctrines, the sannyasin attunes himself or herself with the spirit within, which is divine.
- As divinity develops within, the sannyasin becomes more powerful and can therefore better contribute to the good of others.
- The sannyasin shows through his or her life that religion is not mere words; it means spiritual realization, communion with God.

- Only those sannyasins who attain spiritual realization can communicate it to others. They alone are the beacons of light.

16

Who is Eligible for Sannyasa?

The real concept of a sannyasin is one who has renounced, surrendered or dedicated one's whole life and all of one's faculties to the supreme consciousness, divinity or God. The sannyasin lives, thinks and moves in a higher dimension which is ruled not by 'my will' but by 'Thy will'. The independence which the sannyasin achieves is not freedom of the lower mind and ego, but liberation from the lower mind and its negative and limiting propensities. By attuning oneself with the higher mind, the sannyasin is able to regain his lost harmony, wisdom and spontaneity. Simultaneously his becomes attuned with other people and with the surrounding world.

For these reasons, sannyasa life holds an immense attraction for an increasing number of people today all over the world. However, it is necessary to examine one's motives very carefully before opting for the path of sannyasa. Sannyasa is not suitable for people who actually wish to find a convenient escape from life. Sannyasa is not an escape, nor is it a diversion into peaceful realms of meditation and self-realization. Sannyasins live life just like everyone else, only they are more alert, more active, more aware. In fact, they use the different situations in life to sharpen their awareness and to cultivate discrimination and detachment.

Why sannyasa was adopted in the past

Before the advent of the technological culture, sannyasa was taken for the purpose of attaining moksha or liberation from the cycle of birth and death. The urge to take up sannyasa occurred due to vairagya or the feeling of dispassion for sensual pleasures and worldly life. It could also occur through the development of viveka or discrimination, by reading the scriptures or by experiencing the futility of attachments and desires. In addition, people adopted sannyasa through observation of the ashramas, sannyasa ashrama being the last ashrama or stage of life. In this case, sannyasa occurred as a natural sequence of one's life, whether or not one had developed viveka and vairagya.

People decided to renounce the world and leave society in order to become sannyasins. They undertook vows of celibacy and poverty, dressed in a simple dhoti or loincloth, and led the life of a parivrajaka or wandering mendicant. The sannyasins stayed away from villages and towns, and subsisted on alms obtained from householders. They ate frugally and had almost no other physical needs, nor did they care for them. Their aim was to attain Brahman, the highest consciousness, and establish themselves in that state.

The sannyasins gradually merged their consciousness with the cosmic consciousness by the process of dissolving the ego through austerity and meditation. In this manner, some of the more highly evolved sannyasins were able to reach the acme of human life, while the others remained on the sannyasa path with firm faith that they too would eventually reach moksha. Because the sannyasins of old tried their best to live up to their ideals, they were highly venerated by the people. The sannyasins did not desire anything of the world, yet they gave the treasure of spiritual life to the people and provided solace and guidance to the afflicted.

Why sannyasa today?

Traditionally sannyasa initiation was taken at a mature age, after exhausting all of one's desires and ambitions and having established control over the body and mind. The young people who entered sannyasa life were very few and, like their elders, they were established in discrimination and detachment. Today, however, people of all ages, backgrounds and walks of life are looking to sannyasa as a means of evolving their spiritual awareness. They aspire for the total experience which they are unable to find within society.

Many people today experience deep frustration and lack of fulfilment because they cannot discover any sound basis for their existence. The twin extremes of sensual indulgence and self-denial seem equally meaningless and unnecessary. Yet the individual knows there is something more to live for, to discover and to expand within himself. He knows that his life is very precious, his awareness unique. Yet how is he to progress, how is he to evolve? Most people experience this inner state of self-examination at some stage, but in some it is an inner voice that can hardly be quieted.

For such people, sannyasa is a way of life through which they can discover their creative potential and contribute in a positive way towards the expansion of the collective consciousness of humanity. Sannyasa is a way of life which paves the way to greater self-awareness and ongoing spiritual attainment. It is a path of awakening for those people throughout the world who know they have something more to give, something more to learn, and something more to realize, beyond that which most people consider to be normal.

The desire for sannyasa life grows out of the urge to transcend one's limitations and to do something truly meaningful with one's life. Today there are many intelligent people who are wondering how to change their lives. They cannot accept the life which their parents have led, but want something altogether different. They are searching for knowledge in the universities or leaving their homes and wandering from country to country in search of a greater meaning and purpose in life.

Sooner or later, however, such seekers come to realize that, in order to achieve something worthwhile, something eternal, something which can be of immeasurable benefit to others as well as to themselves, they must look within. Self-improvement is not cultivated externally; it comes about through exploring one's own self. When one realizes this, and feels fully dedicated to the inner quest, then it is possible for one to enter the sannyasa path.

Different levels of sannyasa

In modern society, life has become very complex. Moreover, the political, religious, social and economic values have undergone such tremendous upheavals that people are no longer sure what their aspirations are. The ideal of moksha or liberation from the cycle of birth and death seems to be a very distant goal. First of all, what most people seek is a little bit of peace and harmony. They wish to improve the quality of their life by evolving their spiritual potential and awareness.

Depending on their level of evolution, spiritual seekers are now able to select the stage of sannyasa most suited to their personal aspirations. With these views in mind, a structure of sannyasa as propagated by the Sri Panch Dashnam Paramahamsa Alakh Bara has been outlined below in order to fulfil the different needs of today's spiritual aspirants.

1. *Jignasu sannyasa*: Young people who wish to harmonize their lives by joining the spiritual path may opt for jignasu, or studentship sannyasa. Jignasu is a preliminary before taking a higher stage of sannyasa. These aspirants are committed to becoming good citizens and to serving humanity.

2. *Karma sannyasa*: Many people have a strong inclination towards the spiritual path and ardently desire to involve themselves spiritually. At the same time, they are attached to their families and are very much a part of society for economic and other reasons. Such an attitude often brings conflict because they are unable to balance their family and spiritual life. For such people, the commitment to karma sannyasa, or householder sannyasa, is an important step in

spiritual life. It helps them to lead more purposeful lives and to become instrumental in the upliftment of the family, community and nation.

3. *Gurukul sannyasa*: When an aspirant comes to the ashram and meets the guru, an emotional upheaval usually occurs within. The desire to be near the guru is so over-powering that he takes sannyasa and stays near the guru in the ashram, serving wholeheartedly in his mission. However, many of these aspirants are unable to sever their worldly ties completely. Therefore, they take the commitment of a temporary sannyasa and join ashram life intermittently.

4. *Jnana-vairagya or Rishi sannyasa*: There is another rare type of individual who by his knowledge and experience has understood the futility of mundane life. The usual worldly attractions hold no appeal for him. He has no interest in name or fame, money or power. Although he prefers to remain aloof from society, he still retains some contact and may participate in social functions or activities if he feels so inclined. Such a person usually lives in the country, in the mountains or near the sea. He may stay alone or with his family. In either case, he pursues his sadhana and personal studies. He may become a yoga teacher or preceptor and author of books on spiritual topics. Such individuals are fit for jnana-vairagya or rishi sannyasa.

5. *Vairagya sannyasa*: Very few people are born with utter indifference to the pleasures of the world. They feel detachment or dispassion for the world right from an early age. Their very nature is detached due to their karmas from previous lives. In society they feel like fish out of water. Such persons are able to renounce worldly life completely and take vairagya or poorna sannyasa. Theirs is a life of complete surrender and dedication. The commitment is irrevocable and lifelong. Vairagya sannyasins propagate the guru's teachings and mission, and side by side pursue their own sadhana and personal studies.

6. *Paramahamsa sannyasa*: After completing their work in the mission according to the directions of the guru, some

vairagya sannyasins may qualify for paramahamsa sannyasa. These sannyasins spend the latter part of their lives in the Alakh Bara where they are able to devote themselves totally to sadhana. Thus they will approach the final goal of moksha, or self-liberation.

7. *Pakhand sannyasa*: In each of the six stages of sannyasa mentioned previously, a progressive dawning of spirituality can be discerned. However, there is another category in which there is no discernible spirituality. It is usually for persons who are disillusioned with life due to the death of a close relative, failure in business or profession, disappointment in love, maladjustment in family life, unemployment, loss of property and home. Such persons take sannyasa as a rebound or to lead an easy life. Sometimes persons of ill repute also put on the geru cloth and move about as sannyasins in order to evade the law. These *pakhand* or false sannyasins have done great damage to the sannyasa order which was previously held in very high repute.

Before putting on the geru cloth, one should understand that it represents the highest aspiration, renunciation and total dedication to the guru's mission. It is the traditional dress of those sadhakas who are striving for the upliftment of humanity through the evolution of consciousness. Basically, geru cloth represents an inner attitude which insulates one from worldly values and helps to establish the awareness in the highest spiritual values. If a sannyasin is unable or has no wish to uphold the sannyasa tradition and ideals, then he should remove the geru cloth and wear ordinary dress.

Are you ready for sannyasa?

It is the guru who must decide if you are ready for sannyasa. He understands your personality and spiritual level. He can see the extent to which your worldly attachments are binding. A real guru knows your past, present and future karmas. On the basis of this, he can decide when you are ready to take sannyasa and at which level or category you should enter.

For example, if you are a student or are unmarried and still in the process of establishing yourself in life, then he may initiate you into jignasu sannyasa. If you are married and the guru finds there are many conflicts in your life due to imbalance of spiritual aspirations and worldly commitments, then he may initiate you into karma sannyasa. Similarly, he evaluates your potential for the other types of sannyasa in his own way.

The urge to take sannyasa cannot be explained or rationalized. Therefore, prudence demands that you should answer the following questions for yourself before approaching the guru and asking for sannyasa initiation.

1. Has the decision to take sannyasa come naturally and spontaneously? It should not be a forced one.
2. Are you able to accept yourself and acknowledge your own weaknesses? Self-acceptance is the first step in sannyasa.
3. Are you a person of spirit? Spirituality is a matter of spirit and sannyasa requires a person of spirit. Success in sannyasa life can only come to those who have the courage to strike free of attachments.
4. Are you able to stand alone without depending on others? Sannyasa means pushing into the dimensions of solitude.
5. Can you undergo hardship cheerfully? Sannyasa life can be very tough, tiring and comfortless.
6. Can you accept that sannyasa is beyond religious dogma and belief? Sannyasins have no secular commitments and they follow no religious precepts.
7. Are you ready to renounce your old identity and associations and start a new life? Sannyasa means being born again so that your life can take a more spiritual direction.
8. Are you willing to work hard, engaging all your faculties in selfless service? This is a fundamental requirement for sannyasins of today and without it progress on the spiritual path is very slow.

9. Are you ready to involve yourself totally in the fulfilment of the guru's mission without expecting any gain or reward? This is one of the easiest ways to obtain the guru's grace.

10. Are you able to make the choice between God and the world? Halfway measures do not work in sannyasa.

11. Do you want to take sannyasa in order to become famous, as a means of livelihood, to escape from social or family problems, as a result of sorrow or distress? If so, don't do it. If you take sannyasa under any of the above circumstances, it will be a total failure and bring you much unhappiness.

12. Are you ready to accept the rules of conduct and dedication for the type of sannyasa which the guru may grant you? It is imperative that you follow these rules in order to maintain the high standard of the tradition.

Summing up

Your heart will tell you when the time is ripe for you to adopt sannyasa life. You will be ready when you begin to experience an overpowering discontentment with your present way of life, and when you begin to ponder over the deeper meaning of life beneath the social etiquette and superficialities. In addition, the time will be right for you to take sannyasa when you meet your guru. You cannot take formal initiation into any order of sannyasa without a guru. When you find your guru, an overwhelming desire to surrender to him will surge up in you. When you are ready for sannyasa you will meet your guru, whether you wish to or not.

17

Code of Conduct

FOR SANNYASINS OF THE
BIHAR SCHOOL OF YOGA TRADITION

The code of conduct helps in remodelling behaviour and cultivating those qualities which are conducive to sannyasa life. These rules have been framed so that sannyasins will be more aware of what is expected of them in their daily life. It is required that this code of conduct be followed by all sannyasins with sincerity and earnest resolve. Sannyasa is a noble and inspired way of life. Unless sannyasins respect it and take it seriously, the tradition and lineage will degenerate. Do not allow the high ideals which the geru cloth represents to be lowered by any misconduct on your part.

Once, when asked how a sannyasin should live, Paramahamsa Satyananda replied, "In order to understand the sannyasa lifestyle, observe the process by which the *grihini* (housewife) prepares the rice. Before cooking the rice, she painstakingly removes all the stones and pebbles from it piece by piece. In the same way, you should make a thorough search of all the weaknesses and bad qualities in your personality which are a hindrance to your spiritual development, and remove them one by one. Next the housewife removes the dust, husk and straw from the rice by a process of winnowing. In a similar way, you should remove the subtle portion of your obstacles by the process of discipline. First make an intensive search for the major drawbacks in your character such as jealousy, anger, hatred, attachment, impatience, etc., analyze them, and then exercise

91

control over them by leading a disciplined life. Gradually, bad thoughts, bad speech and bad behaviour will be replaced by good thoughts, good speech and good behaviour. This will help you to develop equanimity and one-pointedness of mind, which is essential for spiritual progress".

The following code of conduct has been designed in such a way that it will be of help to all categories of sannyasins. In order to purify and discipline the mind, the lifestyle must be regulated first. Those activities and behaviours which bring peace of mind and raise the consciousness should be adopted and those which disturb the mind and lower the consciousness should be dispensed with. Different codes are provided for ashram life and home life, which will provide guidance in matters of dress, conduct, karma yoga and sadhana. You may not be able to follow all of these rules in the beginning, but it will become easier as vairagya or dispassion develops. If you are sincere and earnest in your efforts from day to day, you will surely attain the goal.

JIGNASU CODE OF CONDUCT

At home

Daily routine: Go to bed early and get up early so that you can practise your sadhana during the time of *brahmamuhurta*, which is from 4–6 a.m. At this time, the atmosphere is quiet and peaceful and suited for yoga practice. Take a cold bath and commence your asana, pranayama and meditation. In addition, you should light an oil lamp or candle and recite *Saundarya Lahari*, *Guru Stotram*, *Bhaja Govindam* and other selections from *Siddha Prarthana* in the morning and evening, preferably with the family members. Practise *mouna* (silence) for a specific period each day.

Dress: While socializing and at work wear normal civilian clothes. While performing sadhana, anushthana and karma yoga in society, wear a yellow dhoti, kurta (shirt) and upper cloth. Put a single, horizontal line of bhasma (ash) on the forehead. This signifies the sattoguna of brahmacharaya (preservation of alertness and courage).

Behaviour: Attend to all of your duties wholeheartedly and observe the following:

- If you are a student, study with dedication; if employed, work efficiently with the attitude of a karma yogi.
- Do not cause pain or injury to anyone in thought, word or deed.
- Do not use intoxicants of any type.
- Express yourself in a straightforward and honest manner.
- Cultivate self-control, even when being maltreated or abused by others.
- Exercise truthfulness without harming others.
- Be humble and simple, even when success comes to you.
- Avoid temptations and take advantage of opportunities.
- Show perseverance when tackling a laborious and difficult task.
- Be patient when things go against you.
- Look after the needs of your parents, family and friends.

Self-study: For spiritual progress, self-study is essential. Maintain a spiritual diary for this purpose and study the results at certain intervals. Study good books on spiritual topics in order to increase your knowledge. Make an in-depth study of the *Brihadaranyaka Upanishad*, which is recommended for all sannyasins of the Saraswati order.

Karma yoga: Selfless service is an integral part of your sadhana. Work out how much time you can devote to it each day or week. There are plenty of choices available, depending on your inclination and capability. Some of these include: teaching yoga; helping to organize yoga conventions, seminars and camps; writing books and articles on spiritual topics; translating books into the local languages. It is also possible to perform different types of social service. For example, you can help out in adult education programs in your area. You can serve in hospitals and help the patients to learn some basic yoga postures, breathing and relaxation techniques. You can help the old and destitute. You can

93

help in volunteer service during natural calamities such as flood, drought, earthquake, fire, and so on. While performing social service, do not think of yourself as the doer, but as the tool through which guru or God is working.

In the ashram

Daily routine: Total participation without fail in all the activities of the ashram and in whatever duties are assigned to you as karma yoga is compulsory. Follow strictly the rules laid down by the ashram regarding discipline, cleanliness and maintenance of the buildings and grounds.

Sadhana: Practise Gayatri mantra and your personal mantra which was given by the guru in the morning and evening. Practise asana, pranayama and meditation as per the instructions of the acharya.

Dress: Yellow dhoti, kurta and upper cloth should be worn at all times. If you are wearing the sacred thread, you may continue to do so. The head and face should be clean shaven; maintaining the tuft is optional. Put one horizontal line of bhasma on the forehead.

Behaviour: Cultivate awareness in every activity and duty and observe the following points:
• Avoid getting angry, even when provoked.
• Bear physical ailments with fortitude; do not ask for medical treatment unless it is unavoidable.
• Accept whatever food is served in the ashram as prasad.
• The ashram diet is planned for sadhana purposes. Do not expect the same menu as you find in a five star hotel.
• Do not imitate the residents of the ashram.
• Do not waste your time in gossip and small talk.
• Try to spend at least two weeks in the ashram every year.

KARMA SANNYASA CODE OF CONDUCT

At home

Daily routine: Get up at four a.m. and practise your sadhana during the time of brahmamuhurta when the atmosphere is full of sattoguna. Take a cold bath and carry out the practice program given to you at the time of your initiation into karma sannyasa. Light an oil lamp or a candle in the pooja place and recite *Saundarya Lahari, Guru Stotram, Bhaja Govindam* and other selections from *Siddha Prarthana*, in the morning and in the evening, preferably with the other family members. Practise mouna for a specified period every day.

Dress: Wear normal clothes while socializing and at work. During sadhana, anushthana and karma yoga wear geru dhoti, kurta, upper cloth and rudraksha mala. Put two horizontal lines of bhasma on the forehead, signifying the sattoguna of brahmacharya and the rajoguna of karma sannyasa.

Behaviour: Attend to all your duties with the attitude of a karma yogi and observe the following points:

- Do not cause pain or injury to anyone in thought, word or deed.
- Try to live on whatever you receive or earn without craving for more.
- Perform all works without being attached to their fruits.
- Remain calm and collected during happiness and sorrow, honour and dishonour.
- Be intensely aware of yourself and accept yourself.
- Do not depend on anything or anybody other than yourself.
- Try to eradicate the feeling of I-ness and mine-ness.
- Think of yourself as a tool or a medium of the Supreme Self or Paramatma.
- Exercise truthfulness without harming others.
- Avoid temptation and accept opportunities when they knock at your door.
- Practise brahmacharya to the extent possible both in thought and deed.
- Cultivate a sweet disposition towards friends and enemies. It costs you nothing and brings rich dividends to you in return.

- Do not act in a moment of anger. Control yourself and act when you are in a positive frame of mind.
- Serve your parents, family and friends.

Self-study: Maintain a spiritual diary in order to understand your own strengths and weaknesses. Study books on spiritual topics. Try to gain a broad knowledge of world religions, philosophies and spiritual teachings, as well as those within the Indian culture.

Study and reflect on the teachings of the *Bhagavad Gita* and *Brihadaranyaka Upanishad* along with the *Taittiriya, Katha* and *Ishavasya Upanishads*. Also study *Vairagya Shatak* by Bhartrihari, *Aparokshanubhuti* by Shankarcharya and *Karma Sannyasa* by Paramahamsa Satyananda.

Karma yoga: It is very important for a karma sannyasin to perform *nishkam karma yoga* or selfless service as much as possible. You should not be emotionally attached to any work, to anything or to anyone in your life. You should dedicate the fruits of your actions to your guru or ishta, thereby attaining peace within yourself. The most important karma yoga for the karma sannyasin is teaching yoga. It is your responsibility to make your life and your home an example to your community members. Living a yogic life and making the home into a mini-ashram is the best way to show people how they should live and what needs to be changed in their lives.

Karma sannyasins are also responsible for conducting classes on yoga for their community members. In order to transmit the teachings in the best possible manner, you should be well-trained in yoga by attending courses in the ashram. You should also do your own practice regularly with a view to understanding the inner mechanism of the different practices. You should be well read and well versed in different subjects which students may ask about, such as health problems, psychological misunderstandings, spiritual doubts, etc.

As a karma sannyasin you should organize yoga camps and seminars in your area at least once every year and invite swamis from the ashram to conduct the programs. You should also help to arrange and organize yearly conventions in your state in order to make more people aware of the benefits of yoga.

If there is a Yoga Mitra Mandal in the area, it is the duty of each karma sannyasin to support it and take classes there at least once a week and more often if possible. If there is no Yoga Mitra Mandal in the area, then karma sannyasins must try to organize one. This will provide a focus for the yogic activities of the community, as well as a place where classes, satsang, kirtan and bhajan can be held regularly. Karma sannyasins with literary ability may also write books, articles, poems, etc. or translate ashram publications into Hindi or the local language of their area.

Social upliftment is another important aspect of nishkam karma yoga. This involves work with the underprivileged sectors of society, trying to raise their standards of living, improve the educational facilities, modernize agricultural techniques, dig wells, build health clinics and hospitals, etc. The scope for social upliftment in India is very great and this work is your responsibility as a karma sannyasin. You must inspire the people to help fund, organize and carry out this work. Only karma sannyasins will be able to offer relief and assistance where it is needed without any selfish motive. Therefore, the sooner you get started on this work the better. God is not found in the temple or mosque but in the dark and comfortless homes of the poor.

In the ashram
Dress: Wear geru dhoti, kurta, upper cloth, and rudraksha mala. Head and face should be clean shaven. Put two horizontal lines of bhasma on the forehead. Ladies may keep their hair long and wear a geru sari, but they should remove all ornaments and avoid the use of powder, cream, oil, cosmetics and make-up.

Sadhana: Practise according to the instructions given by the guru at the time of karma sannyasa initiation. Try to participate in the Navaratri anushthana at least once a year.

Behaviour: Live in the ashram with the same routine and discipline as the resident sannyasins. Work with them side by side and spend as much time with them as possible. Do not think of yourself as a guest in the ashram. Make every effort to observe the following:

- Follow strictly the rules laid down in the ashram regarding discipline, cleanliness and maintenance of buildings and grounds. Carry out whatever duties are assigned to you with a sense of perfection and dedication.
- Do not consider the ashram as a place to rest or sleep. Ashram means labour in every sense, physically, mentally and spiritually.
- Do not waste your time sitting idle; make use of every moment.
- Bear your ailments with fortitude and do not seek medical treatment unless it is unavoidable.
- Cultivate awareness in all activities, even while relaxing, eating or sleeping.
- Avoid getting angry, even when provoked.
- Accept the ashram food as prasad and be satisfied with whatever you get. Ashram food is prepared simply to meet the needs of the sadhaka.
- Do not imitate the behaviour of the ashram residents.
- Be a model in your behaviour with the brahmacharis, sannyasins and guests of the ashram. Do not waste your time in worthless gossip or small talk.
- All karma sannyasins should live in the ashram for at least one month in the year. The purpose of living in the ashram is to renew your spiritual commitment and to explore the depths of your inner self. Be ready to come whenever you are called by the ashram, for any purpose.

POORNA SANNYASA CODE OF CONDUCT

In the ashram
Sadhana: The sannyasin does not need to practise sadhana as such because his or her whole life is sadhana. The sannyasin

98

has dedicated himself totally to serving the guru's mission and propagating the guru's teachings. Later, when the guru deems him or her ready, the sannyasin may withdraw from active service and spend more time cultivating deep meditative states. However, for most sannyasins, service in the guru's mission is a full-time commitment. Those who are able to dedicate themselves fully to this work for a number of years are able to purify their body and mind to such an extent that all the spiritual experiences come to them spontaneously, because they are ready for them. The mantra of all sannyasins is the Pranava (Aum). Sannyasins should practise Aum chanting aloud and mentally in the morning and in the evening.

Tyaga or renunciation is the basis of sannyasa. Try to cultivate the spirit of renunciation, dispassion and detachment in all actions and interactions. At the same time work conscientiously with perfection and dedication. This is the key to success. Show consideration and care for all beings and attachment for none. Identify yourself with the soul or atma, not with the external body, roles or situations. Purify and spiritualize your vision. See all beings in the light of your own atma. Do not differentiate between I and you. Try to see the underlying unity in all of creation.

Dress: Geru dhoti, kurta and upper cloth are worn at all times. A rudraksha mala is worn around the neck and may also be worn around the arms and waist. The head and face are clean shaven. Put three horizontal lines of bhasma on the forehead. Sannyasins should root out the desire to appear presentable and well dressed; at the same time they should keep their appearance clean and neat. Do not use scent, cosmetics, oil or wear flowers on the body. Do not wear rings or ornaments. Avoid wearing multi-coloured garments. Keep minimum clothing for your daily use.

Instructions: The sannyasin should be a model for all the sadhakas and visitors to the ashram.
• Sannyasins should co-operate fully in all ashram activities.
• Sannyasins should not have a bank account, nor should they keep money with them or receive money from outside.

- In the ashram the sannyasins are expected to take meals with all the inmates and guests.
- Sannyasins should take simple, sattwic food and always eat in moderation. They should not be attached to undereating or to overeating.
- They should be content with whatever food, clothing or shelter comes to them, without making any effort to get something better.
- Sannyasins should not acquire possessions which may cause attachment.
- Sannyasins should not be attached to their name, identity and geru dress.
- After taking sannyasa, they should leave the degrees and titles which they had acquired previously.
- Sannyasins should keep mouna for certain periods, according to their sankalpa.
- Use of intoxicants of any type, such as alcohol, ganja, charas and other drugs is strictly prohibited.
- A sannyasin should have nothing to do with astrology, palmistry, fortune telling, etc. On no account should the sannyasin indulge in the distribution or sale of charms, or of amulets for curing disease or warding off evil spirits.
- Sannyasins should not earn money by doing business in order to maintain themselves.
- It is vital for sannyasins to live in the present. They should forget the past and never try to keep things for the future.
- Sannyasins should have a spotless character.
- Sannyasins should not cultivate relationships with one another or with members of the opposite sex. In sannyasa there should be only one relationship with guru or God; all others are left behind.
- A sannyasin is an embodiment of humility at all times.
- Sannyasins should feel that they are servants of humanity, seeing God in the hearts of all.
- While serving society, sannyasins should follow the orders and disciplines of the ashram implicitly with total attention and dedication.

Points on sannyasa from the Bhagavad Gita

- A sannyasin should be free from desire, fear, anger, hatred, possessiveness, egotism, vengefulness, jealousy, disgust and attachment.
- A sannyasin should be friendly, compassionate, patient, contented, devoted, pure, skilful, indifferent, silent, homeless, steady-minded, virtuous, faithful, given to meditation, free from sin.
- A sannyasin should not be subject to attraction and repulsion, joy and sorrow, pleasure and pain, praise and censure, honour and dishonour, friendship and enmity, heat and cold.
- A sannyasin is constant in the contemplation of the self, and is free from wrong notions or misconceptions about the self.

Conduct during parivrajaka

- Do not visit your native town or village for a period of at least twelve years after taking sannyasa unless instructed to do so by the guru.
- Do not write letters to anybody.
- Do not keep any contact with people of the world.
- Do not talk of, or to, people connected with your previous life.
- Remain alone and independent; do not seek the company of other sannyasins. Two together form a pair attached to each other; three together constitute a village with their bickerings, and more than three is like a city full of bustle and confusion.
- Do not expect reverence, respect and special treatment; your only privilege is to serve.
- Do not speak unless somebody questions you. If anybody speaks to you without proper decorum, be silent and indifferent.
- A sannyasin should conduct himself with dignity, gravity and patience.
- Never wander at night; remain in one place after sunset.

- Do not accept any position or job, even if it is honorary.
- Do not join any social or political organizations.
- Do not care for public opinion.
- Do not try to become a centre of attraction or an object of reverence.
- First analyze your motives and then perform actions that are commendable.
- Do not become dependent upon your devotees or admirers.
- Do not praise a person for the sake of obtaining favours.
- Do not read newspapers, magazines or novels pertaining to worldly matters.
- Do not give lectures or sermons unless you are approached to do so.
- Wherever people are receptive and wish to benefit from your knowledge, hold classes on yoga, give lectures and impart instructions with all the means at your command.

18

Qualities of a Sannyasin

FOR SANNYASINS OF THE
BIHAR SCHOOL OF YOGA TRADITION

In sannyasa life there are certain qualities which have to be cultivated in order to remodel one's behaviour and develop a spiritual approach to life. Anyone who is thinking of entering sannyasa life must become aware of these qualities, so that broadening the outlook and attaining peace of mind become spontaneous. By developing these qualities, the attitude and outlook towards life and oneself changes. These qualities help in dealing with one's own samskaras and karmas, and enable one to increase and direct the awareness in order to became more and more conscious from moment to moment.

Jignasu qualities
The first stage of sannyasa is jignasu, meaning 'aspirant' or 'spiritual seeker'. In this stage of sannyasa, an aspirant needs to develop certain positive qualities and it is not possible to develop them overnight. In the course of time, as we progress on the path and become stronger, these qualities are developed one after another.

The first quality to be cultivated is self-control. When we feel that we are being maltreated by others, we react. That reaction creates certain disruptions in our behaviour, destroys our balance, and induces a state of anxiety, frustration and anger. So self-control at the time of maltreatment is a quality to be developed. We should have a deep understanding of our reactions, so that we are aware of how we respond to different people and situations.

The second quality to cultivate is truthfulness. There are two kinds of truth in the world. One kind is pleasant, the second disturbs the balance of another person. So we have to adopt the middle path and cultivate truthfulness without causing harm or pain to others. If someone is a very bad person and we decide to speak the truth and tell him so, this truth becomes a form of criticism which disturbs his mind. Then he reacts against us negatively and we have to deal with his reactions. Therefore, the concept of truthfulness in yoga is not to cause injury to others but to convey our message positively, which helps to improve interpersonal communications.

The third quality to be cultivated is humility in success. When success comes, it goes straight to our head. If we are able to maintain this success in our heart, then we can be humble. But if it goes to the head, the ego is developed more. So, in order to control arrogance and ego, we should try to be humble at every step. Humility does not mean that we submit to a feeling or an emotion or to another person. It is a state of self-awareness where we are able to observe our intellect and the interaction of intellect with ego.

The fourth quality to be cultivated is honesty. Be honest with yourself when temptation and opportunities knock at your door. In life we wish to do and achieve many things. When opportunity comes or when we are tempted, we tend to grab that opportunity for selfish reasons. Then many of the values which are necessary for maintaining a harmonious personality and awareness are pushed aside and we tend to adopt a new rule. So, when opportunities arise, we have to observe ourselves and ensure that the concept of honesty is maintained to its fullest extent.

The fifth quality which is essential for continual growth and progress in spiritual life is perseverance. Perseverance is a state of mind control. Whenever difficult or laborious tasks lie ahead of us, we subject ourselves to anxiety and build up states of tension in our own personality, which hamper our spontaneous activity. By persevering, we are able to maintain creativity in every action, and that task becomes a labour of love and perfection. So, here an important aspect of karma yoga has been included.

The sixth quality to be developed is patience. When things go against us we become very impatient and nervous. Years of work and practice can be thrown up in a moment of impatience. Patience is required in order to maintain mental and emotional balance. It is patience which enables us to gradually go deeper and deeper into meditation or any spiritual practice. Patience is necessary at each moment for perfection of our work, whether in the world or in spiritual life. Without patience our aspirations can never be fully realized.

These are the six qualities which must be cultivated by jignasu sannyasins.

Karma sannyasa qualities

After jignasu comes karma sannyasa, which involves greater perception and understanding of life, spirituality and the direction or path which you decide to follow. Karma sannyasa is the second stage of sannyasa where you are committed to the propagation and teaching of yoga, and to converting your home life into ashram life. This does not mean that you give your house an ashram name, but that you live in your home as you would in an ashram, with discipline, control and awareness. You should not watch television until midnight and say, "I went to sleep late, so I will not get up early and do my yoga practices." You must maintain the sannyasa ideals in your lifestyle.

In karma sannyasa you are required to make certain changes in your lifestyle in order to follow the spiritual path while living in the world. First of all, you should cultivate control over craving or the desire to acquire more than you actually need. It is good to strive in order to reach a goal, but to continually crave and desire to the point that it takes up every moment of your life is bad. You should learn to live simply within your means, and control the desire to have more.

Another important aspect of karma sannyasa is selfless service, performance of actions without expecting anything for yourself, but as a duty or obligation to others. In this way, you should fulfil all your duties with the fullest attention and care, but without becoming attached to the results or the fruits of your labour. By cultivating this kind of selfless or detached attitude in your life, you will be able to control the egoistic nature and prevent it from becoming more intense and powerful.

The next quality which must be developed by karma sannyasins is the ability to remain calm and collected in happiness and misery, in honour and dishonour, in loss and gain, in success and failure. This is a difficult thing to cultivate. How can you remain calm and collected in moments of happiness and misery? There is bound to be a reaction of some type. If you can observe that particular reaction and then detach yourself from it, move away from it and try to maintain your inner balance, it shows a state of greater self-control.

Self-observation is another important aspect of karma sannyasa. This should become a part of every moment of your life. Self-observation is not only necessary at the time of sadhana. In order to manifest the creative nature of the Self, observation is necessary. Observation can only take place when there is awareness. The presence of awareness will make you see your thoughts, actions, behaviour and interactions. Therefore, it is said, "Be intensely involved in observing yourself and be aware of yourself from moment to moment in every activity."

The next quality to be developed is independence, not depending on anyone other than yourself. You may live with others in your family and community, you may work with many people in different ways, but always inside yourself there should be a feeling of detachment, of dissociation.

You do your duty and that's all. There are certain relationships which must be maintained in life, but the feeling of attachment should not be there. Attachment leads to dependence, and as long as there is dependence you can never be free because you cannot live in the world without being affected by it.

In order to trim the ego, a karma sannyasin must learn to live without the feeling of 'mineness'. The idea of 'mine' represents the selfish nature. This does not mean that anybody can come and take away all that you own and you will say, "It is all right, it is not mine even though I have spent a lot of money to acquire it." 'Mineness' here represents attachment. If you are non-attached to objects, then the feeling of 'mineness' and ego satisfaction will go away.

It is essential for karma sannyasins to maintain balance in thought, word and deed to the greatest extent possible. Cultivate an agreeable disposition towards friends and enemies. Friends and enemies represent your concept of other people. If somebody does something good to you, he becomes your friend. If, on the other hand, he does something bad, he becomes an enemy. Why should you feel hatred or love for someone or something which is temporary? With this mental concept you are creating further tension, further attachment to friends and hatred for enemies. Therefore, try to maintain an equal disposition at all times towards friends and enemies.

Another very important point that karma sannyasins must remember is not to act on the spur of the moment when you are angry. In a moment of anger you will tend to act with a negative and disruptive state of mind. Anger brings up many negative qualities from deep inside. Try to become aware of these thoughts and feelings when you are angry without acting on them. In the course of time you will be able to control your negative thoughts and feelings and reach a positive frame of mind.

These are the important qualities or points of control for karma sannyasins.

Vairagya sannyasa qualities

Vairagya sannyasa is the tradition followed by those sannyasins who have chosen to live a life of total renunciation. This path differs from jignasu and karma sannyasa in that the sannyasins do not live within the family or society. They may be supported by society but they live apart, maintaining no relations or connections with anyone from their previous life. In the beginning these sannyasins must undergo very strict training in the ashram or math, under the watchful eye of the guru or acharya. During this training period, certain qualities must be developed if they are to continue on this path independently, unsupported by the ashram or mission.

The most important of these qualities is obedience. Obedience is the basis of sannyasa life. Through obedience the ego is slowly rooted out and you can thus command the lower self. Therefore, it is said, "First learn to obey, then only will you be able to command." In true obedience there is no procrastination, no questioning. As a sannyasin you must simply learn to obey without any arguing, thinking or reasoning. Only then will the guru be able to transform your consciousness, not otherwise. It does not matter how intelligent or how dull you may be, as long as you are totally obedient, the guru will transform you into a sannyasin in his own image. He will hold you on the path and you will never feel tempted to turn back.

The next essential quality which must be cultivated throughout sannyasa life is the willingness to work and to follow a discipline. Sannyasa is not an easy or a lazy life. A sannyasin should be able to do the work of five people. He should be able to carry the loads, direct and administrate, teach and inspire, and side by side maintain his own sadhana and discipline. While the sannyasin is in training, the work and discipline are imposed from outside by the guru and by the ashram or mission. Later on, however, the ability to work and follow a discipline must be internalized, so that the sannyasin is able to lead a life of intense sadhana and

108

austerity and ultimately establish himself in the highest consciousness.

Those sannyasins who do not wish to obey, to work or to follow a discipline, usually go off independently from the very beginning. They think they are in a very high spiritual state when they have not even established themselves in spiritual life. They mistake having their own way for spiritual freedom and for this reason they do not grow. Being habituated to idleness and indiscipline they are unable to practise sadhana, to perform seva or to establish themselves in higher awareness. Such sannyasins roam about in a very careless manner, without any aim, talking some nonsense and posing as jivanmuktas. They have no spiritual qualities and no one wishes to support them.

The ability to adapt is another important quality which sannyasins must develop. In the world you may demand and expect a certain standard of living for yourself, but not in sannyasa. Sannyasins are basically homeless. Although you live in an ashram for a number of years, it is not your home and nothing there is your own. You may be asked to change your room, your work, your diet and your discipline any number of times and you must comply with each request. Sannyasa life is one of changes, ups and downs, glorification and abuse.

Whether in the ashram or outside, you never know what to expect in sannyasa life. One day you may be in charge, while the next day may find you out begging for food and taking shelter under the trees. The only thing which should remain stable in sannyasa life is the spiritual vision. All else is subject to change and you must be able to adapt quickly in all situations. This is also the mark of a sannyasin. In order to evolve, you must be able to adapt.

After adaptation comes dedication and it is the quality of dedication which actually determines the calibre of a sannyasin. Whether or not you will reach the goal of sannyasa life depends entirely upon the degree of your dedication. Some sannyasins have no dedication, only the initial attraction which has drawn them to the path. They usually do not last for more than a year. Other sannyasins have partial dedication; they waver on the path. They always feel the pull of their family, of the world, of their desires, and after some years they return to them. Very few sannyasins are fully dedicated to their path, and out of these few one or two may have the dogged determination and the absolute dedication which carries them to the lofty heights beyond which there is no return.

Surrender is another quality which sannyasins must embody. In order to surrender yourself, you must have full faith in the guru and in the path of life which you have chosen. Usually, surrender is spoken of in terms of bhakti and devotion, but here the type of surrender implied is absolute and unconditional. The moment your ego rears its head you must be prepared to cut it off or else the guru will do it for you. It is only when total surrender becomes a part of your life that you begin to live in the spirit of God. Before that, you are walking in the world and trying to be spiritual. It is only by complete surrender that the grace of guru or God is drawn down. It is by this grace that the sannyasin transcends the worldly consciousness and rests in his own Self. Sannyasins must feel the grace at every step and surrender to it.

Preserving the tradition

The sannyasa tradition has a very elevated position in India. Even kings and politicians used to bow down in respect for the tradition that sannyasins represent. It is not a question of who bows before a sannyasin, but the sanctity of the tradition must be preserved through the life and example of every sannyasin. This is the duty of all sannyasins, regardless of their order or sect.

The personal behaviour of a sannyasin can influence others deeply. One thoughtful word or act can guide another to commit himself to the spiritual path, while a thoughtless word or act can discourage or repel him. There should be

110

absolutely no hypocrisy in a sannyasin's lifestyle. Every act should be done with discrimination. If you criticize others, gossip and engage in anti-social activities, then what kind of example and encouragement can you provide for others? That is not your sadhana.

The geru robe represents the highest spiritual tradition. When monks wear their habit, they represent their religion. When sannyasins wear geru they represent a spiritual culture and tradition. Therefore, one thoughtless word or deed will degrade the sannyasin, his guru and the name of the tradition. Although the path of sannyasa is intended to free one from all obstacles and inhibitions, one need not and should not demonstrate this freedom in the market place. Indiscriminate actions in society represent one's immaturity, not one's freedom.

19

Role of the Guru

Sannyasa life is based on the relationship between the guru and the disciple. The literal meaning of *guru* is one who dispels the darkness which is obstructing the passage of growth to higher consciousness, the dispeller of avidya, of ignorance, of ill merit, of psychic darkness. But in worldly terms, the word guru has simply come to mean a teacher. Any teacher, whether of history, maths, music, cooking, gardening or spiritual life, is known as a guru. However, this is a wrong interpretation of the word guru. The word guru means light, illuminator. That light which dispels the darkness, the avidya, the ignorance, the ego, is known as guru.

Therefore, the term guru cannot be differentiated. There is no such thing as satguru or paramguru. Guru is guru, just as light is light. Whether you connect a fifteen watt bulb or a tube light, the electricity, the light coming through both is the same. Both have the power to illumine, to dispel darkness. So the guru is the spiritual light which dispels the darkness of avidya or ignorance. Whether the illumination created by his teaching or by his presence is large or small, he is known as guru. Any other form of teacher, professor or master, no matter how knowledgeable or revered he may be, cannot be called a guru or dispeller of darkness in the spiritual sense.

The guru is the central pivot of every sannyasin's life. Without the guru there can be no sannyasa, for the guru is the embodiment of perfect renunciation. The role of the guru is to realize the karma and total destiny of the disciple. Before the guru initiates the sannyasin disciple, he has to discern the sannyasin's level of evolution. He has to decide to what degree the disciple is attached to worldly things and to what degree he can transcend or transform this attachment. Accordingly the guru decides which path of sannyasa the disciple is fit for. In this matter the guru's decision is final and the disciple should not request him to alter it.

Initiation into sannyasa can only be given by the guru. After that, the guru is instrumental in establishing the disciple on the sannyasa path. The guru instructs and trains the disciple and decides what is best for the disciple to do. By following the guidelines given by the guru, the sannyasin is able to move successfully on the path of sannyasa which has been set out for him. However, in order to ensure his progress, the sannyasin disciple must allow the guru to handle his ego. Only then, through the grace of the guru, is the disciple able to evolve to the higher stages of sannyasa.

The guru has his own methods of progressively whittling away the egotistical tendencies in his sannyasin disciple. He helps the sannyasin to exhaust the karmas and samskaras which bind him. In the later stages the guru may ask the sannyasin to go into solitude to work out his karmas through sadhana and austerity. However, in the early stages, the guru guides the sannyasin to exhaust the karmas through the medium of work or karma yoga. In jignasu and karma sannyasa, karma yoga takes the form of social service and upliftment. In vairagya sannyasa, it takes the form of organizational work and teaching within the mission as well as outside.

Guidance by transmission

In the beginning the sannyasin receives guidance from the guru consciously at the external level. The guru is manifested to the sannyasin through his physical form. At some stage, however, the guru must withdraw his physical form from the sannyasin in order to make him aware of his spiritual dimension. At this point the sannyasin begins to receive guidance from the guru through the power of transmission. The guru may be thousands of miles away, but he is constantly infusing the sannyasin disciple with the vibrations of his being.

Gradually, through his efforts to remember the guru, the sannyasin disciple creates an antenna which facilitates contact. These efforts develop within the sanyasin a sensitivity to the guru and the waves of love and guidance which come from him. The sannyasin learns how to set his mind on the guru's transmission and to keep it there, concentrating on his presence. Slowly the sannyasin learns to adjust the fine-tuning when he has eliminated all competing desires in the mind. Then the sannyasin can enjoy perfect reception of the guru and the guru can transmit spiritual knowledge and power to him.

Types of transmission
In the guru-disciple tradition we find different kinds of gurus who can transmit according to their own siddhis. A few of these have been listed below.
- *Chandan guru* emanates his high consciousness like a sandal tree giving out its fragrance and imparting it to the other trees in its environment. His mere proximity is a catalyst for the liberation of others.
- *Anugraha guru* uplifts by sheer grace.
- *Paras guru* transmutes the disciple through touch.
- *Kachchap guru* redeems the disciple merely by thinking of him, like the turtle nourishing its young ones by thought alone.
- *Chandra guru* melts the being of the disciple with his spiritual rays, in the manner of moonlight.
- *Chhayanidhi guru* confers divinity on the disciple through his shadow.
- *Nadanidhi guru* gives knowledge the moment his call reaches the disciple, like the precious stone of that name.

114

- *Kraunchpakshi guru* confers spiritual elevation on the disciple by his remembrance.

- *Suryakant guru* burns up the sins of the disciple through his glance, like the rays of the sun burning cotton through a lens.

There are numerous examples of these types of transmission, such as Swami Vivekananda who had a superconscious experience after being touched by his guru, Ramakrishna Paramahamsa. Bilwamangal went through a similar experience and later became known as Saint Surdas. However, this type of transmission is not the end. The sannyasin still has to labour hard for further perfection and attainment. Even after receiving his guru's touch, Swami Vivekananda had to struggle for seven more years before achieving moksha.

Ashram life

Brahmavidya, the science of the Self, cannot be understood and realized by mere intellectual study, reasoning or rationalization; it demands perfect discipline and sadhana. One must overcome the sense of duality: this is virtue, that is vice; this is good, that is bad, and so on. It is not an easy path, and the destination can only be reached after tremendous struggle and exertion. At this point most people would ask, "How can we do it?" The best way is to live in an ashram or spiritual community under the direct guidance of a guru or spiritual preceptor. According to tradition, the sannyasin should live in the guru's ashram and perform selfless service for a period of twelve years.

For the newly initiated sannyasin, ashram life can aptly be compared to life in a jungle: struggle for existence and survival of the fittest. The sannyasin needs such an environment where his mind will be laid bare of all its misconceptions and false beliefs, where he must constantly confront conflicts and difficulties. Desire, repulsion, anger, jealousy, greed, and all the other emotions can be experienced with awareness in the course of ashram life and the sannyasin learns, often the hard way, not to be carried away by them. Slowly he learns to be honest with himself, humble, persevering and patient. As his awareness develops more and more, he begins to understand his own mind as well as the minds of others and to accept their faults and weaknesses as he would his own.

Under the vigilant surveillance of the guru, ashram life gives the sannyasin plenty of opportunity to develop the four spiritual qualities: (i) *viveka* (discrimination); (ii) *vairagya* (detachment); (iii) *shad sampatti* (the six-fold virtues: *sama* – calmness, *dama* – sensory restraint, *uparati* – desisting from worldliness, *titiksha* – endurance, *shraddha* – faith, and *samadhana* – mental equilibrium); and (iv) *mumukshutva* (intense desire for liberation). These four qualities are the cornerstones of sannyasa life and it is not possible to progress on this path without making every effort to attain them.

Under the guidance of the guru, the sannyasin sets out to smooth the sharp corners of his personality. As a member of the ashram community, he does not have to labour for himself. Instead of doing work with a selfish motivation, service is now dedicated to the community through the guidance of the guru. This form of dedicated, selfless service gives meaning to the sannyasin's life, especially in the early stages when he is not fit for intense austerities and sadhana. Through work he learns how to discipline and purify the mind, and how to develop awareness. After making himself a fit spiritual vessel through service to the guru, he is ready to serve humanity, seeing God in all beings.

Greatness of guru

While serving the guru, the sannyasin learns to live up to his example and to obey his instructions without asking why or how. In this way, he begins to gain a deeper understanding of his own shortcomings. Then he starts to wonder, "Why does the guru stoop down to help a wretch like me?" The guru showers his sannyasins with an incredible amount of grace and guidance, beyond their deserving. After some time, when the sannyasin reflects upon the continuous inner guidance which the guru has silently given him in countless ways, the meaning of grace dawns on him. This gift of grace awakens in him a sense of gratitude which has no parallel in this world. The grace and guidance of the guru gives the sannyasin an inner support, no matter what problems he may face. He now knows that the guru is the real driver of the car and he is merely occupying the driver's seat.

Great gurus have always put an end to the notion that spirituality can only be attained in caves and on mountain tops. They make their sannyasins learn to find their inner balance in the middle of complicated and demanding situations. The guru knows that the self-mastery earned in difficult circumstances is the most rewarding and enduring. In spirituality, the only knowledge which has any value is practical knowledge which aims at purifying and elevating the mind. The guru allows the sannyasin to continue living in the ashram with him. He leaves the facade of his ego for his use as he copes with different situations. But all the while the guru makes careful preparations from behind the scenes for its ultimate collapse. With a slight nudge from the guru, the sannyasin's ego disappears from sight in a flash.

Exhausting the karma

For the exhaustion of the sannyasin's karma, the guru plays his game called 'guru maya'. He knows the personality of the sannyasin thoroughly and puts him through different types of activities to enable him to shed some of his karma. The guru may assign him any karma yoga, perhaps in the kitchen, garden, press or cleaning the ashram. Each karma yoga demands a different type of awareness and can be used as a means for him to carry out an introspection of the mind. The guru may also instruct him to keep mouna or silence while performing these tasks. This is an effective way to bring deep-rooted samskaras to the surface, helping the sannyasin to shed his karma.

Thus, by putting the sannyasin through different types of work, the guru understands the natural vocation of the sannyasin which will open the way for the exhaustion of his karma. It may be that the sannyasin can best express his latent tendencies as a yogacharya, a writer, a researcher, an accountant, a gardener, a managing director, a secretary, etc. In this manner, as the sannyasin serves the guru, the karmas start flowing out without new karmas flowing in. By using work to express the latent samskaras, the sannyasin is able to make a balanced transition from worldly life to spiritual life, and in this way he a base for higher sadhana is prepared.

Through guru seva, the sannyasin feels more at peace and begins to experience mental vairagya, or detachment, as the karmas are slowly rooted out. As the mind becomes more concentrated and still, the sannyasin is able to meditate more deeply and for longer periods of time. His mind begins to function like a clean mirror, reflecting the teachings and knowledge of the guru and of his own inner being.

Organizational work

The way to succeed in sannyasa life is to become a servant of the guru. This will take you to the door of self-realization. Carry out explicitly and without question the organizational work entrusted to you as part of your own sankalpa. You have to surrender yourself completely and perform the work which the guru has directed you to do wholeheartedly, knowing that it is in your best interests. No work in the organization is small or big, inferior or superior. All work leads to the same goal. The guru always weighs the intent, the inner dedication, while the disciple considers the task to be more important.

From time to time, the guru may shift you from one work to another. He always has good reasons for shifting the sannyasin from one type of work to another. By this shifting the sannyasin comes to know more about himself, his weak points and his talents. In this way the awareness is increased and expanded. By taking part wholeheartedly in the organizational work, the talents of the sannyasin are revealed as well as his samskaras. By knowing them, he can easily use them in the service of the guru. Guru seva brings peace and contentment and ensures that the sannyasin's path is free from obstacles. The guru's grace is the light for which the sannyasin must continually strive in order that the truth may be revealed.

Social service

There is no use in trying to perfect your own sadhana without first contributing to the upliftment of humanity. The more you serve humanity, the more divine energy flows into you. Good karma or works are always encouraged by the guru. However, good works by themselves are not sufficient to remove the veil of ignorance. This can only be done when the sannyasin accepts the tasks assigned to him or her and offers them to the guru and not to anyone else. Good works may be beneficial to society, the sick, the hungry, the ignorant, but they are still in the dimension of maya wherein you can be trapped, as in any other worldly activity. Unless you are serving the guru or God within yourself, then social service in any form cannot be considered as a sadhana, because it produces karma rather than eliminating it.

In the *Bhagavad Gita* (1:47), Lord Krishna says, "You have a right to the work only, but never to its fruits. You should not allow the fruit of action to be your motive, nor should you be attached to the action." A sannyasin should never consider himself as a social worker serving society. He does not serve society, he serves his guru. The guru's mission is to serve all mankind and because of his realization he possesses great power. The guru lives a divine life on the earthly plane. In the guru's service, the sannyasin learns to work with dedication, free from attachments, while working for the welfare of many.

119

Propagation of the guru's teachings

When the sannyasin has completed his ashram training, the guru often sends him outside as a parivrajaka or mendicant sannyasin in order to propagate his teachings. In this way the sannyasin performs an important service to society by moving about from place to place and spreading the guru's mission. He does not stay in any one place longer than is essential to impart spiritual teachings, as per the directions of the guru. While moving about amongst the people, he undergoes many experiences, both pleasant and unpleasant. In this way he broadens his knowledge and concepts about life and humanity.

Through his experiences of pain and discomfort, the sannyasin develops dispassion, endurance and a strong will. While moving about as a beggar, his clothes reduced to rags, all pride leaves him and he develops true humility and self-surrender. By attuning himself to God and the natural forces, he understands how nature helps every living being by its own laws. He realizes that he is not a blind victim of circumstances but of his own thought, word and action. He becomes responsible for himself and learns to depend on no one. He is a friend of all and a friend of none. Gradually all fear and insecurity leave him as the sannyasin realizes that he is not the body but the eternal consciousness, Shivoham, Shivoham.

20

Food for Sannyasins

It is true that food plays an important role in the life of all sentient beings, and much has certainly been written and said about all kinds of diets and food fads, but in sannyasa life, the importance of food must be toned down and minimized. The sannyasin eats to live; he does not live to eat. In fact, he barely has time to eat, and he is not concerned with the food that he eats, except that it should be sufficient to maintain the body. In principle, the sannyasin tries to follow the middle path in regard to diet, neither too much nor too little. Excess food increases tamas, heaviness and dullness; while insufficient food causes weakness and an inability to concentrate. Beyond this basic requisite, the sannyasin thinks very little about his diet.

The kind of diet which a sannyasin should take is often misunderstood by both lay people and sannyasins. Some people think that because the sannyasin is a holy man, he should be provided with the finest foods served in copious quantities. But for sannyasins it is simplicity which is important, not quality or quantity. The simpler the diet, the more suitable it is for sannyasins. Rather than having many costly and complicated dishes, the sannyasin's meal should consist of two or three items which are prepared simply. Paramahamsa Satyananda always advocated that the best food for sannyasins is dahlia khichari, which should be taken several times in the week to maintain the digestive function.

Food as bhiksha

Sannyasins should not be overly concerned regarding the correct balance of proteins, carbohydrates, vitamins and minerals, etc. in the diet. It should be understood by each sannyasin that whatever is grown locally and seasonally in their area contains those particular nutrients which are needed by the body to maintain a state of balance at that time and in that place. Furthermore, as the body and mind become purified, the sannyasin is able to produce the required balance of nutrients, vitamins and minerals inside himself, whatever type of diet he may take. That is how sannyasins of old were said to subsist on just five to eight mouthfuls of food per day.

The first thing that one must be prepared to surrender before entering sannyasa life is all of one's basic concepts regarding diet and one's own personal dietary requirements. If a person enters sannyasa life with certain concepts about diet such as, "I must have lots of protein to keep strong," or "My body requires fruits and raw foods to maintain good health," or "I cannot survive without milk, butter and cheese every day," then he will not be able to endure the rigours of sannyasa life. Food desires and dissatisfaction with the diet offered will slowly turn the mind back towards the world and he will leave the path.

Sannyasins must be able to survive on any diet which is available in any given place, at any given time. Of course, if there is a choice they may choose to take the simpler and lighter foods which are easiest to digest, but generally speaking, sannyasins have very little choice regarding their diet. They are offered food by the institution in which they are living, or by the people of the locality among whom they are moving, and they accept the food offering as *bhiksha*, alms or prasad. There in no place for rejection or complaint; no matter what has been offered the sannyasin must partake of it with gratitude and humility.

Choiceless eating

Some people like to complain when food has been specially prepared, saying, "Oh, I prefer a more simple meal than this. Rich and tasty foods do not agree with my digestion." Others wish to complain when the diet is very simple, saying, "Oh, this food has no taste. It is the same thing which we have been having for the last three days in a row, I am tired of this food." But the sannyasin just smiles, and whatever he is given, he pushes it down. For him there is no good and no bad. Whether feast or famine, it is all the same for him. He takes food for the maintenance of the body only.

Why should he worry? He simply swallows whatever he is given and immediately forgets about it, allowing the body to do the rest. After all, it is not for the mind that we take food, it is for the body. And surprisingly enough, the body remains in better health for many years longer when the mind does not interfere with the dietary selection and digestive process. As long as the diet is kept to a bare minimum, the sannyasin will generally fare well in body, mind and spirit. Sannyasins are not supposed to store up things, and the body should not become a storage bin. Sannyasins are not meant to have large bulky frames with protruding buttocks and paunch.

Four basic instincts

Most people in the world are ruled by the four basic instinctive desires. The first is the desire for food, the second is the desire for progeny, the third is the desire for sleep, and the fourth is the desire for property and wealth. In sannyasa these four desires must be renounced. Unless you are able to renounce the first, the desire for food, then it will be impossible for you to renounce the second, the desire for progeny. You will be unable to maintain brahmacharya. If you are unable to control your diet and maintain brahmacharya, you will not be able to control sleep.

Sleep does not just mean the number of hours which you sleep. Here it means that you must be able to control the consciousness within the state of sleep. The consciousness must penetrate even the unconscious dimension. Otherwise you will be unable to establish yourself in higher meditation, in samadhi, because in order to do so, you have to pass through the threshold of sleep without losing consciousness. When all three desires for food, progeny and sleep are controlled, the fourth desire for property does not arise. Then one can easily lead the life of a sannyasin or a mendicant, otherwise not.

So it is essential to come to grips with the desire for food, as far as sannyasins are concerned, and to practise dietary control, choiceless eating and occasional fasting, even in the early stages of sannyasa. Renunciation of the desire for food is not done with a view to emaciate the body, but in order to gain control over the first and most powerful instinct, so that the other instincts can also be leashed and controlled. You have to begin by controlling one basic instinct, then the others will also fall into line. If you are unable to renounce the desire for food, then the other desires will also be running rampantly out of control. This is not sannyasa, it is just fooling yourself. It is better to be honest with yourself and to practise dietary control.

Diet and the gunas

The relationship between diet and the gunas is too important to be overlooked. When life is seen as a process of expanding the consciousness, of increasing and deepening the awareness of oneself and the universe, then the threefold classification of the gunas in regard to diet can be very helpful. There are three gunas, qualities or aspects of nature, and each being is comprised of different permutations of the three. The three gunas are *tamas* (inertia), *rajas* (dynamism) and *sattwa* (equilibrium).

In regard to diet, those foods which are tamasic tend to cloud the consciousness and create inertia, lethargy, cruelty or temper. Tamasic foods are those which are old, stale and dead. This includes most processed foods, fast foods and junk foods. Rajasic foods activate one's desires and ambitions. They make one restless, irritated and unsatisfied. Rajasic foods are hot, pungent, tasty, spicy, rich and stimulating. Sattwic foods produce calmness, alertness and steadiness. They are essential for the expansion of consciousness and for inner peace. Sattwic foods are bland, simple, natural, pure and nutritious. They are more easily digestible and produce less toxins in the body.

Generally speaking, the dietary requirements vary in the different stages of sannyasa. For example, the jignasu or karma sannyasin will require a diet which can balance rajasic and sattwic tendencies, so that he can continue to fulfil his duties in the world and lead a spiritual life at the same time. The vairagya sannyasin, while living in the ashram and propagating the guru's mission, needs a diet which is less rajasic and more sattwic. The paramahamsa sannyasin requires a purely sattwic diet, and that too in a meagre quantity, as compared with the previous stages of sannyasa.

However, notwithstanding the philosophy of the gunas, it should be remembered that the consciousness is infinitely more capable of influencing the way the body functions and the way it assimilates food than the type of food itself. Therefore, throughout history there have been saints and sannyasins of every tradition who have fasted or subsisted on extremely meagre diets for long periods of time in order to reach higher spiritual states. They have subsisted on the pranic and spiritual energies alone, and such sadhus and saints have lived for hundreds of years.

Diet during intensive sadhana

Sannyasins who practise intensive sadhana must be very careful about their diet. This is because during long periods of meditation, the inner body temperature, which is responsible for digestion, comes down. A heavy diet requires higher body temperature for proper digestion. If the sannyasin takes heavy meals and then practises sadhana, eventually he will suffer from dyspepsia, high blood pressure,

125

rheumatism or coronary problems. With the practice of meditation and japa, not only does the inner body temperature fall, but the digestive secretions and enzymes are also reduced.

For proper digestion, five digestive enzymes are required in the correct proportions along with the correct body temperature, which varies in different parts of the digestive tract. In the small intestine a constant temperature is required for a long period of time. In the stomach a higher temperature is needed for about three hours. If there is a higher temperature in the stomach for longer than three or four hours, then one develops hyperacidity and ulcer. If the temperature is lower, then one will have hypoacidity or indigestion. Similarly, if the temperature in the small intestine is higher, then one will have diarrhoea, dysentery, or colitis. If it is lower, then gastric problems and poor assimilation will develop.

Because these temperatures are affected by prolonged sadhana and meditation, most sannyasins who practise intensive sadhana find it necessary to either adjust or else greatly reduce their diet. Firstly, vegetables should be well boiled so the low temperature of the body does not disturb the digestion. Secondly, some digestive enzymes and acids should be added to the food to aid the digestive function. Certain foods like papaya, pineapple and bean sprouts actually contain digestive enzymes. Spices such as coriander, pepper, turmeric, aniseed, cumin, cayenne, mustard and garlic are all digestives. Herbs such as mint, alfalfa, tulsi or basil and chamomile can also aid the digestion.

How much and when to eat

Food plays an essential role in the life of a sannyasin until he achieves the state of moksha or liberation. The type of food, quantity consumed and the timing of consumption greatly affect the physical and mental balance. Charvaka, a well-known exponent of the ayurvedic system of medicine, says: "One must eat in proper measure, and the proper measure

126

of food is determined by the strength of the gastric fire. The self-controlled man always feeds his gastric fire with the fuel of wholesome food and drink, mindful of the measure and the time." For maximum digestive functioning, it is said that the stomach should be filled fifty percent with solids, twenty-five percent with liquids and the remaining twenty-five percent with air or empty. Generally speaking, this is a good rule for most sannyasins to follow.

Food timing is also very important because the digestion follows the solar rhythm very closely. Hence the peak digestive period is between eleven a.m. and one p.m. This is why sannyasins in the ashram take the main meal of the day at eleven a.m. By so doing they avoid many digestive problems. At six a.m., when the sun is rising, a light breakfast is taken and at five p.m., when the sun is setting, they take a light dinner. In this way the digestive process is completed early and they are able to do their sadhana and sleep with a light stomach and a free mind. Regularity in meals and meal timings is necessary for sannyasins if they wish to maintain a high energy level and progress in their sadhana.

21

Sublimation and Sannyasa

It is undoubtedly true that desire is the root cause of all suffering. Many great masters have proclaimed this. As your awareness develops beyond the instinctive and mundane levels, you can recognize this through your own experience. Desire, however, cannot be escaped simply by taking up sannyasa. In fact, sannyasa is like holding the tiger by the tail, for here it is necessary to witness clearly the power of the desire in operation. If desire remains unfulfilled and misunderstood, it has the power to completely disrupt the balance of the mind, especially in the early stages of sannyasa.

Sexual desire is such a powerful force that it must be handled very carefully and with great understanding. It is at this point that many sannyasins who do not receive training under the guidance of an enlightened guru invariably falter or fall from the path. In sannyasa one must learn to sublimate the sexual desires rather than be ruled by them. This requires a special form of guidance, which only a guru can give.

In sannyasa life, sexual desire is a great power which can neither be suppressed nor fulfilled. When the mind is still uncontrolled there is little that can be gained by gratifying sexual desire. Satisfying sexual desire is like trying to extinguish a fire by throwing petrol onto the flames. At the same time, suppression or denial of sexual energy is a cause of neurosis and illness. This is the dilemma which sannyasins must confront in the process of the ascent of consciousness.

Redefining brahmacharya

The process of sublimation of the primal energy in man is called brahmacharya. In Sanskrit *brahma* means 'higher reality' and *achar* means 'to live in'. Hence, *brahmacharya* means to move, learn and live in the higher reality. This is the great ideal of spiritual life, but religious sects throughout the world have a different explanation for it. For them, brahmacharya or celibacy means complete control over the sexual interactions, because the sexual urge represents one of the strongest instinctive desires in man, which is difficult to control and channel.

Brahmacharya is not attained by suppression, nor can it be equated with strict avoidance of sexual interaction. Suppression is a term belonging to psychology; abstinence is a vow belonging to religion. Neither has anything to do with the process of yoga by which a sannyasin becomes established in brahmacharya. The seat of this energy is not so much in the semen as in the mind. Only by controlling the sexual impulse at its point of origin can the mind be controlled and the state of brahmacharya be realized. In order to achieve this, the point of experience has to be withdrawn. In yoga and tantra, this point is called *bindu*.

The bindu exists in two forms, the white and the red. Through the practices of yoga and tantra, the semen which is produced by the male body is transmuted into spiritual energy which is known as ojas, and the menstrual blood which is produced by the female body is transformed into another form of spiritual energy known as rajas. However, at a subtler level, these two energies exist in seed form as two bindus, white and red. According to tantra and yoga, brahmacharya means perfection in retaining the bindu. The tantric yogi does not lose his bindu because he knows how to hold and sublimate it. Brahmacharya should, therefore, be understood as maintaining a positive state of personality wherein the higher energy is not allowed to dissipate, but is given expression through conscious awareness.

This state cannot be achieved by external observances. It may be seen as celibacy, but that is a gross definition. The most important thing is the mind. If life is designed to avoid sexual interaction but the mind is not free of sexual fantasy, then the sannyasin is not a brahmachari, even if he has practised abstinence for fifty years. On the other hand, if he is able to control the mind and isolate the point of experience, then he is a brahmachari.

Vedic tradition

Brahmacharya is not merely a concept of sexual abstention. In the vedic tradition it was taught in order to create a healthy, disciplined social structure. It may or may not help a person to have a higher experience, but it will definitely help a person to achieve amicability, unity, conformity and purity in their social and personal life. Brahmacharya also gives one the physical benefits of strength, power, heat in the system, vitality, resistance, splendour, endurance and the possibility of choosing the future course of one's karmas.

According to vedic tradition, one should not touch a man or woman before attaining the age of twenty-five. Until then, the individual does not possess the necessary maturity of the various physiological, psychological and emotional aspects of life. Having attained full maturity, a person can successfully understand and integrate the sexual experience into their life. Therefore, from the age of eight until twenty-five, every individual was dedicated to studies and this part of life was known as the brahmacharya period.

For the first twenty-five years of his life, the individual lived a life of complete brahmacharya or sexual abstinence. In the next twenty-five years, he fulfilled his dharma by involving himself in sexual interaction, whether it was for progeny, pleasure or self-elevation. He was obliged to live like that, and even a spiritual aspirant had to pass through this stage. In the following twenty-five years, husband and wife had no more physical contact and lived together like brother and sister, friend and friend, guru and disciple.

Total concept of brahmacharya

Many different ideas have been expressed down through the ages regarding the concept of brahmacharya, but the best is found in tantra and yoga. Have a passionless mind with an attitude of worship towards your partner. Give your respect and devotion to every member of the opposite sex, whoever they may be. Your relationship with the opposite sex can be based on many ideas. You can be a total friend to your wife/husband, your mother/father, daughter/son and sister/brother, and you can give them immense love, total love. Sex is not the only way of interacting.

All other definitions of brahmacharya seem to have an unscientific basis. Many create conflicts but, according to the yogic view, there should be no suppression, contradiction or licentiousness. The sannyasin may be leading a life of strict continence, a moral, ethical and spiritual life, but what is the value if it is only a process of suppression which is being followed? Understanding the concept of brahmacharya is one thing, but the process of attaining this state is another, and it is by no means easy. Brahmacharya is a state of control which develops through rigorous training under the supervision of a guru. Without a disciplined lifestyle, whereby the energies can be properly balanced and controlled, it is not beneficial to undertake complete brahmacharya.

Followers of modern Western culture do not understand brahmacharya and that is why a lot of psychological problems and difficulties are faced by them today. Many who have tried to become brahmacharis could not do so because the conditions prevailing in society are not suited to complete abstention. When they could not manage it properly, their behaviour reflected this mismanagement. Sexual abstention has a definite effect on the quality and structure of awareness as long as there is no suppression. Due to suppression, often a breach of trust is created and guilt develops.

One must have a total concept of brahmacharya from both the physiological and psychological viewpoints. Sexual

131

behaviour is influenced by various hormones produced within the body. One must have a basic understanding of these hormones and their effect on the body. How do they influence the gonads and the testes in the male body and the ovaries in the female body? In response to what kind of stimulation are these hormones released in the body? Do they stimulate the testes? How? Do the testes create seminal fluid? How does seminal ejection create an experience of orgasm? How does this experience come to an end? How does one fall prey to the emotional states related with sex? What is the influence of all these factors on the mind? All these aspects must be taken into account as one re-evaluates the meaning of brahmacharya.

How to establish sexual continence

Finally brahmacharya has to become part of human consciousness. The best way to be established in brahmacharya and to be divine is to have the attitude of passionlessness, reverence and worshipfulness. There has to be mastery in an act of passion, for without this brahmacharya is self-deception. There is no doubt that if one can observe brahmacharya totally, not merely refraining from sex, but also redeeming oneself from sensual fantasies and channelling the mind towards creativity, the speed of progress will be very fast. What a non-celibate achieves in six years' time, a celibate can achieve in one year.

Brahmacharya includes and incorporates in itself proper observation and expression in the world of the senses, control and channelling of all sensory and sensual indulgences or *bhogas* (experiences and cravings of pleasure). Certain guidelines have been given in the spiritual tradition for establishing brahmacharya and these are enumerated below.

1. Control your diet. A high protein diet stimulates the sexual hormones.
2. Organize your day. Make a timetable of your daily routine.
3. Redeem yourself from sexual fantasies, lust and desire.

4. Dissociate yourself from sexual acts and amorous advances.
5. Avoid sexual contact, sexual conversations, sexual pleasantries, sexual looks, sexual mannerisms, sexual novels, sexual films, sexual music, etc. Avoid toying with yourself and with others. Be natural and just forget about it.
6. Make certain disciplines for yourself and follow them quietly.
7. Change your soft bed. Use a proper, firm bed.
8. Avoid constipation.
9. Practise asana, pranayama, mudra and bandha to rechannel dissipated energies.

Necessity of work
During the process of sannyasa training, sexual energy must be dealt with almost constantly. It cannot be denied expression without impairing the natural life processes, depleting vitality and leading to depression and mental problems. Medical science has also taught this. However, this same energy which is expressed on the mundane level as sexual interaction can be expressed positively and creatively in other ways. When the evolutionary energy is denied expression in the sexual act, it is deflected back into the unconscious (mooladhara chakra). From there it must be redirected through the higher chakras as work, creativity and spiritual activities.

In the process of sannyasa training, this energy is spent every day in hard work and creative activity which demands total effort and awareness, utilizing every faculty and capacity of the mind. By constant practice, sannyasins learn to work with an intensity which rechannels this energy completely. When this complete rechannelling occurs, no surplus energy remains to be consumed in sexual life or in neurosis. That is why the sannyasin remains totally relaxed even in the midst of dynamic activity. The energy is being consumed in the fire of higher awareness.

If the sannyasin does not learn to work in this way every day as a matter of routine, the energy finds immediate expression in erotic play, aggression or inner tension. This is what happens in many monasteries where intense karma yoga is not practised and the young initiates spend all their time devoted to studies and prayer. In order to successfully redirect these powerful impulses for greater experience and purpose, the sannyasin has to eat less, sleep less and be totally occupied in work for many years.

Once the readjustment of energy has been made, the sannyasin becomes firmly established in spiritual life, disciplined and steady in mind and emotions. Then he is no longer compelled to maintain such an intense work schedule. He can sit quietly or work hard all day without any difference, for he is no longer troubled by mental and emotional inconsistencies. He has learned to conduct the life force and lets it flow productively into the creative, mental and spiritual planes.

When the passage of energy is established, the process becomes effortless. Kundalini energy, which operates on the mundane level as sexual activity in ordinary men and women, has been transmuted to operate on the spiritual level. Thus the sannyasin is lifted into a transcendental experience of regenerative bliss, rather than remaining in a diminishing pool of degenerating pleasure. Such sannyasins are jewels amongst humanity. They are able to bestow light, courage, peace and bliss wherever they go. They are the beacons of mankind, living examples of the higher possibilities open to us all.

22

Suppression and Control

In sannyasa life it is very important to distinguish between suppression of desires and their control. There is a very vast difference between the two, although both involve the use of the will to alter the expression or gratification of the senses. Control means to discipline the senses in order to have a greater experience. Suppression, however, means avoiding expression of desires for a different reason, perhaps fear, inadequacy or wrong understanding. This leads to mental disturbance, as the suppressed energy begins to be expressed in negative and distorted thoughts and ideas. In suppression there is a blockage or opposition to your personality because you do not really agree with what you are doing. This creates tremendous tension in the conscious and subconscious personality.

In control, however, there is mutual agreement between both elements of the mind. When the sannyasin exerts control, he agrees with himself totally and uses willpower to attain what he knows is in line with his objectives. In suppression one wants to do something, but still one does not do it. The mind is split into two opposing forces; an eternal war is unleashed. Two opposing forces are in conflict, vying for supremacy. There is tremendous conflict, which is mirrored in a tense and neurotic personality. The self is denied, the vision is clouded and the mind becomes a battleground. But in control, the elements of the mind work

135

harmoniously to attain the objective. The self is affirmed. This is the fundamental difference.

In suppression one does not want to face the negative aspects when they arise into the consciousness. They are either denied altogether or only minimally acknowledged. They are never looked at squarely and evaluated objectively. This denial leads to alienation of a part of oneself. A kingdom divided against itself cannot stand and so it is that a spiritual objective cannot be attained by suppression of part of the mind. When the mind is divided and scattered, so are the physical and mental energies and so is the quest for transcendental understanding.

When suppression is occurring, one is not whole, not together, not in union with one's objectives. When a suppressed person experiences negative emotions, he feels guilty because he thinks he should not feel like that. Whereas the sannyasin, who is working towards control and self-mastery, realizes that negative emotions are bound to arise from time to time. These have to be experienced fully if they are not to remain repressed in the deeper levels of consciousness, causing blockages and problems. One must be able to experience whatever arises, positive or negative, with full awareness, without feeling elated or depressed about it.

Gaining control over the mind

In suppression, thoughts and feelings are denied. This is surely the wrong approach for a sannyasin. It is better to try to become totally aware of the whole dimension of thought and feeling. Only when the whole dimension of thoughts, positive and negative, creative and destructive, can be witnessed objectively, does the sannyasin succeed in the difficult task of directing the whole mind towards the expansion of awareness.

This task starts by accepting the whole mind. It can never start by suppression of a part of the mind. By suppression, one is bound to fail, if not immediately, then surely and inevitably in the long run. Even if one attains spiritual heights, the power of long-suppressed desires will draw the aspirant back down again. It cannot be any other way. This is the difference between sannyasa and religious life. Religious conditioning utilizes suppression, denial and guilt. These may produce exemplary behaviour, even saint-like behaviour, but they do not allow the aspirant to realize the truth, to reach enlightenment, to gain freedom.

Instead there is ultimately a stagnation. The personality fails to develop, but becomes perverse, even cruel. Where suppression is used as a tool for changing the behaviour, the mind ultimately becomes weak because it is being denied its natural expression. That personality is conditioned and ultimately it breaks down altogether because it has suppression as its basis. Therefore, no matter how fine later acquisitions are, the whole spiritual edifice remains shaky. Like a high building with shaky foundations, it is bound to fall down.

Therefore, the sannyasin learns from the beginning to deal with his mind in a different way. He accepts his mind without denying any aspect of it. Why should he feel guilty about anything? The mind may have negative aspects, but these must be accepted, otherwise the personality will be split and weakened from the outset. Thus a sannyasin learns to develop mental strength and control based on acceptance of the mind. A sannyasin does not fear the mind nor does he feel guilty about it.

The sannyasin's attitude towards his mind is one of fearlessness. Whatever comes up, he is ready to face, like a hero in the midst of battle. He is engaged in a struggle with the mind. He may falter, he may fall down, but the sannyasin will always get up again. He knows that victory is his; he has only to keep on with the struggle. Ultimately he will surely reach a state of equilibrium with his mind. This is shanti, peace. It is based on attainment. Peace can never be attained except by engaging in this struggle.

The sannyasin has to be able to see the state of conditioning in which he is bound. Then he can begin to remove it, step by step, fearlessly, with the guidance and blessing of his guru. The sannyasin is a unique personality. He remains absorbed in one-pointedness, balanced and unaffected, in both favourable and unfavourable circumstances. He learns to accept pleasure and pain, satiety and deprivation equally. He remains blissfully in-between.

Who is a swami?

One who is master of their mind is a swami. The sannyasin crosses the great barrier of ego, lust, anger, attachment and desire, through mental strength, equilibrium and tolerance. He remains unaffected, whether people think highly of him or not. He welcomes even miserable circumstances, insults and abuse, taunts, blame and shame, so that he may be strong enough to stand up to any adversity without losing his balance. He maintains equilibrium, stability and inner peace at every step of the way, in the face of any odds. He regards affection, appreciation, recognition and praise as poison. Inwardly he never accepts them.

A sannyasin uses his senses fully, but he remains master of his mind. He avoids sensual indulgence because it leads to attachment, but uses his senses to develop higher awareness. He is not dead to life, but affirms life fully because he understands its purpose. It is not what a person does or does not do which makes him a sannyasin, but the frame of mind he has while carrying out his actions. In the *Ashtavakra Gita*, it is said:

> *Dispassion for objects is liberation;*
> *Passion for things is bondage.*
> *This is knowledge.*
> *Now do as you please.*

A person who has a strong sensual nature should not feel that he is unsuited for sannyasa. He can tread the sannyasa path provided he can master the expression of his senses, rather than serving them blindly. No one should deny himself what he needs, but all sannyasins must use the senses to

138

gain knowledge, rather than for pleasure's sake. The sannyasin must learn to observe the sensory experiences and the reactions of the mind, rather than losing himself in them. This is the way to freedom and bliss.

Many people ask if sannyasa is suitable for those who have a lot of karmas. The answer is that sannyasa is for those who have the willpower and strength of mind to tread the path, irrespective of their karmas. Guru is the one who decides whether a disciple has the capacity to adopt sannyasa life. If he has the strength to handle the onslaught of the mind, the guru lets him enter into this life. Alternately, the guru may advise him to undertake jignasu or karma sannyasa, especially in the beginning, so as to give him a spiritual identity and make him aware of his desire to achieve a higher goal.

23

Keeping a Spiritual Diary

In order to assess and evaluate one's own progress in spiritual life, every sannyasin is required to keep a spiritual diary. The diary is a whip for goading the mind. It is your teacher and guide. It will help you to remove your negative qualities and to be regular in your sadhana. It shows the way to freedom and bliss. Those who wish to evolve rapidly must keep a daily record of all their actions. If you maintain a diary regularly, you will progress rapidly on the spiritual path.

You should record everything in your diary. You should not hide your weaknesses and defects. It is to correct and mould yourself, to remove your weaknesses and defects, to develop a spiritual nature and to achieve self-realization that this diary is maintained. If the sannyasin is sincere, the diary itself will become his silent master which will open his eyes and direct him towards spiritual attainment.

Keeping a diary will teach you the value of time. At the end of every month calculate the total number of hours you have spent in japa, study of spiritual books, sadhana, sleep, etc. Then you will be able to know how much time you are spending for spiritual purposes and how much you are wasting. In this way, you will be able to increase the period of japa and meditation gradually. If you maintain a daily diary without any fault in any of the items, you will not wish to waste a single minute unnecessarily. Only then will you understand the value of time and how it slips away.

Along with keeping the diary you have to make sensible resolves according to your capacity and circumstances, and stick to them at any cost. There are positive as well as negative resolves. For one negative resolve you should make a corresponding positive one. Otherwise the negative resolves will create unwanted complexes. Make as many resolves as possible. You do not become perfect on the day that you make a resolve, but it is better to have tried and failed than never to have tried at all.

You will have to note down all the difficulties and complexes which arise and preserve these notes in your sadhana place. Whenever you feel restless and depressed you should go there, meditate for a while and read over your notes and resolves. This will give you peace of mind and remove feelings of negativity and doubt.

How to make your own diary
Several questions have been compiled in the following pages to suit all temperaments. Put these questions in columns for each week, leaving adequate space after each question for the daily record. After the daily record leave a blank space for totalling up the number of hours spent in sleep, sadhana, number of malas of japa, etc. After a month study the charts made through your sincere and honest self-observance, and trace out your own progress. Another method to assess yourself is to total up the number of hours or the number of 'yes' and 'no' answers pertaining to the various questions, one week at a time and plot them on a graph. After drawing the graph for a period of three months for each quality, you can observe the pattern which has emerged. Based on this, you can analyze yourself. By introspection you will become acutely aware of your behaviour and how your mind functions in different situations and circumstances.

SPIRITUAL DIARY QUESTIONS

1. What time did you get up in the morning?

The purpose of this question is not to compel you to arise early in the morning by launching a fight against your habits, but to refashion the underground structure of the habit itself. You should take a weekly or monthly average of the time of arising.

2. How many hours did you sleep?

Many people get confused about this question because they are unable to decide the minimum and maximum hours of sleep. We need as much sleep as is required for proper de-carbonization of the system, which may differ from individual to individual. The average requirement is six hours for intellectuals, eight hours for manual labours, and four hours for sadhakas. One who has attained samadhi does not need to sleep at all. Those who sleep in excess generally have accumulated toxins in the system. If not, there may be psychological suppressions or deep, ingrained tensions. A normal person does not oversleep. You can minimize the hours of sleep by taking a sattwic diet, removing stress and tension, and practising more sadhana.

3. How long did you practise asana and pranayama?

Select a few asanas which suit you the most, or which have been selected by your guru, and practise them regularly. Afterwards do pranayama. The total duration should be about thirty minutes.

4. How many malas of japa did you perform? How many minutes of meditation?

This is important. Therefore, make a firm resolve that you will practise a certain number of malas or a certain number of minutes daily. Over-enthusiasm is not good. Japa should be done with your guru mantra only.

5. How long did you do karma yoga?

Write down the total number of hours of work. If you do every act mindfully and consciously, it becomes karma yoga. It is karma when you act mechanically. A karma yogi is aware that he or she is doing a particular action; this is karma yoga. When you act without mindfulness, your actions are karmic. Through the practice of karma yoga you will develop the attitude of detachment and not be affected by external influences. When you complete the work with detachment you feel peaceful. Karma yoga is the best method for developing detachment. Every thought, word and action should be accompanied by perfect awareness. If you practise awareness, the quality of detachment will develop in you in no time. Success and failure, victory and defeat, pain and pleasure will not have any effect on your mind.

6. How many times did you get angry? What was the process of self-rectification?

If you get angry, you must rectify yourself. As a token of punishment, the dearest thing must be given up. If you do not discipline yourself for undesirable actions every time you do them, you can impose cumulative punishment for a month of negligent acts. There is no benefit in getting angry, and for this act of indiscrimination and foolishness, you must correct yourself. You must beg the pardon of the offended person and assure him or her that you are definitely going to correct yourself. You have to decide the form of retribution yourself. Remember not to act when you are in an angry frame of mind. Act only when you are in a positive frame of mind.

7. Which good quality are you trying to cultivate?

First resolve to cultivate one good quality, but it should not be a difficult one. For instance, you can resolve to speak less and avoid irrelevant, useless, sensational and futile talk. Then month by month you continue to cultivate virtues like tolerance, helpfulness and so on.

If you were successful in maintaining the desired quality, mark 'yes' in the column; if unsuccessful, mark 'no'.

8. Which bad quality are you trying to eradicate?

Do not take up a difficult quality to start with. Take, for example, "I shall not speak harsh words." Later you can substitute jealousy, criticizing others, etc.

If successful in eradicating the undesired quality, mark 'yes'; if unsuccessful, mark 'no'.

9. Did you fail in brahmacharya?

Lust, attraction or fascination for the opposite sex, and erotic dreams are all lapses in the observance of brahmacharya.

10. Did you experience greed?

Include here greed for food, clothes, position, power, fame, etc.

11. How much time did you spend in self-study?

Swadhyaya or self-study is an important part of sannyasa life. At least one hour daily should be designated for this. Books should be carefully selected for improving your spiritual knowledge and background.

12. How much time did you waste?

Include time spent in gossiping; reading novels, magazines, newspapers; watching television, videos; daydreaming and so on.

13. How much time did you spend in mouna?

Try to set aside a part of each day for mouna, for example, at meal times and/or from six p.m. to six a.m. It is also beneficial to practise one full day of mouna per week.

24

Women and Sannyasa

In most of the world cultures, women have lived under male domination since time immemorial. It was not until the twentieth century that women were finally accorded the fundamental rights of equality. In many of the world religions, women were also barred from higher spiritual life. Perhaps the reason for this was that men wanted to exploit them for their own carnal objectives. If women were allowed to live a spiritual life and encouraged to raise their awareness, then they could not be used or exploited. Therefore, women were relegated to the home, their sole purpose in life being to serve their husband and produce offspring. They were conditioned in such a way that they did not know how to deny, refuse or resist.

In the vedic shastras, women were accorded a different spiritual status from men. They were not given the option for spiritual life or sannyasa as men were. Therefore, although Indian culture abounds with great women who were saints, poets, philosophers and bhaktas, most of them were married, very few were renunciates.

While in the vedic culture women had fewer rights to practise or to live a spiritual life, the tantric culture, which preceded the vedic culture, did not share these views regarding women. In the tantric culture, women were regarded as supreme. They were the initiators, the gurus and the inspirers. This should not be understood as a

145

social claim, but purely in relation to the evolution of consciousness.

Spiritual awareness of women

The mental framework of a woman, her emotions and her psychic evolution are definitely higher than those of a man. Awakening of the spiritual force, that is, the kundalini, is much easier in the body of a woman than in the body of a man. Besides this, there is another important point which must be understood. Generally a man who goes into the deeper realms of the mind and comes out is not able to bring those experiences back with him, but a woman can. There seems to be very little difference between a woman's outer and inner awareness. When a man goes very deep into his consciousness he has certain experiences, but when he returns from that deeper state of mind to the gross awareness, a veil falls in between those experiences and the conscious mind. In the case of a woman, this veil does not fall.

Apart from this, the psychic being of a woman is highly charged with spiritual awareness. The external expressions that you will find in a woman or a girl – love for beauty, tenderness, sympathy and understanding – are expressions of her inner state. If all the women were to leave the world it would become a desert. There would be no fragrance, no colour, no beauty, no smiles. This indicates that the inner awareness of a woman is very receptive and ready to explode. In the realm of kundalini yoga the woman's body is charged by a particular centre. Mooladhara chakra in the male body is intricately situated in a very congested area. Men do moola bandha and still nothing happens. But in a woman's body, you can help to awaken mooladhara with this bandha. Therefore, awakening can take place much more quickly in a woman's body.

The woman comes first

In tantra, the role of creator is shifted from the male to the female. Ramakrishna Paramahamsa always considered his wife Sarada as Devi or goddess. In Sanskrit, *devi* means illumined or illustrious. When Ramakrishna was married he was very young and his wife was still a child, but he always regarded her as the divine mother. That is how he behaved towards her and it is what he considered her to be. In the scheme of evolution, Shakti comes first, and Shiva comes next. She is the activator and he is the participant in every sphere. Even if a man has realized higher awareness, he will still have difficulty in communicating that to others if he does not bring a woman into the picture.

If you look at any of the spiritual movements, you will find women are in the majority. Women have also played a major role in the revival of yoga. Lord Shiva is said to be the Adiguru and founder of tantra and yoga. His first disciple was Parvati, his female counterpart or shakti. If you read the tantric texts, you will find they commence with the words "Parvati asked" and then Shiva gives his reply. Therefore, the knowledge was first imparted to a woman, and in the spiritual culture, when any reference is made to a relationship, the woman is always mentioned first. They say, 'Sita Ram' not 'Ram Sita', 'Radha Krishna' not 'Krishna Radha' and 'Gauri Shankar' not 'Shankar Gauri'.

When Shankaracharya wrote his famous text on tantra, *Ananda Lahari*, he commenced it with a very significant verse: "Without Shakti, how can Shiva create anything?" Shiva is only the silent witness; Shakti is the creator. Therefore, in Hindu life many rituals, religious and otherwise, are mainly conducted by women and the men are the observers. Woman is the commissioner; man is the participant. Whether it is an ordinary social ceremony, a religious ceremony, the worship of a deity or a day of fasting, it is the woman who introduces it. The man just has to follow her. This is the tradition in India known as initiation from the woman to the man.

Revival of the matriarchal traditions

There are two spiritual traditions existing in the world: one is matriarchal and the other is patriarchal. Matriarchal traditions speak of God as the universal mother, the goddess, the force of nature. They are generally more holistic and harmonious, promoting the welfare of all beings rather than any select or elite group. The patriarchal traditions speak of God the father and are generally more hierarchical and punitive. Judaism, Christianity and Islam are patriarchal. Tantra, Hinduism, Buddhism, Zoroastrianism, Shintoism, Taoism and the Native American traditions are matriarchal.

The matriarchal religions teach tolerance, understanding and compassion for others, which reflect the feminine nature. They have been responsible for the beautiful things in life such as fine arts, dance, music, painting, sculpture and so on. Patriarchal religions are more aggrandizing and non-compromising. They have produced religious wars and developed strong administrations. They have also prevented women from coming forward in spiritual life. However, in the twentieth century women all over the world have become more open and have begun to realize the important role which they have to play in the spiritual evolution of humanity. Many are searching within the seeds of the ancient matriarchal traditions for a new basis upon which to build a more harmonious and spiritual world in tune with the values which will enhance the well-being of all.

The tradition of female sannyasins
There has also been a recent revival in the tradition of female sannyasins. For this, Paramahamsa Satyananda was largely responsible. In the early 1960s and 1970s, he began to initiate women into sannyasa. After initiation, the female sannyasins were trained side by side with the male sannyasins, receiving equal opportunities in all aspects of spiritual life. Finding them more capable, dedicated and hardworking than their male counterparts, he often assigned his female sannyasins to the most responsible and respectable positions in his mission. In the beginning this caused a great commotion amongst the orthodox spiritual leaders and they spoke against it. But as the years passed they had no

other option than to follow his example. Now they too have female sannyasins and disciples.

There is no reason why women should be barred from sannyasa life. Women are very spiritual by nature and they must be allowed to raise their consciousness and develop this part of their personality. Why should they not become spiritual power centres, saints and sannyasins, with a compassionate vision? Paramahamsa Satyananda's personal philosophy is that women are very sincere and obedient. They are honest and hardworking and when they work with you, they keep you relaxed all the time. He also says that one of the most important reasons for the success of his work was the introduction of female sannyasins into the movement. He did not mean that men are useless; they have their own place, but in the scheme of creation he believed that women were superior.

. In honour of all women and in order to express his respect for the Shakti tradition as it is upheld by the science of tantra, Paramahamsa Satyananda once wrote the following eulogy:

To all the women
Of all places, East and West,
Of all ages, old and young,
Who serve me,
Who will serve me
And who have served me,
In my parivrajaka life,
In ashram life,
In my wider mission,
As sannyasin and lay disciples;
To all these women
From whom I have learned so much,
Who have above all
Nurtured in me the equipoise
That brings enlightenment,
I offer my salutations.

25

Women Saints and Sannyasins of India

In spite of the many restrictions imposed on women in regard to spiritual life during the vedic and post-vedic period, their quest for spirituality could not be curbed. Now let us trace some of the more notable female saints and sannyasins during the different periods.

VEDIC PERIOD

Rishi patnis such as Anasuiya, Lopamudra and Arundhati were partners of their husbands in the pursuit of spiritual ideals and were pillars of strength in the ancient ashrams. Saunaka, in his *Brihaddavata* (2:82–84), dating back to the fifth century BC, mentions twenty-seven women who were acclaimed as rishis. The most prominent was Vak, the daughter of sage Ambhrina. Her hymn is the famous 'Devi Sukta' of the *Rig Veda* (10:125). She is said to have sung it in ecstasy on realizing her oneness with Brahman. This supreme realization by a woman is unparalleled in the history of world religions.

Gargi and Maitreyi

During the rishi tarpana, a rite in which offering of water libation is done in the memory of great sages, the names of three women sages occur – Gargi Vachaknavi, Vedava Pratithevi and Sulabha Maitreyi. In the *Brihadaranyaka*

Upanishad, Gargi is referred to as an accomplished scholar who, in the court of Janaka, questions Rishi Yajnavalkya, the greatest teacher of the age, at great length upon the origin of all existence.

The second outstanding woman was Maitreyi, one of the two wives of Yajnavalkya. She could grasp the most abstruse philosophy of Adwaita. She refused to accept the property which Yajnavalkya wished to bestow upon her before he renounced the world and took up sannyasa. She asked him, "What shall I do with that which will not make me an immortal? Give me that alone which you know to be the only means of attaining immortality." Yajnavalkya then imparted to Maitreyi the knowledge of Brahman.

EPIC PERIOD

Shabari

In the Ramayana there is a long list of women who led spiritual lives and attained perfection, such as Shabari, the bhakta saint who served Rishi Matang until his death. At this time he made the pronouncement that, "Rama will come. Wait!" True to her guru's last instruction, every day for the rest of her life Shabari cleaned the ashram and strewed flowers along the path in preparation for the coming of Rama. In this way, many years passed and although she was ill-treated and mocked by the other renunciates who lived in that vicinity, still she never lost hope. Finally Rama did come, and through his grace Shabari attained mukti.

Sulabha

In the *Mahabharata*, we find the story of the mendicant Sulabha. She practised yoga and attained that stage of supreme realization in which the finite individual soul becomes one with the infinite universal soul. She travelled widely and one day she came to the court of King Janaka to test his spiritual attainment and benefit from his experiences. After being welcomed as an honoured guest, Sulabha entered the intellect of the king through her yogic power in order to ascertain the level of his enlightenment. During their meeting, the outer frames of both the yogis remained stationary, while soul spoke to soul unheard by mortal ears. At first Janaka felt intimidated by Sulabha's unlawful union and he rebuked her. But Sulabha remained unshaken and silenced him with her superior knowledge, asceticism and spirituality.

BUDDHIST PERIOD

During the Buddhist period, the condition of women was somewhat improved due to the basic principles which Buddha laid down in his teachings. First of all he laid stress on the fact that a woman, like a man, reaps the fruits of her past karma and that she must depend on her own acts for her future salvation. Secondly, he discarded the Brahmanic rituals in which the wife played a secondary part and a barren woman or a widow had no place. Thirdly, he made no distinction between a man and a woman regarding the attainment of spiritual goals. Fourthly, the order of nuns was open to all women whether they were married or unmarried, barren or widowed. Even courtesans were admitted into the order and no disrespect was shown to them. Finally, the education and the training imparted to female novices and nuns was no different from that imparted to their male counterparts.

Mahapajapati Gotami

Many female renunciates attained distinction in the history of Buddhism. The first one amongst them was Mahapajapati Gotami, who persuaded the Buddha to permit women to become bhikshunis. She was the younger sister of Mahamaya, mother of Siddhartha Gautama. Both the sisters were married to King Shuddhodana of Kapilvastu. Queen Mahamaya died seven days after the birth of Siddhartha (Buddha) and her sister, Mahapajapati, took charge of and nursed him as her own. Later she gave birth to a son and a daughter, both of whom she entrusted to the care of nurses, while she herself reared Siddhartha Gautama.

After attaining enlightenment, Gautama Buddha visited Kapilvastu and delivered discourses. At that time King Shuddhodana became a lay disciple and the son of Mahapajapati entered the order. After the death of the King, Mahapajapati decided to renounce worldly life. She and five hundred companions cut their hair, donned yellow robes and set out to join the Buddhist order. At first, Buddha was not willing to allow them to join the order, but he could not turn down the request to give women equal opportunities to those of men for the attainment of salvation. So at last he permitted women to become bhikshunis. Under the direct supervision of the Buddha, Mahapajapati Gotami soon attained perfection. She lived up to the age of one hundred and twenty and was declared by Buddha to be the oldest and most experienced of his bhikshunis.

Kshema

Kshema was born in the royal family of Madras and in the course of time was married to Bimbasara, the king of Rajgriha. Queen Kshema was very proud of her beauty and when she came to know that the Buddha condemned infatuation with one's personal appearance, she refused to meet him. As the king was the chief lay supporter of the Buddha, he felt it was improper for his queen to approach him and so he arranged for the queen to be brought to the Buddha indirectly.

While the queen was approaching, the Buddha changed himself into an exquisitely beautiful woman and made the queen fan her. The queen was taken aback by the beauty of the woman and felt that her own beauty was less than that of a maidservant in comparison. While standing there observing the charms of the beautiful woman, the Buddha changed her into a middle-aged woman, then into an old woman, and ultimately made her fall down on the ground with the fan still in her hand. While still pondering over the fact that the body must pass through these changes, Kshema heard Buddha utter the following verse:

> *Those who are given to attachment*
> *fall into the stream of repeated existences,*
> *like the spider caught in its own net.*
> *One who has no attachments*
> *gets rid of his suffering,*
> *and goes out by tearing the net asunder.*

On listening to this utterance, the queen obtained perfection then and there. As she could not remain a householder after that, she decided to take ordination at once and upon her return to the palace she asked the king for his permission to become a bhikshuni. The king consented to her request and sent her to live with the order. She became very learned in the shastras and was accorded a high place amongst the *theris*, or female renunciates.

Subhadda

Subhadda Kundalakesha was another notable female renunciate. She was born at Rajgriha in the family of a rich banker. In her youth she fell in love with a boy of bad character who tried to kill her for her ornaments. After this incident, Subhaddha made up her mind to become a recluse and practise rigorous asceticism. She joined the order of Nirgranthas by taking ordination. But each time her hair was removed, it came back again in curly clusters. For this reason, she was called *Kundala-kesha*, curly-haired.

Subhadda studied dialectics and learned the art of disputation. She became a great disputant and no one could defeat her. Wherever she went she would make a sand heap, fix a jambu branch on top of it and announce to the people residing there that anyone who dared to dispute with her was invited to trample upon the jambu branch. Then she would wait for seven days. If none came forward, she would depart for another place with the jambu branch.

In this way, she finally reached Shravasti where the Buddha was residing. The sand heap that she put up there was noticed by Sariputra, the chief disciple of Buddha, who immediately trampled it. When Subhadda learned that she had been challenged, she immediately went with a large following to debate with Sariputra. She was defeated by him and acknowledged him to be her master. Afterwards she was taken to the Buddha, who opened her eyes and soon she attained perfection. Buddha gave her ordination with two words, "Come lady." For fifty years she roamed about in Anga, Magadha, Vajji, Kashi and Kosala, living on alms.

JAIN PERIOD

Mallinatha

Women were highly regarded in the Jain tradition and several Jain bhikshunis were known for their learning and intelligence. Mallinatha, the nineteenth Tirthankara, was the daughter of Kumbha, the ruler of Mithila. She was exceedingly beautiful and learned, and her fame attracted the kings of countries near and far. They all sought her hand but Kumbha refused them. Enraged at this, they attacked Mithila. When Kumbha was on the verge of defeat, Malli requested her father to invite all the kings to her apartment.

When they entered her private hall they were taken aback by the charming figure of Malli standing there, but soon this illusion was dispelled as the real Malli entered by another door and told them that what they had first seen was a lifelike statue. At the same time, she opened a lid on the statue's head from which an extremely foul smell issued. Some days before the statue had been filled with eatables which had become rotten by then. Malli told her suitors that beneath the external charm of her own feminine body lay an equally foul mass of filth of a transitory nature. Therefore, she wished to renounce worldly pleasures and become an ascetic. The kings were filled with remorse and decided to follow Malli in adopting the ascetic order.

Yakini Mahattara

The bhikshuni, Yakini Mahattara, also deserves special notice. Haribhadra-sura was a Brahmin scholar, well-versed in the shastras, who declared that he would accept as guru the person who could defeat him in argument and whose speech he could neither explain nor understand. It was the Jain bhikshuni, Yakini, who defeated and converted him. The greatness of Yakini can be better understood by realizing the immense contribution of the scholar Haribhadra-sura to Indian literature.

He wrote on ethics, yoga, logic and rituals. He also wrote commentaries on older texts as well as stories. He reformed the Jain order by opposing the monks who adopted residence in shrines or kept money. It was not such an easy task to defeat and convert such a scholar to the extent that he would take special pride in calling himself Yakini Mahattara-sunu, the son of the great Jain bhikshuni Yakini. She must have been a genius and must have contributed a great deal to the training of Haribhadra-sura.

It was not uncommon to find bhikshunis of high calibre and great learning amongst the Jains. Guna Sadhwi, for example, who prepared the first copy of that monumental allegorical work of Siddharshi, the *Upamitabhave-prapancha-katha*, is addressed by Siddharashi himself as the goddess of learning incarnate. In the age of Siddharaja Jayasimha, two bhikshunis, Mahattara and Ganini Viramati, actively helped Maladhari Hemchandra in the composition of a lengthy commentary on *Visheshavashyakabhashya* of Jinabhadra.

SHAIVA AND VAISHNAVA PERIOD

Lalla

Between the twelfth and eighteenth centuries, the conquest of India by Muslims made the position of women even more difficult than before. Spiritual idealism, however, was kept alive by the Shaiva and Vaishnava schools. Among the women saints who lived during this period was Lalla (Lal Ded), the prophetess of Kashmir. She was a Shaivite mendicant ascetic who wandered about preaching yogic doctrines as the best means of ultimate absorption into the supreme. She was always naked and when her devotees would ask, "Lalla, why don't you put on clothes?" she would reply, "Why do you see only my body? Why do you not see my soul?"

Mirabai

In the Vaishnava tradition we find the highest expression of bhakti and renunciation in Mirabai of Rajasthan. All her life she sang in praise of Sri Krishna, her lord and sovereign deity. Soaring above the temptations of a royal household and overcoming the importunities of persecutions by relations who wanted her to be worldly, with unflinching faith she devoted herself entirely to the Lord. She mixed freely in the company of holy men, not deterred in the least by the criticisms she received for it. The myriad poems and bhajans which she bequeathed are still highly appreciated for their simplicity and depth of devotion.

Muktabai

Muktabai of Maharashtra was the youngest sister of Nivritti, Jnanadev and Sopan. All four were said to have attained self-realization in childhood. Their father, Vitthalpant Kulharni, was a brahmin who had taken sannyasa after his marriage and then, by the order of his guru, had returned to grihastha life in order to produce children and fulfil his obligation to his wife. When the children were born, however, the townspeople treated them as outcasts because they said that a sannyasin cannot return to householder life without incurring sin. When asked what form of atonement he should perform, the father was told none except the ending of one's life was recommended in the scriptures.

Both the parents threw themselves into the river, leaving their four small children to fend for themselves. At that time, Muktabai was not more than six years old. During the following years of great trial and hardship, Muktabai was looked after by her brothers. Although their parents had performed the final atonement, still the children were denied initiation into the brahmin caste. It was only by dint of their superior knowledge, spiritual powers and perseverance that they were finally able to secure a position of acceptance and respect in the society which had so cruelly rejected and ostracized them from their birth.

Jnanadev completed his studies of Vedanta and other philosophies before the age of sixteen and became a great scholar. He wrote his famous *Jnaneshwari*, an exposition of the *Bhagavad Gita*, in the Marathi language. He began to hold discourses on the Puranas and spent his time in the company of Namadev and other saints. Muktabai also received her share of admiration and honour. She was said to posses supernatural powers like her brothers. She became a saint and initiated others into spirituality. There are many legends about her ability as a spiritual guide. She was also known for her *abhangas*, or devotional songs.

Venabai and Akkabai

Two other saints of Maharashtra, who lived several centuries after Muktabai, were Venabai and ·Akkabai. Both were widowed in childhood and became disciples of Ramdas at a young age. Seeing their abilities, he admitted them into his order and trained them to propagate his teachings. Venabai was sent to Miraj where she laid the foundations for a monastery and served for over twenty years. Akkabai proved herself to be one of the ablest and most trusted disciples of Ramdas. She became the head of the monasteries at Chapahal and Parli and managed them for over thirty years, even during times of great trouble and unrest.

MODERN PERIOD

Sarada Devi

Sarada Devi of Bengal was one of the greatest female saints of this era. She was born to a pious brahmin couple in the village of Jayrambati and was married at the age of six to a madman of God, Gadadhar Chattopadhyaya. By the time she was old enough to join her husband, he had already taken sannyasa and his name was Ramakrishna Paramahamsa. At the age of nineteen she travelled from her native village to Calcutta in order to stay with her husband who was a poojari at the Dakshineshwar temple.

After her arrival, one of the first questions Ramakrishna asked his young wife was, "Have you come here to drag me down to the worldly plane?" To this question she replied, "No, I have come only to serve you so that you may go ahead on your chosen path." After this, the relationship of preceptor and disciple was superimposed on the marital one, both living together as sannyasins and vowed to lifelong celibacy. This spiritual couple developed a deep affection for one another, purged of all impurities and mingled with deep reverence. Each perceived in the other a clear manifestation of the Divine Mother.

On one auspicious occasion, Ramakrishna made Sarada Devi sit before him and worshipped her as the Divine Mother, observing the rituals prescribed by the tantras for *shodashi pooja*. By the time it was completed, she and Ramakrishna had fallen into a beatific trance. Thus transcending the sensory world, the supernormal couple shed the last vestiges of duality and merged their original Self. Ramakrishna concluded the ceremony by prostrating himself before her and uttering the prescribed salutations. After this, Ramakrishna always gave the same respect to Sarada Devi as he gave to the Divine Mother.

For fourteen years, from the age of nineteen to thirty-three, Sarada lived off and on with the master, whom she served assiduously with one-pointed devotion. To look after his health, to hear his voice and to see him from a distance would give her intense joy. Being a purdah woman, as were most of the village women of her time, she could not sit freely with her husband when his disciples and devotees were near, thus exposing herself to their gaze. So she kept

159

herself hidden away for most of the day, spending her time in japa and meditation from early morning and cooking for the master and his devotees during the day. Engrossed in her labour of love, her heart would always remain pinned to the master. Her mind followed him so closely that she was able to hear from a distance what he said in his own room.

After Ramakrishna's death, when Sarada was removing her bangles to put on widow's garb, the master suddenly appeared before her saying, "Where have I gone? I have just shifted from one room to another." This vision was enough to assure Sarada that she need not behave like a widow. Such repeated contacts on the subtle plane made her feel his constant presence by her side and filled her with the intense delight of spiritual vision. One day she lost herself completely in an ecstatic trance and behaved exactly as the master would have done when in that mood.

As the visions and ecstasies increased, a great change took place in her mental outlook and behaviour, enabling her to utilize her divine power for the upliftment of others, filling the vacant place left by Ramakrishna. Soon all of his disciples and devotees had rallied around her. Thus at the age of thirty-five, Sarada began her spiritual ministrations, quenching the thirst of many aspiring souls.

People came to her from every walk of life to remove their sufferings, and she became the refuge of them all. Cast in the mould of absolute egolessness like Ramakrishna, she stood out in unique splendour as an endearing mother, enfolding all who came to her with her boundless affection.

Anandamayi Ma

The life of Nirmala Sundari, 'Immaculate Beauty', later known as Anandamayi Ma, 'Blissful Mother', abounded with psychic and mystical phenomena of every kind. She was renowned, however, not so much for such phenomena as for her ceaselessly happy and tranquil state and the motherly graciousness with which she received the thousands upon thousands who sought her blessings.

160

Born with the same realization that she enjoyed as an adult, she was married at the age of twelve to a little-educated brahmin like herself, whom she later renamed Bholanath. When her husband approached her to consummate their marriage, he received such a terrific electric shock that he never did it again. From that day he vowed to be her spiritual disciple and the couple remained celibate throughout their marriage.

During her twenties, she took up yoga sadhana and spontaneously displayed a great array of mudras and kriyas of which she had no previous knowledge in this life. Various mantras and Sanskrit compositions poured from her mouth. These experiences led her to a more complete knowledge of her spiritual unity, and after this she began to attract a small following. At first she was not eager to function as a guru, and she would only see people because her husband intervened on their behalf. Under his direction she began to mix more freely with those who came to her for healing, guidance and spiritual inspiration. During these years extraordinary ecstasies began to manifest regularly in which her entire body would be utterly possessed by a divine force.

When her devotees constructed their first ashram, she was not particularly pleased, saying that the whole world is an ashram, so what need had they of a special place of their own? When the ashram was completed, rather than settle herself there, her divine inspiration moved her to travel, which she continued to do until her death at the age of eighty-seven. As a result of her wanderings, twenty-five ashrams were eventually established. However, she never considered any of them to be hers. She travelled continuously without plans or possessions, and those who wished to accompany her had to do the same.

Although the ashrams were established by strict brahmins along traditional lines, she herself never conformed to caste rules. She touched and fed members of all castes. Most of the people who came to her sought her blessings, her healing power, her advice and her sympathy. All of these she gave endlessly, with patience and compassion. Serving and enlightening humanity, she made herself available to devotees every day of the year without caring for her own privacy. Although she was never formally initiated into sannyasa, throughout her life she demonstrated the qualities of total dedication and self-abnegation which are the basis of sannyasa life.

Paramahamsa Atmananda

Kamla Gidwani was born in a large Sindhi family which had migrated from Sind during the partition. Her father, a devout and spiritual man, had brought his guru, Beriwale Baba, along with his entire clan to India. All the Gidwani children were drawn towards Beriwale Baba, especially Kamla who always found time to serve him. As she tended his dhuni, brought his food, listened to his satsangs and upadesh, slowly the light of jnana awoke in her. However, when she asked him for diksha he said, "Your guru will come. He will be dressed in geru and be radiant like the sun. You must wait for him."

Years later, after Beriwale Baba had attained maha-samadhi, Paramahamsa Satyananda visited the Gidwani house, and when Kamla went for his darshan, she knew at once that Beriwale Baba's words had come true. Her guru had come, and when she asked him for mantra diksha, he told her, "I will give you mantra diksha and higher dikshas also. Be ready!" Gradually Kamla realized that she really wanted to dedicate her whole life to serving her guru's mission as a sannyasin. So, in 1965, she became the first sannyasin disciple of Paramahamsa Satyananda and was renamed Swami Atmananda Saraswati.

In the guru's ashram she did all kinds of duties from serving Paramahamsa Satyananda to administering the ashram. Often she travelled with Paramahamsaji to seminars, lectures and conventions. After her period of service to guru was over, she travelled to Ireland and founded an ashram. From there she travelled all over Europe, drawing thousands of people to the path of yoga.

From Europe, she went to the Far East where she established an ashram in Singapore and travelled throughout Malaysia, Hong Kong, Indonesia, the Philippines, as well as Middle Eastern countries. Thousands of people flocked to her for guidance and she made disciples from every caste, creed and religion, thus proving that yoga is truly a universal science. Many of her followers were Muslim, Buddhist and Christian.

In 1990, she returned from Singapore to meet Paramahamsa Satyananda and expressed her desire to renounce everything and come to live near him in seclusion. Paramahamsaji told her, "Yes you can come to live here, not as my disciple, but as an individual pledged to sadhana and spiritual life. Live here like a paramahamsa, one who does not care for money, status, disciples or ashrams. Do not think even for a moment that by coming here you will be able to live close to me, for you will not even see me. If you can renounce everything that you have created and live here alone, devoting your time to sadhana, then come, not otherwise."

Swami Atmananda at once accepted this proposal and thus became not only his first sannyasin disciple, but also the first disciple to follow him when he adopted the life of a paramahamsa.

Swami Dharmashakti

Basanti Devi was born in Madhya Pradesh. In her early childhood, her mother, sensing a future full of struggle, inculcated in her the teachings of the Ramayana and other spiritual literature, as well as the lives of great saints. At the age of thirteen she was married to Satyabrat Srivastava whose open, friendly and spiritual nature was an important influence in her life. Satyabrat became a disciple of Swami Sivananda and in 1957 the couple went to Rishikesh for darshan and diksha. When Satyabrat was receiving mantra diksha, he looked around for his wife, but Swami Sivananda said, "She will not take diksha from me. Her guru will come to her at her home".

Paramahamsa Satyananda came to Rajnandgaon in 1958. On the Shravan Poornima day he initiated Basanti Devi and she became Dharmashakti. During the same year, Dharmashakti and Satyabrat went on a pilgrimage to Uttarakhanda with Paramahamsa Satyananda. In Gangotri, Dharmashakti had many spiritual experiences and a sankalpa came to her mind which was to shape the direction of the rest of her life. She resolved that, "Should I bear a child, I will give him to Paramahamsa Satyananda." This sankalpa she later communicated to Satyabrat who endorsed it with repeated affirmations.

After twenty-four years of marriage, on the 14th of February 1960, at the age of thirty-six a son was born to Dharmashakti. Five weeks after the birth of the child, Paramahamsa Satyananda came to remind the couple of the resolve they had made and said, "Fulfil your sankalpa. In your lap is lying the valuable treasure of humanity. Place this jewel in the hands of the sannyasin as promised." The couple looked at each other and Dharmashakti lovingly placed the child in the extended arms of Paramahamsa Satyananda saying, "Oh Prabhu, please accept my offering."

The guru looked into the child's eyes and named him Niranjan. Then he returned the child to his mother's lap and said, "Dharmashakti, from now onwards, you and Satyabrat are the Nanda and Yashoda of Rajnandgaon. In your lap is blooming the promise of the future. Look after him very well with care and respect. Do not identify yourself with him, he will be the ordainer of a new culture of humanity."

The dharmic couple thereafter became actively engaged in spreading the guru's mission. In 1963, the magazines of Paramahamsa Satyananda's mission began publication from Rajnandgaon, and Dharmashakti served as editor, publisher and distributor. Rajnandgaon became the headquarters of Paramahamsaji's International Yoga Fellowship Movement, and Dharmashakti was its first secretary.

On the 20th October 1967, Paramahamsa Satyananda arrived at Rajnandgaon, and at the station itself, witnessed by thousands, Dharmashakti placed Niranjan, then a small boy of hardly seven years, in his hands. Thereafter, Niranjan began his gurukul training in Munger under the guru's supervision, and Dharmashakti saw very little of him. On Basant Panchami in 1971, Niranjan took sannyasa at the age of ten years, and within two months he had been sent overseas so that he could assist in the propagation of his guru's mission.

In the meanwhile, Satyabrat had been initiated into sannyasa and was actively engaged in propagating the guru's mission in Madhya Pradesh. The inauguration of the Rajnandgaon Yoga Ashram in 1971 further increased Dharmashakti's responsibilities. At the end of that year, her husband met with an accident and died. Dharmashakti was deeply shaken by this experience but, having the mettle of a true disciple, she continued to serve her guru's mission.

For the next fifteen years, she worked relentlessly and was the pillar of her guru's mission. In 1985, she finally came to live at Ganga Darshan. During the same year, she took sannyasa diksha and Paramahamsaji commented, "You were a sannyasin right from the beginning. Sannyasa does not come with geru clothes or with long matted locks. The sannyasin is a person who is always dedicated to guru seva, whose life is meant for service. You have given a new meaning and value to sannyasa."

Today we can rightfully say that Swami Dharmashakti is one sannyasin who has stood the test of time. She is the first disciple whom Paramahamsa Satyananda initiated and perhaps the only disciple who, in times of great adversity, always remained a strong and true supporter of her guru's mission. Although her life was full of suffering and hardship, her faith in guru never wavered. She is an ideal example of simplicity, saintliness, total dedication and renunciation. She gives satsang, darshan and diksha and is a source of spirituality and inspiration to all.

Sannyasa Lineage

Dattatreya

26

Dattatreya

Compiled by Swami Dharmakeerti Saraswati

Na Janami Gadyam, Na Janami Padyam,
Na Janami Shabdam, Na Janami Artham,
Chiteka Shadasya Hridi Dyotate Me
Mukham Issarante Giraschapi Chitram.

I do not know the rules of poetry,
prose, words and meanings.
In my heart, I see the six-faced one,
and words flow from my mouth
much to my amazement.

Adi Shankaracharya

"MOTHER! WHAT IS THE TRUTH?"

It was daybreak. The golden rays of the sun streamed into
the nests of doves and nudged the little ones awake, swept
over the creeper that lay in profusion near the cowshed,
prodded a multitude of jasmine flowers into opening their
eyes and poured in through nooks and crannies, washing
the eager, laughing faces of the children going for their
morning ablutions to the river. Slowly the hermitage woke
from slumber. Young girls picked up pots, set them on their
hips and heads and walked together to fetch water from the
Ganga. Others were picking flowers for the morning rituals.
Yet some, under the watchful eyes of the rishi patnis, traced

169

yantras or mystical diagrams in rice powder on the fresh soil that had been cleaned with cow-dung.

The silver bells on the necks of the cows tinkled in the morning breeze as they were being milked. Every cow's forehead was adorned with sindhoor. Everywhere there were groups bursting into merriment and happiness. To the inmates of the hermitage, every day was a celebration of life, moments of simple joy and contentment, a contentment that comes when one has known no anguish, a contentment that is part of the surface of life, when one has not plumbed the depths.

Everyone seemed to be laughing and joyous, all but Anusuiya. Was it only yesterday, she thought, that she had come as a young bride into the home of Atri? The second daughter of Kardama Prajapati and Devahuti, Anusuiya had walked with a shy tread and downcast eyes towards the agni kund. The flowers were in bloom. Her black tresses, adorned with jasmine, reached to her ankles, gently swishing her silver anklets that made music as she moved, against her soft, fair feet which had been coloured red with henna. She had been aware of a feeling of expansiveness within even then, as if she were at the end of a pilgrimage, on the threshold of the divine.

Devahuti saw the radiance on the face of her daughter and caught her breath with wonder. Never had Anusuiya shone so. As a child, unenvious in disposition, she had been extraordinarily giving in nature. Nothing was so special to her that she held on to it if another wanted it. As she grew older, many came to her to share their difficulties. She was a willing listener and when they left, they walked with a lighter step. Anusuiya had healed them with her compassion. Often, as she reached out to remove some small burden from Devahuti's shoulders onto her own, the latter had wondered who was mother and who daughter!

"She has been named well, Devahuti," her husband would say. "Anusuiya is totally without envy." But today she seemed as if her soul were on fire with a total self-giving.

Her mother remembered Anusuiya as a child watching her father perform yajna. "Mother," she had asked, "why does father light the fire when he performs yajna?" "The fire, my child," Devahuti had replied, "is to remind us of the inner fire into which we offer all that we are." "Why do we offer ourselves and what is the inner fire?" Anusuiya had asked, with wide, luminous eyes.

Devahuti had known that this, her second born, was special. She had always asked questions. She was thirsty for vidya, the higher knowledge. She had asked wandering sages about Anusuiya's curiosity. Who would be the guru who could fulfil the innocent child's yearning? Always the answer had been the same. Always they had smiled and said, "A great destiny awaits Anusuiya. Her life will be her sadhana."

"Mother, Mother," Anusuiya had tugged at her, "what is this inner fire?" "Within each of us, Anusuiya," Devahuti had replied, "there is a divine power. It is awareness. It is not our mind. It watches our mind, all our thoughts, our feelings, our actions. It is untouched by them. Agni, this fire, is the guardian of this divine awareness, which is truth. Day and night, when we play, when we eat, when we sleep, this eternal light is always burning. It lights our way on the pilgrimage of life."

"What pilgrimage, Mother?" the child had asked. "We are pilgrims, travellers, moving towards the truth, all of us," Devahuti had replied. "And what is this truth, Mother?" Anusuiya had gone on relentlessly. Devahuti had no words. What words can describe the truth, the vast, the limitless, the eternal? "You will know when you find it, Anusuiya," she had said.

In all her games and household chores, while she learned the art of cooking, music and the shastras, while she was running with her sisters or serving food to a guest, she always played a little game with herself. She had been aware: "Am I standing before the truth?" her young mind would frequently ask. "Not yet," something inside would whisper. As she watched and watched, the little flame of awareness grew into a raging fire.

171

"Mother, see," she would say with wide eyes, "the fire from the yajna kund has entered my heart. Can you see the flame?" And today, seeing Anusuiya in her bridal finery, Devahuti remembered. She looked at the fire in the agni kund and the glow on her daughter's face, and she whispered within herself, "Yes, my child, I can see the flame!"

Devahuti's thoughts went back to yet another day, when she had first seen her Lord, Rishi Kardama. Many years ago, her father, Swayambhu Manu, and mother, Shatrupa, had taken her to the ashram of the sage in accordance with her own desire. Kardama had just finished the agnihotra. Having done intense tapasya, he was glowing like the fire itself. And yet, with all humility, he had offered to the monarch, Manu, the traditional *arghya*, offering water, and *padya*, washing of the feet, and welcomed him. Manu had prostrated at the sage's feet and received his blessings. Kardama had seated the king and asked him about the welfare of his kingdom and the well-being of his people.

"O King," he had said, "a monarch is like a sannyasin. He has no personal life, no attachments. His subjects are his children. He cares for them like a mother, protects them like a father. He sees the atman in all. His path is that of karma yoga. His prana shakti and manas shakti are in balance. His might and valour blend with his gentleness and compassion like the play between the sun and the moon. He puts down evil like Yama and protects dharma. He is Narayana's representative. He is the guardian of tapasvins. Please tell me why you have come."

The king spoke softly, "With the blessings of the Lord and of tapasvins like you, my kingdom prospers. My subjects are healthy and prosperous. I have only one personal desire. I have two sons, Uttanapada and Priyavrata. It is not of them that I am concerned. A father is always anxious about his daughters. He wants them to be married in such a house where dharma will be a living tradition. My daughters, Akuti and Prasuti, have been given to Sage Ruchi and Daksha Prajapati. This one, my Devahuti, chose you as her Lord

172

when she heard your name from Sage Narada. I wish to give her in Kanyadaan to you. Please honour her by taking her hand."

Kardama had accepted with a smile. However, he had told the monarch in her presence, "I will accept your daughter on one condition. The purpose of human life is the quest of Brahman. We purify ourselves by the four stages of life: brahmacharya, grihastha ashramas, vanaprastha and sannyasa. The first three stages are to purify us for the fourth. It is this understanding that has kept the rich tradition of *brahmavarta* alive. I will live with Devahuti in grihastha ashrama until she becomes the mother of my children. After that I will take sannyasa and seek the Lord." Devahuti was then married to Kardama and stayed with him in his ashram at Bindusaras while her parents went back to Barhismati, their city.

Devahuti remembered the years of loving service to her husband, the austerities she had observed, while she had prepared herself physically and mentally for spiritual awakening. She remembered too, how she had, on her husband's asking, expressed her desire to be a mother. Kardama had in his own compassionate way rewarded her for the years of devoted service. Days and nights of joy followed. She was the mother of nine daughters. And then in the twinkling of an eye, it was all over. She remembered what Kardama had said before he had married her, "I will live with Devahuti in grihastha ashrama until she becomes the mother of my children. After that I will take sannyasa and seek the Lord."

She had waited for him to return from his meditation. With folded hands and tears brimming from her eyes she had spoken, "Lord, I have had every possible pleasure in life, all my desires are fulfilled. Yet the thought of your leaving fills me with sadness. My associations with you. all these years should have prepared me for this, and yet I am tossed by my own inner storms. What use have my desires been for me? Everything seems worthless now. I understand the transitoriness of desires and their fulfilment and yet I have not transcended them. How will I face the ocean of loneliness when you are gone? How can my ignorance be washed away?"

Kardama knew that his wife was passing through a normal state of unhappiness. It was inevitable, it was necessary. Such is sorrow that it prepares the ground for viveka and vairagya. "Devahuti," he said, "you will have yet another child, the great Kapila. Prepare yourself to receive the supreme in your womb. Kapila will teach you Brahmavidya. This will be your liberation. Through you he will establish the great Samkhya yoga. Only then will your suffering cease."

Devahuti had obeyed her husband. She had practised ekagrata sadhana. In waking, in sleep, she had continued intense concentration, and even now when she was with child. With a deep sadness and a great longing, she looked forward to the day when he would answer her own inner question voiced by her daughter so many years ago, "Mother! What is the truth?"

"LORD, WHAT IS THE TRUTH?"

Gentle hands lifted the veil from her face. Anusuiya looked into the face of her husband. The fire within her blazed and as she saw the tejas on Atri's face, she did not know whether it was the light within her that threw a reflection on him, or his light that had turned her heart into molten gold. So powerful was this glow that enfolded them both, she knew in a moment that she was in the presence of truth.

For many years she had marvelled at this man who could be so gentle with her and yet so ruthless with himself. His name, Atri, he had told her meant 'traveller' or 'devourer'. He had a devouring desire for the truth. "You have walked seven steps with me," he had said, referring to the *saptapadi*, a ritual of the marriage ceremony, "we will be friends for life, fellow travellers, moving towards the truth." Now Anusuiya learned that there was more to the truth than she had imagined.

174

Patiently Atri taught her spiritual practices, guiding her constantly while she served him with total devotion. Together they went to the Ruksha mountains. She had been spellbound by the green verdant forests. Every day she would go to the Nirvindhya river at dawn, stand waist deep in the water and offer her prayers to the accompanying music of the birds. As she emerged from her worship, the gentle rays of the rising sun would bathe her in silent benediction. The ashram was an abode of peace. She would worship the inner atman in the cows and then set about milking them. As she walked past, the flowers that grew in such profusion would reach out to touch her, as if to feel the softness of her feet with their petals.

Atri, with his senses under control, practised the *panchagni vidya*, knowledge of the five fires sadhana. On all four sides of him were lit fires and with the sun shining on top, the sage shone like Agni himself. Even as Agni is the inner fire that prepares and purifies, Atri would systematically prepare his body and mind to withstand the rigours of tapasya, while Anusuiya, with her devotion to service, grew in consciousness beside him. Their passions and emotions were purified in the common fire of their spiritual aspirations, and were as smoke. Their lives were offered in the yajna of life to the divine life in the cosmos.

Anusuiya became in her own right a repository of incomparable spiritual power and a model of supreme chastity. On one occasion she had reached out, even as she had done so often as a young girl, to assuage the grief of Sumati, the wife of a brahmin. Kaushika, for he was so called, had given himself over to sensual pleasures and over the years had totally lost control over his desires. He had been enamoured of a harlot who, in the course of time, had sucked him dry of whatever material benefits he had been capable of giving her and then thrown him out of her house. Having neglected body and mind, Kaushika became a leper and still his desires remained unquenched as well as undiminished.

Sumati, who was an epitome of chastity, even as Anusuiya was, carried her husband in a basket and set out to the house of the woman at night. On the way, Kaushika's legs touched a sage who cursed the former to die before sunrise. Sumati, with the spiritual power born out of one-pointed devotion to her husband, willed that the sun would not rise. To bring back order to the cosmos, Anusuiya asked Sumati to withdraw the power of her sankalpa, promising in turn to use her own energy to restore Kaushika to health and life.

A chastened Kaushika acknowledged his wife's *pativratya*, devotion to her husband, and spoke to Anusuiya, "O Mother! Having learned the Vedas, I did not understand their essence. I did not realize that intellect and experience ought to have gone hand in hand. I abused my body and mind. I created war among the energy patterns within myself. Desire is like Agni. It is *anala*, ever hungry, never satisfied. It is the same power that wings us up towards liberation and the truth or pushes us down to darkness and suffering. Alas! I have wasted years of my life pursuing the transient, the maya. Mother! I want to be cured of avidya. I want to achieve that state of consciousness that is always serene, unaffected by the ravages of fickle time. Foolish that I was, my mind was clouded by the sense of 'I' and 'mine'. I was the personification of tamas, ignorance and stagnation. I beg you, please enlighten me, so that I may not be ensnared by samsara anymore."

Anusuiya looked at him with compassion and said, "O Kaushika, do not be distressed. The mind is slave to the play of the gunas: tamas, rajas and sattwa. You are not the mind. Disidentify yourself from the actions of the body and mind. You are the sakshi, the eternal witness. Meditate on the *sakshi bhava*, the awareness. We are but instruments of a higher consciousness. Your body and mind have paid for their misuse. You are now born again. Place your devotion in Narayana, the all-pervading consciousness which is in you, in me, in the whole world. Instead of using your body and mind to search for transient pleasures, use them to

176

search for the eternal, the unchanging self. Surrender is the highest form of bhakti."

Embracing Sumati, Anusuiya said to her, "Sister, it is women like you who uphold the dharma of the universe. Because you protected the dharma, it protected you – *Dharmo rakshati rakshitaha.*" Their tears mingled and Sumati and Kaushika left for their homes in peace. For a long time afterwards, Anusuiya remembered the days of her childhood and her sisters Kala, Poornima, Devakulya, Shraddha and Havirbhu. She remembered how they would finish off their household chores so that they could sit near the flowing river at Bindusaras, the beautiful and picturesque spot. They would then talk about dharma and adharma, their own emotions, sometimes laughing, sometimes with great seriousness. Often intellectual conversations were a mask drawn over an inner emotion or yearning. Anusuiya, with her penetrating mind, would pick up the heart of the matter and offer advice and guidance.

Being the second child, she often took the role of a mother while the others would come to her with their difficulties. Yes, Anusuiya remembered the days of her childhood. "Anusuiya's child will be lucky," Shraddha had said on one occasion. No sooner had the memory come when there arose, unbidden in her heart, an unfulfilled yearning. It was a great ache that shook the very foundations of her composure and tranquillity. Disturbed by the painful longing within her, she turned to Atri. "Lord!" she said, "why have I now lost my inner peace? I have served you with complete devotion and in all these years I felt I was closer to the truth than ever before, But now, for no reason at all, I feel disturbed. Have I fallen from the path? Are all the years of tapasya and sadhana wasted?"

Atri, who could see into the future, smiled and said, "Do not worry, Anusuiya. It is natural for you to long for a child. Even that desire would not have arisen in you but for the will of the higher consciousness. Each of us functions at two levels. At one level are the individual aspirations, dreams and desires. Some are samskaras, little ripples that arise and subside. Some are deep-seated vasanas, giant waves that are not easily stilled. They rise, crash into other waves and create new patterns and effects. They stop when they have totally exhausted themselves. You are neither the ripple nor the giant wave. You are the ocean that is unmoved by the play on the surface. You are also the cause of the play.

"Seeing Sumati triggered childhood dreams. These dreams are part of a greater pattern. Our small limited minds cannot fathom the movements of the cosmic mind. Trust in the supreme. Light the fire of *shraddha*, faith. Surrender all thoughts, all feelings to the absolute one. There is a purpose in everything. No thoughts or feelings could have risen in you without the will of He who guides the universe. You are an instrument in the hands of the divine. Be a graceful one. Let your music be as He wills, not in accordance with your preconceived, limited ideas of truth. The truth can manifest in millions of ways. Identify only with the witness. Accept whatever manifests through you but do not identify with it."

How strange it was that Anusuiya, who was so highly evolved on the spiritual dimension and was herself a guiding light to hundreds of seekers, should herself falter in her *ekagrata*, her one-pointedness! Such is the power of maya that it shakes even the greatest of souls. And yet, without it, there can be no growth, no opening into the divine. Everything in the sadhaka is perfected and then the perfected is offered into the flame of Agni. Again and again at different stages in life, Agni appears and asks for all that one has. All one's sense of security, all one's foundations, all one has, is offered as oblation into the raging fire, anala, until one has the courage to stand naked, supportless, anchorless, without identity, without ego. Only the truly brave are sadhakas.

"Lord," said Anusuiya, "when will this ache end?" "Anusuiya," Atri said, wiping her tears, "stand steadfast. Strengthen your shraddha. Learn to wait for the truth."

"Lord," she said, "What is the truth?" "You will know when it reveals itself to you," said Atri.

"SON, WHAT IS THE TRUTH?"

Anusuiya continued with her austerities and penance. Atri's tapasya became more intense. Together the holy couple continued their sadhana unabated. Such was the power of their inner worship that the energy patterns of the whole universe were in harmony with them. Their sadhana set them in tune with the vast forces, of creation, dissolution and sustenance in the cosmos.

One day in meditation, Atri had a vision of three devas: Vishnu, the sustaining energy, Brahma, the creative force, and Shiva, the force of dissolution. "We offer ourselves to you," they seemed to be saying. In a blaze of light they entered into him and merged with him. So pure was Atri, so egoless that the truth poured itself into him, or so it seemed. In reality, he had been purified to the extent of becoming one with the higher forces. He was the perfected instrument through which divinity expresses itself totally. As a result of his severe tapasya, Atri was able to grasp the threefold powers of the universe as his own atman. Drunk with divine bliss, Atri rose and sought Anusuiya.

In the ashram, after the day's rituals were over, sitting in her meditation asana with her gaze drawn inward, Anusuiya had a vision in which three strangers stood at her threshold and asked for alms. In the Indian tradition, where the unexpected guest is treated as the Lord himself, *atithi devo bhava*, this was a very auspicious sign.

"Bhavati bhiksham dehi," they said, "feed us, O Mother!" There are two types of feeding. *Bhojanam* is that which the hostess offers and *iccha bhojanam* is the food that the guest asks for. The strangers at the door wanted her to feed them naked. Anusuiya's power was such that she had the *pancha bhutas*, the five elements that make up all creation (earth, water, fire, air, and ether) under her control. She understood

that they wanted her to feed them without the clothing of the ego. They were asking her to stand with an unconditioned, naked and pure mind before them. Although bound by *pativratya* (devotion to her husband), Anusuiya never wavered.

In her vision she saw herself rising to feed them. They seemed to glow as if they were beings of light. The mother in her reached its full glorious flowering and milk poured out of her breasts. The three devas became babies and she fed them until they were satiated and she was satiated. With the milk, she poured all her tapasya, all the fruits of her intense penance over the years into the higher consciousness until she was empty even of a spiritual ego. The glow from the babies seemed to envelop her. She had a deep sense of fulfilment. The vision faded and she was swept into a deep silence, a silence which was not the absence of sound but the absence of the self.

When Atri entered some moments later, he saw Anusuiya with closed eyes and a smile on her lips. When she opened her eyes, they did not need to talk to each other. Both were aware of the momentous happening in their lives. In the course of time, Anusuiya gave birth to Soma, the *amsha,* partial incarnation, of creative energy, Durvasa, the amsha of dissolution, and on a Wednesday, in the auspicious month of Marga Shirsha, on the fourteen day of the full moon, Dattatreya was born.

It was a day of great celebration in the ashram. Mango leaves were strung across doorways. Banana plants were tied to pillars. Yantras were drawn in rice powder on the floors and filled in with saffron and turmeric. The foreheads of cows were adorned with red sindoor. Rishis from ashrams nearby, glowing with tapas shakti, came to see the new-born child. All who saw the child were drawn to his ethereal beauty.

The rishis found their eyes brimming with tears of joy as they exclaimed, "*Atri netra samudbhava* – Truly this child is born from Atri's eyes." They were referring to the *jnana chakshu*, or the eye of knowledge. The child was the manifestation of the power of penance, the flame of Atri's tapasya. The force of consciousness comes out as energy through the eyes. Therefore, sages are said to have *divya drishti*, or divine sight. Datta was the fruit of Atri's expanded consciousness.

Devakulya, who was later to be called Ganga, a niece of Anusuiya, was fascinated by his large, open eyes like full-blown lotus flowers. *"Prafulla kamalakshena,"* she said as she lifted him up in her slender arms, "he shines like the full moon." Anusuiya saw her child, dark-hued like the rain-bearing clouds pregnant with rain, and she knew this was no ordinary boy. He would pour out wisdom and compassion as he grew older, not because he wanted to but because it was his nature, even as the dark heavy clouds poured their waters onto the parched earth. She knew that this was the supreme consciousness descended into the dark womb of matter; she saw his body glow like a sapphire, the gem called *indra nila*. All her yearning to be a mother was set at rest.

As Datta grew older, he was the joy of the hermitage. Even as in later years Krishna was the darling of Gokul, Dattatreya gladdened the hearts of all. He was calm and composed. At the same time, he could be playful and was referred to as Deva, which means both 'light' and 'spirit'. He loved to smear himself with *bhasma*, holy ash.

Once Anusuiya had found him having a serious talk with his playmates who were sitting around him. He had been eight years of age then. "Bhasma has other names," he was explaining. "It is called *vibhooti* because it gives spiritual power, *bhasma* because it consumes all evils and *raksha* because it protects from all fear. Bhasma has the power of fire. Agni, the inner fire, scorches and reduces all impurities to ashes. He who smears ashes on his body is purified as if he has bathed in fire."

One boy had asked Datta, "Do we realize the truth by smearing ashes on our body?" "No," said Datta. "Smear your body with bhasma. Then reflect on the inner meaning of Agni and bhasma. Then you will realize the truth." When the children saw Anusuiya, they got up reverently and ran away to play. They called Datta, *Bhasma Nishta,* one who loves bhasma.

Datta was an ideal son. While his brothers, Soma and Durvasa, left home early, he had stayed back and served his parents with great devotion. Decades later, Krishna was to say to his consort Rukmini, "I run behind my devotees so that the dust from their feet may purify me." Such is the love and compassion of one of supreme consciousness for his devotees that he appears in many guises now as son, now as servant, as teacher, as friend, so that he may serve those who have surrendered totally.

Datta's hair was matted and lay coiled on the crown on his head. Although Anusuiya loved him to distraction, many times she felt she did not understand him. It seems as if he had unending facets to him. Often he would catch her gazing at him. He would then look deep into her eyes and she would lose all concept of time and identity and move into a bottomless well of silence. When she came back to external life, he would be gone and she would be strangely at peace with herself. Such instances were many. Yet it seemed as if he were waiting, for what she did not know.

Even as a child he was a teacher. Tapasvins and yogis of great spiritual stature would gather around him to listen. Occasionally he would realize that their spiritual progress was hindered by their attachment to him and he would go away. Those that followed him and searched for him would come back with strange tales. They would see him sitting under a tree drinking wine with a beautiful woman by his side. But such was their faith in his gurudom they would wait patiently with an innocent openness. He would then be serious and awaken them to higher teachings. Some of the yogis came back with *siddhis,* yogic powers. Some became great bhaktas. They called him, *Vibhu,* the glorious, the gracious. They believed implicitly that his spontaneous grace would give them liberation which their arduous and upward struggle of tapasya in isolation could not achieve. *Bhaktanu-kampin,* they called him, one who is ever ready to pour compassion on his devotees, to protect and guide them onward.

The years had passed all too soon. Dattatreya grew to manhood. One evening he had come to them and, prostrating before Anusuiya and Arti, had said, "It is time for me to leave. I wish to repair to the Sayhadri mountains for tapasya. Give me your blessings." Atri had given his blessings, but Anusuiya was shocked. Lulled into complacency by his filial devotion, she had never envisaged this separation. She felt that her heart would break, and with grief came anger. How could he leave her and go away when she had carried him in her womb and cared for him as a child? *Putramoham,* blind affection, swept away her viveka. In her attachment to her son, she lost all her discrimination.

"O Datta," she wept, "tell me this is a joke. Your body belongs to me. It is I who fed you, cared for you, clothed you. Even if your mind could be so cruel as to leave me and has wandered away, your body has no right to leave my doorstep." "Mother," said Dattatreya with a look of compassion, "look at me." And as she looked, she felt as if his body had dissolved, leaving only its outer covering, the skin. He did not speak, but she knew what he meant. "Is it this body that is dear to you? Is it my mind? Or is it my essence, the truth?"

As the word 'truth' reverberated through her being, she was jolted out of her seeming reverie. "Datta," she said, "forgive me for my anger. Leave you must. But, before you go, tell me what truth is? When I was newly married I was totally fulfilled as a wife. And then the ache to become a mother overcame all other emotions. When you were born, I lost myself in being a mother. Now that you are leaving, I feel a strange emptiness. I understand that these experiences of being daughter, wife and mother were roles that I played so that my vasanas could be fulfilled and exhausted. They were shadowy reflections of the unchanging. But I have not yet realized the unchanging, the truth. Son, what is the truth?"

Dattatreya's face was radiant with his smile of affection. He sat by his mother and said, "I will tell you how to realize the truth, mother. The mind is the cause of bondage as well as liberation. When it becomes attached to the gunas, the atman becomes involved with the emotions. The mind seeks sensory gratification and in that pursuit forgets its own source. The same mind, when it becomes the witness, sakshi, views these emotions from a distance. It then becomes free of the tumults of *kama*, desire, *krodha*, anger, *moha*, infatuation, and other qualities.

"Attachment is the nature of the mind. It is imperishable, while the mind is alive. Therefore, the wise use attachment as an instrument. Mother, let attachment remain. Change its object. Instead of attachment to *maya*, the world of transience and impermanence, turn it to the changeless, the eternal. It is not easy. The path to salvation is arduous, long and often lonely. But keep the company of devotees. Their talk about the divine will keep other thoughts away. It will gladden your heart. It will lead to shraddha, faith. Shraddha ripens into bhakti, devotion. Bhakti will automatically awaken vairagya and choicelessness. Pleasure and pain will not disturb you.

"There is no suffering for one who is a bhakta, and bhakti to the guru is the highest. All suffering is because the *chitta*, the individual consciousness, is divided in itself. It chooses pleasure and rejects pain. To a guru bhakta there is no choice. All is prasadam. Whosoever takes the guru and invokes in him the *vishwadevas*, gods of the universe, with guru bhakti, all the powers of the highest flow into him. Guru bhakti draws jnana like a magnet. The power of guru bhakti cannot be touched. It is *diksha* as well as *raksha*, initiation as well as protection. Wherever the supreme is invoked, He is there, and more so when invoked in guru.

"There are two forms of *gurutwam* or gurudom – vyakta and avyakta. The *vyakta* or the manifest can be perceived by the senses, but *avyakta*, the unmanifest, cannot be perceived by the senses. It can be felt; it can be experienced. Mother, this form of mind that you see is the vyakta aspect. You have seen it change from the time I was born. Who knows more than you the changes of my body and yet you cling to it as if it were all of me. Mother, I am the avyakta. I am the witness of all, the *sarva sakshim*. I am the eternal witness within this body and within all bodies. This body that you have loved so much is my temple. The wise man does not worship the temple. Mother, come into the sanctorum, the *garbha griha*, and meet me. I am in your heart. I am never away from you, I am within you.

"Mother, you are *atma priya*; your love for me is in reality a shadow or reflection of your love for the atman. You are *Shivapriya,* lover of the auspicious. I have no qualities. I am the stainless, *niranjana*. I am equipoise, *samatwam*. I am the perfected one, *siddha*. Because of the purity and the flaming tapasya of Atri, my energy took manifestation in him. Atri was the beginning of the *guru moola peetam*. I am born of tapasya and by tapasya alone can I be intuited and grasped.

"Therefore, Mother, practise tapasya. By my grace you will arrive at the truth. You will then see that the world of millions of forms is in reality the one Brahman, the eternal truth. Realizing the truth is not an arriving. There is really no journey. You are the truth. Tapasya will reveal this to you."

They had talked late into the night, mother and son, disciple and guru. He had initiated her into hamsa vidya or atma vidya. Anusuiya had felt strangely at peace. "O vishwa guru," she had said, "you are the guru of the universe. In my limitation, I treated you as my child alone. But your compassion has swept away my bewilderment. I see the path clearly."

In the morning, before the ashram was bustling with activity, Dattatreya had woken her up to seek her blessings before he left. She had stood alone and watched him walking away, his matted hair on the crown of his head, his body naked, smeared with ash, with space as his garment, carrying with him a *kamandalam*, or water pot, and a japa mala. She stood gazing until he was a tiny speck against the horizon, walking in the direction of the Sahyadri mountains.

Anusuiya spent the rest of her life in accordance with the instructions given by her son. She dressed herself in tree bark, her hair matted. Sitting in siddha yoni asana, with inward gaze concentrating in the region of *avimuktam*, the eyebrow centre or *bhrumadya*, she visualized Dattatreya as guru, day and night. Her mind became still. Avidya was burnt in the fire of tapasya. Very soon even his image faded. She had merged with the highest state of consciousness. From the vyakta she had merged with the avyakta.

"GURUDEV, WHAT IS THE TRUTH?"

Dattatreya proceeded to the Sahyadri mountains and sitting under the sacred amalaka tree was soon immersed in the highest consciousness. Many stories grew around him, some true, some symbolic. Vedic imagery, which is the mother of the Indian psyche, is very symbolic. Fashioned by the ancient rishis for the purposes of helping their disciples understand their inner selves with clarity, it subsequently pervaded the vedantic and puranic age. Even today it is a very significant part of our archetypal dimension or the subconscious and unconscious part of our minds. It always speaks of the struggles between the forces of light and darkness, ignorance and illumination. The spiritual stories provided entertainment for those of a gross consciousness, but always had a message for the discerning. If we look deep into many of our stories, they contain deep truths. The story of Jambhasura is one such.

Once a *rakshasha*, a demon, named Jambhasura, with the strength born of tapasya, attacked Devendra, king of the gods. Devendra, on the advice of his guru, Brihaspati, sought the help of Dattatreya. When he saw the swami, the latter was looking drunk and dancing with Gandharvas. Devendra waited, as he had been warned by his guru of Dattatreya's unorthodox behaviour, and when the swami looked towards him, he implored him to help destroy the demon. Datta agreed and asked the former to entice the rakshasha to Sahyadri.

When the demon arrived he saw the swami with a beautiful lady, Anagha Devi, on his lap. He was captivated by her beauty and, wanting to possess her, asked his attendants to carry her home in a palanquin. While all this was going on, the swami was watching with complete indifference. Along the way, the attendants pushed and jostled each other to get closer to the lovely woman. In their impatience and anger, they fought among themselves and killed each other.

Jambha, in Sanskrit, means 'eating', 'biting', 'a portion'. *Jambhaka* means one who kills, destroys, crushes. *Devendra* is the energy behind the sensory perception which is perfected; it is the illuminated mind. We can see Jambhaka as the power that presides over the illuminated sensory activities of life, whose source is the gross darkness of the subconscious, physical being. The struggle of man is to replace this action by the illumined working of a higher consciousness.

The battle is fought within each person and in the collective consciousness of all humanity. The gods are the higher powers that work through the purified mind. The *asuras* or demons are the destroyers of purity. They have no divine energy. They cannot bring the divine, creative vibration, the mantra, into the mind. The demons are *devadvishah*, haters of light. They are the powers of ignorance and darkness that hate the light of knowledge. They are our tamasic nature at its nadir.

When tamas is so concentrated, it becomes tapas; it becomes powerful. It drags us down to its cesspools of degradation. It kills motivation and all initiative towards growth. But man is not tamas alone. It is also rajas, activity and movement. The gunas within are never stable. Rajas starts the struggle, the battle. When the energy moves, it has glimpses of harmony, sattwa. Sattwa guna draws the higher or divine energy to help in the battle.

The sattwic mind invokes Indra. He is the speed and force of the illumined mind. He is powerful, but not powerful enough. Man has to go even beyond the purified mind, for the devas and asuras are equally matched. They are two sides of the same coin, a concentrated mind. But the purified mind has the grace of the supreme. It appeals to the vishwa guru, Dattatreya. The asuras in the story are drawn not to Dattatreya, the silent and eternal witness, but to his reflection, the beautiful Anagha Devi.

Anagha translates as 'sinless', 'innocent', 'free from dirt', 'without mishap'. Anagha Devi is the manifested divinity and is, therefore, alluring to the senses. She is maya shakti. When even tamas comes close to divinity, it is not the silent witness that it is attracted to, because the gross mind does not even see it. It is fascinated by the world of form, the reflection of the divine and, being the reflection, it is still divinity. Even this nearness to the reflection has its value. All is not lost. Tamas breaks itself up into a million pieces and is destroyed completely, leaving the illumined mind, an instrument of the divine consciousness.

The story is almost an acting out of Dattatreya's instructions to his mother, not to fight attachment but to change the object of attachment to the divine, *pujyeshu anuragaha bhakti*. Both Jambhasura and Devendra are powers within us, either of which we can increase by our own endeavour. But the truth is not a result of endeavour; it is a result of grace, *anugraha*. It pours into us not because of our endeavour or burning tapasya. It is the compassion of Dattatreya that flows into the unconditioned, illumined mind of the sadhaka.

How does the illumined mind open out? Due to the guidance of the deva guru, Brihaspati. Brihaspati is defined in the vedic hymns as the master of the word, the power of the mantras, the primordial vibrations. The power of the mantra awakens the illumined mind and makes it receptive to the divine nectar from above, the truth, through flaming tapasya. Tapasya, represented by Agni in the Vedas, is

188

Tripura Bhairavi in tantra. She is Chidagni, the flame of consciousness in every being. She is the terrible one who destroys all weakness, purifies and prepares the being for receiving the immortal nectar poured down by the grace of the supreme.

The vedic rishis said that an unbaked vessel would break if *soma*, nectar, is poured into it. In spiritual matters, self-effort alone is not enough. The grace of the divine is necessary. It is in this that the guru's role becomes so important. In the Vedas the guru is Brihaspati. In tantra it is Bhuvaneshwari who arranges the tapas and grace of Bhairavi and Sundari. Gurutwam again is a state of consciousness. It presents itself in different forms according to the quality of discipleship.

Dattatreya, the vishwaguru, is a state of consciousness flowing through the body of Dattatreya, the son of Anusuiya. Gurutwam cannot be caught in a shastra or a technique. According to the qualities of the disciples, Dattatreya gave to them and through them. He gave to the world various teachings and disciples.

Dattatreya was closely associated with the Shakta Agamas: Tantra, Yamala and Damara. He wrote a treatise on the worship of Tripura Sundari, the highest truth. He is closely associated with the shakti pithas which he visited frequently, including Kashi, Pandarpur, Kolhapur, Panchaleswar, Tuljapur, Ganagapur, Bilwadi, Hanguti, etc. It was Dattatreya who handed over Sri Vidya to Parashurama and through him to the world. This is why we find Dattatreya worship side by side with Sri Vidya worship. Besides this, Dattatreya has been associated with cults like Atitas, Bhairava, Akhada and Nath.

Dattatreya and Parashurama

Brighu Maharishi had a grandson, Jamadagni, who was known for his flaming tapasya. Jamadagni, the Bhargava, married Renuka, of great spiritual stature. They had five sons Vasuman, Vasu, Vasushena, Rumanvan and Rama.

189

Rama was a brahmin by birth but a kshatriya by nature. He was a great warrior, a partial avatar. In his own right he was the guru of Drona and Karna. He was dressed in deer skin. He had a bow and arrow and an immense axe on his shoulder. Because of this, he was called Parashurama, or Rama of the axe, in contrast to Kodanda Rama, or Rama of the bow.

On one occasion, Renuka Devi, his mother, happened to see the King of Matrikavaha, Chitrangada, and his wife sporting on the banks of the Ganga, and her one-pointed concentration was disturbed. Jamadagni was furious and asked each of his sons to kill their mother. While the older four were numb with shock, Parashurama, with one sweep of his axe swept her head to the ground. Pleased with Rama's obedience, the rishi brought his mother back to life. It is said that at that moment of severance, Renuka ceased to be the mother of Parashurama, and Chinnamasta, the divine energy of the supreme, entered into her.

In this story it is possible to see the head of Renuka as the ego, and with the exhaustion of her karmas, it is severed. The higher consciousness entered the body which had previously been prepared to receive it by flaming tapasya. In the tantras, Chinnamasta is the name given to the energy that is the outcome of the interaction between primordial sound and light, *nada prakasha*, the forerunner of all creation. The speed and force of this energy, referred to picturesquely as lightning and thunder, is of such an intensity that, not only does creation happen, but it is almost cut asunder from its original source, cosmic consciousness. Chinnamasta is the indomitable force, the striking power of the supreme, and is pictured symbolically as the goddess who severs her own head. She is the force in the sushumna nadi and is concentrated upon in the ajna chakra. She is called Shasti because she was the force behind Parashurama, the sixth avatar of Vishnu. She is Ekavira, the single force that is invincible. Ekavira was the presiding deity of the Sahyadri mountains, where Dattatreya was engaged in intense tapasya.

When Jamadagni was killed by kshatriyas who were of the clan of Kartaveerya, himself a disciple of Dattatreya, Parashurama carried the body of his father, on the advice of his mother, to the ashram of the swami and asked him to guide him in the modalities of performing the last rites. Dattatreya, intent on opening Parashurama's eyes, said, "I do not know dharma or adharma. I behave as I please. I follow no rules or regulations."

Parashurama, because of his intense shraddha, under-stood that the swami was drawing his attention to the transcended consciousness that is not conditioned but exists in its own luminosity. With one-pointed concentration, he in turn renounced all conditioning. Pleased with his understanding, Dattatreya instructed Parashurama in performing the last rites. When the fire on the pyre was lit, Renuka Devi entered it and, giving up her manifest form, became an unmanifest force. Parashurama then left the ashram to complete his mission of destroying the evil forces.

When his mission was over, Parashurama came back to his guru, Dattatreya, and expressed a wish to conduct a yajna or sacrifice. Dattatreya consented, and himself agreed to be the chief priest as well as the *yajamana*, the performer, in the celestial Renuka Yajna. Parashurama and the rishis gathered there heard Dattatreya mutter the words, "Renuka, Ekavira, Jaganmata," frequently to himself. All of them thought that the yajna was named after Renuka Devi, the mother of Parashurama. Realizing this, Parashurama enlightened them on the deep significance of the yajna.

"All yajnas," he said, "are sattwic, rajasic or tamasic. Munis perform sattwic yajna. Kings perform rajasic yajna, and lower beings of a gross nature perform tamasic yajna. Sattwic yajna is performed in a sattwic country, in a place hallowed by the spiritual energy of saints, in the sattwic time of uttarayana. Materials collected are earned by righteous means. Vedic mantras are chanted. The brahmin is *shrotriya*, the guide of the yajna, and there is sattwic faith. The rajasic yajna is performed with *abhiman*, conceit and ego. Many presents are given, elaborate decorations are made and animals are sacrificed. The tamasic yajna is done with arrogance, anger and jealousy. It is done with the sole need to annihilate enemies.

"The Renuka yajna is so named because we invoke the shakti that descended into the body of Renuka Devi. But the shakti itself was not conditioned by the body of Renuka. While the higher consciousness called Chinnamasta or Ekavira resided in the body of Renuka, it sanctified this soil of the Sahyadri mountains. The place around the amalaka tree where I sit for meditation is the Renuka Alayam. The pond here is Renuka Tirtha. Invoke in your minds the shakti of Renuka Devi or Ekavira, so that you may purify your being. Renuka is the shakti in the hearts of all yogins. Her energy is pronounced in the twilight times. She is Mahakali in the ida nadi, Mahalakshmi in the pingala nadi and Ekavira in the sushumna nadi."

Parashurama, Kashyapa and all the rishis assembled invoked the energy of Chinnamasta and completed the rites of the yajna under Dattatreya's guidance. Parashurama then stayed in Renukashram and did intense tapas under his guru's instructions. In the course of time, the rajas in him abated. He became purified and serene to a large extent. However, there was still a mild restlessness within him. He was not fulfilled. One day, while walking in the forest around the ashram, he came across an avadhoota, Samvartaka, who was perfectly at peace with himself and seemed to be bathed in bliss. On enquiring from him as to the source of his state of consciousness, Parashurama was directed back to Dattatreya, the guru of Samvartaka.

Parashurama implored Dattatreya to initiate him into higher teachings. The guru, seeing that the disciple was now ready, said, "I have told you about the three types of yajnas: sattwic, rajasic and tamasic. There is yet another variety which is manasic. In this yajna, the mind offers oblations. The mind is the yajamana, the performer of the sacrifices. The presiding deity is Brahmavidya, the sub-

192

stratum of everything. It is *nirguna*, without attributes. The fire is prana into which all oblations are poured mentally."

Dattatreya then initiated Parashurama into Sri Vidya and Tripura Rahasyam. On his instructions, the disciple left for Mahendra mountain to meditate on the Self, the truth. This *upasana*, worship, of Sri Vidya was passed on by Parashurama to Sage Haritayan in the Kardali forest, and the sage imparted it to the world at large.

The yogic guru

In the city of Mahishmatipura, there lived King Kritaveerya and his queen, Sheeladhara Devi. The royal couple had many children but none survived. The queen visited the ashram of Rishi Yajnavalkya and asked the Rishipatni Maitreyi to help her have a child that would not die young. On Maitreyi's advice, the couple performed Anantavrata. The King performed Suryopasana on the advice of Sage Brihaspati. They were soon blessed with a son, Kartaveerya Arjuna, who grew up to be learned and accomplished as a warrior. He was skilled and handsome, but he had one handicap, his hands were maimed.

In the course of time, when his father died, his subjects wished the young prince to ascend the throne. Kartaveerya was hesitant because of his hands. Ganga Muni, who was one of his ministers, advised him to go to the Sahyadri mountains and seek the help of Dattatreya, who was a yoginath. He told the prince that the swami would sometimes project such dismaying appearances that people of a gross consciousness would be frightened away. Only fearless, non-judgemental sadhakas could approach him.

Kartaveerya duly sought out Datta Prabhu and served him with great devotion, despite receiving abuse, beatings and curses, which eventually ended in his losing both hands totally. However, his shraddha, faith, did not waver. Eventually, when Dattatreya had beaten and flattened the prince's ego, he took him to his side and spoke to him with affection.

193

On the eighth day of the first fortnight of the lunar month, the day known as the sacred Anagha Ashtami, he was initiated into the worship of Dattatareya and Anagha Devi. Datta also gave him the *ashtasiddhis*, the eight yogic powers, which made him invulnerable. Every year Kartaveerya observed the Anagha vrat on that day. He was healed and, having made obeisance to his guru, he returned to his kingdom and ascended the throne. He ruled wisely and well and his glory spread to all of Aryavarta.

However, once touched by a guru, no sadhaka rests. The journey stops only when the goal is reached. Thus it was that Kartaveerya grew tired of his wealth, fame and sensual delights, and there arose in him a great urge to know the supreme truth. Once again he went to the Sahyadri mountains and sought his guru. For the first time, he found Datta Swami immersed in a deep silence. Kartaveerya silently invoked the supreme in his guru. "Lord," he said, "you are the unchanging truth. I have wasted my life running after the ephemeral, the changing, the perishable. I am afraid of the ocean of samsara. Only your grace can ferry me across."

Dattatreya opened his eyes and smiled at his disciple in compassion. Taking heart, Kartaveerya addressed him again, "Lord, my mind is confused. Some say dharma alone takes the soul across the ocean of ignorance. Vedantins say that nothing exists except the Brahmin when realization is attained. The Samkhya Yoga darshanas say that prakriti, the manifest, exists for those who do not know the Self. It also exists for those who know the Self, but they cease to have anything to do with it. What system should I follow, Lord?"

Dattatreya saw that Kartaveerya's confusion arose due to lack of sadhana and because of too much intellectual rumination. Often when intellectual discussions fail because they appeal to the head, stories succeed in conveying a message because they appeal to the heart. To explain the simplicity of yoga, Datta narrated to the king a series of seven stories, *Saptodharini*, which once had been described by Brihaspati. These stories described the lives of various sadhakas: Vishnudatta, Vedasharma, Vishalakshudu, etc. Systematically, he prepared Kartaveerya's mind so that the latter developed a proper understanding of dharma and spiritual truths in the context of life.

"The truth," Datta explained, "cannot be described by the shastras. It is very subtle; it can only be experienced. Different shastras explain methods for the purpose of guiding sadhakas of different personalities. Therefore, they seem to differ. The essence is the one truth." Looking deep into Kartaveerya's eyes, Datta asked, "Do you understand the essence from the stories I have told you?" Kartaveerya said, "Lord, my confusion is gone."

Dattatreya further explained to him the relationship between *purusha*, consciousness, and *prakriti*, energy. He explained the interplay of the gunas: sattwa, rajas and tamas. He explained the source of delusion as an experiencing of the transitory world as if it were eternal. He impressed upon Kartaveerya the significance of vairagya. "Every science," Dattatreya said, "has theory and practice. Theory is like a map. You do not reach your goal by just holding on to the map; you have to get up and walk. The walking is yoga." He described the various types of yoga: karma yoga, bhakti yoga, jnana yoga. He then initiated the king into the practices of yoga.

Kartaveerya retired to a cave nearby and there, sitting in padmasana, with head held erect, he practised yoga under the direct guidance of his guru. Slowly his chitta was purified and he attained a very high state of consciousness. Datta now addressed the king and said, "A yogi is like a lotus untouched by the water in which it stands. Now that you are a yogi go back to your kingdom and rule according to the dharma." And as Kartaveerya was leaving, he said, "Be alert."

The king went back and ruled the kingdom for many years in peace. Then slowly he grew complacent. He forgot that his guru had told him to be alert. Once alertness is lost, the inner witness slowly flags behind. Sattwa goes· to the background; rajas and tamas take over. When the time for destruction comes, the higher, discerning mind becomes careless, which encourages tendencies contrary to dharma and thereby hastens the end. Kartaveerya was finally killed by Parashurama, his gurubhai and a disciple of his guru, Dattatreya.

Twenty-four gurus of Dattatreya

Yayati was a rajarishi, an ancestor of the Yadu clan to which Sri Krishna belonged. His queen was Devayani, the daughter of Rishi Sudracharya. The only weakness the king had was desire, and that desire was his undoing. Cursed by the rishi on one occasion to become old before his time unless he could exchange his old age with someone else, Yayati sought his oldest son, Yadu, and begged him to help him out of the predicament.

Yadu, of all the king's sons, was interested in spiritual life. He pondered over the situation. Seeing his father obsessed with youth and desire, Yadu then realized the impermanence of both. He was filled with vairagya. However, he did not want to grow old before his time because he thought, "When old age comes gradually, one exhausts one's desires naturally and, along with them, the karma. Besides, youth is a time for spiritual sadhana, a preparation period for the development of higher consciousness."

Sad at having to disappoint his father, nevertheless Yadu knew that he had to refuse. His father subsequently disinherited him. To Yadu, who was quite disillusioned with the world already, this was a boon. He walked away from the palace and entered the forest, seeking a guru who would initiate him into the mysteries of higher reality.

During his wanderings he came across a naked ascetic smeared with ash, radiant with bliss. Yadu felt drawn to him. "O Rishi," he asked, "Who are you?" "I am an avadhoota," said Dattatreya, for that was who it was. "What is an avadhoota?" asked Yadu in innocent humility.

196

"*Aksharatvat,* imperishability; *varenyatyat,* devout, wishing for – these two words are the essence of an avadhoota," said Datta Prabhu. "One who has cut himself asunder from all things which are transient, one who has shaken off avidya and lives in the bliss of his own atman, is an avadhoota."

"Lord," said Yadu, "I too wish to shake off avidya. I too wish to know the *akshara,* the imperishable. Please teach me." Pleased by the shraddha of Yadu, Dattatreya explained to him the significance of discipleship in a sadhaka and proceeded to give him instances in life where he had learned from twenty-four situations. Life itself becomes the guru to one who is rich in discipleship.

Dattatreya explained to Yadu that discipleship is openness, receptivity, flexibility of mind, the capacity to renounce concept after concept, experience after experience to reach the inner truth. It is the capacity to see beyond forms into their essence. Discipleship is a state of consciousness that is fired with an intense longing to experience the truth as it is and not to be satisfied with its various reflections. It was with this spirit that Dattatreya responded to the entire world around him, the spirit of discipleship that learns from all of existence, with all the innocence of a child.

Earth

From the earth, Dattatreya learned the qualities of forgiveness, unselfishness and the strength to bear burdens. Very often progress on the spiritual path is hampered because a sadhaka is tied to the past. A trauma at some time in life decides one's response to similar situations all through one's lifetime. Nothing is seen with freshness and innocence. Everything is seen through the eyes of fear and suspicion as a result of past conditioning. This quality is not just projected onto the outside but also onto oneself. Inadequacy, lack of confidence and poor self-esteem are in reality lack of faith or trust in oneself. They are a measure of one's own self-rejection.

The earth, burdened by a thankless world, stands firm and proud. She is not demoralized. She does not punish or reject herself. *Darithri*, she who holds, is a reflection of dharma, the eternal one that holds all existence. With immense tenderness she holds the world in her lap, unmindful of assaults on her person. To Dattatreya she was symbolic of shraddha, a capacity to hold together herself and all associated with her, with great compassion, giving herself totally to the situation, and that which is asked of her, with an unflinching steadiness, like the physical body holding divinity within itself.

Air

The air to Dattatreya was a symbol of aliveness, prana carried in its garments. Pervading everywhere, yet uncontaminated, carrying fragrance but not being the fragrance, it reminded him of pure consciousness, present in all manifestation, yet not being affected by the movement, the changes within it. It brought to him the experience of detachment, the stillness in the movement.

Sky

The atman resides in the body, but it is not the body. The sky holds the world like a garment or canopy, but it is not the world. It seems limited, but in reality it is limitless. The sky was his third guru. The deeper mind is like the sky: vast, unseen, holding thoughts, feelings, like clouds, seeming limited but really limitless in its possibilities.

Water

His fourth guru was water. In its very ordinariness water is extraordinary. It supports all life. Some simple organisms can live without air, however, none can live without water. Over millions of years water has been responsible for shaping the earth's face. It nourishes the soil so that mighty forests can grow; it decides the climate; it has great stability; it cleanses, purifies, and refreshes. To Dattatreya it was symbolic of the compassion of a yogi which unobtrusively flows to the world, nourishing and refreshing, purifying and removing sin, promoting new growth in the form of higher awareness.

Fire

His fifth guru was fire, which destroys all that is gross. Like the inner fire of awareness that reduces everything to its essence, bhasma, ruthlessly purifying whatever is poured into it, the fire reminded him of freedom from the defects of avidya.

Moon

The moon seems to wax and wane, yet there is no intrinsic change in it. Likewise, the moods and changes in man are qualities of body and mind, not part of the atman.

Sun

From the sun that takes water from the ocean by evaporating it and returning it as life-giving rain water, Dattatreya realized that through the sense organs one can take in the essence of the objects of perception without getting obsessed with the external form of the object. Its light is reflected in gutters, rivers, streams, puddles and looks different according to the contents and qualities of the water, but in itself it is the same. So too, the atman in different bodies seems to take on the qualities of the body, but in reality it is the same one everywhere. The sun brought to his mind qualities of egolessness and omnipresence.

Pigeon

From a pigeon whose little fledglings cried piteously when caught in a hunter's net, thus luring the mother to her death, Dattatreya realized the dangers of samsara. Too much involvement with samsara results in the destruction of spirituality. It was the attachment to the family that was responsible for the destruction of the bird. Our samsara too, consisting of our prejudices, our desires, our passions, etc., destroy the spirituality within us. Higher yearning is smothered by preconceived notions, rigidity of mind and intellectual clutter.

Python
The ninth guru was a python. Seeing it eat only what came to it, not setting out in search of food, Dattatreya learned the value of surrender.

Ocean
The ocean receives all rivers, all the waters of the earth, some clean, some polluted. Yet it remains unaffected and retains its essential oceanness. Freedom from disturbances was the lesson that Dattatreya learned from the ocean.

Firefly
Seeing a firefly drawn to its destruction by its infatuation with the glittering flame, the yogi realized how desire can lead to destruction.

Bee
The twelfth guru was the bee. Flying from flower to flower, taking pollen only for its immediate need, leaving the flowers unbruised and unhurt, the idea of bhiksha was born to Dattatreya. Not storing for the future, taking what was given voluntarily and offering goodwill in return, was the concept of bhiksha.

Elephant
The thirteenth guru was an elephant that hurtled down to its trap by being drawn to the wooden image of a female elephant. Dattatreya learned that when one has a great passion for the highest truth, one should not be deluded by the distraction of sensual desire. Even a photograph or the thought of a man or woman can pull one down from one-pointedness in one's search.

Honey gatherer

The fourteenth guru was a honey gatherer. The bee spends its time making honey which the honey gatherer enjoys. Dattatreya realized that most often people spend their lifetimes gathering possessions in the faint hope that they will give them happiness and security. Not only do these possessions not give any inner security but the majority of people are so busy gathering possessions that they do not have time to enjoy them. They are enjoyed by other people. What a waste of time, energy and emotional investment felt Dattatreya. Precious time should be spent, not in acquiring, but in reaching the inner self.

Deer

On one occasion the yogi watched a deer. Nimble and swift of foot, it was on guard and alert. A hunter who failed to catch it realized that the animal was distracted by music. Knowing its vulnerability, he distracted it and caught it. Any vulnerability is a weakness on the spiritual path. One loses alertness. Ekagrata or one-pointedness is lost. In no time, the sadhaka who has raised himself with great effort is plunged into rajas and tamas. One should always be aware of one's vulnerable point and be alert on the path so that one does not go astray.

Fish

The fish is caught because the hook with the worm is a temptation. One should beware of the sense organs and desires associated with them, whether it is taste, smell, vision, hearing or touch. The yogi was alert to this obstacle while watching the fish.

Pingala

The seventeenth guru was a courtesan called Pingala. On one occasion Pingala waited for her lover in great anguish and restlessness. Long did she wait, but he did not come. At one point, she was utterly disgusted with herself and thought,

201

"It is because of my desire and expectation that I suffer." At the height of suffering, she turned her awareness within and a great transformation took place in her. "Had I but sought the divine beloved with the same ardour and passion, I would not be in this plight," she thought to herself.

Thus a great vairagya arose in her. Leaving her desire aside, cutting asunder all expectations in one flash with the sword of viveka, she took to the spiritual path. Dattatreya was inspired by Pingala's life, the lessons she learned from her suffering, the ease with which she dropped her ignorance, like dropping a garment, and the height to which her consciousness soared, free of desires, with the twin wings of viveka and vairagya.

Sparrow

Dattatreya watched a small sparrow flying with a piece of food in its beak and saw it encounter a big bird. Pursued by the big bird, the little sparrow dropped its food and escaped while the former swooped on the food. He realized the wisdom behind the instinctive actions of the bird that when the enemy is stronger one should not hang on to possessions. Not only is this true of material possessions but also of the mind. When a strong emotion so overpowers one, it is not wise to fight with the mind at that stage. It is best to let it pass while witnessing it in a detached fashion, so that the energy associated with it settles down.

The sadhaka needs to systematically build up his foundation and stabilize it before being ready to face the giant waves of the ocean of the mind. It is said, "Discretion is the better part of valour," and, "Fools rush in where angels fear to tread." One must be aware of limitations in the early stages of sadhana lest one gets burnt out for lack of patience.

Child

The nineteenth guru was a little child Dattatreya saw playing, relaxed and untouched by the past. A child lives from moment to moment. He does not remember the abuse, the pain of a moment ago, nor does he dream of the future. All of him is present at every moment. There is no tension in play, no competition, just sheer joy and fun and celebration, like the flowering of the trees. The spiritual path too can be light and full of celebration. The sadhaka should be alert against the dangers of succumbing to the heaviness of the ego. It is for this reason that *santosha*, contentment, is one of the qualities of a disciple.

Girl

The twentieth guru was a young girl who was alone at home when she received unexpected visitors. Brought up in a tradition where the guest, *atithi*, is regarded as divine, she seated them with respect and then went into the inner room to prepare food for them. While she was pounding rice, her glass bangles made a noise knocking against each other. One by one she broke them so that the noise would not disturb her guests, until she had just two on her arm. When they made a noise she broke one so that she had just one bangle on her hand.

In a flash Dattatreya understood that one should walk alone on the spiritual path. Even a close, silent companion can create mental noise that prevents the great silence from taking place.

Archer

The one-pointed concentration of an archer reminded Dattatreya of the importance of the sattwa guna and the unruffled ekagrata of a seeker. One is reminded of the *Mundaka Upanishad*: Om is the bow, atman is the arrow and the target is Brahman. He succeeds who possesses a one-pointed mind. The arrow becomes fixed in its mark; he is merged in Brahman. The archer was Dattatreya's twenty-first guru.

Snake

The twenty-second guru was the snake which taught him two things. One was to abandon crowds. The second was

203

that the seeker should not stay too long in one place because familiarity and the known blunt awareness and create attachment. This lesson also applies to the mind. Shun the crowds within oneself, the market place within oneself. Move closer to an uncluttered state of consciousness. Do not hold on to anything known, whether a thought or an emotion. This will help the sadhaka keep his awareness totally in every moment, unconditioned by yesterdays.

Spider
The twenty-third guru was a spider. The spider weaves its web with saliva from itself and when it is done with it, takes it back into itself. This reminded him of Brahman, the divinity that throws the cosmos out of itself and at the end gathers it back into itself.

Wasp
The twenty-fourth guru was an insect, the wasp, *bhramara keelaka*. The wasp is said to take an insect, keep it in its nest, and go on stinging it every now and then until the insect becomes one-pointed with fear. The insect is almost meditating on the wasp in its terror, until it takes on the characteristic of its tormentor and itself becomes a wasp. *Brahma vidya brahmeva bhavati* – "To know Brahman is to become Brahman". The situation is so reminiscent of sambrahma yoga that Kamsa practised. His fear of Krishna made his mind so one-pointed that he attained liberation.

Upon hearing all this, Yadu was enlightened and, paying homage to the guru, Dattatreya, he proceeded on his way.

Discipleship
The story of the twenty-four gurus of Dattatreya has tremendous significance for any disciple. Very often one analyzes and dissects the speech and actions of one's guru, moving from guru to guru, looking through the eyes of the ego. Because one has not become a disciple, one does not have the consciousness to look beyond words into the silence,

204

beyond form into the formless, beyond the periphery into the centre. One keeps missing, again and again.

For a seeker, discipleship is very important. Discipleship is not an emotional intention or an intellectual understanding of gurutwam. Discipleship is a state of consciousness. It is like the opening of a flower. The flower opens desirelessly. Its opening is not calculated; it does not choose the time. It opens spontaneously when the bud stage is over and, as it opens, sunlight streams into it naturally from all sides. The sun does not choose the flower. The sun's rays are present naturally. When the flower opens there is a meeting, a union.

Dattatreya's relationship with each of his gurus did not consist of didactic lectures, intellectual discussions or understanding. They were intuitive flashes of an innocent mind, a mind innocent of concepts and preconceived notions. His consciousness as a disciple was such that gurutwam, the guru quality, streamed into him from every side, from spiders, snakes, courtesans, children, etc. All of existence became his guru because he was a disciple. And because he was a disciple, he was also the Adi guru. The union of discipleship and gurutwam is not physical, mental or emotional. It is a state of consciousness, two great rivers merging to find that the water is one.

THE SIDDHA GURU

Dattatreya took on various guises while he roamed around. On one occasion, he came to Badrivana where a number of siddhas were gathered together, competing for supremacy. Some were naked, some clothed, some with shaved heads, some with matted locks, some silent, some garrulous, but all were egotistical. When they saw the young avadhoota, they asked him, "Who are you?" "I am *avyakta* unmanifest," Datta replied. "What yoga do you practise?" they asked. "That of inaction," said Datta. "What is your path?" they asked. "The nature of bliss," answered Datta. "What is your mudra?" they asked. "Niranjani," Datta replied.

The effulgence of the swami and his answers struck a deep chord in them and his grace melted away their ego. They realized that they were in the presence of Dattatreya. With humility, they understood the pettiness of their quarrels. "Lord," they said, "forgetting our goal, forgetting the essence we set out to know, we were trapped in the mire of our own egos. We converted even spirituality into a commodity and satsang into a market place. Forgive us and bless us that we may not stray again."

Dattatreya then revealed to them his real form and on the full moon day of the Magha constellation, he initiated them into mantra japa with the *beejakshara* (seed syllable of the mantra).

Gorakhnath, who was also a great siddha and one of the greatest exponents of hatha yoga, had many techniques similar to those practised and taught by Dattatreya. Many glorious yogis of the Nath cult, including Matsyendranath, regarded Dattatreya Avadhoota as the symbol of renunciation and yogic skill.

THE ADI GURU

On the full moon day of Ashada or Kataka, Dattatreya was sitting in meditation under the amalaka tree. King Alarka, who was in deep distress over the impermanence of life and transient pleasures, was looking for a guru. Alarka was the fourth son of King Rithudwaja and Queen Madalasa. His brothers had left the palace for tapasya, and the king, in his old age, appointed Alarka as his successor and retired to the forest for spiritual pursuits. Alarka was loved very deeply by his mother. It was she who gave him the name which meant 'mad dog'. Before she left, she wrote something on a locket, and giving it to Alarka said, "My son, in the time of unsurmountable obstacles, open this and read it."

Alarka ruled the kingdom wisely. His subjects were happy and prosperous. In the meantime, his elder brother, Subabu,

206

who was tired of tapasya, came back. On seeing Alarka and his flourishing kingdom, he was torn with envy. Along with the king of Kashi, he waged war on Alarka and defeated him. When Alarka saw his elder brother, who had chosen to give up the kingdom on his own because of spiritual aspiration, come back and conspire to wage a war for the sake of power, he was confused and disheartened. At that time he opened his mother's locket. In it she had written, "It is desire that causes suffering. Seek liberation."

How often it is said that in our most vulnerable moments, when the ego is totally shattered, we are most receptive to the higher truths. Having seen his brother's plight, he knew that it was not enough to practise spiritual techniques. A guru was necessary or one could fall even from a high state of consciousness. In fact, he realized that it could even be dangerous to practise spiritual techniques using one's own ego as a guide. Therefore, he left the kingdom and wandered in search of a guru.

His search took him to the Sahyadri mountains where he found Lord Dattatreya in deep meditation. When Datta opened his eyes, he prostrated before him and said, "Lord, I am in despair and desolate. Help me overcome suffering. Teach me the way. How do I find the truth, the changeless?" Dattatreya laughed and said, "Alarka, you suffer because you are involved with maya. Who are you? You are not the five elements: earth, water, fire, air and ether, which make up your body. You are not the mind that is in turmoil. You are the sakshi, the eternal witness. Meditate on this."

After a period of intense sadhana, King Alarka realized the truth of his guru's words: "I am neither happy nor sad. Honour and dishonour do not touch me. I am not this body or this mind. My avidya has melted by the grace of my guru." He then felt that he had to thank his brother, Subahu, for having been the instrument of his despair and subsequent search for the guru. So he went back to the kingdom and, touching his brother's feet, explained what had happened to him.

To his surprise Subabu said to him, "Brother, both of us were brought up by Mother to look beyond the ephemeral. When I came back from my spiritual pursuits, I saw that you were so contented with the kingdom that you had become complacent. I wanted to save you from being ensnared in the material world. Therefore, it was I that staged the whole war, defeated you and allowed you to be disillusioned so that you would seek a guru. It was the grace of Dattatreya that impelled Mother to open our minds to the higher truths, his grace that drove me back and his grace that drew you to him."

The king of Kashi, who was watching the two liberated brothers thus conversing, felt a deep sense of humility. He questioned his own values and left for Kashi, a transformed man. "Truly," he thought, "Dattatreya is the Adi guru."

BEYOND GURU, BEYOND SHISHYA

On one occasion, Dattatreya was sitting amidst many sages. Pingalinga, a maharishi's son, approached him and asked, "Lord, I do not understand you. You roam around naked, smeared with ash like a sannyasin. Yet there are times when you are seen with wine and women like a grihastha. You are detached and yet you seem attached. What are you? Which ashrama do you belong to? You do not participate in any ritual, yet your diksha is blindingly powerful. Sometimes you are in meditation like a sage, sometimes you roll on the ground like a beggar unconcerned with the dirt and filth. What are you in reality?"

Dattatreya smiled and replied, "The four ashramas of life: brahmacharya, grihastha, vanaprastha and sannyasa, are the four stages in an individual's evolution. Evolution is a product of time. I am beyond time. I am the timeless. I do not need to follow the ashramas. Rituals are for the purpose of concentrating the energies of body and mind, so as to transcend both. I am not the body or the mind. I am the transcendent. Sannyasa is the preparation for merging with

208

the truth. It is liberation from the mundane to aid in the search for the changeless eternal. I am the changeless. I am beyond all ashramas. Yet I am in all these. I am guru. I am shishya. I am also beyond both. I am the *sarva sakshin*, the eternal witness. My roles change according to your needs. No role can hold me. I am the all-pervading consciousness. I am the truth."

TRUTH REVEALED

To his mother, Anusuiya, Dattatreya had said, "I am the eternal witness within this body and within all bodies. This body is my temple. Come into the sanctum and meet me. I am within you." Through the ages, sages and seers have sought the truth and found it within themselves. They have invoked Dattatreya and the energy of the highest consciousness has flowed into them, transforming them. The flaming torch of spiritual heritage has been held aloft and passed on from generation to generation.

According to the needs of the people, organizations came and went and spiritual sadhakas after Shankara catered to the different needs of genuine seekers. But still the lineage or sampradaya of Dattatreya remains to this day, and its story is a marvellous one. The parampara contains a scintillating group of luminaries.

Sri Pada Sri Vallabha was an avadhoota par excellence. Sri Narasimha Saraswati and Swami Ramakrishna Paramahamsa brought out the paramahamsa aspect. Janardhana Swami, Eknath, etc. showed how a householder could live in spiritual consciousness. Eknath and the Varkaris, in reviving the bhakti aspect, reached out to the common people through the dimension of emotion, thus manifesting bhakti yoga in the Datta sampradaya.

Dasopanta brought the Nath cult and sampradaya under one umbrella. Narayana Maharaj added the dimension of karma and hatha yoga. There is a tendency for the common man to believe that the rich man is far from the divine, while the poor are closer. This is not a concept of Sanatan dharma. Many kings have been raja rishis. It is not the external circumstances of a person, such as economic status, education or other considerations, that make one fit for spiritual life. It is a matter of one's level of consciousness.

The external situation is a matter of *prarabdha* and cannot be altered. Manik Prabhu exemplified this in his life. He would wear rich clothes but beg for *madhukari*, alms in the form of cooked food. Neither wealth nor poverty mattered to him. He was beyond duality. Ramakrishna, Shirdi Sai Baba and Noori Baba showed in their lives and in their personal sadhana that the heights of mysticism could be reached whatever one's religion, and that all religions have the same essence. Swami Sivananda Saraswati, himself a medical doctor, brought in the scientific dimension and broke national barriers.

While previously one left the familiar and wandered out homeless in search of the truth, over the centuries each sage, responding to the needs of the collective consciousness, extended the spiritual dimension to different schools and systems. Crossing religion, caste, economic and national barriers, into every ashrama of life, into the world of science, they moved until now the whole of humanity stands on the threshold of a new and expansive consciousness. It is a flowering of the Dattatreya consciousness.

THE LINEAGE

Sri Sri Pada Sri Vallabha, 1300 AD

In Andhra Pradesh, by the river Godavari, was a small town called Pithapuram. Around 1300 AD there lived in this town a brahmin, who was a vedic scholar and tapasvin. His wife, Sumati, was a model of chastity like Anusuiya. Although the temple was very small, there were many temples of Kukkuteshwara (Shiva) and Kunti Madhava (Vishnu). There is a famous tank called the Pada Gaya tank where people from all over the country come to perform shraaddha, commemorative rites, to this day. Pithapuramis considered as holy as Nabhi Gaya and Shiro Gaya, and is mentioned in the *Skanda Purana*.

One day, after performing the shraaddha ceremony for his forefathers, Appala Raja, a brahmin, went out to find the shraaddha bhoktas, brahmins who would come to eat lunch according to the rules of the rite. It was noon. After having prepared the food, Sumati was alone and was waiting for her husband to return. Suddenly she heard a voice at the gate, *"Bhavati bhiksham dehi."* Hastening out, she saw a hermit of rare effulgence. Without a thought for the rules of shraaddha, where the brahmin bhoktas are supposed to eat first, she fed the hermit in the spirit of *atithi devo bhava* – 'the guest is God'. When he had eaten he asked her what she desired most. "A son like you," was the answer that came to her spontaneously from the heart. "So be it," he said and went away.

When Appala Raja returned, he found his wife on the doorstep, looking dazed, but with a smile of serenity. Tears flowed from her eyes as she recounted to her husband all the happenings of the morning. "The hermit reminded me of Datta Prabhu," she said, "and flouting all the rules of the shraaddha, I fed him with love overflowing from my heart." Appala Raja said, "You are truly blessed. If you had such devotion in your heart without any seeming reason, if your bhakti had invoked the guru, then surely the consciousness of the hermit at that moment must have been that of Datta Prabhu himself."

As the days passed, Sumati found that she was drawn more and more into deep meditation on Dattatreya. Her physical body glowed with a strange radiance. Digambara Datta, the image of the naked avadhoota, was in her heart. Mentally she saturated herself with remembrance of Datta's name. In the course of time, she was delivered of a baby boy. As the emblems of the *shankha* and *chakra*, the sacred conch and discus, were found on the child's feet, he was called Sri Pada. As he was beautiful, he was called Sri Vallabha.

Sri Pada Sri Vallabha was an amazing child. Whatever activity he was engaged in, he did with totality. He had an eidetic memory. One glance and he could remember a whole page. In his seventh year, he was invested with the sacred thread and in no time he was a vedic scholar. When he was twenty-six, his parents felt that the time had come for their son to marry and to live as a grihastha, a householder. The boy gently told his parents, "I am already married to vairagya. Pravritti marga, the worldly path, is not for me. Mine is nivritti marga, the path of renunciation. I am an ascetic. It is time for me to leave home."

Even as Dattatreya had bidden goodbye to his parents so long ago and set out alone, Sri Pada Sri Vallabha Yati took the dust of his mother's feet and, placing it on his head, left Pithapuram. He wandered through Kashi, Badrinath, Kedarnath, in the Himalayas. All along the way, he taught yogis and seekers the highest truths. He then visited all the *punyakshetrams*, the sacred places, in western India. From Gokarna he turned to Kuruvapur, for there an inner voice bade him go.

Kuruvapur was an island on the river Krishna. Many people of all religions, Hindus and Muslims alike, were drawn to the compassionate sage who poured himself and the divine love he had into the lives of those who came to him. Some were blessed with prosperity, some with *santan*, children, some with jnana. No one returned empty-handed. On the twelfth day of the dark half of Ashwin, Sri Pada Sri Vallabha went into samadhi, sitting on the waters of the river Ganga.

Sri Narasimha Saraswati Swami

In Karanjanagar, in the Varad District of Maharashtra, lived a brahmin, Madhava, of the Vajasaneyi lineage and his wife, Amba. It was in the home of this pious couple that Sri Narasimha Saraswati was born. Even as a child, the only word he spoke was Om. On the day of his *upanayanam* (sacred thread ceremony), however, he repeated vedic passages. People who attended the ceremony were astounded. He then asked his parents to bless him so that he could go away to increase the spiritual fire within. As they felt bereft at being separated from Narasimha, on their request he promised them that he would return in twenty years. Reassured, they blessed him and he left.

The boy went to Kashi and. there sat in tapasya. Many years later, Sri Krishna Saraswati, a sannyasin, initiated him into the sannyasa order. Narasimha was an exemplary sannyasin. He always kept moving, like Shankara, teaching people as he went about the inner meaning and the significance of the rituals that they performed mechanically. He revived the tradition of bhasma and rudraksha. His disciples, by his grace, went around the country holding discourses on religious matters, which in turn awoke a deep spiritual yearning among the common people.

The yati marga of Sri Pada Sri Vallabha was slowly transformed into the guru marga. As the consciousness of the common people needed guidance, the guru became a significant feature, and worship of Dattatreya, the vishwa-guru, flourished. Dattatreya's works were expounded to the ordinary folk. "There is no liberation without sadhana and no sadhana without guru," is an ancient saying. Sri Narasimha Swami Saraswati brought this thought to the forefront.

With his yogic powers, many were healed. Suffering was assuaged. Yet Sri Narasimha Saraswati kept repeating to his followers that release from suffering in itself was not the goal. All actions done were for *chitta shuddhi*, purification of consciousness. In those troubled times, many Muslim kings respected him. People moved together into a more open view of spirituality, leaving aside the rigid concepts that existed at that time.

Many people today believe that the Dattatreya consciousness flowed totally through these two sages, and that the parampara itself started with Janardhana Swami.

Janardhana Swami, 1504

Janardhana Swami was born in 1504 in Chaliagaon, Maharashtra. He was a Desastha brahmin of the Ashwalayana lineage. As a youth he led a wild immoral life. When he grew older, he was inspired by stories of Dattatreya and even when he was appointed minister to the Nawab at Daulatabad, he would go for work at noon after intense tapasya in the morning. Soon he had a vision of Dattatreya after which his life was transformed.

Janardhana Swami and many of his followers lived in grihastha ashrama, fulfilling both worldly, *prapanchika*, and spiritual, *paramarthika*, aspects. To Janardhana Swami, there was no situation where the consciousness of his guru was absent. He was beyond dualities such as material and spiritual. For him all action was spiritual. Grihastha ashrama was as spiritual as sannyasa ashrama. For was not the goal the same, liberation from avidya? This gave a new dimension to the understanding of the Dattatreya philosophy. One did not reject anything in life. All situations were God-given and accepted as such. Rejection of God-given life was rejection of God. If everything is pervaded by Datta consciousness, then everything is holy.

The yati and sannyasa concepts of earlier sages of the Datta parampara widened to embrace the grihastha ashrama also. It is consciousness that matters, not what and where it manifests.

Eknath, 1533–1599

By 1533 Hinduism as a spiritual culture had been degraded both by the intellectual egoism of the higher castes and the demoralizing forces of repeated invasions. Scholars quoted scriptures mechanically, but the essence of the scriptures was rarely lived. Their knowledge earned them wealth or power, but it did not touch their hearts.

At this time, Eknath was born in Paithan of a devout couple, Suryanarayanam and Rukmini, both of whom died in his childhood. He was brought up by his grandfather,

Chakrapani, and great-grandfather, Bhanudas, both devotees of Panduranga of Pandharpur.

At six years of age, when his thread ceremony was performed, the child, who was fired by an intense desire for the truth, heard a voice asking him to go to Daulatabad, "For there your guru awaits you." He walked for three days to reach his destination. Such was his faith. He was then directed to Janardhana Swami who, moved by the intense desire for liberation in the child, took him as his disciple.

Eknath was of an emotional temperament and bhakti became his path. "In my purified mind," he was to sing later, "I lit the lamp of dharma and offered the panchapranas to him as homage." His bhakti burned almost all trace of ego in him. Twice he had visions of Dattatreya, once as a hunter and once as a Pathan. Both times, he rejected the forms due to ignorance. In the course of time, he was fully purified. His preconceived notions of good, bad, holy and unholy were washed away. When the Adi guru appeared as a *chandala*, an untouchable, Eknath offered himself as an instrument and with the guidance of his guru, received the blessings of a higher consciousness.

He then practised tapasya on the hill Sulabhanjana and had a vision of Sri Krishna. On the advice of Guru Janardhana, Eknath married Girija Bai and lived an exemplary life as a grihastha. Inspired by his lifestyle, bhakti was awakened in the lives of the common people who had hitherto thought that spiritual life was only for those rare souls who renounced all and retired to the forest.

Eknath's bhakti united the Datta worshippers and the Varkaris. Being a poet, his bhakti burst into songs which thousands joined in. His devotional songs touched the hearts of the common folk and with tears streaming from their eyes, they would sing and dance, day and night, with cymbals and drums. Thus the collective consciousness was elevated. He edited the *Jnaneshwari* and wrote the *Bhavartha Ramayana* and *Rukmini Swayamvara*. He left his body in 1599. His grandson was Mukteshwara, who was born dumb but became a great poet by the grace of Eknath.

Dasopanta

Digambara Pant and his wife, Parvati Bai, were a very spiritual couple. To these two, in Narayanapetta of Andhra Pradesh, Dasopanta was born. He was a clever child and when he grew into a youth, was married. He lived at the same time as Eknath, Janardhana Swami, and Saraswati Gangadhara, who wrote the *Guru Charitra*.

Although he was happy in the worldly life, the influence of the bhakti movement invoked in him a passionate longing for the truth. At sixteen, he left home for the Sahyadri mountains and there sat in intense tapasya for fifteen years. In deep meditation one day he had a vision of Dattatreya who directed him to the river Godavari. "Buried under the sands," the vision said, "are a pair of padukas. Go there and rescue them."

Dasopanta, refreshed, took himself to the Godavari and found the padukas as indicated in his dream. Taking them home, he placed them on an altar and worshipped them. With the grace of Dattatreya, his ishta devata, he was initiated into the Nath parampara. Dasopanta wrote over fifty books including *Hitarnava* written on cloth, *Datta Mahatmaya* and a commentary on the *Avadhoota Gita*.

Niranjana Raghunatha, 1782–1855

Sridhara Panta, a Desastha brahmin, and his wife, Lakshmi, were blessed with a baby whom they named Avadhoota. It was a prophetic name for, as the child grew older, he listened to Thakurdasa, a kirtanist, about bhakti and devotion. Avadhoota's heart was afire with *mumukshutwam*, an intense desire for liberation, and he set out to search for a guru. Discarding his clothes, he sat in meditation at a place called Dehu. So engrossed was he in his ishta devata that his own behaviour changed. When he went for a bath in the morning, he found a *kaupeen* (loin cloth) and *katisutra* (waist thread).

Taking this as prasadam, he vowed to give up his body within a year and seven days if he did not have a vision of Dattatreya.

During his travels, he was in turn respected and jeered at. People thought him mad because he was unorthodox in his manner and behaviour and people found it impossible to understand him. His whole mind was so concentrated on the *saguna* form of the Lord (the form with attributes) that he would act like Dattatreya. Meeting Chandradasa, whose exposition of the *Avadhoota Gita* further inspired him and strengthened his resolve, his sankalpa became so strong that he had a vision of Datta in a dream and in meditation. He then reached Nasik and was initiated by Raghunatha, who gave him the name Niranjan.

On one occasion in meditation his mind threw up images of eight harlots rubbing their breasts against him. His guru explained that this was symbolic of the *ashtasiddhis*, eight psychic powers that are by-products of yoga, but so beguiling that sadhakas become ensnared in their grip. The image also contained Guru Raghunatha on a lotus and a brahmin who was Dattatreya. Niranjan was first and foremost a guru bhakta. He then went towards Girnar and again had a vision of Dattatreya, who gave him a *vastra* (cloth) and *padukas* (wooden sandals). After this last initiation, Niranjan lost body consciousness. He was so saturated with Dattatreya that he would behave like a madman.

During his lifetime he wrote commentaries on *Jnanesh-wari*, *Amritanubhava*, the *Shankara Bhashya*, the *Gita* and the *Mandukya* and *Keno Upanishads*. He sang many abhangas, devotional songs. He lived as a grihastha for year, and was married to Bhagavati Bai. Finally, at the end of his life he took sannyasa and attained jala samadhi.

Narayan Maharaj, 1807–1867

It was Tatya Purani's duty to recite the Puranas at the court of the Maharaja of Jalavana, near Jhansi. The constant repetition of the Lord's name purified his chitta and when he had a child named Narayan, the boy was born with strong spiritual tendencies and a yearning for God.

A day after his marriage he ran away to Brindavan, Mathura, stayed with Govardhan Baba and perfected the practices of hatha yoga. On the advice of his guru, he returned home and after his wife's death a year later, he went to Girnar and did tapasya for a vision of Dattatreya. When he had almost given up hope, Dattatreya appeared in the form of a fakir. The fakir took him to Niranjan Yogi for further guidance.

Narayan Maharaj was a mystic of a high order and many miracles were attributed to him, but he travelled all over the country, emphasizing the role of karma yoga. He won the hearts of the common people to whom he spoke about spiritualizing their daily routine. Irrespective of caste, creed or sect, he initiated all who came to him. His disciples were Sakharama Baba of Kalyan and Narayan Baba of Ratnagiri. His padukas, which he had given to Balaba, one of his disciples, are still preserved in Benares. He wrote poetic works like *Sapta Sagar* and *Karuna Sagar*.

Dattanatha

Dattanatha was an avadhoota. His parents, who had been childless for many years, promised that if they had a child, they would give him to Ananthanatha, a saint. At the age of seven, after his upanayanam, Datta left for the ashram of his guru. He learned astrology, yoga and many other sciences for a few years. Then, on the guidance of his guru, he went home and was married.

Being of a commanding and charismatic personality, Mahadji Shinde, a great warrior of the Maratha clan, built a math for him at Ujjain where he stayed for many years, often leaving to go wandering and imparting knowledge. He died at the ripe old age of one hundred and twenty at Ujjain where his samadhi still exists. His better known disciples were Shivadatta and Atmaram Shastri.

218

Manika Prabhu, 1817–1865

Manohar Nayaka Harakude and his wife, Baya Devi, did parayana of *Guru Charitra* for sixteen years, observing all the rules associated with this worship. In all their meditations they would visualize Datta as a child. Their deep yearning for a child of their own fructified and Manika Prabhu was born. The child was playful and mischievous, ensnaring the hearts of all around him. The village of Ladavanti became a veritable Gokul. The simple folk felt that there was something special about this child and often came to him with their adult problems. When these problems were sorted out spontaneously, their faith in Manika Prabhu grew.

He knew many languages such as Persian, Urdhu, Marathi, Kannada and Sanskrit, all of which he learned on his own. As he grew older, his behaviour became unorthodox. He would place his slippers on the head of the idol in the temple. Initially people were worried, but their faith in the goodness of Manika Prabhu was a reassuring factor. Such is the spiritual soil of India that it is the consciousness that is always respected. External behaviour is not judged in exclusion to the inner person. A spiritually awakened person does not need temples, idols, rituals or religion. He is the living temple, enshrining the truth. Whatever he does is the doing of a higher consciousness working through him. He is simply an instrument.

On one occasion when a brahmin family accosted by dacoits in a temple called out to Manika Prabhu, the dacoits were confronted with a vision of the yogi richly attired in magnificent jewels, and they beat a hasty retreat. Manika Prabhu's appearance was strange. Unlike most sages who were attired either in nothing or in simple clothing, he was always dressed in rich clothes, begging for madhukari. Spirituality holds within itself all apparent contradictions. In truth there are no contradictions. The external appearance or habits of a sage are the result of prarabdha karma of his body or mind. His consciousness is choiceless and beyond dualities.

219

Manika Prabhu was totally detached. His spiritual splendour influenced Hindus, Muslims and Sikhs. Guru Nanak, Basaveshwara, the founder of the Lingayat Sect and a Shiva bhakta, saw him as a gem of rare spiritual glory. Manika Prabhu helped many siddhas like Hamsa Raja Swami and Suraja Sadhananda gain self-realization. He wrote a book, *Kalpataru*, and attained samadhi at the age of forty-eight on Dattatreya Jayanti at Manik Nagar.

Swami of Akkalkot

Swami Samartha's life is a strange one. It is strange to limited minds that would like to categorize, label or pigeonhole the physical dimension of a consciousness that is untrammelled and free. Nothing is known of the swami's antecedents. When asked about them, he gave different answers. He said to one that his name was Narasimha Bana and that he was born four hundred and fifty years ago. To another, he said that he was from Kardalivana in the Himalayas and was a wandering ascetic. To yet another, he was a *mehar*, an outcaste. To a fourth, he said that he was a brahmin of the Yajurveda branch. Perhaps he wanted to shift the preoccupation of his devotees from the physical body to the consciousness behind it. Perhaps it was factually true. After all, each man contains within himself, the brahmin, the kshatriya, the vaishya and the shudra, according to the guna and the karma of the moment. Space and time are not restricted to a consciousness that encompasses the timeless. Such sages do not speak untruths. It is we of limited dimension who do not know the truth or its all-encompassing dimensions.

The swami was in turn like a madman and a child. His consciousness was not confined to his body and so he did not have body consciousness. His spiritual energy spilt out and touched anyone who came into his presence. Therefore, people flocked to him to be healed, to be rid of their suffering or to quench their thirst for knowledge. Most came because they could not help it, but were drawn there. Many who lived in the places associated with Dattatreya, like Girnar, Ganagapur, etc., had dreams in which Dattatreya asked them to go to Akkalkot. The swami wrote nothing and taught nothing. Sitting in Akkalkot, just by his presence hundreds were transformed. He passed away on April 30th, 1878.

Vasudeva Saraswati (Tembe Maharaj), 1854–1914

Vasudeva was born at Managaon, a small village near Savantawadi. Having lost his father at an early age, he was brought up by his grandfather. When he grew up, he was married to Annapurna of Narasobawadi. He was initiated in a dream by Dattatreya into mantra japa, and soon attained mantra siddhi.

When a son of his died, he gave the highest knowledge to his grieving wife. To his credit stands the Dattatreya temple at Managaon. When his wife died, he took sannyasa and wandered through the length and breath of the country, inspiring and guiding. He worshipped an idol of Dattatreya and wrote in detail on Datta worship. He wrote in Sanskrit and Marathi. He wrote the *Dattatreya Mahatmaya* and translated the *Guru Charitra* and *Guru Samhita* from Marathi to Sanskrit. He also wrote the *Datta Puranam*. In 1914 he went into samadhi at Garudeshwar on the Narmada.

Sri Ramakrishna Paramahamsa

Gadhadhar was born in Bengal in 1836. Married to Sarada Devi, he lived like a sannyasin in grihastha ashrama. Yearning for the Divine Mother from his childhood, he synthesized all religions in his various sadhanas, including the Christian and Muslim disciplines. He was initiated into Adwaita by Totapuri, a naked and wandering ascetic, and practised tantra under the guidance of Bhairavi Brahmani.

Though unlettered, he could expound the subtlest aspects of Vedanta because of his personal experience. At times he was naive like a child. At others, he would seem drunk with love of the divine mother, going into an altered state of consciousness at the very mention of her name. He

221

was truly a paramahamsa in every sense, taking the essence from any situation. He was a beautiful blend of a parabhakta and a jnani with tremendous viveka and vairagya.

His simplicity and spiritual power brought devotees from all over the country. But it was left to Swami Vivekananda, his chief disciple, to storm the world with his guru's message and inspire hundreds of young men and women, both in India and abroad, to practise karma yoga and raise the consciousness of society. The Ramakrishna Mission is the legacy of Swami Vivekananda to the world in memory of his master.

Shirdi Sai Baba

No words can describe Sai Baba of Shirdi. His parentage is shrouded in mystery. Some say his parents were brahmins and some say they were Muslims. When asked, he said, "The world is my home. Brahman is my father and Maya is my mother." People of all faiths were drawn to him, Hindu and Muslim. Sai had the qualities of a Sufi. He was a model sannyasin and avadhoota. He was like a Buddhist bhikku and his compassion was Christ-like. He held within himself all faiths. He wrote nothing. His compassion brought about many, many miracles.

He was called Sai, the one who cares. All who came to him, the criminal, the diseased, the grieving, were transformed. Everyone was his child. His actions were incomprehensible. He moved in mysterious ways. If Dattatreya were to walk the earth, truly this would be he. He entered mahasamadhi in 1918, on a day when Buddha Jayanti, Dassara and Moharram coincided. A mandir and masjid grew up at Shirdi. Thousands of Hindus and Muslims flock to his samadhi today in harmony. Sai belonged to all. His message was that love cuts across all barriers, regardless of religion and sect.

Noori Baba, 1869–1923

Born at Ahmedabad in 1869, his antecedents were Taber Baba and Rofan Baba. As a child, he met Fakir Peer Ibrahim Oolai of Kanpur and was transformed by the effulgent glow of the saint. But it was Fakir Abdul Hussain Noori of Merhera who initiated him into the Noori sect. Noori Baba drew to himself both Hindus and Muslims, being able to explain the essence of both religions with equal ease. His mission was an effort at synthesizing various religions. It is interesting to note that when a photograph taken of Noori Baba was developed, it showed three faces like pictures of Dattatreya. He passed away in 1923. His *dargah* (burial place) is a pilgrim centre for both Hindus and Muslims.

Sri Ramana Maharshi, 1879–1950

Ramana Maharshi was a rare example of jnani and bhakta. Hailing from Tamil Nadu, he left home at the age of sixteen after an experience with the process of dying which awoke in him the mystical dimension. He was drawn to Arunachala, a hill behind the temple in Tiruvannamalai. He practised intense tapasya, being lost to the world and body consciousness for days and months together. Most of his life was spent in mouna. He felt words were a waste of time and energy. Instead, when asked any questions on spiritual matters, he would always refer the questioner to look within. "Find out who you are and everything will be known," he would say. This was his only *upadesha* (spiritual advice). He did not have a formal guru. The hill, Arunachala, was his guru, his ishta devata. He did not call himself a guru. He sat on Arunachala and the world came to him. Such was his spiritual splendour.

THREE MORE RENUNCIATES

Gorakhnath

The Nath yogis were Shaivites and they originated in northern India in the eleventh century. Evidence seems to point to Gorakhnath's life during the eleventh century, for example, in Jnaneshwari's introduction to the commentary on the *Gita* written in 1290.

Matsyendranath, his guru, was in Nepal teaching Shaivism when Gorakhnath went to him to be initiated. The local stories of Nepal talk about Avalokiteshwara who went as a Shaivite to Nepal in the form of Matsyendranath, and is still the guardian deity of Nepal.

Gorakhnath is said to be the first writer in Hindi. He had Hindu and Muslim devotees. Jalandharnath, king of Jalandhar, and Bhartrihari, king of Ujjain, were his disciples. Both of these kings were famous in their own right.

The Gorakhnathis wear earrings like Shiva and call themselves Shivagotra. They wear a sacred woollen thread with a ring and a whistle. The ring is called darshana and those wearing it are called Darshanis.

The Nath yogis worshipped Shiva and Shakti as two aspects of the highest truth which was neither dual nor non-dual. Shiva is pure consciousness in the body and Shakti is nada. As part of his training to be detached, Gorakhnath repeatedly said, "A tree by the river bank and a man by the side of a woman cannot expect to last long."

Some of his works are *Yoga Martanda*, *Viveka Martanda* and *Yoga Siddhanta Padhati*. Gorakhnath's mystical writings in the form of a discussion between him and his guru can be found in *Gorakh Bodh*, a work that so inspired Guru Nanak a few centuries later that he adopted its style.

Gorakhnath was very popular among the masses because he spoke to them in their language, Hindi. He travelled all over India, building shrines, establishing monasteries and reviving Shaivism. His disciples can be found to this day from Nepal in the north, through Punjab, Sind, Assam, Bengal, Uttar Pradesh and Maharashtra, down to Tanjore in the south.

Sadashiva Brahmendra Saraswati

During the years 1684–1712, Shahji, the Maratha king of Tanjore, gave away the village of Shaprarapuram to forty-six scholars. Among these scholars was Moksham Somasundara Avadhari. He was duly ordained into the Avadhoota Order of sannyasa by Paramasivendra Saraswati as Sadashivendra Saraswati. His evolution on the spiritual path was rapid. His knowledge of the shastras was excellent. On being rebuked by his guru for entering into intellectual debates with visitors to the ashram, the yogi gave up speech altogether and became a muni.

He soon reached the stage of total indifference to the body, clad in space, wandering oblivious to everything around him, frequently going into samadhi for days at a stretch. However, he left behind a number of works on the Upanishads and Brahma Sutras, Atmanusandhana. In the *Atmavidya Vilas* he describes himself as follows:

> *Avadhoota karmajalah*
> *Jadabadhirandhopainah kopi,*
> *Atmaramo yati rad*
> *Atouikohes vatannaste*

"The quarters are his garments; desirelessness his ornaments; the palms his vessels; his abode is the foot of trees. As he lies on the soft sand dunes of river beds, vayu fans him and the full moon holds the lamp."

His sadhana was nada vidya and he has many musical compositions to his credit. His writings and compositions were brimming with Adwaita bhavana. He took samadhi on Jyeshta Suddha Dasami, in the last part of June.

Kararkkal Ammaivar

Punithavati was born in Kararkkal, Tamil Nadu, during the Chola period. The daughter of Danadatta, a rich merchant, she was married to Paramadatta, a merchant. Realizing that his wife was no ordinary woman, but a person of tremendous spiritual stature, he renounced family life and prostrated before her as one would before a saint.

Knowing that her worldly life was over, Punithavati became Kararkkal Ammaiyar, and was lost to body consciousness. Directed by a vision of Shiva to Tiruvalangadu, she reached the town where day after day she witnessed the cosmic dance of Shiva amidst burning corpses, hovering vultures, howling jackals and skulls.

She lived like an avadhoota, constantly in a dimension of consciousness that embraced the terrible and the beautiful as one. In many visions of Shiva she saw the *trimurtis*, Brahma, Vishnu and Shiva together. She called herself 'the disembodied one'. The *shmashan* (burial ground) was her temple. In many of her poems, she describes the terrors and horrors of the place where, untouched, she watches her Lord dance in beauty with his uplifted hand carrying the eternal fire, *kalagni*. She had no disciples.

TIRTHA KSHETRAS

As Dattatreya was an avadhoota who wandered all over the country, certain places came to be venerated because he had used them for specific activities. The Sahyadri mountains are revered as his dwelling place. Mahurghad is worshipped as his birthplace and the place where he slept. This town is also sacred to Atri and Anusuiya. It has one of the three famous shaktipithas of Maharashtra, the other two being Kolhapur and Tuljapur. It is here that Dattatreya is said to have imparted spiritual knowledge to Parashurama after the cremation of Renuka Devi. Here Renuka Devi is worshipped as Elamma.

Girnar and Ganagapur are both famous as Dattatreya's place of meditation. Ganagapur is situated near the confluence of the rivers Bhima and Amarg. There is a huge hill of bhasma that devotees take as prasadam when they visit the kshetra. This hill has never dwindled in size. Girnar is an ancient place where Datta's padukas are worshiped. Many sadhus have had the *sakshatkara* vision (direct experience) of Dattatreya here. It is a pilgrimage centre for Jains, Vaishnavites, Devi bhaktas, Muslims and Buddhists.

Haridwar Ganga is worshipped as the place where Dattatreya had his morning bath. Kurukshetra is where he did his *achamanam* (sipping water from the palm of the hand). Dattapapeshwara is where he smeared ashes on his body. Karnataka is said to be the place where he performed his morning sandhya. Kolhapur is where he went for bhiksha. Pandarpur is where he applied tilak. Panchaleswar is where he ate food. Tunga is the place where he drank water. Garnedshwar, on the banks of the Narmada, was made popular by Swami Vasudevananda Saraswati because of his worship of Dattatreya.

Suchindram, at the southern tip of the country, is sacred to Atri and Anusuiya as they were said to have had realization of the energies of Shiva, Vishnu and Brahma and the promise of the birth of Lord Dattatreya there. Ujjain is where Dattatreya Akhara is located. Narasoba Hi Wadi, Ganagapur and Kurwapur are Dattatreya pilgrimage centres because of the penance of Sri Pada Sri Vallabha and Sri Narasimha Saraswati. Akkalkot was sanctified by the Swami of Akkalkot, who is considered as having realized the shakti of Dattatreya within himself.

MURTIS OF DATTATREYA

There are three types of murtis:
1. Brahma, Vishnu and Shiva standing side by side as Dattatreya
2. Vishnu sitting in padmasana as Dattatreya
3. Dattatreya with three heads, four arms, six arms or eight arms.

The oldest murti is in the Peshawar Museum. It was found at a site called Balahisar near the rivers Swat and Kabul in Peshawar. Other murtis are found in temples of Orissa, Saurashtra, Mahabalipuram, at Kailasa of the Ellora Caves, at Matikoral in Gujarat, in the Elephanta caves and on top of Neel Parbat in Trayambakeshwar.

DATTA UPASANA

The formal sadhana of Sri Dattatreya was laid down by Sri Narasimha Saraswati. One should begin the sadhana on a Thursday at an auspicious time. Place a photograph of Sri

Dattatreya or one's guru before one, light a lamp, burn incense and offer flowers. Invoke the energies of Brahma, Vishnu and Shiva through the mantra: *Guru Brahma Guru Vishnu Guru Devo Maheshwaraha Guru Sakshat Para Brahma Tasmai Sri Guruve Namaha.* Offer *naivedya,* prasad, of sweets and make a sankalpa.

On the first day read seven chapters of *Guru Charitra.* On the second and third days read four chapters each. After this read two chapters every day. When the reading is over, feed three pious brahmins or one sadhu or any poor man, imagining him to be Sri Guru Dattatreya.

As the sadhana evolves, the sadhaka's awareness also grows until he or she is saturated with Datta consciousness. Other details of the sadhana are to be sought at the feet of one's guru. It has always been an oral tradition passed on from guru to qualified disciple and is never found in books.

RULES OF SANNYASA

Swami Narasimha Saraswati also laid down the rules of formal sannyasa. They consist of the following acts:

- *Prayaschitta*: Atonement for all one's acts of unawareness during all births. In essence it is an act of looking back on one's mechanical way of functioning and finding that it has led nowhere. Make a sankalpa to act in awareness of a higher consciousness with shraddha, faith.
- *Ashtashraaddha*: Funeral rites done for all worldly relations including one's previous self. One cuts off totally and irrevocably with one's past.
- *Virajahoma*: Offering oblations to the fire which is symbolic of crossing the river of death.
- *Gayatripravesa*: Entering into the spirit of the mantra or allowing the vibrations of the mantra to saturate the body and mind.
- *Yeshanatrayatyaaga*: *Putreshana,* renouncing one's relationship with progeny (one's future), *viteshana,* renouncing

material possessions (security), and *lokeshana*, renouncing attachment to place (one's past).

- *Bhuradi sannyasa*: The sadhaka should be choiceless. He is prepared to renounce or become inwardly detached from the pleasures of the external world or sensory experience and from the non-sensual experiences of the mind and deeper psychic realms, the siddhis, etc. With the mantra: *Om bhur bhuvah swaha sannyastam maya*, the seeker indicates his willingness to renounce all attachments towards all outer and inner happenings, in other words to try to be choiceless, in all the dimensions of his consciousness.

- *Shika sutra sannyasa*: At the time of formal initiation, sannyasins shave off the tuft of hair and remove their sacred thread, both symbols of caste. The act symbolizes the readiness of the sadhaka to go beyond all barriers towards that consciousness that is unlimited and unconditional.

- *Guru upapati*: The sadhaka then goes to a guru who imparts to him the four mahavakyas: *Prajnanam Brahma* – highest knowledge is Brahman; *Tat Twam Asi* – Thou art That; *Aham Brahmasmi* – I am Brahman; *Ayam Atma Brahma* – this Atman is the Supreme. In the *Viveka Chudamani*, Shankaracharya says: *"Vedantartha vicharana jayate jnanamuthamam"* – Jnana arises from sincere contemplation upon the meaning of the Upanishad mantras. The mahavakyas are meant to inspire the sadhaka to find his own true nature.

- *Yoga patta*: The aspirant is given the title of a monk.

- *Paryankasaucha*: Only one's garment is used for sleeping; the bed is kept pure.

- *Swadharma vichara*: Constant contemplation on the spirit of sannyasa, the goal for which one is initiated, the contemplation of one's inner nature, or the true self.

Formal initiation and rituals are for the purpose of purification of the sadhaka, to heighten his receptivity to the higher teachings and to serve as a guideline for his pilgrimage on the spiritual path. After this, the sadhaka is on an inner journey which is uncharted and beyond all rituals. All initiations after this are subtle, internal break-throughs.

•

Shankaracharya

27

Shankaracharya

Who am I? And who are you?
Where is the place from which I came?
Who is my mother? Who is my father?
Pondering thus, perceive all things
As fancies only, without substance.
Give up the world as an idle dream.
Worship Govinda, worship Govinda.

Adi Shankaracharya
(Bhaja Govindam)

RENUNCIATION

In the early hours of the morning, as birds were leaving their nests in search of food, and the rising sun coloured the eastern sky with brilliant colours, a lone figure of a lady stood under a coconut tree with tears in her eyes, totally oblivious to the soft breeze murmuring through the leaves. She was gazing at the figure of a boy no more than eight years old, with shaved head and dressed in ochre robes. Holding a staff and a kamandalu in his hands, he was walking away with determined steps towards an unknown destiny. She watched him until he was swallowed up in the distance by the tall mango, coconut, betel nut and other tropical trees surrounding the tiny village of Kaladi in Kerala.

231

For a long time she stood there, hoping against hope that the child would return, although in her heart she knew it was not to be. She wiped the tears, stifled a cry and murmured softly, "Shankara, may Lord Ashutosha protect and guide you." Later, she sat in front of her hut thinking about her son, Shankara, who had left home and village that morning. Where he had gone she did not know. In search of guru and truth, so he had said. She felt drowsy and in that state she remembered events leading to his birth. What a joyous time that was, unforgettable.

Shankara's father was named Shivaguru, and he was the only son of Vidyadhara. Although Shivaguru had not wanted to involve himself in householder life, at the request of his father he had returned from his guru's ashram and married. After the death of Vidyadhara, apart from fulfilling the responsibilities and obligations towards his small family, Shivaguru dedicated himself to the study and teaching of the shastras. When Shivaguru and his wife, Vishishta Devi, were reaching middle age, they both yearned for a son. After discussing the matter, they had gone to the Vrisha mountain near the village. There, in the temple, they had worshipped Lord Chandra Maulishwar Shiva with all their devotion. How hard those days had been! They survived on berries, roots and the fruits of trees, and worshipped, prayed and fasted. Their bodies were greatly affected by such a rigorous discipline.

One night, before the end of their austerity, Shivaguru had a dream. In this dream, Lord Shiva appeared before him and said in a voice full of compassion, "My son, I am pleased with your devotion. Tell me your wish and I shall fulfil it." In the dream Shivaguru had fallen at the feet of his Lord and had said, "Bless me with a long-living, omniscient son." Smilingly the Lord had replied, "If you want an omniscient son, then he shall have a short life span. If you want a long-lived son, then he shall not be omniscient. Tell me whether you wish for an omniscient or a long-lived son." Shivaguru prayed that his son would be omniscient. The

Lord said, "Your wish shall be fulfilled. You shall have an omniscient son. I myself will come to your family as your son." So saying, the Lord disappeared.

Shivaguru woke up from his reverie, and told Vishishta Devi about the dream. How happy they were that the Lord's grace was with them. Soon they completed their worship and returned to the village. Vishishta Devi remembered well the day of Shankara's birth in the year 788 AD on the twelfth day of Vaishakh Shukla Panchami. People had said that the sun had stopped moving in the sky to gaze at the face of the newborn babe. Birds flocked to the house and sang the praises of the child while the wind gently caressed his body. All the brahmins of the Nambudiri clan had gathered to bless this divine child. How happily his father had given away land, wealth and cows to the brahmins and, after observing the auspicious signs of Shiva on the body of the child, they had named him Shankara.

Her child was very special. As he grew, everyone noticed that he was silent, daring and of very sharp intellect. He had been able to read and remembered by heart much of the literature in his native tongue, Malayalam. He had also read and remembered the ancient Vedas, Vedanta, Upanishads, Ramayana, Mahabharata and the Puranas. His abilities knew no bounds. Sivaguru was delighted with this divine ability of the God-child. He had decided that after Shankara reached the age of five, he would perform upanayana samskara, and send him to the gurukul for further training. But Sivaguru died soon after, and upon completing his last rites, Vishishta Devi left with Shankara for her father's place. However, she never forgot the last desire of her husband, and when Shankara was five years old, she came back to her village home, performed his upanayana samskara, and sent him to the gurukul.

She remembered what the people who commuted between the ashram and village had told her about Shankara, how he had surprised everyone with his clear, sharp understanding and pronunciation of the scriptures. Whatever he was taught he remembered and he soon became the joy of his teachers. In a short span of two years, he had completed studies which would normally take twenty years, and had mastered the Upanishads, Puranas, Itihasa, Dharmashashtras, Nyaya, Samkhya, Patanjali, Vaisheshika and other traditional literature.

Somebody had recently told her that Shankara also possessed miraculous powers. They had told her that, as per the rules of the gurukul, the disciples had to go for bhiksha. Once, while Shankara was collecting bhiksha, he had come upon a very poor family who had given him an amla fruit, as they had nothing else to give. Moved by their great poverty and devotion, Shankara had prayed to Goddess Lakshmi, and soon the hut of that poor family was covered with golden amlas which had rained down from the sky. This news had travelled all over the country.

Shankara was a gifted son, she mused. How otherwise would he be able to bring the river to their doorstep? She remembered that once while she was going to take a bath in the river Alwai, which flowed near the village, she had swooned and fallen to the ground. Shankara, aged seven, had found her and carried her home. Afterwards he had decided that by propitiating Lord Ashutosha, he would bring the river to the door of their home, so that his mother would not need to undertake the arduous journey every morning. He had prayed and prayed, and sure enough, after the next monsoon the river had changed her course and had begun to flow in front of their home.

One day some learned brahmins had visited their humble abode and, charmed by Shankara's wit, wisdom and intellect, they had asked to see his horoscope. They had said that he would be a teacher of great renown and a parivrajaka, and that his life would be short. He would die at the age of eight, sixteen or thirty-two. They had left after giving their blessings to the family. Since that day Shankara had not been the same. He had expressed his desire to take sannyasa. He had said that without sannyasa there was no scope for self-knowledge and without self-knowledge, no scope at all for moksha. She had very firmly stated to Shankara, "As long as I am alive I cannot give you permission to take sannyasa."

How she had misunderstood Shankara. Had she forgotten that he was the Lord himself in the form of her son? Her motherly affection wanted Shankara to be the bastion of her old age, but the Lord had wanted him to be the bastion of humanity. One day she had gone with Shankara to the river Alwai for a bath, when a crocodile had grabbed hold of Shankara's foot and was pulling him into the deep waters. Shankara had cried to his mother, "Mother, a crocodile is pulling me in. This is the last moment of my life. Permit me to adopt sannyasa, for without it there is no liberation. If you so permit, I shall remember the good Lord, take the sankalpa of sannyasa and thus die happily, knowing that I will attain moksha."

She had felt the pang of utter grief and desolation after seeing her beloved Shankara in the clutches of the crocodile. Not a single bather or fisherman was able to help Shankara out of his predicament. Sobbing, she had said, "So be it, my son. I give you permission to take sannyasa." Then she had fainted and had been unable to remember what had happened afterwards. People had told her later that some fishermen had come and captured the crocodile in their nets and had brought Shankara to the river bank where a local doctor had administered healing balms to his wounds. Rumours were going around that after Shankara had taken the vow of sannyasa, the crocodile had vanished. Some speculated that a divine hand had intervened in this episode. It did not matter to her what the truth was, for her beloved Shankara was alive.

When she was returning home with Shankara, he had said, "Mother, I cannot enter the house now as I am a sannyasi. I shall stay under a tree." She had become speechless and had replied, "What are you saying? How long do you think I will live? Renounce home after my death, but remain with me for as long as I live. Do you not have certain obligations towards me?" Shankara's reply had been full of love and compassion, and he had convinced her of his determination by saying, "On your instructions by the river, I took sannyasa. The Lord has saved me from the crocodile and it is his wish which I must now obey. With your blessing I shall attain yoga siddhis and tattwa jnana. In your last hours, you just have to remember me and I shall appear beside you and you shall have darshan of your Lord. He is the source of everything that is holy and auspicious. Believe me, Mother, what I am saying will happen. Bless me so that I can unhesitatingly tread the path of dharma and sannyasa." She was silently listening to her young boy saying these unbelievable things. Could she believe her ears? She did believe, after all, he was a God-child and she was his mother. She had blurted out, "So be it. I give you my blessings, so that you can achieve whatever you aspire for."

This event had happened yesterday. After reaching home, he had helped her to organize a proper sannyasa ceremony. This morning he himself had lit the fire and, as per tradition, initiated himself. She had dressed him in his ochre-coloured robes, given him a staff and a kamandalu. The whole village had come to see this event, and later they had all followed Shankara to the edge of the village and watched him depart. When he could no longer be seen, they had all returned, sad and in tears. Only she had remained standing under the coconut tree, hoping against hope that her son, Shankara, would return.

She opened her eyes and looked at the veranda where she sat alone, and where she had sat so many times before with Shivaguru and, later on, listening in rapture to Shankara reciting Sanskrit mantras from the Vedas. Today she was alone, but she knew that the Lord was with her, just as he was with Shankara. Filled with the warmth of the Lord's glow inside her, slowly she got up and whispered softly, "May the Lord guide your every step, my Shankara."

Training with the guru

It was dark inside the cave. Oil lamps were burning in the corner, giving just enough light to see the outline of those who were sitting there. In the dim light one could make out two people. One was ancient and ageless, with matted hair and a white beard. Ochre-coloured robes covered his frail body and he was sitting on a raised pedestal covered with a tiger skin. Beside him were a staff and kamandalu. Sitting below him was a boy of not more than eleven years. Dressed in the robes of a sannyasin, he was listening silently and intently to what the ancient one was saying.

"You were born with the grace of the Lord to re-establish the vedic precepts. I have waited many years at the instructions of my guru to convey to you the precepts of dharma. Now that you have learned everything, my duty is over and I am now free to attain samadhi. You will proceed to the eternal Kashi and there have the darshan of the Lord, who will guide your future work." Govindapada, the ancient one, then closed his eyes. Shankara, the young boy, bowed before his guru and silently left the solitude of the cave beside the river Narmada at Omkareshwar.

Govinda heard the silent footsteps of Shankara leaving the cave and his mind was diverted from samadhi to his young disciple. He remembered how he had come out of his year-long meditation on the day Shankara had reached this cave at Omkareshwar. The Lord had willed it to be so. He had heard stories that it had taken Shankara only two months to walk from Kaladi (Kerala) to Omkareshwar, beside the river Narmada (presently in Madhya Pradesh). This was an incredible feat for someone as young as he had been, just eight years old.

Where was the Narmada? Who would guide him there? Shankara had known that the Narmada was somewhere north of his village. He had heard of an ancient guru who was supposed to be waiting for someone. How much difficulty he had faced when crossing deep forests and jungles, rivers and mountains, encountering wild men and animals, but nothing had deterred the young boy. Shankara was very brilliant. All the elders, sannyasins and other disciples admired and respected him. In just three years he had mastered everything. The first year he had mastered hatha yoga, the second year raja yoga. As a result he had attained many spiritual powers and siddhis. The third year, Govindapada had taught Shankara the highest truth of jnana yoga, aparokshanubhuti, and the secrets of dharana, dhyana and samadhi.

It was indeed an honour to have such a disciple. In these times of degenerating values, a lot of hopes had been pinned on the young boy's shoulders. He also remembered that during the monsoon season that year, when he was sitting in samadhi, the waters of the Narmada had started to rise as if to inundate the cave. There was panic and pandemonium amongst his disciples. Shankara had calmly put an earthen pot in front of the cave and all the waters of the flooded Narmada had been drawn into it. How surprised everyone had been to witness this miraculous feat that he had performed so effortlessly.

Afterwards, when Govindapada heard of this event, he blessed Shankara by saying, "I had heard from my guru, Gaudapada, and he had heard from his guru, Sukadeva, that one would come who would contain the hundred currents of the Narmada in an earthen pot. That person shall assimilate all the vedic teachings in the *Brahma Sutras* to revive the dharma. I know now that they were referring to you. I bless you in your work."

Acharya Guru Govindapada was satisfied with Shankara. He was an incarnation of the Lord and would set things right. Govindapada had completed his mission, his waiting was over and he would now enter mahasamadhi. He concentrated his mind at the eyebrow centre, bowed mentally, offered prayers to his guru and the Lord, centred his pranas in sahasrara chakra and attained mahasamadhi.

MISSION

It was afternoon and although the sun was shining high in the sky, it was quite dark inside the small hut. Within, one could make out two old figures, one lying on a bed covered with blankets and the other crouching beside the prone figure on the bed. The figure, crouching beside the bed was an old maid who served Vishishta Devi, the mother of Shankara, and the figure on the bed was Shankara's mother, who was sick, delirious and unconscious. The whispered name of "Shankara" escaped from her lips from time to time. Doctors had come, given her treatment and medication, but nothing seemed to work on her frail body.

Ultimately the doctors had said that only the grace of Lord Ashutosha would be able to return her to health. Thus they had slowly left the hut, leaving Vishishta Devi in the care of the maid who had served her since the day Shankara was born. The old maid knew about the promise that Shankara had made to his mother when he had taken sannyasa and left home in search of his guru. "In your last hour, you just have to remember me. I will appear beside you and you will have darshan of your Lord." But where was he now? Why hadn't he come?

She knew that Shankara would come, but when? "Shankara, please come," was the only thought that kept appearing in her mind over and over again. News of Shankara's achievements and glory had preceded him. He was the talk on everyone's lips. How happy his mother used to be whenever someone brought news of Shankara from far away lands. She would hear the news with silent tears of joy in her eyes, then go to the temple and offer worship to Lord Ashutosha and distribute prasadam to all the children in the village.

After the mahasamadhi of his guru, Govindapada, Shankara had left Omkareshwar with some sannyasins and gone to Varanasi. There he had chosen a solitary place near the Manikarnika Ghat for his stay. Daily he would give discourses to aspirants who would come to him, many times out of curiosity, and many times with an earnest desire to imbibe his wisdom. Slowly his fame began to spread. Many used to come with the purpose of trying to defeat Shankara with their arguments and debates, but in the end they were defeated and would feel blessed to hear the truth from one so young. It was at Varanasi, the maid mused, that Shankara had met a boy named Sanandan, another young prodigy who had come to study the scriptures and had become a disciple of Shankara. Later on he was named Padmapada.

Stories were told that at Varanasi, Adya Shakti Bhavani and Lord Mahadeva had blessed Shankara. The Adya Shakti had appeared in the form of a woman mourning over the corpse of her dead husband, which lay on her lap, and asking for assistance to perform his final rites. Shankara was going to take a bath with his followers and had asked the lady to move the corpse from the path. She had replied, "Why don't you ask the corpse to move?" Shankara had said, "Mother, why are you so disillusioned? How can a corpse move? It has no power, no shakti." That woman had answered, "Then why, O Yogi, do you profess that Brahman without Shakti is the Creator?" Shankara was astonished, and the woman along with the corpse just vanished before his eyes. He realized that it was Adya Shakti who had come to open another dimension of reality for him and had thus blessed him.

On another occasion when Shankara was again going for a bath, Lord Mahadeva had appeared in the guise of an ugly chandala (untouchable) accompanied by four dogs. Shankara had addressed him, saying "Move out of the way." The chandala had laughed and said, "Who are you asking to move, the body or the spirit? The atman is omnipresent and the body its container. From the atmic viewpoint is there a distinction between a brahmin and a chandala? Is there a distinction between the reflection of the sun in the waters of the Ganga and the reflection of the sun in wine?" Shankara was aghast as the realization dawned on him. He had bowed before the chandala, who disappeared, and Lord Mahadeva appeared in full glory. The Lord blessed and instructed him to re-establish the vedic precepts and to propagate them amongst the masses. Shankara was asked to write a commentary on the *Brahma Sutras* of Vyasa. The Lord said to him, "You were born of me for the welfare of mankind."

At Kaladi, his mother had heard that after this encounter with the Lord, Shankara had decided to go to Badarikashram to complete the mandate of the Lord. He had left Varanasi with his followers and had travelled on foot passing many towns and tirthas, giving discourses, inspiring people to renovate temples, organizing systems of worship according to the vedic tradition. What an enormous task and arduous journey for someone just twelve years old! She was proud to be his mother. Eventually Shankara had reached Vyasashram in the Badarika area. This was where sage Vedavyasa had dictated the great epic *Mahabharata* to Ganesha, who became his scribe. Here Shankara spent four years, taught his followers the vedic truths and wrote commentaries on the *Brahma Sutras*, twelve Upanishads, *Bhagavad Gita*, *Vishnu Sahasranama*, *Sanatsujatiya*, Srutis and Smritis. Afterwards he had travelled to pilgrimage centres in the Himalayan region.

After completing his travels in the Himalayas, Shankara came to Uttar Kashi and there, as if knowing that his lifespan of sixteen years was coming to an end, lost himself in contemplation of the supreme Self. People said it was here that Sage Vedavyasa had come to Shankara in the guise of an old man and, after a lengthy discussion with Shankara, had been very pleased with his commentary on the *Brahma Sutras* and other texts. He had blessed Shankara with another extension of sixteen years and had instructed him to guide the masses, who had deviated from this original path due to the power politics of many sects and traditions, back into the fold of spiritual and vedic precepts. Hearing this story Vishishta Devi's joy knew no bounds. She knew that with the blessings of the gods and saints, Shankara was going to live and that he had a great mission to fulfil.

After having received instructions from Sage Vedavyasa, Shankara travelled with his disciples and followers through the regions of northeastern India and came to Prayag, where Kumarilla Bhatta lived. He had waged an interminable war against foreign and non-vedic influences which were trying their best to destroy the foundations of vedic dharma. In the course of his drive to re-establish vedic precepts, Kumarilla Bhatta had offended his own teachers and, as repentance for this sin, he was about to undergo self-immolation. It was at this time that Shankara came to discuss the Sanatan ideals with him. Kumarilla Bhatta had told Shankara to find Mandan Mishra, who would be able to discuss these ideals with him, and by defeating Mandan Mishra in debate, Shankara would thus become the champion of the vedic cause.

The old maid remembered the day when some travellers had come and told them about the defeat of Mandan Mishra and Shankara's miraculous powers. How had the story been told? The maid started to think that Shankara had reached Mahishmati town, located between the Narmada and Mahishmati rivers, and there had requested Mandan Mishra to enter into a debate with him, as that was the will of Kumarilla Bhatta. Mandan Mishra was a disciple of Kumarilla Bhatta and accepted the debate as it was the will of his teacher. The debate between the two started, with Mandan Mishra's wife, Ubhaya Bharati, who was very learned and considered to be an incarnation of Goddess Saraswati, as the judge.

The debate was very dynamic and interesting and continued for eighteen days, at the end of which Mandan Mishra conceded defeat and, as per tradition, offered himself as a disciple of Shankara. Ubhaya Bharati had then come forward and asked Shankara for an opportunity to enter the debate as, according to the Sanatan ideals, the wife is the other half of the husband. So her husband would not be fully defeated unless she could be defeated also. Shankara agreed and the debate between the two continued for another eighteen days. Finally, Ubhaya Bharati questioned Shankara about the erotic arts and sciences, at which time Shankara had become silent, as he had no knowledge of them. Hence he had asked for one month to find the answers, which was granted to him by Ubhaya Bharati.

Shankara had left Mahishmati and gone to a cave where he had sat in meditation. His disciples had brought him the news that a king named Amarak from a nearby province had just died. After leaving his ascetic body immobile in the care of his disciples, Shankara had immediately taken this opportunity to transfer his soul into the body of the dead king. In a short time, he had learned all there was to learn in the royal palace about the erotic arts and sciences. Before the completion of the month, he left the body of the king and re-entered his own body which was still lying inert in the cave. Then he went to Ubhaya Bharati, answered all her questions and won the debate. Mandan Mishra became a disciple of Shankara and was named Sureshwaracharya.

Listening to this incredible story, the maid was astonished that the toddler who had played in her lap, now had the ability to transfer his soul from one body into another. "Wonders never cease with Shankara," she thought.

After Mahishmati, Shankara had journeyed with his increasing number of followers towards western India and visited many *tirthas*, holy places, before coming to Sri Shaila. People talked amongst themselves that at Sri Shaila, a bad kapalika by the name of Ugra Bhairava had become a disciple of Shankara, with the purpose of eliminating him at the first opportunity. "How low can a person fall?" the maid had thought. Shankara, so young and inspired, had not suspected anything and soon Ugra Bhairava had invited him to a kapalika ritual where he intended to make him the sacrifice. Shankara had readily consented to accompany him to his cave. If it had not been for Padmapada, who was ever alert in guarding the welfare of Shankara, and who saved him by invoking Narasimha (the man-lion incarnation of Vishnu), he would surely have died at the hands of the kapalikas, his sworn enemies. How the maid had shuddered at this terrible thought. "May God forbid!" she had muttered under her breath.

During his travels, Shankara had come to Harihara Tirtha, and there as he was going to the temple for the darshan of Ambika, a young couple had come with their dead newborn child. They had placed him at the feet of Shankara, begging for his life. Shankara in his compassion prayed to Goddess Bhagavati, and in front of the multitude of followers, disciples and visitors to the temple, the child moved its body, opened its eyes and began to wail.

Shankara had given life to a dead child. Had he not also given speech to a dumb boy? Yes, he had. The maid tried to remember how this had transpired. Shankara had gone to Sri Beli accompanied by hundreds of followers, and there a brahmin family had brought their boy of thirteen, who had been dumb since his birth, to be blessed by him. Shankara had asked the boy in Sanskrit: "Who are you? Whose son are you? Where are you going? Where have you come from? What is your name? Answer me, for I get a special feeling when I see you." That young boy had brightened up upon hearing Shankara's questions, and had replied in clear Sanskrit: "I am not a man, nor divine nor spirit, neither brahmin, kshatriya, vaishya nor shudra, neither brahmachari, householder, renunciate, nor ascetic. I am an embodiment of the Self." Thus the mute boy had spoken, and his parents then offered him to Shankara, who later initiated him and named him Hastamalaka. Shankara had then come to Sringagiri (Sringeri) where he established a Math and a temple where he installed Sri Yantra and invoked Goddess Saraswati. There another boy joined him, who was later initiated and named Trotakacharya.

"At present, Shankara is in Sringeri," thought the maid. There was a soft knock at the door. The maid came out of her reverie and looked at the prone figure on the bed. The blanket had slipped. She gently covered the body with the blanket and heard Vishishta Devi murmur the name of

Shankara. "Was he going to come as promised?" thought the maid. Again there was a knock at the door of the hut. Who could be there at this hour? It was evening and the people of the village were winding up their activities of the day and preparing for the evening meal.

She got up, adjusted her sari and went to open the door. Outside it was just evening and in front of the door a God-man was standing, young and radiant like a mini-sun. She was stunned! Who could he be? The God-man bowed before the old figure of the maid and said, "How is Mother?" The maid, recognizing the young man, gave a cry of joy. Tears broke from her ancient eyes. Shankara had come at last. How had he come? Well, all those questions would wait. She grabbed the young hands of Shankara with her ancient, withered hands and pulled him towards the bed where his mother lay.

Shankara lovingly placed his hands on top of his mother's head and in a soft voice full of love said, "Mother, your Shankara has come." The words brought an instant reaction and the eyes of Vishishta Devi had fluttered open. In the meantime, the maid lit a lamp and brought it near the cot, so that mother and son could gaze at each other. Vishishta Devi's eyes were moist with tears of joy at seeing her son now grown up and acclaimed by the masses everywhere as the vishwa guru, guru of the universe. She clasped his head, covered with saffron robes, in her trembling hands, pulled it to her and smothered his forehead with kisses.

Shankara said to his mother, "I have come to serve you and to remove all your sorrows so you will get well soon." His mother replied, "My son, seeing you all my sorrows have disappeared. I am happy. The body is suffering due to old age. The near and dear ones have caused a lot of trouble. If it was not for the faithful maid and her care, I would have died a long time ago. Look after her when I am no more. Now have a bath and a meal." After the bath and the meal which the maid had hastily prepared, Shankara returned to his mother's side.

245

His mother then said to him, "I am preparing for my departure. My last desire was to see you. You have come and now nothing remains for me. I only wish to attain the abode of my ishta." Shankara lovingly said, "Mother, once you know the ultimate Self, you will attain liberation." And he started to impart the transcendental wisdom to her. Vishishta Devi said to him, "I am not versed in this lore. I am uneducated. How will I realize the Self which is beyond speech and mind? My Shankara, show me the divine form of the Lord so that I can look upon it with my eyes and consider myself blessed."

Shankara remained silent for a few moments and then he said, "Mother, close your eyes and merge your mind in your ishta devata. That way you will have his darshan." Then, in a voice full of compassion, he prayed and invoked Mahadeva and Narayana. His mother had the divine darshan of her Lord in full blazing glory, not even remotely comparable to the brilliance of a thousand suns in the heavens. Afterwards she blessed Shankara by placing her frail hands on top of his head and said, "May the Lord Ashutosha protect and guide your destiny, and may you be an able instrument of his will." Thus saying, she gave up her mortal frame on the lap of her beloved Shankara.

"I must walk alone"

The sun was reflected in the snow-capped mountains and the sky was clear blue. Wisps of white cloud hung in the heavens and the few high-flying birds made the glory of the Himalayan sky even greater. It was a desolate region where there were hardly any trees. The terrain was barren, with pieces of rock jutting out from the ground like eternal sentinels guarding the mountains passes. The whole scenery was vibrating with an inner beauty. Padmapada, along with Sureshwaracharya, Hastamalaka and Trotakacharya, watched the receding figure of their master, Shankara, walking alone and barefoot on the snow-clad Himalayan mountains towards Kedarnath, a solitary place which Shankara had decided would be his final resting place.

246

At the age of thirty-two, the final year of his life, Shankara had come with a multitude of his disciples to Badarikashram. Here he had given final instructions to his disciples to carry on with the work of propagating and preserving the Sanatan vedic precepts, which by now had taken a great hold over the masses throughout the country. All opposition from non-vedic, foreign influences and sects had dwindled away. Afterwards he had called his four close disciples and had said, "The purpose of my adopting this body is over. Now all of you prepare yourselves to become living examples of the highest Vedantic truth and propagate this doctrine in all four-corners of the country. The divine will which directed this self will also continue to guide you. Now let me go."

Thus saying, he had left Badarikashram with his four disciples, heading towards Kedarnath, over the snow-laden mountain tops. At one point he had stopped them from proceeding further with him by saying, "The path which I shall walk now will be without human company, so you must stay here." The disciples had begged Shankara to allow them to go further in order to help him, but he had said, "I have no use for human companions, for the Lord will lead me now." And declining all help, he went on alone. The disciples, now alone, sat on the snow from where they had watched their guru go towards the deep Himalayan ranges, each one lost in his own thoughts. They had a mission to fulfil now which had been assigned to each one of them by Shankara.

Their minds went back to the time when Shankara was at Sringeri, discussing and teaching Vedantic reality to his followers. Suddenly he had adjourned the class in the middle of his discourse and had gone to his room. The four disciples had also followed him and there he had told them that his mother was on her deathbed. She was remembering him and so he was needed there. They could follow him as soon as they were able to manage the affairs of the math which had recently been established. They had asked how he would be able to cover that long journey without having made any prior travel arrangements. Shankara had laughed and said, "The Lord will provide a way." Then he had closed himself in the room and when the room was again reopened by his disciples, Shankara was not found there. People believed that he had flown with the help of his yogic powers to his ailing mother.

When the disciples had arrived at Kaladi, they had found that Shankara's mother had left her mortal frame. It was Shankara himself who had performed her final rites, as per her wishes, and had then given the family wealth to the old maid and made her comfortable. While Shankara was in Kaladi, the king of Kerala, Rajashekhar, had approached him and requested him to stay on for a longer period to reorganize the vedic tradition in the state for its social development.

After spending some time in Kerala, Shankara had left with his followers to travel and to rekindle the faith of the masses in the dharma. He was accompanied by King Rajashekhar of Kerala and King Sudhanwa of Karnataka with all their retinue. The chanting of mantras by Shankara's disciples vibrated through the hearts and minds of all who met them. They visited town after town, village after village, and countless tirthas and temples, until a new direction had been given to the people.

They had reached Madhyarjuna tirtha, where Shankara addressed a large group of pundits on Adwaita Vedanta philosophy in the temple of Lord Shiva. When questioned on the validity of his Adwaita system, Shankara had meditated and prayed to the Lord to give the wise some sign, and a divine voice was heard from the heavens saying, "Adwaita is the Truth." This voice was heard by all present.

After this event, Shankara had gone to Sri Rangam via Rameshwaram. There he had had a debate with the head of the Vaishnava sect along with his followers and had taught them the five mahayajnas: (i) *Brahmayajna*, study of scriptures; (ii) *Pitriyajna*, offering to the ancestors; (iii) *Homayajna*, agnihotra, etc.; (iv) *Baliyajna*, serving the creatures of the

Lord; and (v) *Nriyajna*, service and care of guests. Many of the Vaishnavas at Sri Rangam had become his followers.

Then, travelling northward, Shankara had come to Prayag and Varanasi, where he had held discussions with the heads and followers of the Samkhya system, Shaivas, Shaktas, Mimamsakas, Charvakas, ritualists, yogis, followers of various tantric branches, worshippers of Lakshmi, Saraswati, Ganapati, etc., and infused them all with vedic aspiration.

From Varanasi, Shankara had gone to Saurashtra and visited many tirthas in that region, establishing another math at Dwarika, and holding debates with the followers of Samkhya, Buddhist and Jain schools of thought. After that he had travelled on to Kashmir where, in a temple at Srinagar, he had composed the famous hymn, *Saundarya Lahari*. Afterwards he had travelled to Bihar, Bengal and Assam, where he won the hearts of everyone with his clear concept, understanding and teaching of the vedic tradition and dharma.

It was in Pragjyotishpur (Assam) that Shankara was taken ill with fistula. He recalled his disciples, still sitting on the big, snow-capped hills of Kedarnath. Assam was famous for its Buddhist tantric practitioners, especially the region around Pragjyotishpur, known as Kamaroopa, where Shankara had visited the famous temple of Kamakhya. It was here that the Buddhist tantrics led by Abhinava Gupta had come to challenge Shankara to a debate, and were defeated by his deep insight and wisdom. Unable to accept defeat, they had performed tantric rituals and Shankara had started to feel the pangs of fistula. Pus and blood began to flow, accompanied by terrible pains. The disciples were concerned, but Shankara, despite his suffering and deteriorating health, remained equipoised and calm. At that time, his disciples had felt that he would not live long. Once again it was Padmapada who had come to know of the malicious intention of Abhinava Gupta and had performed the Shanti karmas to neutralize the effects of the tantric influences. Sure enough, Shankara had soon regained his health and vigour.

After this episode, Shankara had come with his disciples to Gaudadesha (presently northern Bengal) and inspired the king to propagate Vedantic precepts in the region. It was here that Shankara had the darshan of his grandfather guru, Acharya Gaudapada.

One evening when Shankara was contemplating alone beside the river Ganga, the radiating figure of an ancient, ageless sage materialized in front of him. Shankara had bowed before him. The figure had said, "Dear Shankara, you have received the ultimate knowledge for liberation from my disciple Govindapada. I am content that you have performed the great feat of re-establishing vedic dharma and have written commentaries on the scriptures. Ask something of me." Shankara had replied, "O great guru, your vision is like the living vision of the Supreme Lord. Grant me the boon that I lose myself in the contemplation of the Supreme Self, which is truth, consciousness and beatitude." Gaudapada then blessed Shankara with raised hands and the vision dematerialized.

After a few days, Shankara travelled to Nepal and Tibet and awakened the zeal of dharma in the people of those states. Then, slowly but surely, he directed his steps towards Badarikashram and Kedarnath.

The sun was slowly setting and a soft chilling breeze began to blow in the hills where the disciples sat with heavy hearts, looking again and again at the footsteps of Shankara imprinted on the snow, going towards infinity. Finally, they got up and bowed to the footprints. Just one sentence formed on their lips, "Victory to Shankara, the Vishwa Guru, the Acharya, the Preceptor of the Kali Age. Victory to Shankaracharya." Slowly they walked down towards Badarikashram. They had a mission to fulfil and many miles to walk before they could rest.

Work and establishments
There are many different accounts concerning the final departure of Shankara. Some say that Shankara left his

mortal frame at Mount Kailash after visiting the cave of Dattatreya, where he was blessed by him. Others believe that he left his mortal frame in Kanchi, while yet others believe that he merged his body with the deity at Parashuram temple at Trichur in Malabar State. However, most historians agree that it was in the region of Kedarnath that Shankara attained the ultimate merging with the Supreme.

Whatever the belief, all accept that no one else could have done in many lifetimes what Shankara was able to do in his short lifespan of thirty-two years. He changed the total religious and spiritual structure of India, reorganized the scattered groups of sannyasins and gave a solid and clear direction to the vedic movement, which is still being followed today with full enthusiasm by countless aspirants and seekers all over the world.

With far-reaching inner vision, this great God-man organized the ancient tradition of sannyasa, collecting all the ascetics, renunciates, yogis and sadhus who wandered aimlessly through the length and breath of India, under the one banner of the vedic tradition. In the course of his wanderings he established four pithas or maths in the four corners of India: Sharada Math in Dwarika in eastern India; Govardhan Math in Puri in eastern India; Jyotir Math in Badrinath in northern India; and Sringeri Math in southern India. In each math, one of his disciples was installed to lead the sannyasins and to guide the propagation of the vedic precepts. Details of each math are given in chapter 11.

Views on sannyasa
Shankaracharya was a great spiritual leader and a revolution-ary. He fought against all the ideas, philosophies and religions of his era which he did not feel would lead people to the highest realization. His idea was to form a nucleus of sannyasins who would have a relatively higher awareness than the average person and who could also teach and inspire others to follow a way of life which would allow free expression to their innate, spiritual potential, and which

251

would have nothing to do with the prevalent religious concepts of those times. To achieve that end, he debated with all the great scholars and pundits just to prove the futility of their intellectual argumentation: Brahmins fighting against Buddhists, Buddhists fighting against Jains, Jains fighting against Muslims, and so on.

Shankaracharya was a teacher who did not emphasize intellectual awareness; rather, he emphasized intuitive awareness. He also realized that, in order to introduce people to this new concept of intuitive awareness, which is based on pure knowledge of the original scriptures as they came out from our superminds, the right atmosphere for the process of learning was essential. That atmosphere was an ashram or math and the central figure there was the guru or acharya. Shankara started teaching people in an ashram environment in his four main centres which, in his day, became highly respected places of learning.

By Shankaracharya's time, the vedic tradition, the rishi parampara, had deteriorated drastically, because as people lost their spiritual awareness, they developed worldly awareness. So Shankara said a definite 'no' to the rishi culture. In his sannyasa order, he wanted only celibates, unmarried sannyasins who would follow the precepts set by him very strictly. He said that for them there was no need to go through brahmacharya, grihastha or vanaprastha ashramas. He initiated his disciples into sannyasa directly. However, it was not that sannyasa which had been practised previously by hard-headed ascetic recluses that Shankara advocated, but a new sannyasa with a different aim and direction.

Before Shankara's time, sannyasa had been for personal gain only. Shankara felt that by such rigid renunciation, neither the sannyasin nor the society benefited. Hence he conceived a new order of sannyasins who would become the spiritual torchbearers for future generations. The purpose of this order was to preserve the right knowledge, the right understanding, the proper means and the techniques for attaining altered states of consciousness, so that people would be able to experience the highest reality.

He slowly taught his sannyasins how to discover their insight, their own inner consciousness which would ultimately lead them to the experience of reality. This was the whole teaching of Shankaracharya, the Adwaita philosophy. In any type of sannyasa this training is essential so that one can become aware of the unifying aspect, the unifying force within everything. If we study the scriptures seriously and deeply, observing what is written in them, we find an invisible chain linking everything in life, every part of creation, every action, thought, emotion, desire and feeling. This also becomes a form of introspection for aspirants once they realize that there is something more to human nature that that which they can perceive with their normal understanding.

Shankara had to utilize the knowledge of all the different religions, philosophies and thoughts and give this to his sannyasin disciples as well, so that they would see the similarity in everything and not think that one thought was final. For that, he used practically every scripture, Vedas, Upanishads and Gitas, which represented the discovery of truth by different superminds.

In regard to karma, Shankara said that the atman should and can be realized only through knowledge and not by ritual. He asserted that with the dawning of knowledge, karma naturally and necessarily ceases to function. Karma of any kind is a hindrance to the final emancipation, and the performance of karma involves one in the cycle of samsara, the manifest, gross world. It is Brahmajnana that removes ignorance and bestows moksha.

Shankara said that sannyasa is absolutely necessary, whether it be vividisha sannyasa (renunciation while living in the world) or vidvat sannyasa (renunciation due to parvairagya). Without perfect renunciation, it is impossible to pursue the path of Brahmajnana. The necessary qualifications for sannyasa which he emphasized are as follows:

- Discrimination between the one eternal substance and the appearance of ephemeral phenomena.
- Dispassion for the enjoyment of objects of pleasure in this world and in the other.
- Possessing the qualities of (i) tranquillity of mind, (ii) control of the senses, (iii) cessation from all worldly activity, (iv) capacity to endure the pairs of opposites, i.e. heat and cold, pleasure and pain, love and hatred, etc, and (v) ability to concentrate the mind.
- Yearning or desire for knowledge and liberation.

Shankara said it was foolish to cite examples such as Janaka who did not take sannyasa but remained in the world, and yet possessed Brahmajnana. Such instances are quoted by people who do not want to leave their attachments, for knowledge alone enables one to transcend all worldly attachments. Without renouncing attachment to worldly life, knowledge of the Self cannot be pursued with vigour. This does not mean, however, that a sannyasin undervalues human society and discards all people without helping them. A sannyasin transcends the different stages of spiritual evolution and exercises a silent, unnoticed but powerful influence for the good of humanity.

Becoming one of the devas in heaven is not the highest endeavour of mankind. There is something beyond karma, higher than the transitory earthly life, more transcendental than heavenly enjoyment. Even the devas are subject to the misery of heavenly samsara and they are not immortal in the real sense. The Srutis declare that Brahman alone is above samsara, above all experiences. One who is intent upon realizing the peace, the bliss, the One without a second – Shantam, Shivam, Adwaitam, is the most powerful and useful friend of the world.

Being alone was in the beginning, One without a second.

Chandogya Upanishad VI: 2–1

In the beginning all this was the Self, only One.

Aitareya Aranyaka 114–1

This is the Brahman without cause and without effect, without anything outside or inside, this Self is Brahman, perceiving everything.

Brihadaranyaka Upanishad 11–5–19

28

Swami Sivananda

Throughout the ages, the world has been guided by spiritually illuminated people who come from time to time to raise man's consciousness and to remind us of the path we must traverse. Swami Sivananda was one great soul who was born to give the word of spiritual life to thousands and thousands of people all over the globe. He never came to the West and he never went to the East, but today he is everywhere.

Swami Satyananda Saraswati

BIRTH AND BOYHOOD

It was early in the evening of Tuesday, 16th July 1963. A small group of sannyasins refreshed their aching bodies in the holy water of the Ganga at Rishikesh. An air of melancholy hung over them, as one by one they finished their baths. They sat together on the banks of the river, contemplating the setting sun lost in their thoughts. At last one of them spoke, a young man whose feelings showed clearly on his face. "Oh Swamiji," he cried, turning humbly to the eldest sannyasin in the group. "What a hard day for us all!" "Indeed," agreed the elder, "but we must not grieve, for although our guru has gone, his mission will remain, and it is now for us to uphold the mission in Swamiji's name."

Swami Chidananda, for this was the elder's name, was referring to the mahasamadhi of Swami Sivananda, which

Swami Sivananda

had taken place in a miraculous fashion the night before. These disciples, gathered in companionship, had spent the night beside the body of their guru, placed in the lotus position, softly chanting the maha mantra and guiding the many residents of the ashram who came to pay their last respects. As morning broke and as conches were blown and bells chimed, they had lifted the bier and borne it slowly towards the Ganga, where Swami Sivanandaji's holy form was ceremoniously bathed. Continuously reciting holy mantras, they carried Swamiji's body into the ashram on Vishwanath Mandir Hill and placed it tenderly in the samadhi shrine, its final resting place.

Many of the younger disciples, encouraged by the words of Swami Chidananda, were now quietly speaking amongst themselves, commenting on these events. After a few minutes one of them turned again to Swami Chidananda and said, "Swamiji, many of us have only lived in the ashram for a short time and, although we have seen the kindness and divinity in Swamiji with our own eyes, we know nothing of his earlier life, of his childhood, of the path he took to renunciation and the beginning of the ashram where we are now. Please, if you can, tell us something about our master."

Swami Chidananda smiled lovingly at the eager faces turned beseechingly towards him. "With pleasure," he replied, "to speak of our guru is, for me, always the greatest of honours." And settling himself more comfortably, he began to speak.

"Swamiji's birth and childhood were simply a preparation for the role he was to fulfil in later life. But he himself often spoke to me of those early days, and so I can give you some idea of how his greatness gradually came to manifest itself. He was born on the 8th of September 1887, in the early hours of the morning in a village called Pattamadai on the banks of the river Tamraparni in South India. His father, Vengu Iyer, was a devotee of Shiva and descended from an erudite saint scholar, Appaya Dikshitar, and his mother was a village woman. Both were simple, devout and religious, and rejoiced greatly at the birth of their third son, naming him Kuppuswami. Having many good omens before his birth, they even believed he was a reincarnation of Appaya Dikshitar, who, as a Shaivite had entered a Vaishnava temple and changed the murti of Venkateshwara into the form of a shivalinga and then back again. This prophecy was later to be fulfilled when Swami Sivananda, ignoring the differences between all creeds and sects, also proclaimed the oneness of God.

"Love for God was inborn in little Kuppu. He delighted in fetching leaves and flowers for his father's Shiva pooja, in listening raptly to his chanting of vedic mantras and hymns, and in accompanying his mother daily to the temple. It was not long before he too was participating in prayers and kirtan with, I suspect, all the enthusiasm of an adult.

"I have heard tell that even from these very early days, Kuppuswami rejoiced in giving. He used to pity the poor, distributing food generously to servants and beggars whenever he could. Animals showed no fear of him and would eat peacefully from his hands. On one particular festive occasion, Kuppuswami was wearing new clothes but, spotting a naked beggar outside, he immediately stripped and gave away his new dhoti, responding to his mother's protest with the words, "But he is so happy with it, Amma. See how proudly he wears it, and he needs it far more than I do.

"Indeed, Kuppuswami's mother was often to be found wringing her hands with worry over her small child. For Kuppuswami's love of adventure would often draw him into early morning expeditions. On one occasion, when he walked twelve miles away from home to the temple at Kazhugumalai, she waited anxiously for three days, longing for his return. But it was only on the evening of the fourth day that he reappeared, hungry and exhausted, but happy and shining with devotion." Swami Chidananda paused, lost in memories of his master. "Please go on," prompted the young disciple. "Tell us about his studies. Did his love of adventure also lead him to miss school?"

Swami Chidananda, roused from his reverie, shook his head. "Oh no," he answered, "at school Kuppuswami put the same energy and enthusiasm into his studies as he did into loving others. And, as you all know, for him studies included a sound training in gymnastics and sports. He used to rise from his bed as early as three a.m. and slip off to the gymnasium where he would engage in vigorous exercises. But before leaving the house, he would place a pillow on his bed and cover it up with a blanket to give the appearance of his innocent self sleeping soundly!" The disciples laughed, recognizing in this tale, the mischievous quality which they had known and loved in Swami Sivananda.

"While fellow students were dreaming of degree courses in the arts and sciences, hoping to make their mark in the world," continued Swami Chidananda, "Kuppuswami rejected such dreams of moving the world, professing instead that it is our hearts which should be moved at the sight of the suffering in this world. He decided to do medicine and to try his best to reduce the sufferings of his fellow man. And so, despite some opposition from his parents, Kuppuswami joined the Tanjore Medical College and began his studies with intense interest and zeal. Throughout his time there, his imposing figure would often be seen in the corner of the operating theatre, or bent over his books during the recess, even in the holidays, when the other students went home to relax and enjoy themselves.

"I believe that it was during this period that he had an encounter which was to remove the veil of caste distinction from his life once and for all. He had started learning fencing from an untouchable teacher and during one lesson was rebuked by a brahmin onlooker, 'Oh Kuppu, how can you, a caste brahmin, become a student of an untouchable?' On returning home, Kuppuswami pondered deeply over what the brahmin had said. As he was immersed in meditation, the image of Lord Shiva, which he used to worship in his father's pooja room, appeared majestically before him, and entered into the heart of the untouchable.

At once, Kuppuswami went with some flowers, sweets and clothes, garlanded the untouchable, placed flowers at his feet and fell prostrate before him. Thus did God come into Kuppuswami's early life to demonstrate the inequities of caste distinction, later allowing him, as a doctor, to treat all the sick alike, both the brahmin and the untouchable."

Again Swami Chidananda paused, a little breathless as the effort of speaking for so long had overcome him. "Please," he said, turning to Swami Krishnananda, who sat on his right listening intently to his friend's words, "you tell the story of Malaya. You know of his work there. Tell these young sannyasins of Swamiji's work and his selfless actions in those difficult circumstances." Krishnananda nodded in acquiescence and willingly took over the story.

DOCTOR IN MALAYA

"After graduating with astounding brilliance, Dr Kuppuswami joined a doctor in Tiruchi as his assistant. Realizing, however, that as part of his service to the suffering he also needed to teach them how to avoid illness, he started a medical journal entitled *Ambrosia*. The motto of the journal was thus: "Prevention is better than cure." Over the next few years, although he was happy in his work, Kuppuswami felt an increasing need within him to give more, to do more to reduce the suffering of others. Hearing of the deplorable conditions in which thousands of Indian workers lived on the rubber plantations of Malaya, he decided to cross the seas to serve the needy. At a farewell party, the young doctor told his friends, 'Book knowledge will not take us far. I studied anatomy, I dissected the human body, but I could not find the atman within.' 'The atman can only be seen when the ego is destroyed,' interjected a friend. 'True,' agreed Kuppuswami, 'and selfless service is the most potent weapon to thin out the ego.'"

"But his family," objected one young disciple who had only recently left his home and family for the ashram life, "were they willing to let him go?" "Not so easily," replied Swami Krishnananda. "Once again his mother was distraught. The poor woman pleaded with him not to leave her, and she argued that crossing the seas was prohibited in the shastras. But Kuppuswami had resolved to cross the sea to serve humanity, and the shastras would not stand in his way. Eventually, his mother accepted his decision and gave her blessings, beseeching God to stay with him in his noble mission. And so, one twilit evening, she said goodbye to her son as he embarked on his mission, knowing, her heart filled with pride, that her son was made for the Lord's service.

"After a lengthy sea voyage, during which Kuppuswami volunteered his services to passengers, treating them kindly and free of charge, he arrived in Malaya. There he was immediately appointed to the Senawang Estate Hospital where he worked ceaselessly dispensing medicines, keeping the accounts and personally attending to patients. Hopeless cases often came to him, but success was sure. Everywhere people declared that he had a special gift from God for the miraculous cures effected in the patients and acclaimed him as a very kind and sympathetic doctor with a charming and majestic personality. He continued to give endlessly, not only his services but often his money.

"I have even heard tell that once a poor man, drenched to the skin, came to the doctor at night. His wife was in the agony of labour pains and needed urgent attention. The doctor went at once to her aid and, after attending to her, stayed outside the hut in spite of the heavy rain. Only after the safe delivery of the child, did the doctor return home next morning."

At this point, the chiming of bells was heard in the ashram, as the devotees gathered together for evening kirtan. The sound of chanting reminded Swami Krishnananda that, even in Malaya, his guru's spiritual yearnings could not be forgotten. And so he spoke of those yearnings to the group now seated at his feet. "Throughout this period," Krishnananda went on, "the relentless drive towards

261

renunciation was stirring within Swamiji. He became gradually more thoughtful and pensive, and meditated on the uselessness of material pleasures and the need to attain everlasting peace.

"As if sent by God, it was at this point in his life that Dr Kuppuswami had the opportunity of hosting a noble sadhu who had fallen sick. The doctor served him with great reverence and devotion and on his recovery, the sadhu gave him the book *Jiva Brahma Aikyari* by Sri Swami Satchidananda, saying, 'I am highly pleased with your services. There is something noble and great in you. You will shine as a world teacher. Read this book well and it will help you.' Inspired by this, Kuppuswami began to study the books of Shankaracharya, Swami Rama Tirtha, Swami Vivekananda and many, many others. Increasing daily his intensive practice of sadhana, he felt less and less able to discharge his duties at the hospital satisfactorily. Realizing that he could offer no lasting solution for disease, he resigned from his job and returned to India to set out on the path of renunciation, in search of immortality."

The sun had sunk low behind the hills surrounding Rishikesh and the sky was infused with a beautiful red glow, which reflected off the waters of the Ganga, illuminating the faces of the disciples. "Enough," said Swami Krishnananda, "you shall hear more tomorrow. Now it is time for satsang, and telling stories of our master must not become a replacement of our sadhana." "No, no," agreed the others, rising hurriedly and gathering their dhotis about them. Together they proceeded up the steps of the ghat and made their way to the samadhi shrine of their master, as devoted to him now as they had been during his lifetime.

RENUNCIATION

The following morning the disciples rose as usual in the quiet, early hours of the morning, when the only sounds to be heard in Rishikesh were the chiming of bells, the chanting of mantras and the rushing waters of the Ganga. They spent many hours that day sitting in meditation by the samadhi shrine, contemplating their master's greatness, as it had been revealed to them by Swami Chidananda and Swami Krishnananda the day before. As the evening approached, they rose as if of one accord and having taken their ritual bath in the Ganga, they again gathered together in eager anticipation of the story to come. Once again Swami Chidananda took up the tale, this remembrance of his master which had become a tribute far exceeding his original intentions.

"On his return to India," he began, "the delight of Kuppuswami's mother at seeing her son again was short-lived, for he chose to slip away quietly without even having entered the family home. She waited for him, but in vain. Empty-handed, Kuppuswami began to wander in search of God, heading towards the sacred city of Varanasi. His fellow travellers were amazed at his beatific absorption and his apparent unconcern with the comings and goings around him. On arriving in Varanasi, Kuppuswami, now a pilgrim, bathed in the holy Ganga and was blessed with the darshan of Lord Vishwanath. 'O Lord!' he prayed, 'I now take refuge in thee! Guide me in my quest for the truth.' Varanasi, although a holy city, was not the quiet and secluded place which Kuppuswami was seeking and so he continued on his way towards Rishikesh. Leading the life of a mendicant, on some days he went without food, walking mile after mile. But he faced his hardships gladly, grateful for the opportunity to prove his devotion.

"Shortly after his arrival in Rishikesh in March 1924, Kuppuswami met the sadhu who was to initiate him into Sannyasa Dharma, Sri Swami Vishwananda Saraswati, giving him his ochre robe and the name Swami Sivananda Saraswati. His sannyasa initiation rites were performed at the Kailash Ashram by His Holiness Sri Swami Vishnudevanandaji Maharaj. From that moment on, Swami Sivananda dressed to clothe himself, ate to live and lived to serve humanity. A small, dilapidated kutir, not used by others, and infested with scorpions, protected him from rain and sun. He would walk four miles every morning, singing and chanting Om in his ebullient way, for his alms of four rotis and a cup of dal. He practised intense tapasya, observed mouna and often fasted for days together. In the early morning hours he would stand in the icy cold Ganga up to his hips and commence his japa." The disciples shivered in the warm evening sun, knowing how cold this could be.

"Despite this intensive sadhana, Swami Sivananda continued to treat sick pilgrims and mahatmas, believing strongly that realization only comes through selfless service. He visited the huts of sadhus with medicines, served them and massaged their legs. He begged food on their behalf and fed them with his own hands when they fell sick. He brought water from the Ganga and washed their kutirs. Using his savings from Malaya, he provided medicines and printed spiritual leaflets. So famous did he become that the authorities directed visitors to him for darshan, saying, 'He is the only great mahatma and yogi in Swargashram'.

"One of the mahatmas in this neighbourhood, Swami Kalikananda, watched with interest the selfless services rendered by Swami Sivananda and, thinking that the opportunity should not be lost, he approached him with a proposal to run a charitable dispensary. Thus, in 1925, the Satya Sevashram dispensary came into being. Here Swami Sivananda continued to work for others, putting them before himself." "Tell them the story of the pilgrim," interrupted Swami Krishnananda, "they must know to what extent their master's devotion went." "Yes, indeed," continued Swami Chidananda and he told the story to the waiting group.

"One evening a pilgrim en route to Badrinath came to the dispensary for help. Later it occurred to Swami Sivananda that he should have given a different medicine which would have been more helpful. So, early next morning, even before dawn, he took the correct medicine and started at a ready uphill run to catch up with the traveller. When he reached the next halt, he found that pilgrim was an even earlier riser and had already proceeded on his way. Never daunted Swami Sivananda caught up with the pilgrim near the fifth mile and there gave him the medicine."

"Was that back when you joined the dispensary, Swamiji?" asked one listener, knowing that at some point Swami Chidananda had been entrusted with the management of the dispensary. "No, my child," replied Swami Chidananda, "this was many years before I arrived here. I remember being told that during this time, Swamiji refused to accept disciples, claiming himself to be a common sadhu and a friend of all, not a guru. It was only later, after a vision of Lord Krishna requesting him to share the divine nectar that he possessed with all those around him, that he began to teach yoga and meditation. But he never lost his own inner peace, and on days when too many callers posed a threat to his spiritual routine, he would disappear into the rocky ledges of the Ganga or the forests on the Manikoot hill slopes. In deep meditation he questioned his own soul and the truth began to manifest."

Silence descended on the group as they imagined how their guru had been in those days. Just as they were all sinking into their own reveries, Swami Krishnananda began to speak. "Remember," he admonished them, "that your master never forgot others." Knowing that there was a great need for him in the outside world, in 1931 he began to mix with the masses, touring extensively in Uttar Pradesh, Bihar, Punjab, Jammu-Kashmir and Andhra Pradesh. Everywhere he went he delivered fiery speeches, demonstrated asana and pranayama, and conducted ecstatic kirtan. He visited schools and colleges, pouring forth all his energy, and people became devoted to him from all corners of the country. Even the British and those who came to criticize him were inflamed by the passion of his presence and would come to the stage and dance with Swamiji, singing the Lord's name." The listening disciples laughed, amused at this picture of the divine inspiration which Swami Sivanandaji had often caused others to feel.

"For five years he travelled the whole length and breath of India, not only speaking to the people but also visiting important places of pilgrimage in the south, including Rameshwaram near his home town." Krishnananda paused, noted the setting sun and the tired faces of his listeners and decided that, for the moment, they had heard enough. "His work and his energy should be an example to us all," he said. "But do not forget that Swamiji was a God-man and we are but children in comparison. Let us then go to bed, where we can each marvel alone at the stories we have heard this evening." After a short prayer, the disciples dispersed for the night, comforted and consoled for the loss of their master by the tales which his dearest and closest followers were now telling.

MISSION

"Quickly, quickly," urged the young sannyasin who only two days earlier had been overcome with grief, and now skipped nimbly down the steps of the ghat. "If we hurry and are ready early perhaps our storytellers will also come and we shall hear more of the great deeds of our master." Infected by his spontaneous enthusiasm, the others plunged into the waters of the Ganga and within minutes were once again seated in a group, waiting expectantly. Swami Chidananda and Swami Krishnananda walked slowly down the steps, immersed in deep conversation. "Ah!" cried Chidananda looking up to see the welcoming crowd, "I see you are keen and eager to hear the rest of the story. Such enthusiasm shall not be disappointed. Wait for one moment and I shall be with you." And after they too had taken their baths, the two senior sannyasins settled down amidst the group to continue the story.

"The ashram, as you know it now," began Swami Chidananda, "came from very humble beginnings." After

266

Swamiji's tours, be begun to feel the need to establish himself independently in the interests of the spiritual upliftment of the large number of seekers who came to him. And so, in 1934 he and his disciples crossed to the right bank of the Ganga and, finding an old, dilapidated and disused cowshed, they settled down to work, sowing the seeds of the present Divine Life Society.

"The ashram grew very quickly. Devotees soon offered to build kutirs. Materials and workers came streaming in and the humble beginning exploded into a world in miniature. But Swami Sivananda never allowed a pause for consolidation. He kept on pressing for greater and greater service. Hence the ashram suffered from an almost perpetual financial crisis which he encouraged so that the inmates would have to work harder. 'Work, work and work for the welfare of humanity,' was then, as always, his maxim. Once, a shopkeeper in Rishikesh refused to supply provisions unless the earlier balance of Rs.20,800/- was cleared. The secretary swami of the ashram approached Swami Sivananda and pleaded with him to keep only the senior inmates and to send the rest away. Swami Sivananda refused, saying that God had sent them here and he would provide. Miraculously, the next day, an ardent devotee of Swami Sivananda came to the ashram and offered money, exactly the same amount that the ashram owed!"

"If he was so busy, when did Swamiji find time to write all those books we see in the library?" asked one astonished sannyasin. "Heaven knows," interjected Swami Krishnananda, taking over the story line. "You must all have seen how tirelessly and ceaselessly he used to work. But he always considered the gift of knowledge as the greatest gift and sought to share it with others to the maximum extent possible. He started a printing press at the ashram to aid him in this task, and everyone who wrote a letter to him or sent the smallest donation received some leaflet or pamphlet. Whenever he went out on tour, he made sure that spiritual literature was printed for free distribution. Typically,

267

however, he was not satisfied even with this, and with the growth of the ashram he felt that something must be mailed regularly to his correspondents. Thus in September 1938, *The Divine Life*, the monthly magazine of the Divine Life Society was born. Then, in 1939, his first book was published. For more than two decades he had to have his books printed by outside presses. Even after the ashram press was started, it could not cope with all the publications that he wanted undertaken." "Don't you remember," Swami Krishnananda said, turning to Swami Chidananda, "when we arrived, you in 1943, I in 1944, how the press was never shut down, even when there was a financial crisis in the ashram?"

"Oh yes," replied Swami Chidananda, "the speed with which Swamiji brought out books was phenomenal. Generally, he worked on three or four volumes at a time. I think that overall he must have written more than two hundred books, including commentaries on the *Bhagavad Gita*, the principal Upanishads, the *Brahma Sutras*, Patanjali's *Yoga Sutras* and the *Narada Bhakti Sutras*; scores of books on the practice of yoga and on Vedanta, and many volumes on health and vigour. He used every form of literary expression to convey his point to the reader. Poetry and drama, letters and essays, stories and parables, aphorisms and lectures were all adopted by him to spread knowledge of divine life.

"Perhaps you have heard about the All-India-Ceylon Tour which Swamiji undertook in order to bring about a mass awakening and a further dissemination of knowledge. From 9th September to 8th November 1950, Swami Sivananda travelled, addressing hundreds of civic receptions and public gatherings, schools and college students in almost all the important cities and towns. And en route, at every station where the train halted, thousands of devotees had Swamiji's darshan and heard his kirtan. At the end of the tour, when Swamiji returned to the ashram, how proud we were of him and what a warm reception we gave him! The effect of this tour was tremendous. Since then the flow of devotees to the ashram for darshan and guidance from

Swami Sivananda was ever on the increase. Eminent people from all walks of life were drawn towards him."

"Is it true," asked one young devotee, "that he welcomed everyone to the ashram and gave mantra diksha to anyone who asked for it?" "Of course," interposed Chidananda. "Swamiji also gave sannyasa diksha liberally, and I am sure that in India's spiritual history no other saint turned so many into monks. He gave sannyasa to men and to women; to Indians and to foreigners; in person and by post. To some who had worldly responsibilities, he gave mental sannyasa. He coloured their minds. He told them to live in the world, but not be of it. Furthermore, Swami Sivananda did not impose too many rules and restrictions on his disciples. He asked them not to think too much about their body or bread, but to dwell constantly on the all-pervading Brahman. His instructions to all were: Serve, Love, Meditate, Realize."

The disciples nodded in recognition of their master's words. And then one by one they began to voice memories of their own. One spoke of the Yoga Vedanta Forest Academy established in 1948 to give systematic training to the resident sadhakas and visiting seekers. Another praised the way Swamiji had advocated the fundamental unity of all religions, and described the World Parliament of Religions, convened at the ashram in 1953. Gradually, the talk moved closer to the present and the sannyasins reminded one another of how their master had seemed in recent months to know that the end of his life was approaching, and how on the day of his mahasamadhi, he was able to swallow a glassful of Ganga water, having rejected all other food and drink for days.

One inquisitive member of the group turned to Swami Chidananda and asked if he knew what Swami Sivananda's last words had been. Chidananda was quiet for a moment and then, speaking in a voice full of tenderness and love, said, "'Happiness comes when the individual merges in God'. This was his last message to us." The disciples fell silent and calm seemed to descend on their troubled minds.

269

Rishikesh too had subsided into quietness during the long hours of storytelling. Only the stars seemed to be moving, sparkling in the night sky, and for a moment the disciples felt that their master was amongst them, that his love surrounded them and that it would always be so.

Work and establishments

Swami Sivananda founded the Divine Life Trust Society in 1936 with the aims of worldwide dissemination of spiritual knowledge and service to mankind. The ideals of the society were lofty, practical and within the reach of every human being, irrespective of caste, colour, country or creed. It catered to the needs of all people, whatever class they belonged to.

As early as 1936, branches were established at Munger (Bihar), Jangh Maghia (Punjab), Akidu (A.P.), Ambala City (Punjab), Mandya (Mysore) and Madras in India, and at Jaffna in Ceylon, Riga in Latvia and Heidelberg in Germany. Abroad, branches of the Divine Life Society grew in number and strength from year to year, some becoming large and dynamic centres of training such as the Divine Life Society of South Africa (Durban) and the Divine Life Society of Malaysia (Kuala Lumpur).

The Sivananda Publication League was established in 1939 to revive spirituality worldwide through publication of books, journals and pamphlets dealing scientifically with all aspects of yoga and Vedanta. Over the years, all the books authored by Swami Sivananda were published by this organization.

In 1942, the Bhajan Hall opened, and in 1943, the *Akhanda Mahamantra* kirtan (non-stop chanting of the mahamantra around the clock) was commenced in the Bhajan Hall. The Lord Vishwanath Mandir was begun with regular worship three times daily in the same year.

In 1945, the Sivananda Ayurvedic Pharmacy was established to serve the people with genuine herbal preparations.

In the same year, Swami Sivananda organized the World Religions Federation, and in 1947, the All World Sadhus Federation.

The Yoga Vedanta Forest Academy was set up in 1948 to give systematic training to the resident sadhakas and visiting seekers.

The Yoga Vedanta Forest Academy Press was established in 1951, as a means for the wide dissemination of spiritual knowledge.

In 1953, Swami Sivananda convened the World Parliament of Religions at Sivanandashram.

The Charitable Dispensary that had been inseparable from Swami Sivananda ever since the early 1930s grew slowly and in 1950 it was upgraded to a general hospital with X-ray and other facilities. The Sivananda Eye Hospital was opened in 1957.

In 1958, the Sivananda Literature Research Institute was formed in order to have all the works of the master translated and published systematically in all the regional languages of India. In 1959, the Sivananda Literature Dissemination Committee was established, which had regional committees for each regional language.

Thus Swami Sivananda saw the fulfilment of his mission in his own lifetime before he attained mahasamadhi in 1963.

Worldwide awakening

From within the four walls of his small kutir on the banks of the Ganga, Swami Sivananda's influence spread throughout the world. He understood the problems of people living in countries he had never seen and guided them along the spiritual path. The ashram, the inmates, the Divine Life Society and other institutions founded by Swami Sivananda were only instruments for the spiritual awakening of mankind at large. It was not enough for the aspirants who had gathered around him at the ashram to elevate themselves. Swami Sivananda never let them forget for one moment that their own salvation lay in the spiritual awakening of humanity.

271

He distributed so much spiritual literature and deputed so many disciples that yoga became a byword in every nook and corner of the world. By making use of every possible method and every available avenue, he flooded the world with spiritual knowledge. He acquainted thousands with the facts and details of spiritual life. He constantly raised the goal of God-realization before the eyes of the people as the only real purpose of human birth.

His mission was to bring about a needed transformation in mankind, to eradicate the lower qualities and unfold the divinity. This transformation was needed universally, and his mission therefore attracted seeking souls from all walks of life and from every country. He trained many sannyasins of a stupendous calibre, and it would not be an exaggeration to say that on his attainment of mahasamadhi, he verily entered those sannyasins in and through whom he carries on his mission, in a more vigorous manner, even to this day. Notable among his sannyasin disciples are: Swami Chidananda, Swami Krishnananda, Swami Venkatesananda, Swami Vishnudevananda, Swami Satchidananda, Swami Nadabrahmananda, Swami Sivapremananda and Swami Satyananda.

PHILOSOPHY OF SANNYASA

Sannyasa is a life of renunciation. Without perfect renunciation it is impossible to pursue the path of Brahmavidya. The sannyasin is dead to the world and his family. He renounces the whole universe at a stretch and has nothing to do with anything except the one Self. To the sannyasin, name and fame are equal to faecal matter. Therefore, renouncing name and fame he wanders freely.

The sannyasin has only three duties to perform: shaucha, bhiksha and dhyana. There is no fourth duty for a sannyasin. Meditation is his duty, meditation is his food, meditation is his life. He lives meditation, breathes meditation. He is ever intent upon the realization of the supreme Brahman. The sannyasin lives at the height of wisdom, like a fool, like a child. Blossoming with knowledge, he behaves like an idiot. Absorbed in the atman, the sannyasin speaks not a single word.

Qualifications for sannyasa

Sannyasa is open to a brahmachari, a grihastha or a vanaprastha alike. One can take sannyasa either directly from brahmacharya or otherwise one should qualify oneself with sadhana before entering into sannyasa. There should be perfect renunciation born of discrimination. The vairagya, or dispassion, should not be mild and half-hearted. It should be a burning flame of disgust for everything that is seen and not seen. Nothing but the state of *kaivalya*, or final liberation, is to be the ideal of attainment. There should be no desire for wife, children and worldly activity. The sannyasin must be encircled by the fence of dispassion from all sides.

The self-arrogating faculty is to be finally reduced to naught. Love and hatred should be effaced completely. The aspirant must be above the tricks and bondage of samsara. As soon as disgust arises in the mind for all objects of the world, then one should take to sannyasa without any further hesitation.

If you like seclusion, if you are free from raga or passion, worldly ambition, karmic tendencies and attractions of this world, if you are reticent and serene, if you have disciplined yourself while remaining in the world, if you can live on simple food, if you can lead a hard life, if you have a strong constitution, if you are not talkative, if you can remain alone without company and talk, if you have a meditative temperament or reflective nature, if you can bear all the difficulties in the spiritual path, if you can live like an ascetic until the end of your life and if you can bear any amount of insult and injury, then you can take to the path of renunciation. Only then will you be benefited by embracing sannyasa.

You should actually lead the life of a sannyasin for one or two years in the world itself. Otherwise you will find it extremely difficult to tread the path. For a person of dispassion, discrimination and strong will, this path is all joy and bliss. A passionate man should not take sannyasa. A person who takes sannyasa even when he is being overpowered by passion goes to the region of darkness and gloom. That man whose tongue, genital organ, stomach and hands are properly disciplined is fit to take sannyasa.

When women are equipped with the four means of salvation, they are also eligible for sannyasa. They are as efficient as men in the field of spirituality. When one is born with sannyasa samskaras, no force on earth can prevent him or her from taking sannyasa. Even if you keep a hundred guards to prevent such a person from leaving the house, they cannot check him or her.

Young people are also most fit for sannyasa. Young people can practise intense sadhana and tapasya. What can an old man do? When he is about to die, someone will utter the mahavakyas in his ears which have already gone stone-deaf. Of what use is such sannyasa? Sannyasins like Swami Vivekananda, Swami Rama Tirtha, Swami Dayananda, in fact most of the noteworthy sannyasins, renounced the world in their youth.

The role of sannyasins in society

Every religion has a band of anchorites who lead a life of seclusion and meditation. There are bhikkus in Buddhism, fakirs in Mohammedanism, sufis in Sufism, priests in Christianity. The glory of a religion will be absolutely lost if you remove the hermits or sannyasins or those who lead a life of renunciation and divine contemplation. It is these people who maintain and preserve the religions of the world. It is these people who give solace to the householders when they are in trouble and distress. They bring hope to the hopeless, joy to the depressed, strength to the weak and courage to the timid by imparting spiritual knowledge.

Sannyasins live on a few pieces of bread and, in exchange, move from door to door spreading the teachings of Vedanta,

274

the philosophy of realization of Brahman, through the length and breath of the country. The world is indebted to them. Their writings still guide and inspire us. If you study a few slokas of the *Avadhoota Gita*, you will at once be raised to the magnificent heights of divine splendour and glory. Depression, weakness, anxiety and tribulations will vanish.

A real sannyasin is the only mighty potentate on earth. He never takes anything; he always gives. It was only sannyasins who did glorious, sublime work in the past. It is only sannyasins who can work wonders in the present and in the future also. It is only bold sannyasins who have cut off all ties and connections, who are fearless, who are freed from delusion, passion, selfishness, who can do real service to the world. A sannyasin alone can do real *lokasangraha* because he has divine knowledge, and he is a totally dedicated person! One real sannyasin can change the destiny of the whole world. It is the mighty Shankara who established the doctrine of the Kevala Adwaita philosophy. He still lives in our hearts. His name can never be obliterated so long as the world lasts.

Just as there are research scholars or postgraduates in science, psychology, biology, and philosophy, so there should be postgraduate sannyasins who will devote their time to study and meditation, in research of the atman. These postgraduate sannyasins will give the world their experiences and realizations in the spiritual field. They will train students and send them into the world for teaching. It is the duty of the householders and the administration to look after the needs of these sannyasins. In turn these sannyasins will take care of their souls. Thus the whole world will revolve in a smooth manner. There will be peace in the land.

Necessity for sannyasa

I do not believe it when people say that they have given colouring to their hearts. This is timidity and hypocrisy. If there is real internal change, the external change is bound to come. The inner nature will not allow us to keep an opposite nature outside. I do not think that a mere attempt at eradication of egoism, sankalpa and vasana constitutes sannyasa. Progression through the four ashramas is absolutely necessary. Why did sages like Shankara and Sri Ramakrishna take sannyasa? Why did Yajnavalkya take sannyasa, even after realization of Brahman? What is the necessity for this order?

There was no greater karmakandi or follower of the pravritti marga than Mandan Mishra. He was the greatest votary of karma. He had argued with Shankaracharya for days together on the point that sannyasa is not necessary. He wanted to establish that we can attain *mukti*, salvation, by *karma marga*, the path of action, and that *nivritti*, renunciation, is not absolutely essential. But at last, Shankara defeated Mandan Mishra, and Mandan Mishra also became one of the four disciples of Shankara. When such a mighty man became a sannyasin, are we able to say that sannyasa is unnecessary?

Geru and shaven head

The geru colour of the sannyasin indicates that he is as pure as fire itself. He shines like burnished gold, free from all impurities of desires and vasanas. It denotes purity. For the aspirant who has taken to the path of nivritti marga, it is a help. He will swerve and shrink from evil actions. This cloth will remind him that he is not entitled to worldly enjoyments. Gradually his nature will be moulded. This geru-coloured cloth serves as an external symbol to show that one is a sannyasin.

A sannyasin shaves his head completely. This removes all longing for beauty. He will not take much care about dressing his hair with oil, etc. This shows that he has renounced all external beauty and that he dwells in the self which is the beauty of beauties. This *mundan,* or shaving of the head indicates that he is no more of the world. He should not desire any sensual objects. It is only an external symbol of the mental state of complete dispassion for the pleasures of the world.

The mental state

Of course, sannyasa is not only geruing your clothes. Sannyasa is a mental state. He is a veritable sannyasin who is free from passion and egoism and who possesses all the sattwic qualities, even though he lives with the family, in the world. Chudala was a queen yogini-sannyasini, although she ruled a kingdom. That sannyasin who lives in the forest, but whose mind is full of passion, is worse than a householder and a worldly-minded fool. Sikhidhvaja was a worldly man, although he lived naked in the forest for many years.

True renunciation is the renunciation of all passions, desires, egoism and vasanas. If you have a stainless mind, a mind free from attachment, egoism and passion, you are a sannyasin, no matter whether you live in a forest or in the bustle of a modern city, whether you wear white cloth or an orange-coloured robe, whether you shave your head or keep a long tuft of hair.

Someone asked Guru Nanak, "O saint, why have you not shaved your head? You are a sannyasin." Guru Nanak replied, "My dear friend, I have shaved my mind." In fact, the mind should be cleanly shaven. Shaving the mind consists of getting rid of all sorts of attachments, passions, egoism, infatuation, lust, greed, anger, etc. That is the real shaving. External shaving of the head has no meaning if there is internal craving, *trishna*.

Many people have not understood what true renunciation is. Renunciation of physical objects is not renunciation at all. True renunciation lies in the abnegation of the mind. It consists in renouncing all desires and egoism, not worldly existence. The real tyaga consists in the renunciation of egoism or ahamkara, then you have renounced everything else in the world. If the subtle ahamkara is given up, *dehadhyasa,* or identification with the body, automatically goes away.

Sannyasa and Vedanta

Sannyasa and Vedanta go hand in hand. One is not complete without the other. Wherever there is real sannyasa, there is practical Vedanta. Wherever there is practical Vedanta, there must be sannyasa of the highest type. Sannyasa without Vedanta becomes fruitless. Vedanta without sannyasa becomes mere intellectualism. When sannyasa and Vedanta merge into one, there crops up a sage of supreme wisdom.

Sannyasa empties the individual of ego and the negative phenomena, and Vedanta fills one with positive truth. Sannyasa without Vedanta remains empty and does not serve its purpose. Even so, Vedanta without sannyasa becomes essenceless and loses its meaning. Vedanta cannot be grasped without emptying the ego through sannyasa, and sannyasa becomes a waste without getting at the supreme ideal through Vedanta.

Vedanta does not want you to renounce the world. It wants you to change your mental attitude and give up this false illusory I-ness and mineness. If you remove these two poisonous fangs of the mind, then you can allow the mind to go wherever it likes. Then you will have samadhi always. You must renounce *tyaga abhimana*, the pride of renunciation, also. Tyaga abhimana is very deep-rooted. You must renounce the idea: "I have renounced everything. I am a great tyagi." This pride of the sadhus is a greater evil than the pride of householders: "I am a rich man; I am a brahman, etc."

Not by carrying a *danda* (wooden staff), not by shaving the head, not by wearing geru cloth, not by egoistic action, is liberation attained. Wisdom is the sign of a sannyasin. The wooden staff does not make a sannyasin. He is the real sannyasin of wisdom who is conscious of his absolute nature even in his dream, just as he is during the waking period. He is the greatest of Brahma jnanins. He is the greatest of sannyasins.

Swami Satyananda

29

Swami Satyananda

Let me decorate many hearts and paint a thousand faces with colours of inspiration and soft silent sounds of value. Let me be like a child, and run barefoot through the forest of laughing and crying people, giving flowers of imagination and wonder that God gives free.

Shall I fall on bended knees and wait for someone to bless me with happiness and a life of golden dreams? No. I shall run into the desert of life with my arms open, sometimes falling, sometimes stumbling, but always picking myself up, a thousand times if necessary. Often life will burn me; often life will caress me tenderly. Many of my days shall be haunted by complications and obstacles, and there will be moments so beautiful that my soul shall weep in ecstasy.

I shall be a witness, but never shall I run or turn from life, from me. Never shall I forsake myself or the timeless lessons I have taught myself, nor shall I let the value of divine inspiration and being be lost. My rainbow-covered bubble shall carry me further than beyond the horizon's settings, forever to serve, to love and to live as a sannyasin.

Swami Satyananda

DEPARTURE

August 8th 1988 was a normal day at Ganga Darshan. All the sannyasins and inmates of the ashram were busy with their daily duties, opening their departments, sorting through piles of mail, reading proofs, typing manuscripts, packing parcels, teaching classes, attending to the needs of visitors. Nobody was aware that in Sri Niwas, the apartment of Gurudev at the top of the Ganga Darshan complex, destiny was about to completely change the order of their lives.

There was some commotion in Gurudev's apartment, a wave of tension in the air, as he hurriedly packed his two dhotis into a small jhola and called two or three of his younger disciples to issue some last minute instructions. Anybody would have thought that perhaps he was going out for the day as he often did to inaugurate some seminar or program nearby.

A short time later, the clack clack of Gurudev's kharau could be heard moving fast out of the front door of the main building and down the wide road lined with palm trees, leading to the gate. Nobody was around to notice except for a few sannyasins who happened to be working in the garden at that time. At the sound of the kharau, they were on their feet and rushed to pranam Gurudev, as they would normally do, feeling most pleased with themselves for having spotted him on his ashram perambulations. The thought that this would be the last opportunity they would get to touch Gurudev's feet never crossed their minds.

As the disciples hurriedly bent forward to touch his feet, there was the usual smile of encouragement on Gurudev's lips, but his gaze was far off in the future, where the glimpse of some new destiny was about to unfold. Quickly, with folded hands, he dismissed the disciples and proceeded further towards the gate. At that time, unknown to anyone in the ashram, the small metal door at the side of the main gate slowly swung open and Gurudev stepped outside, never to look back.

Days slipped by, then months. Although the sannyasins were totally occupied with their duties, still they began to ponder, "Where is Gurudev? Why has he not come back?" They all knew there were no scheduled programs for him in that month or in the months that followed. Generally he did not travel during September. So where could he be? It was all the more baffling as Gurudev had never stepped out before without at least informing someone. The idea that he had renounced his lifetime's work, as well as his disciples, had not yet occurred to them.

Of course, the writing on the wall had been clear for many years. Had Gurudev not recalled Swami Niranjan from America in 1983 and announced that he would succeed him and take over all his responsibilities. After this, Gurudev had travelled abroad for several years as a 'royal mendicant', returning to Munger only intermittently. Then he had renounced even this and had taken up a semi-reclusive life in the ashram, meeting people only once in fifteen days, once in a month, once in three months. Again and again in satsang he had expressed his wish to renounce the institution and live alone. But still, the sannyasins were not ready to accept all this. Nobody ever suspected that one day Gurudev would actually leave and never come back. It was unimaginable.

So it came as a hard blow to all the disciples and inmates of the ashram when Swami Niranjan finally announced two months later on 8th October 1988 that Paramahamsaji had left the Munger ashram as a parivrajaka, a wandering mendicant, for a pilgrimage of the siddha tirthas in India. He had carried only a single jhola and one hundred and eight rupees, which was the amount given to him by his guru, Swami Sivananda, when he had left Rishikesh. He firmly declined any further assistance. Swami Niranjan also related that, when asked if he would return to Ganga Darshan, Paramahamsaji had clearly stated, "I have no further obligation or attachment with the gurudom of Bihar School of Yoga. The first phase of my mission culminated with the foundation of Ganga Darshan, and the next phase of my mission has begun with my parivrajaka life. Now, wherever I shall visit, it will be in the capacity of a sadhaka and not as a guru."

It took several months for the sannyasins to recover from the impact of this message. Most of them felt as if the sun had gone out of their world. The one who had given so much meaning, purpose and inspiration to their lives was with them no longer. Everyone became very pensive, and disappointment mingled with sadness weighed heavily on the minds of all. Nobody smiled. Every sannyasin was engaged in the same thought, "Why has Gurudev left us?"

Then, in order to lighten their mood, Swami Niranjan used to sit outside on the lawn in the evening, discussing the events of the day, telling stories or playing games with all the sannyasins. On one such evening some sannyasins asked Swami Niranjan, "Although we have lived in the ashram for several years, still we know very little about Gurudev's early life. Please tell us something about his childhood and how he found his guru." Swami Niranjan looked a bit reticent then said, "Yes, the life of Swami Satyananda is an inspiration to us all and it will give me great joy to relate it to you. But first let us all go inside the Jyoti Mandir."

CHILDHOOD

All the sannyasins and inmates of the ashram quickly trooped in and sat down in the cool, quiet atmosphere of the sadhana hall, illumined only by the jyoti in the front, symbolic of Gurudev's divine inspiration since the beginning of his mission. All eyes were riveted on Swami Niranjan as he settled himself and began to speak.

"Gurudev was born in a village of Almora district in the foothills of the Himalayas. In this picturesque atmosphere of rolling green hills, far away from modern civilization, the boy grew up in perpetual satsang, being surrounded not only by the invisible guiding spirits of sages of bygone days, but by living mahatmas and sannyasins. The soil was rich with the spiritual samskaras acquired in previous births through tapasya and renunciation, and the spiritual seed in this birth was sown quite early.

"His parents aptly named him Dharmendra as if they intuitively realized that this boy would one day shine, not only as a resplendent being with the senses under full control (Indra), but as a sovereign whose very being would be filled with dharma. In fact, his mind was shaped and moulded even before he knew it by spiritual influences, so that the young boy's vision itself was different from others, and he did not have to battle with wrong samskaras when he consciously stepped into the arena of life.

"Paramahamsaji's parents were both Hindus. His father belonged to the Arya Samaj, which is a special movement opposed to traditional idol worship. Their daily practices included *havan* (fire ceremony) and chanting of Gayatri and other Sanskrit mantras. His father, Sri Krishna Singh, was a devotee of Shiva and the follower of a guru. His mother was a Gandhian in outlook, being a co-worker of Mahatma Gandhi. She wore only khadi, which she would weave herself. This was a noted characteristic of the Sarvodaya movement in which she was active.

"Paramahamsaji's family were kshatriyas and landowners. They had several villages and large numbers of livestock including ponies, sheep, goats and cattle. His father, by profession, was a police inspector for the British administration while his mother, being a patriot, participated in the Satyagraha movement as a humble volunteer. Thus what usually happened was that the father arrested the mother, sent her to jail, then released her after some time, and both lived together again at home with their opposing political views.

"Even as a small boy, Paramahamsaji was very responsible and hardworking. He managed his family estates and properties from the age of eight as his father used to be on duty and his mother was either in jail or out working for the freedom movement, so she never had any time for household work. This made him practical and independent and gave him managerial skills, which he was later able to put into excellent use as a spiritual leader and founder of an international yoga movement."

"It seems to me," remarked one of the swamis, "that from both sides, the stern disciplinarian father and the patriotic, revolutionary mother, Paramahamsaji received the qualities which would later take him so far in his life as a spiritual leader and as an ascetic."

"Yes, but what about his spiritual development?" asked another swami, "Were there any particular events or experiences in his early life which led him to the path of renunciation and indicated his brilliant future?"

"From the stories which Gurudev has told," replied Swami Niranjan, "we can assume that from early childhood he was spiritually inclined. Regarding his mission and the founding of Ganga Darshan, I can remember him telling me that as a small boy of five, he used to draw and build a seven-storey building, saying that it was his. He used to dream of travelling in planes to far off places.

"When he was six years old, he began to have spontaneous experiences where he lost all consciousness of the body. When he was ten years old, the same thing happened. His father had no understanding of these strange lapses which his young son experienced from time to time. These were unusual experiences which can be defined as disembodiment, where the *chetana*, or consciousness, sees the body as something apart from itself, as a *sakshi* or witness. However, yogis passing through his village described them as a spiritual state which they called 'samadhi', but being a small boy, Paramahamsaji had no control over this state. They advised that the young boy should undergo spiritual training, and so from that time onwards his spiritual life began.

"After this his father would take him to meet sannyasins or saints who were passing through the area. He also encouraged him to study all the spiritual texts such as the

Bhagavad Gita, Ramayana, Mahabharata, Bible, Koran, etc. Even at this early age Paramahamsaji's comprehension of such lofty topics was remarkable and, being gifted with a photographic memory, he was able to learn many of the difficult Sanskrit texts by heart.

"Around this time, Anandamayi Ma, an enlightened lady saint, was touring in the area. Paramahamsaji's father decided to take his young son to meet her in order to ask her advice regarding his mysterious out-of-the-body experiences. She also told his father that the boy was not suffering from any kind of possession or mental aberration, but that due to his positive samskara, his spirit had begun to awaken spontaneously. She placed her hand on Parama-hamsaji's back and blessed him saying, 'Do kirtan, become a saint and a sannyasin'."

"After such experiences," asked one of the swamis, "what sort of education did Gurudev receive? Did he exhibit any special gifts during his student days?"

"About his formal education," Swami Niranjan replied, "we know that he was sent to a convent school in Nainital and thereafter to the government Intermediate College in Almora. He was an extremely bright student with an innate talent for language and literature. He soon acquired such a mastery over Hindi, Sanskrit and English that he could spontaneously compose beautiful and inspiring poems which floated to him as if from on high, and they were almost always mystical and highly spiritual.

"Paramahamsaji published his poems in several school journals and they always created an uproar. People could not believe that such beautiful and uplifting poems had been written by a mere school boy. Later, Paramahamsaji began editing his own journal which he called *Bharat*. Once, when the renowned poet Sumitranandan Pant came to Almora, Paramahamsaji showed him his journals. He admired Paramahamsaji's work and said of him, 'This boy will definitely make great contributions in the field of literature.'

285

"Paramahamsaji wrote in Sanskrit as well as in Hindi, and at one time he was even thinking of publishing a journal in English as well. However, his mind was not on his other studies. During the periods of algebra and geometry, he used to sit on the last bench in the class and write poems or correct stories and articles for the journal. He showed that if he liked a subject he could master it in no time, acquiring greater brilliance than his masters, but what he did not like, no one could make him learn.

"That was, however, only one of the many signs of inner awakening in the young man. His spiritually illumined soul refused to accept life as others do. The boy began to question life itself and discovered many idiosyncrasies. Hence, viveka, discrimination, slowly gained strength and percolated deeper."

At this point one of the sannyasins asked, "Swami Satyananda was always regarded as one of the leading exponents in the field of tantra. Were there any particular incidents in his childhood which may have awakened his interest in this subject?"

"Yes," Swami Niranjan replied, nodding his head, "I can think of several important incidents. I can remember one story that he told us about an experiment he had done with shmashan sadhana when he was about twelve years old. It seems that he had met a tantric yogi who advised him to bring the ashes of a dead body and chant a certain mantra over them, so he started doing it. In the night he would go to the burial ground and practise this sadhana along with some other things which he had learned from the tantric yogi.

"One day, however, his father found out what he was doing. Being an Arya Samaji, he never believed in these things, nor did he approve of such rituals. He told Paramahamsaji to stop these practices or else he would throw him out of the house. But Paramahamsaji had been instructed that he must finish that round of practice. He had already practised for about twenty-five days and he had

286

fifteen more days to go in order to complete the round. So he brought the ashes of the dead body from the burial ground in a clay pot and hid it on the terrace of his house.

"At night, when everybody was asleep, he would go up to the terrace and do all the mantra chanting and invocations. One night his father was awakened from sleep by the sound of chanting and pounding on the roof, as though someone was up there dancing. His father thought that it must be thieves, so he got out his rifle and went up to investigate. Not finding anyone on the roof, he went back to bed, only to be disturbed again by the renewed sound of dancing on the roof.

"He went up and inspected the roof a second time and again found nobody. By this time he began to think that some funny business was going on there, so he called Paramahamsaji and asked him what was happening. Paramahamsaji acted like an innocent fellow and said that he did not know anything about it. However, in the morning, when his father went up to the terrace to inspect it again, he found the pot of ashes and put two and two together. He was terribly angry by this time and flung the pot as far away as he could, scattering the ashes to the wind."

"What a precocious boy," said one of the swamis, "I bet he was disappointed."

"Yes," Swami Niranjan replied, "this turn of events disappointed Paramahamsaji because he wanted to know how to handle this particular experience by himself. This began a new relationship between the father and son. At this point the idea of sannyasa came into his mind. He decided not to lead the usual type of life, but to dedicate himself totally to the discovery of that experience, and to informing people that this experience exists and can be realized by everyone."

"Did Paramahamsaji continue to explore the practices of tantra and yoga after that?" one of the swamis asked.

"I think it was an ongoing process for him," replied Swami Niranjan. "At the age of fifteen, while still at school,

Paramahamsaji started practising kundalini yoga, which gave him some deeper understanding. Around this time he had another experience. He was sitting quietly when suddenly, without any effort, his mind turned inwards. He immediately saw the whole earth with its oceans, continents, mountains and rivers crack into pieces. He did not understand this vision until a few days later when news came that the Second World War had broken out. This experience really made him begin to wonder."

"Did the coming and going of these visionary experiences worry Paramahamsaji?" asked one of the swamis. "After all, he was still a young boy."

"He definitely wanted to know more about them and he read many books, from hypnotism to Vivekananda, searching for some answers. Then one day he happened to meet a swami passing by on his way to Mount Kailash. His name was Nityananda. He mentioned his condition of uncontrollable lapses into unconsciousness to him. Swami Nityananda also told him that this was not an illness but an altered state of consciousness. He recommended that Paramahamsaji practise meditation and taught him how. The form of meditation he taught him was laya yoga or suspension of thought. But the state beyond this, he said, could only be achieved with the help of a guru."

"Did Swami Nityananda become Paramahamsaji's guru?" asked one of the sannyasins. "No," Swami Niranjan replied, "but he showed him the path. Paramahamsaji began his sadhana at home through Nityananda's inspiration between the years 1938 and 1940."

"Were there any more yogis or renunciates who influenced Paramahamsaji during the years before he left home?" asked a swami.

"Yes," Swami Niranjan said, "when Paramahamsaji was eighteen or nineteen, Sukhman Giri, a sannyasin from Nepal, came to stay on his estate. She was a renunciate, belonging to one of the tantric sects. Although totally illiterate, she was nevertheless deeply spiritual with complete mastery over the esoteric aspects of tantra. She taught Paramahamsaji much about the secrets of tantra and gave him profound experiences. Under her guidance he began to explore the dimensions of consciousness and he had many inner illuminations. At the time of her departure she told him to search further for a master with greater control over the unconscious mind."

"Paramahamsaji certainly had some remarkable experiences as a young boy," exclaimed one of the swamis. "Yes," said another, "but how did the turning point come, when he actually left home in search of a guru?"

"Even as a young boy," Swami Niranjan replied, "Paramahamsaji knew very well that family life was not for him. He always wanted to live alone and wander alone. He never wanted anyone to protect him, help him or sympathize with him. Neither did he care for money, property or friends. So really, the only way left for him was sannyasa. By the time he was seventeen, Paramahamsaji was asking questions which nobody could answer. He wondered about things, like the difference between perception and experience. He talked about such topics with his maternal uncle and his sister, but this did not quench his thirst, and he knew that he would have to go out and discover the answers for himself."

"You mentioned Paramahamsaji's sister," said one of the swamis. "Can you tell us anything about her? It seems she was one of the few people he was able to confide in."

"Yes," said Swami Niranjan, "he had one sister of whom he was very fond, and four brothers. It seems that he had little in common with any of his brothers, but he and his sister had similar temperaments and natures. Whenever they were together, they thought about doing things which involved revolution, social service and spiritual transformation. But one thing bothered him greatly. His sister wanted to take sannyasa and the Hindu religion would not permit this. So she became a Christian nun. Then an unexpected event occurred which was a turning point in Paramahamsaji's life. His sister died suddenly in 1942. Soon after her death the idea of leaving home became uppermost in Paramahamsaji's mind."

"Perhaps," mused one of the female sannyasins in the group, "that is why Gurudev was one of the first spiritual leaders to initiate female sannyasins and to encourage them to lead a life of total dedication and renunciation."

"Yes, definitely," Swami Niranjan said. "It was not long after his sister's death that Paramahamsaji left home and went in search of a guru. He was just nineteen years old at that time. Before leaving home, he informed his father of his intentions. His father replied, 'You have made the right choice. If I had not indulged in other activities, perhaps I would be on the same path. But do not tell your mother about your departure, because she may try to block your way.' His father gave him ninety rupees and saw him off at the bus stop. The last advice he gave to his son was, 'Do not write letters, do not look back and do not retrace your steps.'"

"So, Paramahamsaji never returned to his home again after that, not even for a visit?" asked a sannyasin.

"No, never," replied Swami Niranjan, "and now it is getting late so we must end this session. But we will meet again tomorrow and I will tell you about Gurudev's life with Swami Sivananda."

GURU SEVA

In the evening after dinner, all the sannyasins and inmates of the ashram quickly made their way to the Jyoti Mandir for the continuation of Gurudev's life story. After they were all seated, Swami Niranjan entered the hall and took his seat in front of the jyoti. There was pin-drop silence as he closed his eyes and began to intone the shantipath. After the chanting, he resumed the narrative, while the sannyasins listened with rapt attention.

"Paramahamsaji left home in 1943 and took a train to Udaipur. He was just following his unconscious inspiration,

290

without a particular aim or direction. After wandering about for a while, he reached an ashram where a sadhu who was a master of Kaula tantra lived. Paramahamsaji stayed with him for six months and learned more about the theoretical aspect of tantra. After that he wandered about in Rajasthan and Gujarat, often in the company of saints and sages. Being full of knowledge and spiritual light, he was often requested to stay on by the acharyas of the different maths which he visited. Sometimes they even offered to make him their successor if he would remain there. But his purpose was different, and so he moved on from one ashram to another, until he reached Rishikesh.

"In Rishikesh, Paramahamsaji first stayed at the Kali Kamliwala Kshetra for a few days. There he met a man from Almora who directed him to Kailash Ashram where he met the Mahamandaleshwar Sri Vishnudevanandaji. He did not initiate Paramahamsaji, but advised him to go to Swami Sivananda. Upon hearing his guru's name, Paramahamsaji was filled with peace and he felt as if he had found his real home. So he immediately set out for Sivanandashram which was only about two kilometres away. He arrived there on the morning of 19th March 1943, walked up the stairs and entered the Bhajan Hall where kirtan was going on. The vibration which he felt in that hall was the most divine atmosphere he had ever experienced.

"Paramahamsaji was met there by Swami Narayan, who was the vice-president of the Divine Life Society, and then taken to meet Swami Sivananda. When asked by Swami Sivananda why he had come, Paramahamsaji said that he was a spiritual seeker searching for a guru. He also explained that during meditation practice he was able to reach a point of *shoonya*, or mental vacuity, but was not able to go beyond that. At that time Swami Sivananda instructed him, 'Live in the ashram, work hard, and have absolute faith in God.' On that day, Paramahamsaji's search for a guru came to an end."

"What sort of influence did Swami Sivananda have on Paramahamsaji, and what kind of life did he lead after that?" asked one of the young swamis who had been following the narrative intently.

"Paramahamsaji had practised yoga and meditation before coming to Swami Sivananda," replied Swami Niranjan. "The early spiritual experiences which he had had were very powerful and allowed him to reach a point of meditation far beyond the mind. Not only once but many times he had crossed the barriers of the mind and gone beyond his own ego and consciousness. Still, the things he was searching for were not in sight. He had not been able to arrive at any real understanding of his experiences until he came to Swami Sivananda.

"Swami Sivananda's influence was spontaneous and total. At the first glimpse of him Paramahamsaji realized that Swami Sivananda was his guru. He did not have to assess him, he did not have to decide whether to stay with him or not. In Swami Sivananda's presence, Paramahamsaji's analytical mind became stilled, and his heart was awakened. He experienced surrender for the first time in his life, not that surrender of prostrating before a man, but total, unconditional surrender of the ego and intellect. Under the guru's guidance, his consciousness underwent a process of metamorphosis. His whole attitude was completely changed."

"What was the Rishikesh ashram like in those days?" asked the swami who was sitting nearest to Swami Niranjan. "It must have been very different to what it is today."

"Yes, definitely," replied Swami Niranjan. "At that time, the ashram at Rishikesh was in the early stages of development and no amenities were available there as you find nowadays. The whole ashram was surrounded by forest and there were plenty of mosquitoes, scorpions, serpents and monkeys. The Ganga, in which all the swamis bathed early in the morning, was very cold. There were no toilets; one had to walk a mile to find a suitable place in the nearby forest. The ashram life was so different and so difficult that it kept Paramahamsaji constantly alert and aware. It developed in him a strong body and mind, and a total

292

dedication to guru. At times it was so hard that he had to awaken his prana just to survive."

"What about karma yoga?" asked one of the younger swamis. "Paramahamsaji must have done plenty of that!"

"Yes," Swami Niranjan replied, "during his years with Swami Sivananda, Paramahamsaji did not have any time to study hatha yoga, raja yoga, bhakti yoga, tantra, Upanishads, Vedanta, Gita or Ramayana. From dawn to dusk and sometimes during the night as well, he worked and worked and worked and worked. He worked like a donkey because his guru had given him just one command: "Work hard, then you will be purified. You don't have to bring the light; the light is within you.'

"So, for twelve years he lived a transcendental life which was above time and space, and worked as one possessed by guru's grace. He did everything from cleaning the toilets to managing the ashram. He worked so hard he completely forgot himself in karma yoga. He never knew that he was working. He used to feel as if work was relaxation. And during those years he never suffered from mental turmoil. Even if something troublesome was inside, it never dared to raise its head. His one watchword in life was service to guru, without any motive and without any expectation. This was his passion, his joy and his pleasure."

"What was the procedure for taking sannyasa in those days?" asked one of the swamis. "Was it compulsory to undergo a period of training first or did Paramahamsaji take sannyasa straight away?"

"Generally, the sadhakas living in the ashram who were unmarried were given brahmacharya diksha as a preliminary to sannyasa," Swami Niranjan replied. "Seeing a high calibre of spiritual aspiration in Paramahamsaji, Swami Sivananda initiated him into the order of brahmacharya in 1945 and renamed him Satyachaitanya, but he always called him Satyam."

"Then after working hard for a couple of years and living the life of a brahmachari, Satyam suddenly got the idea that for self-realization, sannyasa was not necessary. He reasoned that anyone could attain moksha whether he had a wife or not, children or not, whether he was a householder, a brahmin or non-vegetarian. So, without telling anyone, he applied for a job as a sub-editor to a newspaper in Lahore. After receiving a letter of acceptance, he went to Swami Sivananda and told him of his intention.

"Swami Sivananda said, 'Oh, now you are going!' You have lived in the ashram for several years and you have done a lot of work, constructed so many buildings, printed books, managed all the departments – kitchen, office, accounts and press. So, before going, we will give you a farewell party which will be arranged in one week's time.' Satyam said, 'All right,' and then he began to prepare for his departure.

"One week later, on the morning of 12th September 1947, Swami Sivananda called Satyam and said, 'Get yourself ready, you are going to take sannyasa. Your destiny is sannyasa. You do not have to worry about self-realization. You have a mission to accomplish.' The barber was already there. The geru dhotis were ready. The acharya who chanted the mantras for sannyasa was waiting nearby. Everything was prepared. Satyam looked around him and said, 'But you were going to give me a farewell party.' 'Yes,' Swami Sivananda replied, 'farewell to the old and welcome to the new.'

"So, on the occasion of Swami Sivananda's Diamond Jubilee Birthday, Satyam was given Paramahamsa sannyasa and renamed Swami Satyananda Saraswati, a name which denotes his inner nature more than any biographical sketch could. Into his affectionate heart, cosmic love came to dwell. Into his searching eyes entered equal vision. His questioning mind questioned itself out of existence, and in its place Swami Satyananda realized the Truth, the substratum of all being. At the time of his initiation, as an indication of his future, Swami Sivananda said to him, 'You are serving here as a part of your training. However, even as the saplings of a tree are removed and planted elsewhere so shall be your destiny be.'

"After his sannyasa initiation, Paramahamsaji remained in Rishikesh for many more years, serving his guru. He became a pillar of the Divine Life Society. As a sannyasin, he touched guru seva at the greatest number of points. He washed his guru's clothes, cooked for him, attended upon his guests, served as his private secretary, typed his manuscripts, translated his books into Hindi, looked after the Publication League, supervised the printing of books outside, established and managed the ashram printing press, worked as the mandir poojari, and thundered forth his divine life message during tours, seminars and conventions.

"In spite of all this work, Swami Satyananda remained entirely detached mentally and was a supreme example of karma yoga in every respect. He did everything very well and then offered it to guru. Therefore, he was ever cool, introspective and contemplative. He had the knack of getting work done. He was original in his thought, speech and methods of work, but he was not proud or vain. He had one-pointed application to any task which he undertook. His needs were few, and even those he was ready to renounce at any moment. He was humble and simple, but fearless. He loved everyone but he calmly bore any criticism. He was an all-rounder and an ideal sannyasin."

"Please tell us some stories of Swami Satyananda's life with his guru," asked one of the young swamis who had been listening most intently.

"Ah," said Swami Niranjan, "there are many beautiful stories like that, but I remember one which relates to obedience. Swami Satyananda was very fond of visiting different pilgrimage places such as Kedar, Badri, Gangotri, Yamunotri and Haridwar, especially on the occasion of the Kumbha Mela when thousands of sadhus and devotees gather for a dip in the sacred Ganga. But Swami Sivananda always disapproved of his going and on such days he would give him extra work to do in order to keep him in the ashram. However, not wishing to be thwarted, Swami Satyananda would stay up all night in order to complete the work assigned by his guru and then set off in the early morning for the mela.

"On one such occasion, after arriving in Haridwar he had been trapped in the surging throngs. While moving en masse towards the river, suddenly his upper cloth slipped off and he was unable to retrieve it. As the crowd arrived at the riverbank, he was pushed and jostled into the water. While dipping, his bottom dhoti got stuck under somebody's feet and was quickly carried away by the current. After this, as he tried to regain his footing and return to the river bank, in the rush the upper end of his loin cloth came untied and before he could even reach for it, it was gone. In such an enormous crowd, on a cold winter's morning, how could he remain in the water for long? He thought of joining the group of naga sadhus passing by but his mind was very disturbed.

"After passing some time in this distressful plight, he spotted someone amongst the jostling crowds whom he knew from Rishikesh. Slowly he made his way towards his friend, hoping that no one would notice his nakedness. Fortunately, his friend was able to give him some cloth to cover himself, and feeling much relieved, he quickly made his way back to Rishikesh. When he reached the ashram, Swami Sivananda was standing at the gate. 'Well, Satyam,' he said, 'shall I give you some cloth?'"

"As Swami Sivananda was a medical doctor," asked one swami, "did he expect his disciples to serve the sick also?"

"Oh yes," Swami Niranjan replied, "his sannyasins were always on call to sweep, clean and wash the rooms and clothes of the sick, to feed them and even to massage their feet. Swami Sivanandaji used to say that there was no better way than this to erase the ego."

"What are some other lessons which Swami Satyananda learned from his guru?" asked the swamis.

"There were so many," replied Swami Niranjan, "I'm sure they would fill a book. But as we are all sannyasins, I will tell you about the time when Swami Sivananda taught him about tyaga. You see, Swami Satyananda had always been a tyagi, even in his childhood, but tyaga is not so easy to practise. He was not the type of babu sadhu that we find in many ashrams today. You know, the types who dress very well and keep all manner of things in their rooms. In his room he kept only one chowki. There was no mattress, no blanket, no mosquito net, no glass, no water pot. In fact, his room was absolutely empty, he did not even lock it.

"One day Swami Sivananda went around to visit the rooms of all the swamis. When he came to Swami Satyananda's room, he looked around it and asked, 'Is this all you have?' Swami Satyananda thought that his guru would be very happy to see that his room was absolutely empty, but instead Swami Sivananda said, 'From now on, you must keep a few glasses, a kerosene stove, some tea and sugar, a few blankets and mattresses in your room, so that if any guest arrives in the night, you can give him something.'

"This was another definition of tyaga that Swami Satyananda learned from his guru. From that time he remained totally detached, even though he kept many things in his room because he was keeping them for the sake of others. He was not keeping them for his own enjoyment or satisfaction. In the course of time, his room became a place for everybody. All the sick people in the ashram would go there to drink tea. If somebody had malaria, they would go to his room for medicine. If money was needed, one was sure to get that also. This is another view of sannyasa."

"What about the spontaneous spiritual experiences that Paramahamsaji used to have in his childhood?" asked one of the swamis. "Did these experiences keep coming?"

"Yes," replied Swami Niranjan, "they continued to come and go with far greater intensity. I remember him telling me about an experience he had while sitting on the banks of the Ganga late one night after completing his duties as night watchman. He was thinking of some mundane affairs when his mind spontaneously started going in and in. Suddenly he felt as if the earth was slipping from under him and the sky was expanding and receding. A moment later, he experienced a terrible force springing from the base of his spine like an atomic explosion. He felt that he was vibrating very fast; the light currents were terrific. He experienced the supreme bliss, like the climax of a man's desire, and it continued for a long time. His whole body was contracting until the feeling of pleasure become quite unbearable, and finally he lost complete awareness of his body.

"This was the third time it had occurred. With the first experience he didn't know what had happened, with the second experience came the awakening of his fantastic photographic memory and with the third came complete and total awareness of vairagya. After returning to consciousness, he was listless for many days. He could not eat, sleep, move or even go to the toilet. He saw everything but nothing registered. The bliss was a living thing within him and he knew that if he moved, this wonderful feeling would cease. He would lose the intensity of it all. How could he move when bells were ringing inside? This was the awakening of his kundalini.

"After a week or so he returned to normal and then he started to study the deeper aspects of tantra and yoga. He practised hatha yoga in order to purify his entire system, then he began to re-explore the fantastic science of kundalini yoga. What was this power which awakens in mooladhara chakra? His interest was aroused and he put much effort into trying to understand this marvellous force."

"How interesting," exclaimed one of the swamis. "Now we can begin to understand how Swami Satyananda became such a great exponent of kundalini yoga and tantra."

"I would like to know," said another swami, "if Swami Satyananda was fond of kirtan because he certainly sings very well."

"Oh yes," Swami Niranjan replied. "In Sivanandashram from 1943 onwards, *akhanda kirtan*, unbroken kirtan, was going on twenty-four hours a day, day in and day out. The Maha Mantra 'Hari Rama, Hari Rama, Rama Rama, Hari Hari, Hari Krishna, Hari Krishna, Krishna, Krishna, Hari,

Hari' was repeated in the Bhajan Hall before two burning lamps. In the beginning there were only four or five swamis to conduct the kirtan and Swami Satyananda had to do kirtan sometimes for six or eight hours a day continuously. Once he relieved all his gurubhais and sat down in the Bhajan Hall from morning to evening singing the mantra. He had a very nice experience while doing that and afterwards when he went to his room and lay down, he felt wide-awake. He tried to simply be aware of his body, but instead of experiencing his physical body, he experienced the body made of light particles. That experience continued all night."

"Was there ever any thought that Swami Satyananda would succeed his guru, as you have succeeded him?" asked one of the swamis.

"Swami Satyananda's association with his guru was very deep," replied Swami Niranjan. "During the days when he lived in the ashram at Rishikesh, he was innocent as a child and Swami Sivananda took great care of him. Swami Sivananda never wished to part with Swami Satyananda, but for the good of humanity he did so, knowing that his disciple had a great destiny which had to be fulfilled. Swami Sivananda used to say, 'To keep Swami Satyananda here would be like trying to accommodate an elephant in a tiny match box.' In a tribute to his beloved disciple, Swami Sivananda wrote, 'Few would have such vairagya at such a young age. Swami Satyananda is full of the nachiketas element. Yet any work that he takes up, he will complete in a perfect manner. He does the work of four people and yet never complains. He is a versatile genius and a linguist too. Yet he is humble and simple, an ideal sadhaka and nishkama sevak.'"

"Please tell us one thing more," asked a swami. "When did Swami Satyananda finally depart from his guru's ashram?"

"Swami Satyananda served in his guru's ashram for the traditional period of twelve years, from 1944 to 1956. After this period, he went to Swami Sivananda to tell him he was going. Swami Sivananda gave him one hundred and eight rupees and told him he could go. Then he called him into his room and gave him instructions on a very old tantric practice, kriya yoga. It took hardly seven or eight minutes for Swami Satyananda to learn all the kriyas. Before his departure, Swami Sivananda just looked at him for several minutes, and when he bent to touch his guru's feet, at once the thought came into his mind very clearly, 'Find a mission for yourself.'

"With that, Swami Satyananda's ashram life came to a close. Now we must end this session, but we will continue tomorrow evening. Please get ready for shantipath." As the vedic mantras were intoned, each sannyasin was thinking about the life of Gurudev.

> *When a sannyasin is denounced,*
> *He does not defend himself,*
> *When he is criticized,*
> *He does not clarify himself.*
> *When he is hit,*
> *He does not retaliate.*
> *He considers praise and respect*
> *As maya, which is false, not true.*
>
> *The property, disciples and followers*
> *That the sannyasin receives*
> *Do not belong to him.*
> *He has no right to enjoy*
> *Money, name and fame.*
> *Ashrams that are given to him*
> *Are not meant for his gratification.*
>
> *Everything the sannyasin has is in trust.*
> *Once the sankalpa is made before guru:*
> *"I give my life to sannyasa,"*
> *The money, property, intelligence*
> *And whatever faculties he possesses*
> *Are no longer to be used for himself,*
> *But for the upliftment of others.*

Swami Satyananda

PARIVRAJAKA LIFE

The sun was just about to set, spreading its last rays like molten gold over the Ganga, as the sannyasins assembled in the sadhana hall to hear the continuation of Paramahamsaji's life story. On this evening, Swami Niranjan entered the hall, followed by Swami Dharmashakti who seated herself by his side. After closing his eyes, he began intoning the Om mantra. When the chanting was completed, he opened his eyes and began to speak. "Until now I have been narrating the story of Paramahamsaji's life. However, we have come to the part where Swami Dharmashakti has first-hand knowledge, as she spent many years in his service and company during this period. So she will narrate this part of the tale."

With this brief introduction, Swami Dharmashakti began to speak. "After twelve years of dedicated service and hard work for his guru, Paramahamsaji left his guru's ashram and mission for the life of a wandering ascetic. The parting words of his guru were, 'Go and spread the message of yoga from door to door and from shore to shore.' So, in April 1956, Swami Satyananda, glowing in the light of the wisdom imparted by his guru, set out. For nine years he moved all over the Indian subcontinent, travelling by foot, bullock cart, train and any other means available. In the course of his wandering, he did not view the social condition with the eyes of an ordinary person, but with the vision of a seer.

"From Rishikesh, he first went to Delhi, where he conducted yoga classes and satsang for two months. While in Delhi, some devotees invited him to visit Rajnandgaon. He arrived there in June and within a few days had won over the hearts of all the people. Before departing for Benaras two months later, Paramahamsaji decided to make Rajnandgaon his base. While he was wandering, letters could be directed to him there and the devotees would chalk out his programs.

"In November, Paramahamsaji returned to Rajnandgaon, held a few satsangs and proceeded to Amravati. After

301

conducting programs there, people from Durg, Raipur, Bhilai, Shakti and Rewa organized programs for him. His discourses were written up by the local newspapers, which gave his teachings more publicity. From Rewa, Paramahamsaji returned to Rajnandgaon, and decided to visit Bhagalpur in March, followed by Gangotri and Yamunotri in May. Then he resumed his wandering.

"In March 1957, after a visit to Jabalpur, he went to Bhagalpur at the request of some devotees whom he had known from his Rishikesh days. From Bhagalpur he went on to Aara, Chapra, Muzaffarpur and Munger, where he visited Karna Chaura, the site of Ganga Darshan, feeling intensely drawn to the place as if by some invisible force. In mid-May, Paramahamsaji left Bihar for Delhi, enroute to Gangotri."

"Did Paramahamsaji face many difficulties during his wanderings?" asked one of the swamis.

"Yes," Swami Dharmashakti replied. "He often faced difficulties, but he would always remain cheerful. On most occasions the only familiar person would be the sponsor. The rest would all be strangers, who often argued and made fun. However, one meeting would suffice to transform these people.

"Paramahamsaji never accepted gifts from anyone. If someone put money at his feet, he would distribute it among children. He carried a simple jhola, containing two dhotis, one kurta, one chadar, toothbrush and paste. If someone presented clothes, he would give them to the poor. He would walk on foot from one village to another and sleep under trees. The poor people sometimes gave him some simple fruits or a bowl of milk. The rich generally gave him harsh words.

"Once he was roaming about in a town which he had never visited before. Feeling tired and hungry, he approached the shopkeeper of a large shop and said, 'Hari Om.' The shopkeeper replied, 'Go away. Find someone else to feed you. A young man begging, have you no shame? Learn to work.' His devotees would be very upset to hear about such treatment, but Paramahamsaji being unmoved by both praise and blame, would just laugh.

"Sometimes while travelling from village to village by foot, Paramahamsaji would go into the interior of the jungle and stay with the *adivasis*, tribal people, who considered him as a god just descended from heaven. Ordinarily the adivasi diet consisted of rats, snakes and crabs, but for Paramahamsaji they would buy flour from the market and bake round balls of dough over a fire. In the evening they would all assemble and Paramahamsaji would talk to them about Rama and Krishna, and they would sing kirtan and bhajan. Thus he was at ease in both huts and palaces."

"Was Paramahamsaji travelling more or less continuously at this time?" asked one of the swamis.

"Yes," replied Swami Dharmashakti. "He would only stop in one place for a few days in order to conduct a program and then move on. After leaving Bihar, he travelled to Delhi and up to Rishikesh where he met Swami Sivananda and received his blessing. From there he proceeded to Gangotri on foot. After a forty-five day, two hundred and seventy mile journey, Paramahamsaji returned to Rishikesh and gave his guru the water brought from Gangotri. Afterwards he toured Haridwar, Delhi, Mathura, Vrindavan and Agra. Then he proceeded to Amar Nath via Jammu, Kashmir and Vaishnav Devi. From there he proceeded to Rewa.

"In Raipur, workers of the Bharat Sewak Samaj requested him to help educate the villagers of that area, who were extremely backward. During the monsoon season, Paramahamsaji would often tour for miles in a day with the workers, moving from village to village in wet mud, meeting the people. In two months he toured sixty villages. Often it rained and he would get wet, but he still continued to move about regardless of the weather or the inconvenience.

"In the spring of 1958, Paramahamsaji conducted a yoga camp at Amarkantak on the banks of the Narmada.

Afterwards he travelled through Rewa to Benaras, Rishikesh, Badrinath and Kedarnath. Then he went to Rameshwar and many nearby places. In July he proceeded to a village called Farhad where he stayed for chaturmas, the rainy season. In November he returned to Rajnandgaon for a yoga conference. After the conference, he established the Mahila Yoga Mandala and began a monthly bulletin of twelve pages called *Divya Jeevan Sandesh*. Then he left for Bombay. In December he went to Burhanpur, then to Indore, Khamgaon and back to Rajnandgaon.

"While travelling, he would send copies of his discourses to his devotees in Rajnandgaon who would file them and also publish them in the newspapers. There were also many letters to be answered and programs to be arranged. Whenever he had time, he would go through the files, answer the letters and compile the lectures into books for publication. By 1959 his work had really started expanding."

"Paramahamsaji must have encountered many different kinds of people in the course of his travels," said one of the swamis. "Yes," Swami Dharmashakti replied. "Once Parama-hamsaji was invited to visit a village in Rewa by the younger brother of a dacoit, who used to terrorize all the villagers and steal their belongings. When Paramahamsaji arrived at the village, the dacoit was very angry to see him there, but when he heard that his younger brother had invited him, then he asked Paramahamsaji to stay for one day.

"The next day when Paramahamsaji was about to leave the village, the dacoit asked him to stay on for another day. Paramahamsaji said, 'If I stay, there will have to be satsang, but nobody will come here. We will have to hold the satsang at the crossroads.' The dacoit was determined to invite everyone in the village to the satsang, although the people were so frightened of him that the women would not come out into their own courtyards even in broad daylight, girls would not go to school and everyone carried pistols.

"The dacoit was a transformed man. He kept Parama-hamsaji in his home for three weeks. Soon everybody began to attend the satsang, girls began to go to school and the women came out into their courtyards. When Paramahamsaji was leaving the village, the dacoit offered him five hundred rupees, which he refused to accept. Then the dacoit tried to force him to accept the money at gunpoint, but Paramahamsaji was undaunted. He called the man's son and after explaining to him how to deposit the money in a bank account, he departed."

"Did Paramahamsaji often go off to unknown places?" asked one of the swamis.

"Yes," Swami Dharmashakti replied. "Since Paramahamsaji left Sivananda Ashram in 1956, there have been many periods when he would just disappear for months without informing anyone of his whereabouts. Only when he returned from such tours would we come to know that he had visited sadhus, saints, pilgrim centres, ashrams and monasteries, in Pakistan, Afghanistan, Nepal, Bangladesh, Burma and so on.

"The following year, in May 1959, Paramahamsaji conducted a sadhana camp at Bandha Bazaar in M.P. Afterwards he went to Mount Abu and toured many places. In July, he went to Bandha Bazaar for chaturmas where he remained on mouna, eating only fruits and practising sadhana for three months. Afterwards he went to Bombay, Poona, Nasik, Trayambakeshwar and Allahabad.

"In February 1960, Swami Niranjan, a symbol of the blessings of guru, was born, and Paramahamsaji came to Rajnandgaon in March to bless him. Afterwards he was off to Bhilai, Raipur, Bilaspur and Raigarh. His work area was constantly expanding and his programs were in great demand. Then he went to Bombay and from there in July to Neemgaon (Barad) for chaturmas. In October he returned to Rajnandgaon to see the copies of his first yoga publications: *Lessons on Yoga* in English and *Kurukshetra ki Ladai* and *Yoga Asana* in Hindi.

"In November he went to Gondia for a program and from there to Nagpur and Amravati. Then he went to

305

Bombay where he held discourses in many places. The devotees there compiled his satsangs and lectures into a book, which was called *Discourses on Yoga*. After two months in Bombay, he returned to Rajnandgaon and said, 'Now books will be printed continually, so we must set up a printing press.'

"In January 1961, he went to Bihar and toured Chapra and nearby villages. After a month he came to Munger, where he stayed at Ananda Bhavan, which overlooks the Ganga. There he practised sadhana and held satsang in the evening. He was enchanted by the natural, scenic beauty of this place and he compiled *Siddha Prarthana*, the book of bhajan and kirtan, there.

"An added attraction was Karna Chaura, the ancient stone platform located on a nearby hilltop, which had a commanding view of the Ganga. There, according to legend, Raja Karna of Mahabharata fame used to sit in court and distribute gold coins to all who asked. Paramahamsaji used to roam about on the hill or sit on the historical platform and meditate. He had many experiences and visions there. Once he saw a luminous white figure loom up out of a crack in the platform. The figure said to him, 'Yoga will be the culture of tomorrow and this place will become the centre of yoga.' Then the figure disappeared. At such times, Paramahamsaji would decide not to go to Karna Chaura again, but he was always drawn back.

"At that time his host in Munger wanted Paramahamsaji to stay on and offered to build an ashram for him, but Paramahamsaji was not in favour of this. His base in Bihar was Munger. From there he would go to Bhagalpur, Chapra, Katrasgarh, Sitamarhi, Patna and many other places, then return to Munger. Here he translated his book *Lessons on Yoga* into Hindi, which was called *Yoga Sadhana Part One*, and for Part Two a compilation of letters was prepared.

"In 1961, Paramahamsaji regularly went to Bombay, Amravati, Khamgaon, Nagpur, Rajnandgaon, Bhilai, Bilaspur, Raigarh, Calcutta and Allahabad for programs. In

Bombay, the devotees were preparing four books for publication, containing compilations of his discourses. At the same time, he was constantly receiving invitations to visit new places. His sphere of contact was increasing rapidly."

"When was the International Yoga Fellowship Movement established?" asked one of the swamis.

"In January 1962," Swami Dharmashakti replied. "At that time, Paramahamsaji was inspired to start an institution. So he consulted with the people connected with his work and explained his plans to all. It was then decided to prepare the blueprint. Afterwards Paramahamsaji went to Nagpur for a yoga camp and from there to Bombay where eight books were being printed. Five books were also being printed in Bihar and a Publication Society was formed at Rajnandgaon."

"In February of that year Paramahamsaji spoke in Rajnandgaon on the necessity of a printing press. He said, 'We are printing many books and we don't know how many more we will have to print. The foundation of our mission rests on books.' At that time he also spoke of his plan to begin publication of a regular yoga magazine. After explaining all the work, he went on to Bombay, then to Munger and Sitamarhi where he held a program during March. When he returned to Rajnandgaon at the end of March, the International Yoga Fellowship was formalized. At that time he explained the future course of action and went on to Nagpur and Bombay where he stayed for one month. In May, he received his guru's blessings for founding the International Yoga Fellowship Movement."

"That year Paramahamsaji decided to stay at Ananda Bhavan in Munger for chaturmas. During this period he performed *kaya kalpa*, an intensive purificatory practice, and ate only fruits once a day. In October, a yoga camp was held at Rajgir, which was attended by devotees from Bhagalpur, Chapra, Bombay and Khamgaon. A meeting of the International Yoga Fellowship was held and the agenda was decided. Paramahamsaji asked that the printing press

307

should be installed at Rajnandgaon without delay, as there were many books waiting to be published and many others on the way. By this time, Paramahamsaji's mission was already off the ground. Fifteen books had been published which he went on distributing and everything was set up for the publication of a monthly magazine.

"In 1963, the January edition of *Yoga Vidya* in Hindi and *Yoga* in English was printed in Bombay. Later, when the Yoga Vidya printing press was installed at Rajnandgaon, the magazines were printed there. All the devotees, disciples and friends of yoga received copies of the magazines. Everyone cooperated and gave all possible assistance for the success of this endeavour.

"That year Paramahamsaji was again staying at Ananda Bhavan in Munger during chaturmas. On 14th July at midnight, while practising his sadhana, he had an inner awakening, in the form of a dream, but it was as real as if it were happening physically in front of him. In that dream he saw Swami Sivananda travelling in a steamboat from Sivanandashram to Swargashram on the other side of the Ganga. From the steamboat the sound of bugles, conches and drums could be heard. Swami Sivananda was sitting alone on the steamboat. He was the only passenger.

"Paramahamsaji was witnessing the whole scene from the bank in front of Darshan Maha Vidyalaya, which is a little above Sivanandashram. While crossing, the flywheel of the steamboat splashed a little bit of Ganga water on him and his experience finished. Immediately he understood that his guru had left the body. When the Ganga water was splashed on him, Paramahamsaji saw Swami Sivananda looking at him. Otherwise he was looking towards the other side. With the splashing of water, Paramahamsaji realized that he had been anointed or appointed. His guru's grace was upon him, and he would have to start working earnestly for the propagation of yoga.

"The next day Paramahamsaji left Munger for Delhi and Rishikesh. As soon as he arrived at his guru's ashram, he found that his dream was correct. Then he returned to Munger and informed his host that he would settle there. Sannyasins have a tradition that wherever the disciple happens to be staying when his guru leaves the physical body, no matter where it may be in the world, the sannyasin should establish himself at that place. So Paramahamsaji said, 'I will abide by the tradition and do my duty. Because I was blessed by my guru for the last time in Munger, I will stay in Munger.' This was the opportunity that his host had been waiting for and he immediately agreed. It had always been his earnest wish that Paramahamsaji would settle in Munger. So, under his patronage, the construction of an ashram began.

"In October, Paramahamsaji went to Rajnandgaon and told his devotees there that his wandering life would end in December. From January, he would be staying in Munger where the ashram was being built. Then he went on to Bombay, Poona, Amravati, Khamgaon, Neemgaon and the caves of Elephanta and Ellora. It was at this time that he again received his guru's darshan and special instructions. He also received the blessings and darshan of many divine forces and the state of paramahamsa was conferred upon him. From that moment, Paramahamsaji renounced the wearing of kurta, chappals and watch, and restricted his dress to a dhoti and an uppercloth for many years.

"Afterwards, he went on to Nagpur, Gondia, Dongargarh, and back to Rajnandgaon, where a tremendous crowd had gathered from many places for his darshan. Then he passed through Durg, Bhilai, Raipur, Bilaspur, Raigarh, Bhuvaneshwar, Calcutta, Chapra and Bhagalpur, on his way back to Munger. With this he concluded the chapter of his life as a wandering sannyasin. The ashram was nearing completion and the devotees were busy organizing for the inaugural function and the reception of guests. On 19th January 1964, Basant Panchami, Paramahamsaji inaugurated the ashram. He lit the akhanda jyoti in memory of his guru and offered the first *ahuti* (oblations) into the fire.

"From that time, Paramahamsaji found that every now and then his soul would open. He would find his guru there who would tell him what he had to do. In this way, over the next twenty years he was able to establish the Bihar School of Yoga, Sivananda Ashram and Ganga Darshan, and become the guide for hundreds of ashrams and centres throughout India and the world. He always said that this work was not an outcome of his own experiences or abilities, but it was because of the instructions and guidance which his guru whispered to him from time to time. Such was his link with the guru."

THE MISSION

In the evening the swamis again assembled in the sadhana hall, and waited with a quiet feeling of expectation to hear the next chapter of Gurudev's life. Soon Swami Niranjan entered the hall and took his seat. After intoning the mantras, he began to speak.

"Just as the history of any institution is usually related to one particular person, in this way the history of this ashram is related to Swami Satyananda Saraswati. On 19th January 1964, Paramahamsaji established the Sivananda Ashram in a small building near the Ganga at Lal Darwaja, Munger. In the first few years of its establishment, the ashram grew very slowly. The facilities were very simple and there were no private rooms. Everybody lived together in the sadhana hall and slept on blankets on the floor. At the far end of the ashram was a mud hut which we used to call Paramahamsaji's kutir, because he lived there.

"A few devotees would come to live in the ashram from time to time with the idea of learning yoga practices. Thus more rooms were added slowly one by one. At the end of 1965 an annexe to the main hall was constructed. The first two rooms were called Panchavati and Yoga Nidra Vihar. In April 1967, this annexe was further enlarged to include a third room called Ganga Sagar and a small room at the end with an underground room just below it for Paramahamsaji's sadhana.

"There may be dark clouds in the sky, but they cannot prevent the sun from giving light. When flowers bloom, it is not necessary to beckon the bees. In this manner, people came and Paramahamsaji started teaching. His aim was to offer something useful to society so that every human being could evolve. He was not only a yoga teacher, but a siddha yogi. People used to come to him with all their problems, asking him to perform some miracle to make them fit. He would immediately reply, 'I am not the swami who performs miracles. If that is what you wish, please go elsewhere.'

"Paramahamsaji was always very practical. He used to say 'If an individual is not practical and does not try to do something useful, how can he be called a sadhaka?' This was the first lesson we received from him. We did not receive the sort of teachings which you get today. You can ask the sannyasins who are present if they ever received any sadhana from Paramahamsaji."

"Starting in such a lonely and backward area," one swami, asked, "how was Paramahamsaji able to expand the teaching activities to such an extent that within a few short years his institution had gained worldwide renown?"

"First of all," Swami Niranjan replied, "in order to celebrate the annual meeting of the Bihar School of Yoga and the International Yoga Fellowship Movement, an international yoga convention was organized every year from 1964 onwards. In this way more people came to the ashram, and their experiences were such that the ashram life became known all over the world.

"In November 1964, the First International Yoga Convention was held at Munger. It was inaugurated by the governor of Bihar and the chief guest was Paramahamsaji's gurubhai, Swami Chidananda of Rishikesh. Then, in November 1965, the Second International Yoga Convention was inaugurated by the Shankaracharya of Puri and closed by the Governor of Bihar. The Governor of Rajasthan was

311

chief guest. In November 1966, the Third International Yoga Convention was held and many Western aspirants participated in the function. In November 1967, the Fourth International Yoga Convention was held at Gondia.

"The first intensive nine month Yoga Teacher Training Course was held in Munger from 1st July 1967 to 31st March 1968. This course was attended by many aspirants from India and abroad. It was a tremendous success and through these first teachers whom he had trained, the seeds of Paramahamsaji's mission and teachings on yoga began to spread world-wide. During this course the students received much more than mere techniques. They gained a deep understanding of the integral system of yoga as a science, a philosophy and a way of life. The lectures given by Paramahamsaji during this period were later on to form the basis for several books, including *Four Chapters on Freedom* and *Early Teachings of Swami Satyananda*.

"By 1968, the Bihar School of Yoga was well established and Paramahamsaji decided that the time was auspicious to spread the message of yoga 'from door to door and from shore to shore'. In March of that year he visited Swami Sivananda's samadhi at Rishikesh, travelling with seventy disciples, to seek guidance and blessings for his forthcoming world tour. For one week Paramahamsaji fasted and remained in seclusion inside Swami Sivananda's samadhi. He never came out or met with anybody. When he came out after one week, he said, 'I have received permission to go.' Within one week, his passport and ticket were prepared, contacts were made and he started on his tour. In April he departed from Bombay for Malaysia and Singapore. From there he toured Australia, Japan, USA, Canada, England, France, Holland, Sweden and Italy. The tour was very successful and lasted for five months. In his absence the swamis in the ashram resolved to build a three-storey building for accommodating the students who would come to learn yoga. The building was completed within three months and students were already living in it by the time Paramahamsaji returned.

312

"Paramahamsaji returned to India in October and in November he conducted the Fifth International Yoga Convention in Raigarh. The chief guest was Swami Satchidananda, his gurubhai and the head of the International Yoga Fellowship in USA. After the convention a three month Yoga Teacher Training Course began in Munger, in which trainees from all parts of the world participated.

"In 1969 Paramahamsaji was very active. In May he presided over the Jaipur Yoga Vidya Sammelan. In June, he toured India extensively, conducting yoga programs in Bhagalpur, Patna, Muzaffarpur, Dhanbad, Calcutta, Tatanagar, Raigarh, Bilaspur, Sambalpur, Raipur, Gondia, Rajnandgaon, Bhilai, Nagpur, Amravati, Bombay, Poona, Ahmedabad, Jaipur, Delhi, Bhopal, Sagar and Jabalpur.

"In August he embarked on his second overseas tour, during which he conducted yoga programs in England, Ireland, Denmark, France, Belgium, Germany and Switzerland. In September he presided over the Sixth International Convention which was held in Richmond, Australia, and organized by Roma Blair (Swami Nirmalananda). Guests included Swami Gitananda from Pondicherry, Swami Karunananda from Australia and Swami Venkatesananda from Mauritius.

"In January 1970, he commenced an all India tour with his disciples. During this extensive tour which lasted for four months, he conducted yoga programs in Patna, Delhi, Jaipur, Calcutta, Bhopal, Sagar, Giridi, Saharsa, Forbis Ganj, Kisanganj, Tatanagar, Kharagpur, Chaibasa, Goa, Sambalpur, Dhenkanal, Angul, Athmallik, Nagpur, Amravati, Bombay, Poona, Ahmedabad, Jabalpur, Indore, Bilaspur, Bhatapara, Raipur, Bhilar, Durg, Gondia and Rajnandgaon.

"In May, he departed on his third overseas tour. After visiting Ireland where one of his sannyasins was establishing a yoga ashram, he presided over the Seventh International Yoga Convention in Paris. Afterwards he toured the USA.

"In June, he returned to India and opened the Sivananda Kutir Yoga Ashram in Munger in the Fort area to cater to the needs of the local people, as Bihar School of Yoga was now flooded with interstate and foreign visitors. In July he inaugurated the Yoga Research Library where books on yoga could be researched and written.

"In August, he conducted yoga programs in Chatarpur, Tikamgarh, Panna, Shajapur, Katni and Shadol. In September he went abroad again, visiting England, Ireland, Denmark, Belgium, Germany, Switzerland and Austria."

"What about the sannyasa training?" asked one of the swamis. "When did that begin?"

"Sannyasa training was one of the most important aspects of Paramahamsaji's mission," replied Swami Niranjan. "By 1970, there was a growing demand in many parts of the world for more experienced yoga teachers and sannyasins who could guide people in their own localities. For this reason, Paramahamsaji conducted an international three year sannyasa training course for those aspirants who wished to make sannyasa their lifestyle. This course commenced in September with one hundred and eight trainees from all parts of the globe taking part, under the direct guidance of Paramahamsaji.

"During the three year sannyasa course, Paramahamsaji conducted all the classes himself. There was one month of asana, one month of pranayama, one month of bhajan, one month of sadhana, and in this way he covered all the topics that he wished to teach. These classes later formed the basis of several Yoga Publications Trust publications, including: *Asana Pranayama Mudra Bandha*, *Meditations from the Tantras*, *Prana Vidya* and *Yoga Nidra*."

"During the sannyasa course," asked one swami, "did Paramahamsaji remain in the ashram or continue with his tours?"

"He stayed in the ashram most of the time," Swami Niranjan replied, "but at intervals he still continued to conduct outside programs in India and abroad. In March 1971, he travelled to England and Ireland, accompanied by his youngest disciple, who was me. I stayed on in Ireland

314.

and Paramahamsaji returned to India in April to inaugurate the Yoga Convention in Sambalpur. He then travelled to Raigarh and Bilaspur where he inaugurated a forty day diabetes camp. Then he went to Korba and on to Rajnandgaon where he stayed for one month with forty-five sannyasin disciples. From Rajnandgaon, Paramahamsaji returned to Sambalpur in May to light the jyoti at the ashram. Afterwards he flew to Belfast to inaugurate the ashram there and stayed for the month of June, conducting a yoga teachers training course. In July he returned to India and inaugurated the ashram at Rajnandgaon. In November he sent several sannyasin disciples to Colombia to start an ashram.

"In March and April 1972, Paramahamsaji toured Raigarh, Rajnandgaon, Nagpur, Gondia, Betul, Satna, Rewa, Jabalpur, Mirzapur and Gaya.

"In January 1973, Paramahamsaji conducted Bhumi pooja at the site of the Raipur ashram. In March he travelled to Australia. In April and May he travelled to South America and Europe. On his return he established a printing press at Bihar School of Yoga to print the pamphlets and yoga publications in preparation for the Golden Jubilee celebration.

"In October 1973, the Golden Jubilee was celebrated at Munger in the form of an International Yoga Convention. Delegates from abroad arrived on chartered flights and a large number of delegates from all parts of India participated. Gurus, swamis and saints from all over the world came together during this event to celebrate the fiftieth year of renunciation of Swami Sivananda and also the fiftieth birth anniversary of Paramahamsaji. At this function Paramahamsaji was acknowledged as the foremost exponent of yoga. Included amongst the guests were HH Jagadguru Swami Shantananda, Shankarcharya of Jyotir Math, Sri B.K.S. Iyengar, Swami Chidananda of Rishikesh, and countless other sannyasin disciples of Paramahamsaji, who by then had become yoga teachers in their own right.

"In February and March 1974, Paramahamsaji travelled through central India with a team of swamis conducting yoga programs at Ambikapur, Korba, Janjgir, Bilaspur, Raipur, Bhilainagar, Mahasmund, Dhamtari, Jagdalpur, Rajnandgaon, Gondia, Balaghat, Panhmore, Jabalpur, Sagar and Satna. In April Paramahamsaji travelled to South America and on his return, he went to Sambalpur to inaugurate the Yoga Convention there. In September, Paramahamsaji travelled to Germany and then on to Colombia. In October he returned to India and went to Dhanbad to conduct the World Yoga Convention. In December, he sent one of his sannyasin disciples to Australia to start an ashram there.

"In March 1975, Paramahamsaji presided over the All India Yoga Convention in Bilaspur. He then inaugurated a seminar at the Bhilai Steel Plant. In October, Paramahamsaji travelled to Bogota, Colombia, for the Silver Jubilee Celebration. Afterwards he visited Equador, Peru, Brazil, Chile, Panama, Argentina, Guatamala, Uruguay, El Salvador, Paraguay and Mexico, and then went on to Trinidad, Barcelona, Copenhagen and Paris. In November, after returning to India, he inaugurated the Yoga Convention in Rajnandgaon. In December, he conducted a yoga seminar in Bombay.

"By 1976, the small ashram in Munger, which Paramahamsaji had started twelve years earlier, seemed to be even smaller. It was always overflowing with devotees, guests and sannyasins. There was no room for all the new applicants who wrote and arrived daily seeking admission.

"In February and March 1976, Paramahamsaji conducted yoga programs in Asansol, Calcutta, Allahabad, Supaul, Sambalpur, Raigarh, Rajnandgaon and Barhaiya. In May, he inaugurated programs in Hazaribagh, Kumardubi and Sambalpur. In July and August, Paramahamsaji presided over the Guru Poornima functions in Raigarh. Afterwards he conducted a program in Ranchi and then toured South India, visiting Calcutta, Kharagpur, Cuttack, Visakhapatnam, Madras, Mahabalipuram, Hyderabad, Nagpur, Jabalpur and Bhopal. In November and December, he conducted the

National Yoga Convention in Raipur, the Steel Yoga Convention in Bhilai, and a yoga seminar in Bhopal.

"In 1977, Paramahamsaji upgraded the BSY printing press called Ashram Graphics, in order to take over the publication of *Yoga* and *Yoga Vidya* magazines, which had been printed in Rajnandgaon since 1963. The work of compiling, editing and printing the magazine was done as karma yoga by all the sannyasins of the ashram. In February, a new floor was constructed on top of the press building to house the BSY Research Library and the despatch office. Overcrowded living conditions continued to worsen. However, as numbers of applications for admission increased, Paramahamsaji announced that the ashram gates were closed to new arrivals. All applications were referred to the outside ashrams such as Dhanbad, Raipur, Rajnandgaon and Sambalpur, but still people kept coming and begging to be admitted, although there was no accommodation.

In February 1977, Paramahamsaji went to Kathmandu. In July he presided over the Guru Poornima celebrations at the Mangrove Mountain Ashram in Australia. In August he inaugurated the Calcutta ashram. In September, Paramahamsaji went to Zinal, Switzerland to address the delegates of the Second International Yoga Week, sponsored by the European Union of National Federations of Yoga. In October he presided over the National Yoga Convention conducted at Sambalpur. In December, he travelled to Colombia.

"In 1978, after much consideration, the decision was made to acquire the property of Karna Chaura, a hill just opposite the original ashram overlooking the Ganga, in order to build a larger ashram complex with adequate facilities to accommodate the ever-increasing number of yoga aspirants. Later in the same year, the legal transactions were completed and this ancient and historical site was handed over to Bihar School of Yoga. Paramahamsaji renamed the place Ganga Darshan. He drew up plans for the Sadhana hall which would be built on the site of the ancient Karna Chaura platform, and for large residential blocks.

317

"In January 1978, Paramahamsaji conducted yoga seminars in Athens and Barcelona. In February and March, he inaugurated a yoga camp for diabetes in Sambalpur and then he went on to Raigarh. Afterwards he conducted programs in Calcutta, Poona and Bombay. In July, he conducted a one month seminar for European yoga teachers. Guru Poornima marked the opening of Ganga Darshan. Thousands of people came to celebrate the event and Paramahamsaji conducted the Pratishtha ceremony.

"In October, Paramahamsaji presided over the World Yoga Convention organized by the Australian Ashram. In November, he travelled to Colombia. In December, he inaugurated the All India Yoga Convention at Thane. Afterwards, special kriya yoga courses were conducted in Munger for large groups coming from Australia, Spain and South America.

"In February, March and April 1979, Paramahamsaji conducted yoga programs in Sagar, Bhopal, Jabalpur, Khamgaon, Bombay, Poona, Bangalore, Secunderabad, Rajnandgaon, Raipur, Sambalpur and Raigarh, returning to Munger. In May, he travelled to Bombay, Singapore and Australia. On his return he presided over the Patna Yoga Convention. In June, Paramahamsaji conducted a yoga program in Medellin, Colombia. In July he presided over the Guru Poornima function held in Bilaspur.

"In July, August and September, Paramahamsaji conducted yoga programs in Singapore, Athens, Barcelona, Antwerp, Zinal, Copenhagen, Paris and London. Afterwards he presided over the International Yoga Convention organized by the Belfast Yoga Centre and addressed the delegates at the Fifth International Yoga Week sponsored by the European Union of National Federations of Yoga in Zinal.

"By 1979, the construction of Ganga Darshan was in full swing. Most of the sannyasins were living at Ganga Darshan by that time, supervising building work.

"In 1980, Paramahamsaji started one month yoga teacher training courses in Munger so that the basic yoga practices could be propagated by people at community level. In January, he inaugurated the Bolangir Ashram in Orissa and presided over the Bolangir Yoga Convention and the Kahalgaon Yoga Convention. Paramahamsaji toured Europe in April and May, visiting Athens, Rome, Frankfurt, Vienna, Zurich, Brussels, Copenhagen, Stockholm, Paris, Barcelona and London. In July he presided over the Guru Poornima celebrations in Satna. In August and September, Paramahamsaji returned to Europe where he conducted the Intercontinental Yoga Seminar at Chamarande, France. After this he addressed the delegates of the Sixth International Yoga Week, sponsored by the European Union of National Federations of Yoga. Then he toured Spain, conducting yoga programs in many major cities. In October, Paramahamsaji presided over the International Yoga Convention in Colombia. In November, he inaugurated the District Yoga Convention in Bariarpur, Bihar.

"In January, February and March 1981, Paramahamsaji toured South India, conducting programs in Bombay, Madurai, Madras, Neveli and Hyderabad. Afterwards he went to Patna, Delhi, Ghaziabad, Bhopal and Raipur, where he inaugurated the Bhilai Steel Plant Yoga Convention. In April he flew to Europe and conducted a yoga seminar in Italy. Afterwards he presided over the First Pan-Hellenic Convention on Yoga and Health organized by Satyananda Ashram, Greece. On his return to India, he conducted a yoga program at the Bhagalpur Engineering College.

"In July 1981, yoga students from Switzerland, Colombia, Brazil and Italy came to Munger for a sadhana course which culminated in the Guru Poornima celebrations at Jabalpur, presided over by Paramahamsaji. Afterwards he flew to Europe where he conducted yoga programs in Finland, France, Belgium and Italy. In November he inaugurated the Singapore ashram and in December he toured South America.

"In May 1982, Paramahamsaji flew to Japan, the USA and then South America. In Japan, he visited Tokyo and spoke with Dr Hiroshima Motoyama in relation to yoga and

319

research. Afterwards he gave talks on yoga in Kyoto, Nagasaki and Hiroshima. In the USA, he conducted programs in Los Angeles and San Francisco. Afterwards he flew to Medellin, Colombia, and proceeded to visit the ancient cultural site of San Augustin, which houses many archaeological artefacts that indicate the tantric origins of the pre-Colombian culture. Then he proceeded to Santo Domingo where he inaugurated a yoga convention and conducted television programs on yoga.

"In July, Guru Poornima was celebrated at Ganga Darshan and at this auspicious time, Paramahamsaji laid the foundation stone for the seven-storey main building which would be built on top of the hill and which would stand as a beacon of yoga for generations to come.

"In August and September, Paramahamsaji toured the USA and spoke on yoga at the following places: Elizabeth, New Jersey; Monroe, New York; Charlottesville, Virginia; Washington D.C.; Ann Arbor, Michigan; Denver, Colorado; Los Angeles, Ojai, San Jose and San Francisco, California; and New York City. Afterwards he flew to Europe where he conducted programs in Italy, Spain, England, France, Switzerland, Yugoslavia and Greece.

"In October, Paramahamsaji returned to India and conducted programs in Delhi, Dhanbad, Rajnandgaon, Athnair, Agra, Gondia and Sambalpur. In November and December, he travelled to Santo Domingo and then to Puerto Rico for the International Yoga Teachers Association Convention. From there he went to Pointe-a-Pitre and then to Medellin. In December, he returned to India and inaugurated the National Yoga Convention in Thane."

"When did Paramahamsaji decide to renounce his mission," asked one of the swamis, "and how did he decide upon his successor?"

"When Paramahamsaji realized that he had completed his duty with regard to his guru," replied Swami Niranjan, "he decided to renounce the mission. Paramahamsaji's life is made up of twenty year cycles. He was born in 1923, he joined his guru's ashram in 1943, this ashram was established in 1963 and he handed over complete charge to me in 1983. After handing over the ashram to me, however, he remained for five years longer, mainly in solitude, because I needed his guidance.

"In November 1982, when Paramahamsaji went to Puerto Rico, I accompanied him. An International Convention of Yoga Teachers was being held in Puerto Rico and during the convention he asked me, 'Will you come to India?' I immediately replied, 'I do not wish to return. However, if it is your wish, then there is nothing that can stop me from coming back.' He asked, 'Why don't you want to return?' I said, 'What will I do there? I want to live in that part of the world where you are not physically present so that I can serve you and carry on with your work. Of course, if it is your order, I will come.' He said, 'All right,' and dropped the subject. After a few days he returned to India and I returned to America.

"One month later I returned to my ashram from a tour and found a telegram waiting for me. The telegram read, 'Reach Munger by 16th January.' I had received an order. I quickly closed the ashram and bought a ticket for the 14th January. I reached Ganga Darshan on the 16th. I thought I had come on temporary leave and that I would return soon. However, on the 19th of January, there was a meeting of the executive body of the Bihar School of Yoga. Paramahamsaji called me into the meeting and told me, 'From today, BSY is your responsibility and you are the President.' I felt that I was going to pass out, but I had to obey the order of my guru. Then I requested Paramahamsaji to stay on until I became used to my new responsibilities. He replied, 'All right, I will stay back for some time because it is your request, otherwise I would have left the ashram today.'"

"It is most unusual for a guru to appoint a successor while he is still living," said one of the swamis. "Why did he do this and how did he adjust himself to this radical change in the direction of his life?"

"Most gurus and spiritual leaders remain in their positions until they die," replied Swami Niranjan, "because they are attached to their mission and work. Paramahamsaji, however, was not. He had a very clear sense of direction about his life and had always told us, 'To become a guru, to collect disciples, to work for some goal, was not the purpose which brought me to sannyasa. The purpose was discovery of the Divine. All this that I am doing is to exhaust my karmas and when I am ready my destiny will guide me.'

"Paramahamsaji continued to live on in the ashram much as he did before, but slowly he withdrew himself from the management of ashram affairs. He still went out on tours, however. In February and March 1983, he toured England, France, Italy, Switzerland and Spain. In April and May, he toured Australia. In July, he presided over the Guru Poornima celebrations in Raipur.

"In 1983, construction was the main feature of Ganga Darshan's activities. The press building with the second floor residential block and the three storey residential building near the kitchen were both completed. The press was shifted from its old quarters in Sivananda Ashram to its new quarters in Ganga Darshan and the foundations of the main building were also completed.

"In 1984, Paramahamsaji conducted programs in Europe from April to August. He toured Greece, giving lectures in Crete at Hania, Rethymno and Iraklia, and on the mainland he lectured in Thessaloniki, Rhodes, Mytilini, Alexanderopolis and Athens. He was the chief guest at the Annual Convention of the Italian Yoga Federation in Ciocco. Then he toured France and inaugurated the ashram at Toulon. In July, he presided over the Guru Poornima function at the Greek Ashram in Athens. Afterwards he conducted seminars throughout France and an intensive sadhana course in Switzerland.

"In October 1984, under the inspiration of Parama-hamsaji, two associated institutions were formed at BSY: Sivananda Math, a charitable institution, and the Yoga

Research Foundation. It was necessary to develop, not only the spiritual aspect of yoga, but the social and scientific aspects as well. For this reason he started these two brother and sister institutes, Sivananda Math for social development and the Yoga Research Foundation for scientifically establishing the efficacy of yoga through controlled clinical trials.

"During 1985, Paramahamsaji stayed quietly in Ganga Darshan giving darshan, diksha and satsang to devotees and disciples. In 1986, he rarely went out and spent more time in seclusion. At first he met people only once in fifteen days, then gradually he extended the periods of seclusion to several months at a stretch.

"In 1987, on Basant Panchami, Paramahamsaji took up residence on the top floor of the Ganga Darshan Main Building from where he viewed and inspired the whole ashram throughout the year. His sadhana and periods of seclusion continued; he met with outside people and sannyasins less and less. He did not leave the ashram during this year for any outside programs or tours. In July, he presided over the Guru Poornima celebrations at Ganga Darshan to which thousands of disciples and devotees thronged for his darshan.

"In July 1988, Paramahamsaji presided over the Guru Poornima celebrations for the last time. During the program he sang and danced to the delight of his devotees. In August, he departed from the ashram, unknown to anyone, on a long pilgrimage of the siddha tirthasthanas of India."

"Didn't Paramahamsaji inform even you about his intended departure?" asked one of the swamis.

"On 7th August, Paramahamsaji decided on his departure," Swami Niranjan replied, "and he called a few of us to say that on the following morning he would be leaving the ashram. All night long I paced up and down in my room praying that the sun might never rise. I was restless, wondering how I could stop a wandering yogi from wandering, a flowing river from flowing."

"In the morning, I went to meet Paramahamsaji and he said, 'Namo Narayan. I am going.' I asked him if I should make any arrangements, but he said, 'No.' About the mission, he said only this, 'If you are able to look after the work well, it will grow. If you are not able to look after it, let somebody else do it who can.' That was all, and then he was gone."

"From all of your experiences with Paramahamsaji," one of the swamis sitting near the back asked, "what are the special qualities of his nature which have inspired you most?"

"The quality that inspired me the most," replied Swami Niranjan, "was his ability to always live as a disciple at heart. Externally he lived like a guru, but in his mind and heart he never considered himself to be a guru. He played a role for us, not for himself. There was never any show of ego or any pompous air that he was a great man. In his heart and mind he was never a great or a learned man, he was always a seeker. He did not allow himself to ever reach a state where he could say, 'Okay, I know the answer.' He gave us all the answers we needed, but within himself he always searched. He had the quality of being naturally in tune with a higher reality, which is a very beautiful attribute. He had a simplicity of heart with which he could communicate with his own guru, with his ishta devata and with God, and he received definite directions from them.

"Paramahamsaji had very strong convictions about what he had to attain and achieve in life, as if the path was laid out since the day of his birth and he knew exactly where he had to go. We might say, 'Let's wait and see what the future holds.' He would never say that. There were no limitations for him in his mind or in his life. People have had utmost respect and love for him and have also disliked and rejected him. But he always knew that 'this is where I have to go'. Possibly because of his nature, he always sought out the best in everyone he met. He used to say that when a person came to him full of faults and defects, if he saw one single good quality hidden behind the layers of defects, he would try to develop that one good trait and forget all the faults.

324

"Paramahamsaji was very practical in every way. He could accept the glory and the dishonour thrown at him by people without being affected by it, without going into a state of depression or anxiety that his image, mission or life had been tarnished. He never dwelt in the past, he was always here and now in the present, having a clear vision of what had happened, what was happening and what was going to happen. He saw his own life and the life of every person laid out before him.

"These are some of the qualities which I have seen in him, but if I try to recall everything it will be an endless story. Now it is time to end this session, but we will continue later when more is known about Gurudev's future mission."

The hamsa has flown away.
Soaring high with its wings spread
Across the infinite sky.
It has been searching for its ultimate abode
For many yugas.

Knowledge it has received in abundance
From the jnanis of the world,
Grace and blessings of the divine too.
Still, today it is restlessly flapping
Its wings in search.

Looking down at its own creation
Of the three worlds
Etched across the horizon,
Yes, it is flying high
And flying ceaselessly in search,
Witnessing the world down below as lila.
Alone all alone, in the infinite sky,
My soul is flying to unite with its beloved.

Swami Satyananda

THE TRANSITION

The next chapter of Paramahamsaji's life was revealed slowly, as news of his travels and of his new mission reached the ashram. One evening in satsang, one of the sannyasins in training asked Swami Niranjan, "Please tell us about Paramahamsaji's life after renouncing the role of guru and head of the mission. How did he become a paramahamsa?" Swami Niranjan sat quietly for a few moments and then he began to speak.

"Sannyasa does not end with initiation or putting on geru robes. It is an ongoing process of achieving harmony, perfection and cosmic unity. In the course of his life, a paramahamsa who is sincere in his quest has to go through different and intense kinds of sadhana, which can take any form according to the instructions of his guru. The sadhana of a paramahamsa is never written down. It is a tradition that passes from mind to mind, not like yogic sadhanas which are described from yama and niyama to samadhi. These yogic sadhanas are defined for ordinary people like us. However, as the evolution of mind, consciousness and perception takes place, and as we exhaust our samskaras and karmas and open ourselves up to experience the higher qualities and realities of nature, then the sadhana and lifestyle has to undergo a change."

"Why is it," asked one of the students, "that most of the sannyasins today do not attain the state of paramahamsa?"

"Many brilliant sannyasins," replied Swami Niranjan, "like Swami Vivekananda, Swami Sivananda and others living in the world today could not make the transition from vairagya sannyasa to paramahamsa sannyasa despite their attainments and knowledge, because of their karmas. The story of Swami Vivekananda is an example. He experienced the vision of God with one touch from Ramakrishna. But despite having that vision, he had to come back and live like an ordinary person and struggle for money, disciples and mission.

"In Paramahamsaji's life the transition happened as a natural process, although it was totally unexpected. Even in the early days of the ashram, from 1963 to 1965, he used to say, 'The ashram is not my life, yoga is not my goal; they are but a means to enter into the next stage.' So, finally, when Paramahamsaji heard the inner call and received the instructions from his ishta devata, he left.

"For one year, he toured all the traditional tirthasthanas, sacred places, and eventually reached Rishikesh, where he stayed for a few weeks, not as a guru but as a disciple. At first his gurubhais, Swami Chidananda, Swami Krishnananda and Swami Madhavananda, did not recognize him. Some of Paramahamsaji's disciples were living there and they also did not recognize him. He moved about incognito, changing his role and vision of life, from guru back to sadhaka and disciple."

"What were the different tirthasthanas to which Paramahamsaji travelled?" asked one of the swamis. "Was there any significance in this?"

"Yes, there was," replied Swami Niranjan. "When Paramahamsaji wandered throughout India for nine years after leaving his guru's mission, he visited all the tirthasthanas. At that time he made a promise that when his life's work was completed, he would again return to surrender himself fully. Therefore, after leaving Munger he began this pilgrimage. At times, he used to send us short accounts of his travels which were later published in our magazines, so that all those who had known him could follow his journey.

"In September 1988, he visited the temple of Lord Vishwanath in Kashi then Vindyavasini and Sankat Mochan. Afterwards he bathed in the Sangam at Allahabad. In Kathmandu he offered his obeisance to Pashupatinath and then proceeded to Vaishnava Devi. Afterwards he took a dip in Brahma Kund in Haridwar. Then he had darshan of Yamunotri, Gangotri, Kedarnath and Badri Vishal. Finally, he went to Sivanandashram in Rishikesh.

"In October, he visited Vasukinath near Deoghar where he had a vision of a hooded serpent coiled around his neck and he heard the clear instruction: 'Become a chakravarti.' Then he went to Kamakhya where he performed the Navaratri anushthana and on Dashnami he worshipped Devi, the incarnate *kanya* (virgin), and performed the ritual of washing her feet. Afterwards he stayed for a few days in Calcutta. There, at Kalighat he had darshan of Kali, the destroyer of kala (time) and destiny.

"In November, he proceeded to Jagannath Puri where he sat amidst the grove of trees in the temple precincts for hours and transcended himself. From there he went to Khajuraho, a tribute paid to Lord Shiva by the Chandelle Dynasty. Here he experienced the temple depictions as a sublime prayer to the cosmic process of creation, revealing every aspect of life as a means to reach God. Next he visited Chitrakoot, the site where Sri Rama played his leela with Sita and Lakshman. It was here, at the ghat of Chitrakoot, when all the saints gathered to watch Sant Tulsidas grinding chandan paste to anoint a tilak on his ishta devata, Sri Rama, that the Lord revealed Himself in person. Afterwards he went on to Maihar, where he made the long, steep climb up to the shrine of Sarada Devi and offered his salutations to the goddess of knowledge, music and the arts.

"In December, he visited Amarkantak, 'the forest of the immortals', where tapasvis, rishis and munis have practised sadhana from time immemorial. Here he had a dip in the Narmada Udgam and at Kapil Dhara, where the icy cold Narmada falls freely. Then he proceeded to the eternally sanctified city of Ujjain. There he performed bhasma abhishek on Mahakaleshwar, the swayambhu jyotirlinga of Lord Shiva. Then he proceeded to Kala Bhairava where he offered all his spiritual intoxication, saying that this was all that he had left to give.

"From Ujjain, in mid-December, he proceeded to Omkareshwar, the sacred Om shaped island on the banks of the Narmada. Here, in a cave overlooking the Narmada, Adi

Shankaracharya received diksha from Guru Govindapada and later performed the miracle of absorbing Narmada in his kamandalu, transforming faith into a living experience. Standing inside the cave with folded hands, he heard a voice from within saying, 'What do you seek? Ask and it shall be yours.' In an outburst of Sanskrit he replied, 'Digvijay – No; Immortality – not possible; Prosperity – had plenty; Moksha – it is in me. I have come here merely to fulfil my promise which I made to you years ago to return when my work was over.' Then he followed a secret passage which led from the cave to the Garbha where he had darshan of the jyotirlinga of Omkareshwar, which he experienced as eternally luminescent in sahasrara. Afterwards, he went to Datia and visited the Pitambari Peeth of Shakti, where he had stayed for four days with his third tantric guru during his parivrajaka life.

"In early January 1989, he was in Vraj or Mathura where he enacted the whole playful lila of Krishna with Radha. He also visited Brindavan, Gokul and Barsana. It was here too that he had darshan of the great saint, Devraha Baba. Afterwards, he went to the Kumbha Mela at Allahabad and took part in two *snan parvas*, or bathing festivals, that of Makar Sankranti on 14th January and Somavati Amavasya of 6th February. The charged waters of the Sangam electrified his whole body and he could easily feel the truth of the saying that a bath here gives man rebirth in this very life itself. This year was especially auspicious as Somavati Amavasya took place after one hundred and seventy-two years.

"I went to be with him for this momentous occasion and to have darshan of Ganga, Yamuna and Saraswati Devi. During the day we jostled with millions of devotees from every culture, race and creed, all with just one thought in mind, to bathe at Prayag. This gave us the unique vision of witnessing faith in motion, and we could easily conceive the idea of that faith which is a dynamic principle and which has been known to move mountains.

"In mid-January, he went to Datia for three weeks to perform the anushthana of Tripura Sundari who is enshrined at the Pithambari Pitha. In February, he returned to the Kumbha for a second bath and then went on to Katni, where he made the sankalpa to throw off the mantle of guru and take up the life of a parivrajaka. From Katni, he went to Dwarka, the land to which Krishna migrated from Mathura with the entire Vrishni clan. Then he proceeded to Somnath, one of the Dwadash jyotirlingas, having a history which fades into legend. It is said that this temple was originally constructed by Somraj, the moon god, himself.

"In March, he visited the town of Shirdi, which resonates with the spiritual vibrations of the great saint, Sai Baba. There he had darshan of the samadhi and sat at the eternally lit dhuni of Baba. In early April he had darshan of the jyotirlinga of Mahabaleshwar, which is said to be the source of five rivers: Savitri, Krishna, Venya, Koyen and Gayatri. He spent many hours walking through the forests of Mahabaleshwar, which are beautiful but sinister and few venture there.

"In mid-April, he proceeded to Nasik and Trayambakeshwar, where the river Godavari originates. It was in Panchavati that Sri Rama spent eleven years in exile. Then he had darshan of the jyotirlinga of Lord Trayambakeshwar, which is unique on account of three lingas emerging out of a single stone. Here he conducted a special pooja with chants of Rudrashtakam. Later he did *parikrama* (circumambulation) of the mandir and had darshan of many mahatmas residing there.

"In early May, he travelled to Bhimashankar which was a journey back to nature. Surrounded by lush green forests, unspoiled by modern civilization, is the jyotirlinga of Bhimashankar. The temple itself is very ancient and, unlike other tirthas where one has to ascend to worship the deity, here the devotee has to descend a flight of steps before having darshan of the jyotirlinga. It was there that Lord Shiva rested after slaying the demon Tripurasura.

"From Bhimashankar he went to Ghushmeshwar, named after a bhakta called Ghushma. The jyotirlinga there was a boon which Ghushma received from Shiva for her unflinching devotion. It is also known as Shivalaya because Shiva promised her that he would be eternally present there. This temple is situated near the famed Ellora caves which he visited after many years.

"In mid-May, he went to Nathdwara, the seat of the Vallabha Sampradaya, renowned for the rites and rituals adopted by the Pushti Margis. In Nathdwara, he actually had the feeling of being in the presence of Lord Krishna. A little further down from Nathdwara is Kankroli, another important seat of the Pushti Margi sect, where he had darshan of the image of Dwarkadheesh. There he sat for hours in the temple precincts amidst the singing of Krishna bhajans in the local dialect. From here, he visited the temple of Eklingi which houses images of almost every deity. The main deity is a four-faced image of Shiva emerging from a black marble shivalingam. To enter the *garbha griha,* the inner chamber, he was given a special robe by the poojari and he had personal darshan of Eklingi Maharaj.

"From Eklingi, he went to Pushkar, which is said to be the guru of all teerthas. No pilgrimage is complete without a visit here. The only Brahma temple in India is found here. After a dip in the Pushkar lake and in the Agastya kund, he had darshan of Brahmaji and conducted a special pooja in this beautiful temple. From Pushkar, he went to Ajmer where he offered a chadar or upper cloth, to the *dargah,* burial site, of Khwaja Moinuddin Chisti. Thousands come to this place, forgetting their caste and religion. Here, filled with devotion and faith, he practised japa and dhyana.

"Afterwards, he went to Mount Abu. There in the majestic Jain temple of Dilwara, he meditated in front of the large image of Lord Mahavir, and was inspired to walk further along the path of self-discovery, filled with renunciation, *tyagabhava.* There also he had darshan of the cave where Dattatraya performed austerities. Many years ago, during his wanderings, he had stayed here and he felt that his future was being directed by Lord Dattatreya.

"In June, he terminated his pilgrimage with a visit to Rishikesh, Gangotri and Badrinath. I accompanied him on this trip. Many saints and mahatmas met Paramahamsaji and he bathed in the icy cold waters of the Gangotri and the steaming hot water of Tapt kund at Badrinath. He also had darshan of Saraswati Udgam at Manas where she emerges with full force out of the mountain, which was a sight to behold."

"At what point during this spiritual journey," asked one sannyasin, "did Paramahamsaji's future become clear?"

"After his yatra of the tirthasthanas," Swami Niranjan replied, "Paramahamsaji went to Trayambakeshwar for chaturmas. He decided to spend the monsoon months in the place of his ishta devata, Lord Mrityunjaya. He had been invited by the Mahant of Juna Akhara to stay at Neel Parbat, which is itself a jagrat and siddha place. He chose to stay in a small room, eight feet square, in the *goshala* (cowshed) at the base of the hill for two months and perform his sadhana.

"It was here in Trayambakeshwar many years ago that his first mission was revealed to him. It was here too that he had made a promise or sankalpa to return and seek further instructions, after renouncing all his achievements in the propagation of yoga. Soon after his arrival in Trayambakeshwar, Paramahamsaji went to the temple and renounced his geru cloth and watch. Placing them in a bundle near the shivalingam, he said, 'These are my clothes and my wealth. You gave them to me for a purpose and I have fulfilled that. Now I am returning everything to you.'

"After this he stayed alone on Neel Parbat surrounded by the Brahma Giri hills, meditating and awaiting his next command. At midnight, on Guru Poornima, there was a cyclonic storm and the command was clear: 'Perfect the unbroken awareness of your guru mantra with every breath and beat of the heart. That is your mission now.'

"His mission was clear, but still the question, 'Where to fulfil it?' was haunting his mind. Many places were offered, a beautiful cave at Gangotri on the bank of the Ganga, a kutir at Kedarnath, but he had reserved his decision until the direction was made clear to him from within. On 8th September, he woke up at midnight. The sky was quiet; the translucent rays of Ashtami were shining through the small window of his kutir. He found himself enveloped by a strange light and again the command was clear, 'Go to my cremation ground, the *chitabhoomi.*'

"That morning, a swami arrived from Munger and the first instruction Paramahamsaji gave was to find that place for him. He gave a glimpse of what he had seen and described the setting and topography. The swami left barely three hours after arriving in search of the place of his description. On 12th September, Paramahamsaji's sannyasa initiation day, he was informed that the exact setting in Lord Shiva's smashan bhoomi for his further mission had been located. That evening he performed poornahuti for the fulfilment of his prayers and the revelation of the divine place and a clear-cut path, just as BSY and Ganga Darshan had been revealed to him twenty-five years before in the same place by the same Lord Mrityunjaya."

> *Om Namo Narayana*
> *O Lord Mrityunjaya.*
> *I have worshipped you*
> *as Kaal Bhairava with one tattwa,*
> *as Kaamakshi with five tattwas,*
> *as Vishnu with flowers, fruits, water and milk.*
> *In many forms, in many ways*
> *and in many places*
> *I have worshipped whatever form*
> *you have revealed to me as your own image.*
> *And now, at your burial ground*
> *I will worship you with every breath.*
> *This I promise.*

Swami Satyananda

PARAMAHAMSA SANNYASA

Some time later, Swami Niranjan was preparing a group of students for their first darshan and blessing of Paramahamsaji. On this occasion he was accompanied by Swami Satyasangananda. The students were very eager to ask questions as they were anticipating the long awaited journey to Deoghar on the following morning.

"Please tell us something about Deoghar?" one of the students asked.

"Yes," Swami Niranjan replied, "but let us ask Swami Satsangi to answer this question because she has done a lot of research into the history of this locality." So, Swami Satsangi agreed and, after reflecting for a few moments, she began to speak.

"Mythologically, Deoghar is known as Lord Shiva's chitabhoomi or cremation ground. At first we were surprised that this rural area of Bihar was chosen for Paramahamsaji's sadhana, when there were so many spiritually awe-inspiring places which he had been offered. But after some time, as we watched the unfoldment of a paramahamsa, we began to understand why this place was indicated to him. Deoghar is ideal in many ways for Paramahamsaji. It is located about one hundred miles from Munger, on top of a high plateau in southern Bihar. Climatically it is suitable for sadhana because the air is dry, and even on the hottest days the breeze is cool.

"Rikhia, the actual location of the Paramahamsa Alakh Bara, is located about six kilometres outside Deoghar. The name Rikhia is derived from the word *rishi*, meaning 'seer'. At one time this place was a dense forest and no one dared to roam about there. Many rishis were attracted to the place as they always preferred to remain in solitude to practise their sadhana. So, Rikhia was a place where rishis used to live. In more recent times, Sri Aurobindo lived there before setting off to start his mission in Pondicherry. Sri Rabindranath Tagore had originally chosen this place for his university, which was later founded at Bolpur and named Shantiniketan. Mahatma Gandhi also had an ashram there which was visited by all the great Indian leaders of the freedom movement. A sannyasin by the name of Satyananda, whose guru was Swami Sivananda of Ramakrishna Math, also came to this place to live in seclusion and practise his sadhana.

"Today Rikhia is a small hamlet, containing many villages, including Pania Pagaar where the sadhana *sthal* (place) of Paramahamsaji is situated. Paramahamsaji had once said that when choosing a place for sadhana, a sadhu should have only one consideration in mind, and that is an abundance of water. A roof over the head is not as important as a plentiful supply of water. The name of this place is, therefore, befitting. *Pania Pagaar* means 'plentiful water.'"

"Did Paramahamsaji encounter any problems while establishing the Alakh Bara on the land which was acquired there?" asked one of the students.

"There were absolutely no problems whatever with that land," replied Swami Niranjan. "Anything that is planted just shoots up. Paramahamsaji says that in each and every tree of that place there resides a particular deity, devata or tree spirit. There is a well on the property, which is filled with crystal clear water all year around. This well is only about fifteen feet deep, which is remarkable when you consider that the land is up in the mountains. Once we decided to bore a well in order to get more water for irrigation, but we had to go down three hundred feet, while in the natural well which we found on the property, water was available just a few feet below ground level. How such things happen is really amazing.

"Another amazing thing happened when Paramahamsaji first arrived on the land. He saw a huge, glittering geru-coloured serpent emerge from a hole beneath the rudraksha tree at the centre of the property. The serpent slowly did a parikrama or circumambulation of the whole property three times, while Paramahamsaji watched. Then it returned to the hole and slid back down, never to be seen again. Paramahamsaji recognized the serpent as a manifestation of Nag Nath which had come to bless him and the land for the success of his spiritual endeavour."

"Why are visitors prohibited from entering the Alakh Bara?" asked one of the students.

"During the period of sadhana," replied Swami Satsangi, "no one is allowed to enter the Alakh Bara. For Parama-hamsaji, sadhana is a way of life which consumes his entire day. It is not restricted to a few minutes or hours. Parama-hamsaji has always said that the only difficulty he faces in his sadhana is the constant stream of visitors who wish to have his darshan. He has no problems with his body, mind, emotions or spirit. They are all firmly set on the path of self-realization. However, the frequent darshanartis do pose a problem, as meeting them causes a break in his sadhana.

"Paramahamsaji has said, 'I have nothing more to say to anyone and no further guidance to give. For twenty-six years I lived with people, answering their questions and helping them on the spiritual path. Those who are receptive will surely benefit from what I have taught them. But those who are not receptive will now have to find their own way. I do not wish to give darshan now; if I did I would have stayed in Munger. I want to live in solitude. If I am disturbed here, I will go elsewhere to a place where no one will find me.'

"Throughout the year, Paramahamsaji remains alone at the Alakh Bara. His sole companion is a ferocious dog. Dogs are the vehicle of Bhairav Nath. At all Shiva temples you will find Bhairav Nath in the outer precincts. First you have to pay obeisance to the security officer and then to Lord Shiva. The security officer of Paramahamsaji is called Bhola Nath. He remains around him the whole day, guarding his dhuni and mandap. He barks fiercely and attacks if anyone dares to enter that area uninvited. At the sound of the *damaru,* drum, and *shankha,* conch, Bhola Nath knows that Parama-hamsaji has commenced his sadhana and he positions himself near the *vedi,* the altar, in order to guard him."

336

"Please tell us more about Paramahamsaji's lifestyle in the Alakh Bara," asked one of the students. "What kind of sadhana does he perform there, and what are the effects of these austerities on his health?"

"Paramahamsaji leads a very simple life in the Alakh Bara," replied Swami Niranjan, "although he is very disciplined. He remains outdoors all the time during the summer and winter months. It is only during the period of chaturmas that he performs *purashcharana* (observance consisting of mantra repetition) in his thatched kutir. At other times he stays outside near his dhuni, which is called the Mahakal Chitta Dhuni, or else at the vedi where he performs Panchagni Vidya. Paramahamsaji does not wear a dhoti anymore; he just wears a loin cloth. Even this he does only for social reasons, otherwise he would prefer to live like an avadhoota, without any covering.

"The sadhanas which are prescribed for paramahamsa sannyasins are different and vary according to the season. In summer, Paramahamsaji performs the Panchagni sadhana where he sits underneath the blazing sun, in the heat of the day, with four fires burning around him. The temperature can go as high as eighty or ninety degrees Centigrade. We used to wonder how Paramahamsaji could survive such heat, sitting there for hours, days, weeks and months at a time, without it adversely affecting his body. I studied *Brihadaranyaka Upanishad* and it said that only those who have overcome the five fires that rage inside: *krodha*, anger; *lobha*, greed; *kama*, passion; *moha*, attachment, and *mada*, arrogance, can survive the sadhana of the five fires outside.

"We were very inquisitive about the effects of his sadhana. From our analysis we felt that only a person who has achieved control over the natural elements and the mind can survive such an intense routine. Paramahamsaji is not a young man, he is nearly seventy. The body usually has many limitations at that age, but not his body. He has never been sick despite the exposure to the elements. He sleeps on a mattress of gunny bags, out in the open, no matter what the season.

337

"In winter, instead of Panchagni, he keeps water in earthen pots and takes a cold bath outside under the stars at midnight. Then he sits in the freezing air and starts his sadhana. The emphasis of sadhana in winter is on the practice of pranayama. He does about two thousand rounds of bhastrika a day and other higher pranayamas which are not revealed in the books but are handed down from guru to disciple. He also practises one hundred and eight rounds of surya namaskara at a stretch.

"To us this path of sadhana sounds a bit strange, extreme heat during summer and extreme cold during winter, but it is not strange to the sannyasin or yogi who knows the process of spiritual transcendence. Paramahamsas have to undergo that process. They have to come to that stage in order to perfect the awareness of divinity. At that moment every atom of their being is charged with cosmic, universal energy and power. Many times when Paramahamsaji finishes his sadhana, his body is just glowing. It is difficult to look into his eyes, they seem to go straight through you."

"We always regarded Paramahamsaji as a highly realized being even before he started all this sadhana," said one of the devotees. "What is the need for him to practise these austerities now?"

"Many people question the need for Paramahamsaji to do all these sadhanas and live in austerity when he has already proven his spiritual calibre," replied Swami Niranjan. "In answer Paramahamsaji says, 'I receive clear mandates from above, and I do nothing of my own accord except follow these commands. I was asked to renounce my disciples and mission, because I cannot be both a guru and a disciple. Then I was instructed to repeat the name with each breath. The third instruction was to remain in seclusion and mouna. I am a slave, and for a slave there is no rest.'

"Apart from the fact that the path of sadhana and tapasya has been divinely ordained, it is also a way of life which is most suited to Paramahamsaji's nature. Furthermore, his sadhana and lifestyle set the example for other sadhakas and sannyasins so that later they may themselves undergo the disciplines necessary for attaining the state of a paramahamsa. It is out of his infinite compassion and grace that he has paved the way for sincere sannyasins to follow in the future.

"Since he arrived at the Alakh Bara, Paramahamsaji has never stepped out. He says, 'A paramahamsa has nothing to do with the world.' He lives simply with the minimum comforts. His bed is the bare grass and his clothing is his own skin. He sustains the body on a frugal diet and prepares himself for total transcendence. He does not give upadesh, darshan or diksha, nor does he pose as a great mahatma; rather he lives away from the glare of public life. The divine qualities he attains through sadhana, he uses for the fulfilment of the highest spiritual goal. One who has attained the state of paramahamsa is a liberated being."

ODE TO TAPASYA

Aeons passed. The tapasvi was scorched by the fire of the sun. In winter he shivered to the bone. And when it rained he remained drenched in water. Decades flew by, yet he remained in tapasya. He lived on leaves, water and air, and one day Tapasya appeared before him in his small, dilapidated hut. Her radiance fell on his worn-out body and his life shone and glittered with a new light. At the sight of Tapasya, the tapasvi became overjoyed. Song burst forth from his lips. His life was anointed.

> *O Tapasya!*
> *Where have you come from today*
> *to sing your song of celebration*
> *in the torn and tattered hut of this ascetic?*
> *For which bygones*
> *have you come to offer solace*
> *with auspicious symbols in your hands,*
> *a golden lamp*

and nine crest jewels
on a platter of glittering gems?
This ascetic has endured heat
and on shivering winter nights, the cold too.
Many storms and hurricanes
have swept past his dhuni.
Its flames rose high and fell.
Many oblations have fallen into these flames.
And how many lives have been nurtured by it?
Many sorrows of the suffering
have been burnt here too
and their ill-fortune averted.
This tattered geru robe
has seen precious wealth.
Many have bowed and prostrated before it.
But this tapasvi remained
unmoved, unaffected, unclad,
swallowed up by water,
scorched by the heat of burning hot sands,
consumed by the fire of his austerity.
This tapasvi remained enraptured in meditation.
He lived on leaves, water and wind.
But now if the wind is silent
let there be no wind,
for this tapasvi's meditation has deepened.
O Tapasya!
This ascetic has read the Vedas
Shastras, Vedanta and Nyaya too.
Logic dawned
and his intellect was formed.
Jnana was awakened
and meditation flourished.
The spirits were under his control
and he became endowed with the power of mantra.
He overcame the desire for pleasure
and emancipation.
For he had become liberated and pure.

Renouncing all pleasures and ceremonies,
today he walks on the sacred path.
The mere flick of his eyebrow
can send all of creation
to total destruction.
For he is the emperor of all that he beholds,
these mountains and oceans and Shivalaya too.
Power and fame are now spreading
like blazing fire,
consuming the earth
and lighting up the sky.
And today you have come carrying a lamp,
awakening a new glow in his hut,
compelling compassion to flow
in the hard life of this ascetic.
Gyan will now awaken
in the heart of this ascetic,
and celebration will fill his life.
Standing at the threshold of many lives,
today this tapasvi will tune his instrument.
For you have come to awaken him
and to make him laugh.
Today this ascetic is content.
Let us go and celebrate
in the torn and tattered hut of this ascetic.
Let us all celebrate!

Swami Satyananda, 1956

Sannyasa Upanishads

30

निर्वाणोपनिषत्
Nirvanopanishad

The *Nirvanopanishad* is the forty-seventh among the one hundred and eight Upanishads and forms part of the *Rig Veda*. It enunciates in the style of aphorisms (sutra style) the progress of the *paramahamsa parivrajaka*, the self-realized mendicant monk. A paramahamsa has attained the highest state of consciousness, where one is able to discern the unreal from the real, and where one gains realization of the divine. A parivrajaka has no possessions, is non-attached and is not bound to any one place. The external accoutrements of patched garments, the emblematic staff, the sacred thread, etc. are all merged in the state of self-realization. He is a *jivanmukta*, liberated while alive. He observes no religious vows and worships no gods. He is ever in the state of bliss and has realized the non-duality of the Self and of Brahman.

The commentary on the Nirvanopanishad by ParamahamsaNiranjanananda resulted from informal satsangs with sannyasin disciples. Swamiji's intention is to clarify the vision of paramahamsa sannyasa as explained by the seer of this Upanishad. Although there have been many commentaries, the format of this one is different. Here a paramahamsa is describing the actual states of experience on the path of nirvana and, therefore, the commentary has taken the form of a personal descriptive experience rather than a philosophy. It is also relevant as a guideline for serious spiritual aspirants.

निर्वाणोपनिषद्वेद्यं निर्वाणानन्दतुन्दिलम् ।
त्रैपदानन्द साम्राज्यं स्वमात्रमिति चिन्तयेत् ॥

Nirvaanopanishadvedyam Nirvaanaanandatundilam;
Traipadaananda Saamraajyam Svamaatramiti Chintayet.

The *Nirvanopanishad* is worth knowing. It is full of the bliss of nirvana (like the big belly of a contented man). It is the kingdom of the bliss of the *traipada* (Aum). It should be reflected on as the Self only.

शान्ति पाठ
SHANTI PATH

ॐ वाङ् में मनसि प्रतिष्ठिता मनो मे वाचि प्रतिष्ठितमविरावीमं एधि। वेदस्य म आणीस्थ: श्रुतं मे मा प्रहासी:। अनेनाधीतेनाहोरात्रान्संदधाम्यृतं वदिष्यामि। सत्यं वदिष्यामि। तन्मामवतु। तद्वक्तारमवतु। अवतु मामवतुवक्तारमवतु वक्तारम् ॥

ॐ शान्ति: शान्ति शान्ति

Aum Vaang Me Manasi Pratishthitaa Mano Me Vaachi
Pratishthitam Aaviraaveerma Edhi; Vedasya Ma Aaneesthah
Shrutam Me Maa Prahaaseeh; Anenaadheetena Ahoraatraan
Sandadhaamyritam Vadishyaami; Satyam Vadishyaami; Tanmaam-
avatu; Tadvaktaaramavatu; Avatumaamavatu Vaktaaram Avatu
Vaktaaram.

Aum Shaantih, Shaantih, Shaantih

Aum. May my speech be fixed upon my mind and may my mind be fixed upon my speech. O Self-luminous Brahman, be Thou revealed to me. May both mind and speech make me able to understand the truth of the Vedas. May the vedic truth be ever present in me. Day and night I shall dedicate to this endeavour. I shall think the truth and speak the truth. May That (Brahman) protect me. May He protect the teacher. May He protect me.

Aum peace, peace, peace

Mantra 1

अथ निर्वाणोपनिषदं व्याख्यास्याम: ॥ 1 ॥

Atha Nirvaanopanishadam Vyaakhyaasyaamah. (1)

Translation
Now we shall expound on the Nirvanopanishad.

Commentary
Nirvana means realization and liberation, freedom from the bondage of birth and death. A person who has attained that higher state of consciousness and realization is not bound by the same laws that govern us. Rather, they have come to a stage where they are the lawmakers. They have merged with the divine and become divine.

Mantra 2

परमहंस: सोऽहम् ॥ 2 ॥

Paramahamsah So'ham. (2)

Translation
The paramahamsa said: I am That.

Commentary
How does a person of that level of enlightenment feel, behave and act? In vedic terminology 'That' generally refers to the Supreme Being. The Supreme Being is envisioned as Brahman, the ever-expanding consciousness, containing the attributes or the powers of omniscience, omnipresence and omnipotence.

This concept of Brahman is a *nirakara* concept, meaning that it is not definable by name, form or idea. It is something, which is not defined, which cannot be described as having this name, this form or this idea. Brahman is just a state of realization of the omniscient, omnipresent and omnipotent nature of divinity. So, the paramahamsa's statement 'I am That' describes the process of nirakara realization, which is realization of the formless, attributeless God – One who is everywhere.

Mantra 3

परिव्राजका: पश्चिमलिङ्ग: ॥ ३ ॥

Parivraajakaah Pashchimalingaah. (3)

Translation
After the marks of renunciation comes the stage of parivrajaka (the mendicant monk).

Commentary
After the statement 'I am That' the paramahamsa states, "After the marks of renunciation comes the stage of *parivrajaka*," meaning the mendicant monk. Generally, we think of a parivrajaka as a person who is wandering from place to place, but in this context parivrajaka means something else. The statement is that after the marks of renunciation comes the stage of parivrajaka. What are the marks of renunciation? They are the actions of renunciation, renouncing the attachments of the world, renouncing the craving of the body, renouncing the craving of the senses, renouncing the craving for pleasure and the repulsion of pain.

After having renounced all these things and having become detached from the world of objects and senses comes the stage of parivrajaka. A parivrajaka means a person who has no base anywhere. From the spiritual point of view, having a desire can be a base, a basis for some kind of attraction, attachment or bondage. Being free from this craving or desire, not being bound to one place in the spectrum of the mind, nature or consciousness, where one is subject to the same kind of experiences day in and day out, is parivrajaka. In this sense, parivrajaka means "liberated", not bound by time, space and object, being free from these. This is the state of parivrajaka.

In this context, the parivrajaka, the liberated person, is on the same level as a paramahamsa. A paramahamsa has the discrimination to distinguish the difference between the unreal and the real, and the parivrajaka is free from every kind of earthly, material, sensory and mental bondage.

Mantra 4

मन्मथक्षेत्रपाला: ॥ 4 ॥

Manmathakshetrapaalaah. (4)

Translation

I am the protector of the field in which ego identity is destroyed.

Commentary

Remember that it is the teaching of a paramahamsa parivrajaka sannyasin that is being given in this text. This sutra comes after the statement 'I am That', meaning the divine. So, speaking from the level of that divine consciousness, from that state of universality, the paramahamsa says, "I am the protector of the field, the dimension of experience or that spiritual consciousness, where ego identity of body and mind, or individuality, is destroyed."

In the spiritual dimension, after one has attained realization of the divine, there cannot be a place for any kind of ego manifestation or ego expression. That state is pure ground, a pure field where no earthly weed can grow. Earthly weeds will only grow when ego consciousness or 'I' consciousness exists. When there is 'I' consciousness, desires and actions will become the seeds, which will grow like in the form of weeds, grass, shrubs and trees. However, if the basic ingredient for the growth of these weeds, the ego, is destroyed, then only pure nature remains. This statement means that, I am the protector in that level of realization, of the field in which impurity does not exist, where there is total purity and no ego related with individuality.

Mantra 5

गगनसिद्धान्त: ॥ 5 ॥

Gaganasiddhaantah. (5)

Translation
My established truth is all-pervasive like space.

Commentary
The paramahamsa continues: "My eternal truth, the eternal truth which I have realized, is all-pervasive, like space.' Generally, the concept of truth which we have is still limited according to our perceptions and knowledge. Truth can appear in many shades, colours and views. The following story illustrates this point.

One day a person saw a reptile sitting on a rock. Describing the reptile to the people in his town, he said, "I saw a reptile which was yellow in colour." Fortunately, another person had also seen the reptile. This person said, "Yes, what you say is true. I saw the same reptile in the same spot, but its colour was brown." As luck would have it, a third person was also there and he said, "What you both say is true, but the reptile is neither yellow nor brown, it is green." They were talking of a chameleon, the lizard that changes colours.

All three were speaking the truth. One said the colour of the lizard was yellow and gave a perfect description. Another said the colour was brown and gave a perfect description, and a third said the colour was green and also gave a perfect description. For each one, their realization, according to their perception, vision and wisdom, was the final truth. However, for a person who has been liberated the truth is not

350

confined to his or her perception, vision or wisdom, but is all-pervasive. It can be or it cannot be; both possibilities are there depending on the circumstances prevalent at the time. Therefore, the paramahamsa states, "Established truth, the eternal truth which I have realized is all-pervasive, like space."

Mantra 6

अमृतकल्लोलनदी ॥ 6 ॥

Amritakallolanadee. (6)

Translation

(My heart) is the river of immortal waves.

Commentary

Nadee means river. *Kallola* means ripples or waves playing on the surface of a body of water, like a river. *Amrit* means immortal. The paramahamsa states, "My heart is the river of immortal waves," meaning his attitude and outlook towards everyone contains the feeling of immortality, because he does not see the decaying principle, the decaying nature in any individual.

If one puts on rose-coloured glasses, the world is seen as rose-coloured. If one puts on green-coloured glasses, the world is seen as green. A realized being has immortal-coloured glasses, so he sees everybody as immortal beings. He does not see the body or how a person stands, walks, lives, thinks, acts or behaves. The realized being sees the nature of spirit. The nature of spirit conveys the same feeling of happiness, light, joy and immortality.

The statement, "My heart is the river of immortal waves," means that the feelings that come up from within him are the same for everyone. He does not have compassion for one and repulsion for another, or love for one and hatred for another, the same feelings arise. for everyone and lead to immortality; the realization of the undying principle, which is God.

351

Mantra 7

अक्षयं निरञ्जनम् ॥ 7 ॥

Akshayam Niranjanam. (7)

Translation

(My heart) is imperishable and unconditioned.

Commentary

The paramahamsa is saying that the feeling and the vision
he has for everybody in the world does not change according
to circumstances. It is imperishable and unconditioned. It
is one and the same.

Mantra 8

नि:संशय ऋषि: ॥ 8 ॥

Nihsamshaya Rishih. (8)

Translation

(I am/my acharya, teacher, guru is) the rishi (realized sage)
free from doubts.

Commentary

This sutra can be explained in two ways. Firstly, that "I am
the seer who is free from doubts". *Rishi* means the seer,
one who can see. One who can see does not have any
doubts; doubts exist only if we cannot see anything. In the
absence of vision, doubts come. If he is the seer of the
eternal process, then there is no doubt within him. If he
has attained that state of realization where he is one with
God, then he is also the seer and has no doubts because he
has become one.

The second way of understanding this sutra is: 'My
teacher is the seer without any doubt.' This means that once
he has accepted God as his teacher, he accepts that He is

omniscient and he has no doubt in God or Brahman. Therefore, he has accepted That as his teacher, God as his teacher, who is a rishi.

Mantra 9

निर्वाणोदेवता ॥ 9 ॥

Nirvaanodevataa. (9)

Translation

My divine being is nirvana (beyond sound).

Commentary

Here the paramahamsa states that his ultimate God, his divine being, his deity whom he worships, and whom he has attained, is named nirvana. *Nirvana* means beyond sound, beyond speech, beyond any kind of description of the senses and the mind.

The process of recognition implies the aspect of description. If one recognizes something, then one also has the ability to describe it. Recognition and description both go together, but here only recognition is given. There is no description because there is total dissolution of the physical and mental senses. Nirvana, the state of liberation, is a state which cannot be defined by speech, words or sounds. That undefinable entity, that undefinable state, is God, whom the paramahamsa worships.

Mantra 10

निष्कुलप्रवृत्ति: ॥ 10 ॥

Nishkulapravrittih. (10)

Translation

By nature I am free from family (and all ties).

Commentary

This is a reconfirmation of renunciation, *tyaga*. This is the nature of a paramahamsa. He does not have any ties or attachments with the family. Here family does not mean brothers, sisters, mother and father. Family means what one brings with oneself: the five *karmendriyas* (organs of action), the five *jnanendriyas* (sensory organs), and the four *manaschatushtaya* (mental aspects) – *manas* (analytical mind), *buddhi* (intellectual mind), *chitta* (subconscious mind), *ahamkara* (egocentric mind). These are the fourteen members of our family which always travel with us. We can leave behind our worldly family members – husband, wife, children and relatives, but these fourteen family members continue to follow us right until the end.

So, saying that he is free from all family ties means that the fourteen members within him are powerless. They do not tie him down in any way. He is beyond their influence, he is liberated, he is free.

Mantra 11

निष्केवलज्ञानम् ॥ 11 ॥

Nishkevalajnaanam. (11)

Translation

My knowledge is complete.

Commentary

This statement is a reconfirmation of the second sutra, *So Aham*, 'I am That'. If he is That, how can there be any kind of incompleteness in him? If he is That, then his knowledge is complete. There is nothing he can be taught. There is nothing he can learn. His knowledge is complete because he *is* the knowledge. There is nothing remaining for him to know. He is all. The statement, "My knowledge is complete," means that since he is one with the divine, and he is the

354

divine, there is nothing remaining for him to know, to realize, to understand, or to learn. Since nothing remains, he is the complete knowledge.

Mantra 12

ऊर्ध्वाम्नाय: ॥ 12 ॥

Uurdhvaamnaayah. (12)

Translation

(I study and transmit) the higher scriptures (on Brahman).

Commentary

The paramahamsa states that if there is anything remaining for him to study and transmit, it is only knowledge of the Self, of Brahman.

Mantra 13

निरालम्बपीठ: ॥ 13 ॥

Niraalambapeethah. (13)

Translation

I myself am the seat of learning without the support (of institutions).

Commentary

The paramahamsa states that he is knowledge. He studies and transmits knowledge of the higher Self. He is a source, a centre of learning, which does not have a structure, base, an institution or an ashram. He is self-contained.

Mantra 14

संयोगदीक्षा ॥ 14 ॥

Samyogadeekshaa. (14)

Translation

Upon union there is initiation. (If a worthy disciple comes in contact with the guru, initiation happens spontaneously.)

Commentary

If a worthy disciple happens to come to a guru, then there is spontaneous initiation. There is no need for the disciple to ask or for the guru to give initiation. One example is Swami Vivekananda. When his guru, Ramakrishna Paramahamsa, saw him for the first time, he simply said, "I have been looking for you. Where have you been all this time?" So it can happen that a worthy guru finds a worthy disciple or a worthy disciple finds a worthy guru. When the two meet, the process of initiation is natural and spontaneous, because there is recognition of the disciple's worth on a different dimension.

In the process of learning from a self-realized being, the mentality of the disciple has to be of a different type. Generally, the disciple tries to pull the guru down to his level. He says that such and such a guru is realized and he goes for his blessings. However, he ends up by asking questions which simply fulfil his own desires. No disciple can be called worthy if he tries to pull the guru down to his own level. If he is able to recognize that the guru is on a different plane, and if he has a sincere desire for learning, then he should be receptive to the messages and instructions coming down to him from that level, which happens naturally and spontaneously, without superimposing his own ideas, phobias and desires.

Mantra 15

वियोगोपदेश: ॥ 15 ॥

Viyogopadeshah. (15)

Translation

The instruction is separation (non-attachment to worldly life).

Commentary

What kind of teaching does a teacher give to his worthy disciple? The teaching is of separation, of non-attachment, of disunion. Live in the world, but be not of it. The teaching of non-attachment, or *vairagya*, emphasizes that what is perceived as real in this dimension is not actually real. It is only the appearance which hides the reality. Just as your clothes hide your real body, in the same way, this whole world is hiding a different reality, which is the reality of spirit, the reality of divinity. In order to understand that reality, you have to learn non-attachment, how to separate yourself from the normal experiences, habits, attachments, situations and conditions of life.

Mantra 16

दीक्षासंतोपनानं च ॥ 16 ॥

Deekshaasamtopapaanam Cha. (16)

Translation

Drinking (receiving) the teachings of saints is also diksha (initiation).

Commentary

Drinking means receiving what is taken inside, absorbed and implemented. Real receiving is absorption. It does not happen through the mind or intellect. It happens not only

357

through the head but through the harmony of head and heart, meaning the total self. Real receiving is not just hearing but also digesting the teachings. So, if one is able to digest, implement, absorb and understand the teachings of saints, then that level of understanding itself is a form of initiation.

Mantra 17

द्वादशादित्यावलोकनम् ॥ 17 ॥

Dvaadashaadityaavalokanam. (17)

Translation

(The initiate) perceives (the entire creation) as twelve (changing aspects of the) Sun.

Commentary

The initiate perceives the entire creation as the twelve changing aspects of the sun. The sun moves from one zodiac sign into another, making a complete circle. It is never stationary. In the same way, the entire creation is not stationary. If one feels creation to be permanent, then that is one's perception, but from the perception of prakriti or purusha, Brahman or God, the total creation undergoes transformation or change at different times. The initiate who realizes the changing or transitory nature of the entire creation is that person who has absorbed the teachings and identified the Supreme Being as the non-changing eternal reality.

Mantra 18

विवेकरक्षा ॥ 18 ॥

Vivekarakshaa. (18)

Translation

Discrimination (between the real and the unreal) is (my) protection.

Commentary

If something protects one from again getting caught up in the web of *samsara*, the changing world, the changing appearance, it is discrimination. Discrimination means having the ability to discern the real from the unreal. If one has discrimination, one will always strive to know the real and not be caught up in the unreal. The ability to discriminate between the real and the unreal is protection, as it prevents one from losing awareness.

Mantra 19

करुणैव केलि: ॥ 19 ॥

Karunaiva Kelih. (19)

Translation

Compassion is my joy (sport).

Commentary

We play many games for sport, but compassion is the sport that a realized person enjoys. His compassion reaches out to everyone, without preference or partiality. He views each and everyone with equal vision. There is no better vision than compassion.

Mantra 20

आनन्दमाला ॥ 20 ॥

Aanandamaalaa. (20)

Translation

(I wear) the garland of bliss.

Commentary

What is the purpose of this garland? For a renunciate, a garland or a mala represents a state of achievement or the culmination of the process of becoming. We say, "I have been crowned." In spiritual terms we say, "I have been garlanded." So it is the garland of bliss that the paramahamsa wears, and which indicates his blissful nature, that is being referred to here.

Mantra 21

एकांतगुहायां मुक्तासनसुखगोष्टी ॥ 21 ॥

Ekaantaguhaayaam Muktaasanasukhagoshtee. (21)

Translation

Alone in a cave, in an easy posture, there is intimate conversation (with Brahman).

Commentary

Just as anyone might sit comfortably at home and carry on a discussion with a friend or relative, the paramahamsa is comfortable sitting alone in a cave in a meditation posture, discussing the cosmic situation with the Self.

Mantra 22

अकल्पितभिक्षाशी ॥ 22 ॥

Akalpitabhikshaashee. (22)

Translation

(I) subsist on food which is unexpected (free from craving).

Commentary

Here 'unexpected' means free from desire and craving. Usually we crave for one type of food or another. Craving in general plays an important part in our life. Craving makes us feel that certain things are really essential for living, when actually they are not important at all. So, the paramahamsa says, "I can subsist without craving; I can live without desire. Anything that comes unexpectedly is all right. I am not attached. Whatever happens I accept as an experience of life, and I can subsist on that."

Mantra 23

हंसाचार: ॥ 23 ॥

Hamsaachaarah. (23)

Translation

My conduct is like the hamsa (the swan who takes the real and leaves the unreal).

Commentary

A paramahamsa has the ability to distinguish between the real and the unreal, the true and the false. There is a belief that one kind of swan, which is known as *rajahamsa*, has the ability to separate milk from water. This means it takes the essence and leaves what is unimportant. So here the paramahamsa states, "My conduct is like the swan. The world can offer anything to me and from that I will select what is beneficial, real, true and just, and leave aside those things which are impermanent and unreal."

Mantra 24

सर्वभूतान्तर्वर्ती हंस इति प्रतिपादनम् ॥ 24 ॥

Sarvabhootaantarvartee Hamsa Iti Pratipaadanam. (24)

Translation
I demonstrate (by my conduct) that what is present in all beings is this (reality of Brahman).

Commentary
The paramahamsa demonstrates here the supreme reality by his conduct because he has realized and established it in his own life. This realization is not something that he has simply understood or read about in a book. The supreme reality has been experienced by him in its totality and his entire being has been transformed by that experience. Therefore, whatever he does, he is a demonstration of that higher reality.

Mantra 25

धैर्यकन्था । उदासीन कौपीनम् । विचारदण्ड: । ब्रह्मावलोकयोगपट्ट: । श्रियां पादुका । परेच्छाचरणम् । कुण्डलिनीबन्ध: । परापवादमुक्तो जीवनमुक्त: । शिवयोगनिद्रा च । खेचरीमुद्रा च । परमानन्दी ॥ 25 ॥

Dhairyakanthaa; Udaaseena Kaupeenam; Vichaaradandah; Brahmaavaloka Yogapattah; Shriyaam Paadukaa; Parechchhaacharanam; Kundalineebandhah; Paraapavaadamukto Jeevanmuktah; Shivayoganidraa Cha; Khechareemudraa Cha; Paramaanandee. (25)

Translation

Patience is my covering. Non-attachment is my undergarment. Reflection is my staff. The vision of Brahman is my identity. My sandals are prosperity. To fulfil others' needs is my desire. (The dormant) kundalini is my only bondage. He is liberated in life who is free of speaking ill of others. Union with Shiva is my sleep. (My sadhana is) khechari mudra (drinking the nectar). Supreme bliss (is attained).

Commentary

Dhairyakanthaa means, 'Patience is my covering, the covering of the body.' Generally we tend to become very impatient because we live in a world or a dimension which is limited by time. However, the paramahamsa does not become impatient; his world is not limited by time. He dwells in the absolute, that dimension which is beyond time, which has no demarcations, and patience is, therefore, his external mark or covering.

Udaaseena kaupeenam means, 'Non-attachment is my undergarment.' This is a very pointed statement. We may remove the rest of our clothing, but we are very attached to our undergarment. Here the paramahamsa says that there is no part of his being that he wants to cover with anything. He is not attached to any part of his being, and non-attachment is the undergarment that he wears.

Vichaaradandah means, 'Reflection is the walking staff.' The paramahamsa uses reflection, the thought process, as his staff to help him walk along the path.

Yogapattah means, 'One's own name', 'one's own identity'. Instead of asking, "What is your name?" swamis will ask, "What is your yogapattah? What is your identity?" So here the paramahamsa says, *'Brahmaavaloka yogapattah'*, which means that the identity through which he is recognized is the vision of Brahman, the Supreme. Only because he has that vision of Brahman is he recognized, otherwise he would be an ordinary sannyasin, not a paramahamsa parivrajaka sannyasin.

363

Shriyaam paadukaa means, 'My sandals are prosperity in every respect, external and internal.' The prosperity of a paramahamsa is not physical or material; it is cosmic or spiritual, it permeates his entire being. Just as sandals protect the feet from thorns and stones on the road, so prosperity provides protection to the wayfarer against all the adversities of the world.

Parechchhaacharanam means, 'To fulfil the need of others is my desire'. At that level the paramahamsa still has the recognition that people have certain needs in life and his desire is to help them attain their needs, not their desires. A need is an absolute necessity. A desire can be a necessity, but it is not absolute. An ambition is definitely not a necessity. To fulfil the need of another person is the only desire the paramahamsa has remaining within him as long as he has the use of this body and mind. When he loses this body and mind, then he loses that desire also.

Kundalineebandhah means, 'If there is any bondage in life, it is kundalini.' How can kundalini be a bondage when everyone is trying to awaken the kundalini? The dormant unawakened kundalini is bondage. If the paramahamsa experiences any kind of bondage, it is the dormant kundalini. Once the kundalini awakens, it will always go to sahasrara for union with Shiva.

Paraapavaadamukto jeevanamuktah means, 'Those who are free from speaking ill of others are liberated in life.' Speaking ill of others simply means that we are unable to understand them. If we were able to understand others, there would be no need to speak ill of them. When we are unable to understand what is going on, then criticism or ill speech begins. If we are able to understand others, then there is no need to criticize or speak ill of them. When one has overcome the tendency to speak ill of others, the lower mind has been transcended. With the transcendence of the lower mind one attains *mukti*, liberation.

Shivayoganidraa cha means, 'I rest or sleep in union with Shiva.' As long as I am not united, I have to be awake, active and striving to reach that point of union with Shiva. But once I attain Shivahood, once I become one with the auspicious nature of the divine, then I can rest. In that state I sleep without any fear, with total relaxation and rest.

Khechareemudraa cha means, 'My sadhana is khechari mudra.' The practice of khechari mudra is used in order to drink the nectar, or *amrit*, which drops from bindu chakra. According to kundalini yoga, perfection of khechari brings about transformation of the physical body. The sadhana of a paramahamsa sannyasin is khechari mudra, drinking the nectar, whereby he sheds the mortal body, the mortal clothes, and becomes immortal.

Paramaanandee means, 'By doing all this, supreme bliss is attained.'

Mantra 26

निर्गतगुणत्रयम् ॥ 26 ॥

Nirgatagunatrayam. (26)

Translation

(My realization of Brahma) is free from the (influence of the) three gunas.

Commentary

Everything related with the world and the mind is conditioned by the interplay of the three gunas, but whatever realization the paramahamsa has had is not conditioned by the three gunas of sattwa, rajas and tamas. It is free from all that conditioning and influence.

Mantra 27

विवेकलक्ष्यम् मनोवागगोचरम् ॥ 27 ॥

Vivekalakshyam Manovaagagocharam. (27)

Translation

(My) direction is discrimination which is beyond the reach of mind and speech.

Commentary

Here 'speech' means the externalized sense, while 'mind' means the subtle sense. Speech is used in order to communicate; it is an external process. The mind is used in order to understand; it is an internal process. The paramahamsa's direction is discrimination. The direction in which he has to go all the time is towards discrimination, *viveka*. That viveka is not a realization that can be attained through a mental, subtle experience, or a physical external experience. It is beyond the physical and the mental, beyond mind and speech.

Mantra 28

अनित्यं जगद्यज्जनितं स्वप्नजगदभ्रगजादि तुल्यम् । तथा देहादिसंघातं मोहगुणजालकलितं तद्रज्जुसर्पवत्कल्पितम् ॥ 28 ॥

Anityam Jagadyajjanitam Svapnajagadabhragajaadi Tulyam; Tathaa Dehaadisanghaatan Mohagunajaala Kalitam Tadraj-jusarpavatkalpitam. (28)

Translation

The world which is manifest is as impermanent as an elephant seen in the sky in a dream, and like the illusion of (seeing) a snake in a rope, this body complex is a created network of delusion (infatuation) and gunas (qualities).

Commentary

The world which is seen as manifest is impermanent. Just as if you see an elephant in the sky in a dream, you know it is not real, in the same way the world is also not real. Even the body is not real. This body complex is a created network of delusion or infatuation, and gunas or qualities. If we see a piece of rope lying on the road at night, we begin to think it is a snake. This is a case of mistaken identity. In the same way, if we look at our own body and consider it to be the ultimate creation we are also wrong, because this body is a created network of delusion and gunas, or qualities which keep on changing. They are not permanent. Only the absolute reality is unchanging and free from gunas and delusion.

Mantra 29

विष्णुविध्यादिशताभिधानलक्ष्यम् ॥ 29 ॥

Vishnuvidhyaadishataabhidhaanalakshyam. (29)

Translation

The gods (such as those) named Vishnu, Brahma, etc. and a hundred others culminate in (the one and the same) Brahman.

Commentary

There may be many gods – Vishnu, Brahma, Shiva and a hundred others, but they all culminate in one and the same Brahman. For a normal person involved in the world, there may be a thousand ways of identifying the divine, but ultimately these ways are all manifestations of just one reality, and that is what one has to realize.

Mantra 30

अंकुशो मार्ग: ॥ 30 ॥

Ankusho Maargah. (30)

Translation

The goad (discipline) is the path.

Commentary

A goad is a sharp instrument used to steer elephants. Just as reins are used to direct a horse, an elephant is directed with the help of a goad. The goad is the path. It is through a goad that we control an elephant, which is many times bigger than us. In the same way, it is through the process of discipline that we can stay on the path by controlling the unruly manifestations of our personality.

Mantra 31

शून्यं न संकेत: ॥ 31 ॥

Shoonyam Na Sanketah. (31)

Translation

(The path is) shoonya (the void) without (any) signs.

Commentary

Ultimately, the path is shoonya. Shoonya is the state where there are no signposts along the way. Through discipline we are able to train ourselves in such a way that we experience the state of shoonya. *Shoonya* means nothingness, the dropping away of everything, both material and physical. Once the state of shoonya has been achieved, then the path is just devoid of any and all kinds of signposts or milestones.

Mantra 32

परमेश्वरसत्ता ॥ 32 ॥

Parameshvarasattaa. (32)

Translation

There, the authority of the Supreme rules.

Commentary

Through discipline you can only go to the state of shoonya. Once you reach the state of shoonya and you have dropped everything, only one thing remains, the authority of the Supreme. There, self-effort ceases completely and one moves according to the music which is being played by the divine.

Mantra 33

सत्यसिद्धयोगोमठ: ॥ 33 ॥

Satyasiddhayogomathah. (33)

Translation

The accomplished yoga is the monastery.

Commentary

There are three ideas here: yoga, monastery and accomplishment. The accomplishment achieved through yoga by a paramahamsa is the attainment of self-realization. The sutra then speaks of a monastery, math or ashram. What is the conduct of a person in a monastery where the disciplines of non-attachment, non-possessiveness, truthfulness, and all the yamas and niyamas, are effulgent? When a person has perfected yoga, this disciplined lifestyle becomes an integral part of his own personality. So the statement means that having attained self-realization, the paramahamsa lives as in a monastery where there is total discipline and the spontaneous flowing of the yamas and niyamas.

Mantra 34

अमरपदं तत्स्वरूपम् ॥ 34 ॥

Amarapadam Tatsvaroopam. (34)

Translation

The eternal state is the form of That (Brahman).

Commentary

Amarapadam means 'the eternal state'. *Tatsvaroopam* means, 'the form of That', or 'Brahman'. That eternal state or that eternal reality is only the form of that Brahman which the paramahamsa has accomplished through the practice of yoga.

Mantra 35

आदिब्रह्मस्वसंवित् ॥ 35 ॥

Aadibrahmasvasamvit. (35)

Translation

The eternal Brahman is consciousness itself.

Commentary

That eternal state in which eternity and the existence of Brahman are experienced is consciousness itself. *Svasamvit,* 'one's own consciousness', is that consciousness itself. Through the accomplishment of yoga I have attained within my own consciousness that level of eternity where I experience 'That' and the entire Brahmic creation.

Mantra 36

अजपा गायत्री । विकारदण्डो ध्येय: ॥ 36 ॥

Ajapaa Gaayatree; Vikaaradando Dhyeyah. (36)

Translation

Meditation is on Gayatri (mantra), the staff of (inner) transformation.

Commentary

Ajapa means 'unbroken repetition of the mantra'. Gayatri is the mantra which continues unbroken. The unbroken continuation of the mantra represents the final state of meditation where the consciousness is not dissipated or distracted by the world of name, form and idea. The entire consciousness is just fixed on the contemplation of the mantra alone.

Gayatri is a very specific mantra in which the experience of the divine is expressed. The broad meaning of Gayatri mantra is to perceive the existence of God in every action, whether it be an internal action performed through the senses, mind and ego, or an external action.

Vikaaradando dhyeyah means that meditation on Gayatri is 'the staff of (inner) transformation'. The continuous, unbroken repetition of Gayatri, or the repetition of mantra, is the staff of transformation, whereby the *vikaras*, the traits of mind, are changed, controlled, isolated and made pure. Meditation on the continuous, unbroken mantra is the means of transforming the mental traits.

Mantra 37

मनोनिरोधिनी कन्था ॥ 37 ॥

Manonirodhinee Kanthaa. (37)

Translation

(For a paramahamsa parivrajaka sannyasin) mental restraint is the clothing.

Commentary

This is one of the most important sutras of the entire Upanishad. If the paramahamsa has mental restraint, then that serves as his covering. Some of the different aspects of mental restraint are: complete control over, and total clarity of, the faculties of mind which lead to knowledge of justice and injustice, viveka, and the aspect of awareness, *sajagata*. So mental restraint is the best covering. Clothing provides a kind of protection, security and comfort for the body. In the same way, mental restraint becomes the clothing which a paramahamsa, a liberated soul, wears. In that clothing there is harmony, continuity and discipline in the structure of the mind, emotions, psyche and spirit.

Mantra 38

योगेन सदानन्दस्वरूपदर्शनम् ॥ 38 ॥

Yogena Sadaanandasvaroopadarshanam. (38)

Translation

The vision of eternal bliss can be had through yoga.

Commentary

This statement is clear; it needs no further clarification. Here, the ideas of discipline, following a path, being firm on that path, and adjusting one's lifestyle and mentality according to the necessities along the path, have been defined as yoga. The vision of eternal bliss or Brahman can be had by following the path of yoga.

Mantra 39

आनन्दभिक्षाशी ॥ 39 ॥

Aanandabhikshaashee. (39)

Translation

They receive bliss as bhikshu.

Commentary

Those who have attained the eternal reality receive bliss as the bhiksha. *Bhiksha* means 'alms'. When a poor person begs for alms, that is known as bhiksha. The individual soul is craving for the alms of bliss. Once the vision of the eternal reality is attained, the individual consciousness receives the bhiksha of bliss, *ananda*.

Mantra 40

महाश्मशानेऽप्यानन्दवने वास: ॥ 40 ॥

Mahaashmashaane Api Aanandavane Vaasah. (40)

Translation

(For them) living in this great cemetery (of the illusory world) is like living in the garden of bliss.

Commentary

For those who have received bliss as bhiksha, living in this illusory world, which is referred to here as the great cemetery, is like living in the garden of bliss or the garden of Eden. The world has been referred to here as 'the great cemetery', *mahaashmashaan*. A cemetery represents the place where the individual, the body, the form dissolves. From an entity it becomes a non-entity. Similarly, every kind of dissolution or change from one state of being into another is experienced in the illusory world.

If a person has attained a degree of realization, understanding and compassion, sometimes the feeling arises, "What am I doing in this wicked world?" Limiting or negative traits do not exist in that state of realization. Even feelings of rejection of the world or of the senses do not arise for those who have received bliss as bhiksha. There is no depression, anxiety, frustration or feelings such as, "What am I doing here? I wish I could leave." In this state, even the illusory world, which is the cause of pain and suffering, is seen as the garden of Eden, the garden of bliss.

Mantra 41

एकान्तस्थानम् । आनन्दमठम् ॥ 41 ॥

Ekaantasthaanam; Aanandamatham. (41)

Translation
Solitude (is their) locality where bliss is the monastery.

Commentary
Ekanta means solitude. *Sthaanam* means locality. So the sutra means, 'Solitude is the locality of a person who has had the vision of bliss; it is the monastery where one dwells'. A person who has had that degree of realization will also have the knowledge and awareness that one is really alone, not alone in the literal sense but alone meaning 'one identity'. In that single identity of spirit, the feeling and experience of bliss is the house where a person with that knowledge resides. 'I am one with the spirit and bliss is my residence, my home.'

Mantra 42

उन्मन्यवस्था । शादरा चेष्टा ॥ 42 ॥

Unmani Avasthaa; Shaaradaa Cheshtaa. (42)

Translation

The state of mind is *unmani* (on the threshold of introversion and extroversion) attained through efforts for realization.

Commentary

The state of mind of a paramahamsa is the state of unmani. *Shaaradaa cheshtaa* means 'attained through efforts for realization'. The state of unmani is the threshold between complete internalization and complete externalization. It is standing in the doorway, having the vision of both. We do not experience the unmani state. When we are aware of the external world at any given moment, we are not aware of what is happening inside. If we become aware of what is happening inside, we isolate or cut ourselves off from the external inputs. Our awareness is not developed to the extent that the internal and external worlds are experienced simultaneously. In the state of unmani we are aware of both the worlds because we are living in both worlds. With the body we are living in this external world of the senses, while with the soul we are living in the inner world of spirit. So, the awareness of a paramahamsa is on the threshold, and this state of being on the threshold has been attained through efforts which have been made for realization.

Mantra 43

उन्मनी गति: ॥ 43 ॥

Unmanee Gatih. (43)

Translation

Effort (is) towards attaining the (above) threshold.

Commentary

Effort must be made to attain that threshold state between introversion and extroversion. This emphasizes the statement made in the previous sutra. These sutras state that effort must be made in order to reach the threshold where the gross world and the spiritual world are perceived simultaneously. Effort also refers to the process which is adopted. The basic understanding is that by effort, through the practice of yoga, one attains this level of paramahamsa parivrajaka. Yoga is the means used to attain that state, and the effort made for that attainment also has to be within the framework of yoga.

Mantra 44

निर्मलगात्रम् । निरालम्बपीठम् ॥ 44 ॥

Nirmalagaatram; Niraalambapeetham. (44)

Translation

Their body (is) pure, the seat of the soul without support.

Commentary

The body of the paramahamsa is pure; it is the seat of the soul without support. What kind of body will the sadhaka have who has established himself in the path of yoga, making the necessary effort to attain the state of oneness with Brahman? Body here does not mean the physical structure only, but the entire personality. The physical structure is relevant here because certain sets of discipline are to be followed by the body as well as by the mind. Certain sets of discipline also pertain to the dimensions of emotion and knowledge. Even the emotions and knowledge must have discipline. This total harmony that exists on all levels: physical, mental, psychic and spiritual, results in purity, balance and equilibrium. In that pure state of being the soul resides in its own nature without any support of the external sensory attractions. At that level, the body is pure and it becomes the seat of the soul, which is not supported by the perceivable world, universe or cosmos.

Mantra 45

अमृतकल्लोलानन्द क्रिया ॥ 45 ॥

Amritakallolaananda Kriyaa. (45)

Translation
His activity is joyful on the waves of immortality.

Commentary
The activity of the paramahamsa is joyful on the waves of immortality. A person who has attained that level of purity and oneness with spirit becomes immortal by nature. In this state of immortality, every action which the sadhaka, the yogi, performs becomes an activity of joy which is pleasurable to himself and to others.

The normal activities that we perform as human beings are geared towards providing self-satisfaction. There is very little consideration of whether our actions give pleasure to others. Only by going beyond self-centred ideas, fears and insecurities, by living in the present and expressing ourself in an integrated way, can that expression of the self become pleasurable and enjoyable for others. At that level, the aspect of giving joy and happiness to each and every individual, not limiting it to just one person as in normal relationships, happens naturally and spontaneously, and pervades the entire world.

Mantra 46

पाण्डरगगनम् । महासिद्धान्त: ॥ 46 ॥

Paandaragaganam; Mahaasiddhaantah. (46)

Translation
The space of consciousness is the established truth.

Commentary
Paandaragaganam means 'space of consciousness' and *mahaasiddhaantah* means the 'greatest truth'. The sutra means, 'The space of consciousness is the greatest living truth which one can experience.' In the vision of the space of truth there are no barriers, whether cosmic or individual. It is just one continuity, the state of being, not the state of becoming. In the state of becoming there would be barriers, but in the state of being there is only one continuity. That continuity, eternity or infinity is the truth which has to be realized.

Mantra 47

शमदमादिदिव्यशक्त्याचरणे क्षेत्रपात्रपटुता । परावरसंयोग: तारकोपदेश: ॥47॥

Shamadamaadi Divyashakti Aacharane Kshetrapaatrapatutaa; Paraavarasamyogah; Taarakopadeshah. (47)

Translation
In conduct (they have) divine calmness and self-restraint. They are observant in the field of receiving. Union gives knowledge of opposites (good and evil, or what has been and what will be). The instruction is for emancipation.

Commentary
The sutra *Shamadamaadi divyashakti aacharane kshetrapaatra-patutaa* means, 'In conduct the paramahamsa has divine calmness and self-restraint. He is observant in the field of

378

receiving.' This is followed by *Paraavarasamyogah taarakopade-shah*. *Paraavarasamyogah* means, 'Union gives the knowledge of opposites, good and evil or what has been and what will be.' *Taarakopadeshah* means 'the instruction for emanci-pation.' So the sutra means, 'In conduct the paramahamsa expresses divine calmness which encompasses all spheres of human experience from matter to spirit.'

In this sphere of human experience from matter to spirit, we are subject to ups and downs, fluctuation and dissipation. We are also subject to changing biorhythms that govern our conduct. Because of this fluctuation our state of being is disturbed. There is no coordination between the senses, thoughts and feelings. There is no coordination between feelings, instincts and viveka (discrimination). There are disturbances, distractions and fluctuations in our conduct. Sometimes the animal instincts dominate over our discrimination. Sometimes our knowledge of what is right is clouded by a feeling or a thought.

The life of a paramahamsa, however, expresses that divine calmness which results from the harmony of his activities in all spheres, from gross to spiritual. Self-restraint is the keyword here. Self-restraint implies a state which has to be achieved, an effort which has to be made. Without continued effort, the state of self-restraint will not be attained. So effort symbolizes a process and self-restraint symbolizes the attainment gained through yoga.

The paramahamsa is observant in the field of receiving. Receiving is an art. We tend to receive too many things, even anger, hatred and jealousy. After receiving such negative things, we are affected by them. There is a story from the life of Buddha about a man who was very angry and began abusing him. Buddha listened very calmly to all the abuse and when the man had finished, asked him one question: "Imagine that you give someone a gift. If the person does not accept the gift, what will you do?" The abuser replied, "Well, I would take the gift back." Buddha said, "In the same way, I will not accept your abuse, please take it back."

Buddha had become so transparent. Whatever was hurled at him just went straight past. It did not bother him in any way because he was not a reactive man, he was an active man. Human beings in general are reactive. An enlightened being, a buddha or a paramahamsa, is not reactive but active. Why are these people non-reactive and active? Union gives knowledge of opposites. They must have had some kind of understanding and knowledge. In the absence of knowledge, there would be no distinction between positive and negative activity, positive and negative giving.

So, after having attained the stage of union, they have gained the knowledge of opposites: justice and injustice, good and evil, positive and negative, past and future, which predominate in the domain of prakriti. It is the nature of prakriti to manifest through duality, to express both the black and the white. Prakriti manifests in a definite dimension, shape or form, like a coin with two sides, whereas Brahman, nirvana, or mukti is not defined in any way. 'Neti, neti,' not this, not this, is the last statement of the Vedas.

After having described the supreme reality in four immortal books, the last statement is, 'Whatever I have said is not That. Whatever I have not said may be That or it may not be.' 'Neti, neti' means do not believe what has been said. Follow your own process of realization in which the aspect of total wisdom or omniscience gives rise to the knowledge of the opposites in prakriti. The knowledge of opposites exists and the actions of a paramahamsa are directed according to that knowledge. The instruction is for emancipation. That activity of the paramahamsa, which is being guided by knowledge of the opposites, becomes an instruction for emancipation, mukti.

Mantra 48

अद्वैतसदानन्दो देवता ॥ 48 ॥

Advaitasadaanando Devataa. (48)

Translation

The effulgence (of emancipation) is the non-duality of everlasting bliss.

Commentary

Adwaita means non-duality, *sadaanando* means everlasting bliss and *devataa* means self-effulgence. The sutra means, 'The effulgence of emancipation is the non-duality of everlasting bliss.' Despite having the knowledge of the good and bad qualities, at this level there is no negative reaction, (the quality of badness), and there is no positive reaction, (the quality of goodness). The knowledge is there, that these two opposites exists, that day and night exist. In those states of day and night the paramahamsa perceives the non-duality, the unifying aspect of the everlasting bliss, which is ananda.

Mantra 49

नियम: स्वान्तरिन्द्रियनिग्रह: ॥ 49 ॥

Niyamah Svaantarindriyanigrahah. (49)

Translation

Niyama (the code of conduct) is restraint of one's own inner senses.

Commentary

What is the *niyama*, or code of conduct, followed by a yogi? This has been specifically classified as restraint of one's own inner senses. There are six inner sensory organs, which are the five jnanendriyas and manas, the mind. The five jnanendriyas are the inner attributes of buddhi. They pertain to the dimension of logic and understanding, the process of interaction between an individual and the external world in which he lives. This is the function of the jnanendriyas. *Manas*, in this context, is the aspect which is observing the interactions of the five jnanendriyas and assimilating them, thinking about them and referring to those experiences as its knowledge. These are the six senses which are termed inner senses. Restraint of these inner senses is the niyama, or code of conduct of a paramahamsa yogi.

Mantra 50

भयमोहशोकक्रोधत्यागस्त्याग: ॥ 50 ॥

Bhayamohashokakrodha Tyaagah Tyaagah. (50)

Translation
Renunciation of fear, attachment, grief and anger is real renunciation.

Commentary
The first thing to renounce in the world is fear in its broad aspect. Fear and insecurity relate to the gross mind, the subtle mind and the emotions. There is fear of losing one's own identity, fear of the unknown. We experience fear and insecurity in so many different ways and each expression is equally powerful. Fear acts in different ways upon the human personality, transforming and changing the entire lifestyle and habits. So renunciation of that fear, or *bhaya*, comes first.

Second is *moha*, which means infatuation. Identification with the object of attachment is moha. Attachment to anything may also be termed as *asakti*, involvement. This self-identified attachment to the world of the senses must be renounced. In attachment there is pain and suffering, expression of love and hatred. In non-attachment there is universal vision. Grief, or *shoka*, is the third thing to be renounced. When all the strings of attachment are cut, then grief spontaneously leaves the human personality. Anger, *krodha,* or reactive frustration, becomes the fourth thing to leave.

Mantra 51

परावरैक्यरसास्वादनम् ॥ 51 ॥

Paraavaraikya Rasaasvaadanam. (51)

Translation
Tasting oneness in good and evil (opposites).

Commentary
This is a confirmation of the previous sutras. The opposites are there. All opposites are created by the same nature. Nature is not split into two. The opposites are different manifestations of the same nature. The head and tail of a coin are not split; they are part of the same coin. In that sameness, when the mind is stabilized, there is a pull towards the head or the tail of the coin. Good and bad, positive and negative, do not exist. Here one experiences the oneness.

Mantra 52

अनियामकत्वनिर्मलशक्ति: ॥ 52 ॥

Aniyaamakatva Nirmala Shaktih. (52)

Translation
Real power is the sense of non-controllership (of Self).

Commentary
The eternal fear of losing one's own identity is being dealt with here. When we have the awareness of over-identity, there is the sense of controllership, 'I control myself; I

control other people; I control my thoughts; I don't want to be in control of someone else's thoughts.'

That process of 'I' in relation to the entire cosmos is the sense of controllership. If I am not in control, then some other jiva might be in control, but still there is control. If no jivas are in control, then Brahman will have control. Still there is control. So these are the confined or limited powers assigned to each individual, or *jivatma*.

After having attained universality, real power is knowing and experiencing the non-controllership of the self. I am not the doer. I am not the enjoyer. I am being guided. I am just an instrument, which is played by the musician. A musical instrument is not in control of itself. If you become the instrument and you are aware of the non-controllership of yourself, then this is the state being described here.

Mantra 53

स्वप्रकाशब्रह्मतत्त्वे विशशक्तिसंपुटितप्रपञ्चच्छेदनम् तथा पत्राक्षाक्षिक-मण्डलु: ।
भावाभावदहनम् ॥ 53 ॥

Svaprakaasha Brahmatattve Shivashakti Samputita Prapanchach-chhedanam Tathaa Patra Aksha Akshikamandaluh; Bhaava Abhaava Dahanam. (53)

Translation
In the self-luminosity of Brahman, the illusory world enveloped by Shiva and Shakti dissolves. The existence and non-existence of the created elements and their container is burned.

Commentary
Three ideas have been expressed here: (i) the existence and the non-existence of the elements, (ii) the illusory world of Shiva and Shakti, and (iii) the self-luminosity of Brahman.

In the description of this process, the existence and non-existence of the elements are represented in the aspects of mahat and the indriyas. The jnanendriyas are the organs of perception and knowledge. They are extensions of buddhi, and we can even call them *buddhendriyas*, because perception, awareness and knowledge take place at the level of buddhi. *Buddhi* is derived from the word *bodh,* which means 'to become aware of', 'to know', so buddhi is not the intellect or the intelligence; it is a process of knowing. The sensory perceptions give the external information to the aspect of buddhi within the mind. The other indriyas, or sense organs, are the karmendriyas which are used in order to interact in the physical, manifest world. The jnanendriyas or buddhendriyas, are the perception and awareness of the self interacting with both the manifest and the unmanifest.

In the process of enlightened awareness, the experience of the senses, which are individually identifiable, dissolves. Each sense perception, each sensory action, is a unique field. It is identified by its own independent way of action and reception of knowledge. This process of giving and receiving of the senses dissolves in the process of enlightened awareness. There is homogeneity or harmony in all the expressions of the senses and no individualistic traits remain.

This state also applies to the inner mental faculties because the total mind in itself is a sense organ comprised of four faculties: manas, buddhi, chitta and ahamkara. These are subtle sense organs, giving us the knowledge of 'I am', 'I exist', 'I interact'. So even the 'I' consciousness existing in ahamkara, in manas, in buddhi or in chitta is unique and individually identifiable. However, when that individual identity dissolves in the process of experiencing the continuity of consciousness, then *mahat,* meaning the inner mind, itself dissolves.

The experience of both the existence and the non-existence of the elements dissolves in the continuity of consciousness. The body continues to be governed by the laws that govern the body, and the mind by the laws that govern the mind, but self-identification does not exist. If somebody slaps me, I feel pain. If somebody gives me good news, I feel happy. If I hear sad news, I experience grief. That is all because of self-identification. But at this level there is no self-identification with the body or the mind. Only one continuous flow of consciousness is experienced.

In the next idea, the illusory world of Shiva and Shakti dissolves. When the senses and mind are under control, this state of harmony and integration within our own being is the state of *sanyam*. The first thing we experience in the state of sanyam is the faculty of *viveka*, which means right understanding or discrimination. The second thing to develop is *vairagya*, which means without raga, not attracted towards the sensory world, but towards maintenance of inner balance in a non-attached way. Material things may be there, but we are not attached to them. There is no shutting off from worldly experience; there is acceptance, which does not have any positive or negative influence on the human mind or personality.

When acceptance is experienced without the influence of desire or ego, that is the state of sanyam or vairagya and viveka. This is a very difficult, yet fulfilling and inspiring process. How do we learn to accept without allowing that acceptance to influence our mind, behaviour and action; just acceptance as a reality? Each individual has to find his own way. When this acceptance is experienced, and when one is unaffected by attraction and repulsion, the state of maya, the state of raga and dwesha, dissolves. This is the meaning of the sutra which says, 'The world created by Shiva and Shakti dissolves.'

Shiva and Shakti are the dual forces of creation which have been given different names in different traditions: Brahman and Maya in Tantra, Purusha and Prakriti in Samkhya. In this way, different traditions have described the interaction of Shiva, representing the manifest and the unmanifest, the gross, the subtle and the causal consciousness, and Shakti, representing the manifest and the unmanifest, the gross, the subtle and the causal energy. There is always an interaction between consciousness and energy.

Consciousness and energy interact on many levels: physical, mental, emotional, psychic and spiritual. Depending on the trait, the tendency or the nature of the guna which is predominant in each individual, the manifestation of the power of Shiva and Shakti is different. Again, the individual identity of the trait or nature is dissolved with the attainment of viveka and vairagya. Therefore, the illusory, unreal or sensory world of Shiva and Shakti and their play, or *lila*, is dissolved and one experiences the self-luminosity of enlightened awareness.

Mantra 54

बिभ्रत्याकाशाधारम् ॥ 54 ॥

Bibhrati Aakaasha Aadhaaram. (54)

Translation

Luminous space (becomes) the base.

Commentary

Akasha, or space, in this context, means the omniscient field of consciousness, knowing no boundaries, having no demarcations or definitions. If there are demarcations and definitions in the total field of consciousness, then there will be the experience of duality, this and that. When there are no demarcations, just the one experience of omniscience, then that becomes the base from which all thoughts and actions generate.

Mantra 55

शिवं तुरीयं यज्ञोपवीतम् । तन्मया शिखा ॥ 55 ॥

Shivam Tureeyam Yajnopaveetam; Tanmayaa Shikhaa. (55)

Translation

The auspicious turiya (fourth) state is their sacred thread and complete merger is the tuft.

Commentary

Here the description is slightly symbolic. In the Indian tradition the Brahmins, who are known as the twice born or *dwijas*, wear a sacred thread, which is known as *janeo* in colloquial language and *yajnopaveetam* in classical language. Yajna represents rebirth from fire, and fire represents the dissolution of the old and emergence of the new. The attainment of turiya, which is the fourth state according to the yogic tradition, is the emergence of a new being, combining the faculties of strength (shoulders), compassion (heart) and support (waist), which are the three areas covered by the thread of yajnopaveetam.

The four states of consciousness are: jagrit, swapna, sushupti and turiya. *Jagrit* means the consciousness active in the manifest world. *Swapna* means the consciousness active in the subtle world at the time of dream. *Sushupti* means the consciousness active in the absence of awareness in the state of deep sleep. *Turiya* means transcendental consciousness. In the three lower stages of consciousness, we are still the old self, experiencing the various stages of the jagrit, swapna and nidra states. The different intensities of the evolving states are individual or identifiable experiences.

In turiya, however, there is no such thing as an individual or identifiable experience distinct from the omniscient, omnipotent, omnipresent awareness. So the merger or the dissolution of the three: jagrit, swapna and sushupti, results in the re-emergence of a new self who is the twice born

388

person. He wears the experience of the dissolution of the states of jagrit, swapna and nidra as the yajnopaveetam, the symbol representing the attainment of Brahmanhood.

Tanmayaa shikhaa means, 'Lost in that merger is the shikha.' *Shikha* is the tuft, or the *bindu chakra*, the point where the microcosmos becomes the macrocosmic universe; expression of the individual self become universal. Externally the shikha is the tuft of hair at the back of the head, but the paramahamsa is not talking of external symbols. He has no external identification with any symbol. Shikha here represents the point of bindu, where the merging of microcosmic and macrocosmic existence takes place. So another level of human experience is transcended; the paramahamsa is aware of the oneness of the self in the first, second, third and fourth dimensions, and beyond.

Mantra 56

चिन्मयं चोत्सृष्टिदण्डम् । संतताक्षिकमण्डलुम् ॥ 56 ॥

Chinmayam Cha Utsrishtidandam; Santata Akshikamandalum. (56)

Translation
Chinmaya (Supreme Intelligence) is the staff of higher creation. Continuous awareness is the water-pot.

Commentary
'Chinmaya is the staff of higher creation.' In this context, *chinmaya* represents the power of self-luminosity and omnipotence, which becomes the staff or the magician's wand for higher creation. One becomes 'That', and the experience of becoming 'That' is not only confined to the state of omniscience as previously described. The point has been emphasized here that self-luminosity also encompasses the faculty of omnipotence, and there is identification with that omnipotence as well. There is not only *jnana* but also

shakti, not only knowledge but also power. The absorption of knowledge and power in oneself is the state of chinmaya. That power is the medium through which higher creation takes place.

This sutra continues with *Santata akshikamandalum*, which means, 'Continuous awareness is the water-pot.' *Akshika* literally means 'eye'. Here we should understand the eye as a symbol of humanity's ability to witness, to be aware. The paramahamsa is explaining that the sacred thread, the tuft, the staff and the water-pot, which are the external, recognizable insignia of a holy man in India, are mere symbols of another state or reality. The paramahamsa lives in turiya, the fourth state, or the state beyond, where there is continuous awareness, where there is complete union with the Supreme Intelligence.

Mantra 57

कर्मनिर्मूलनं कन्था । मायाममताहंकारदहनम् ॥ 57 ॥

Karmanirmoolanam Kanthaa; Maayaa Mamataa Ahamkaara Dahanam. (57)

Translation
The uprooting of karma is (unrealistic) talk. Illusion, possessiveness and ego (have to be) burned.

Commentary
This is a very important statement because generally everyone is trying to finish off their karma as soon as possible. But if you cannot finish off the ego, if you cannot control and guide your ego expression and possessiveness, attachment, desire, like and dislike, and if you cannot prevent the mind from becoming clouded, then do not talk about uprooting the karmas. Such talk is unrealistic, just fantasy.

In order to dissolve or uproot the karmas and free yourself from the clutches of prakriti or maya, through whatever process of yogic sadhana you have adopted or been given for your growth, maximum effort has to be made first for the dissolution of *mamata* – possessiveness, attachment, craving, desire, ambition, and the dissolution of *ahamkara* – ego expression in the form of anger, hatred, jealousy and greed.

First these two experiences have to be channelled, controlled and guided, then you can move onto the second level of *maya*, the illusory world. When you come out of the illusory world, only then are the karmas uprooted. As long as you are influenced by the senses and the mind, the karmas cannot be uprooted. No amount of meditation or sadhana will uproot them.

Mantra 58

श्मशाने अनाहताङ्गी ॥ 58 ॥

Shmashaane Anaahata Angee. (58)

Translation
In the cemetery, his body is unhurt.

Commentary
In the cremation ground where the maya influence or unreality, mamata or possessiveness, and the ahamkara or ego are burnt, the body remains unhurt. The body, meaning the identity of the self as an all-encompassing reality, remains unhurt, unaffected. The identified, limited self has to dissolve, but the real Self, known as atma, which is all-encompassing, is not affected by the change that is happening to the gross self. The place where the change takes place is the *shmashan*, the cremation ground.

Mantra 59

निस्त्रैगुण्यस्वरूपानुसंधानं समयम्। भ्रान्तिहरणम्। कामादिवृत्तिदहनम्।
काठिन्यदृढ्कौपीनम्। चीराजिनवास:। अनाहतमन्त्र:। अक्रिययैव जुष्टम्।
स्वेच्छाचारस्वस्वभावो मोक्ष: परं ब्रह्म ॥ 59 ॥

Nistraigunya Svaroopaanusandhaanam Samayam; Bhraanti-
haranam; Kaamaadivrittidahanam; Kaathinyadrirha Kaupeenam;
Cheeraajinavaasah; Anaahata Mantrah; Akriyayaiva Jushtam;
Svechchhaachaara Svasvabhaavo Mokshah Param Brahma. (59)

Translation

The discovery of the form without three gunas is the agreed
truth. This destroys illusion. Craving and other mental
modifications (should be) burnt. Firm steadfastness is the
undergarment. The cloth is bark. The mantra is unstruck
sound. His nature is free action and liberation is merging in
the Supreme Brahman.

Commentary

'The discovery of the form without the three gunas is the
agreed truth.' The gross, subtle and causal forms; the
experiences of jagrit, swapna and sushupti; the attributes of
sattwa, rajas and tamas; the demarcations of conscious,
subconscious and unconscious, do not exist. When they
become non-existent, then the discovery of the form which
is beyond the three attributes governing prakriti is the
established truth, or the knowledge of Brahman. This
destroys illusion, craving, fear, grief, anger and all the other
mental modifications.

'Firm steadfastness is the undergarment.' The sankalpa,
determination or conviction regarding the merger with reality
is the undergarment. The most difficult thing to remove in
public is the undergarment. You can remove your shirt and
even your pants, but if you also remove your underpants,
everybody will mind, starting with yourself. So the sankalpa
or firm steadfastness is as important as the undergarment.

Clothing is like the bark of a tree, and this physical body is like a tree, being an attribute of prakriti. The tree and the body both come under the jurisdiction of prakriti. The soul, atma or consciousness is what uses this covering of prakriti. So anything related with prakriti, meaning nature, is just the covering which the soul, as an enlightened awareness, has around itself.

'The mantra is unstruck sound.' At that time, in the state of omniscience, omnipresence and omnipotence, the *anahata nada*, the unstruck sound, is the mantra, not Aum or Aum Namah Shivaya or any other mantra. The universal vibration, the *spandan*, which is the cause of creation and of dissolution, is the anahata nada, the unstruck or unmanifest sound. Even in the nucleus of the atom, there is a vibration, a pulsation. That vibration has a sound, which is the unstruck, unheard, unmanifest sound. We are using the word sound because, according to both modern physics and the ancient theories, wherever there is movement there is bound to be vibration. Wherever there is vibration there is bound to be sound, but in the state of enlightened awareness, when I become the sound, then I become the nada of the eternal vibration. This is why the nature of a paramahamsa is free action, and liberation is merging in the Supreme Brahman.

Mantra 60

प्लववदाचरणम् । ब्रह्मचर्य शान्ति संग्रहणम् । ब्रह्मचर्याश्रमेऽधीत्य वानप्रस्थाश्रमेऽधीत्य ससर्वसंविन्नयासं संन्यासम् । अन्ते ब्रह्माखण्डाकारम् । नित्यं सर्वसन्देहनाशनम् ॥ 60 ॥

Plavavat Aacharanam; Brahmacharya Shaanti Samgrahanam; Brahmacharya Aashrame Adheetya Vaanaprastha Aashrame Adheetya Sa Sarvasamvin Nyaasam Samnyaasam; Ante Brahma Akhanda Aakaaram; Nityam Sarva Sandeha Naashanam. (60)

393

Translation

His conduct is like skimming (the ocean of samskara) and his collections are brahmacharya and peace. After studying in brahmacharya ashrama (as a student), and vanaprastha ashrama (as a forest dweller), he entrusts all that (is within him to the divine) and that is sannyasa. Finally (he realizes) Brahman is of indivisible form, eternal, and then all doubts are destroyed.

Commentary

The conduct of a paramahamsa is like skimming along the surface of the ocean. Children throw pebbles which skim the surface of the water without sinking, and then when the force is spent, the pebble sinks. In the same way, a paramahamsa lives in the world but does not belong to it. He is like the lotus which grows out of water but to which not a single drop of water can attach itself; it is water-resistant. In the same way the actions, life and teachings of a paramahamsa take place in the mortal world, but that enlightened awareness does not belong to the mortal dimension.

His possessions are brahmacharya and peace. In this context, *brahmacharya* does not mean sensual or sexual abstinence; it means one who is established in the truth. His first possession is that he is established in truth, and his second possession is peace. There is no disharmony within him. Once he has established himself in that truth, there is no disharmony there is peace. These two are the possessions of a paramahamsa.

First, the paramahamsa studies in brahmacharya ashrama. While leading the life of a student or a novice sannyasin, he is inspired to attain knowledge. Then he studies in vanaprastha ashrama, living in solitude. As a student, he aspired to attain knowledge by living in an environment conducive to this, with other people. After having attained that knowledge, he retired into himself and began analyzing and experiencing that knowledge by following a process of sadhana. Next, renunciation of the craving or the aspiration for knowledge also took place, and this renunciation of the process being followed is *poorna sannyasa*, complete sannyasa. With this complete sannyasa, the paramahamsa realizes that Brahman is indivisible form and eternal.

Mantra 61

एतन्निर्वाणदर्शनं । शिष्यं पुत्रं विना न देयमित्युपनिषत् ॥ 61 ॥

Etan Nirvaana Darshanam; Shishyam Putram Vinaa Na Deyam Iti Upanishat. (61)

Translation
This is the Nirvana philosophy which should not be given other than to a disciple or to the offspring.

Commentary
A *shishya*, or disciple, is a person who has decided to follow the guidance and the instruction of the master and who is committed to follow it until the end. A person who is neither committed nor inspired but just wants to chat about spiritual life in order to pass the time is unfit to receive this kind of knowledge. There has to be receptivity, *grahan shilata*, and absorption in order to follow this process. The disciple's mind has to be strong, positive and receptive.

A shishya, a disciple, must have these three faculties. To be strong does not mean that the disciple develops strength and begins to clash with another. Disciples should not become individual mountains; they should become a unified mountain. The disciple also has to be positive. This means he has to be free from guilt, fear, insecurity and other limiting faculties which take us into a state of negativity, depression, anxiety and frustration. Positive does not mean observing the good and ignoring the bad.

The third quality that a disciple must have is receptivity, surrender, the ability to flow with the will that is guiding him. To flow with the will that is guiding him is real surrender. Saying that "I surrender myself, body, heart and spirit" is not surrender whatsoever. Thousands will say it even today and many thousands more will say it in the future, but out of those thousands and thousands only one or two will shine. They are the ones who have surrendered completely, who have learned to flow with the divine will.

Thinking that "From tomorrow I will follow my guru's every instruction" is duping oneself. Surrender is a very important quality for a spiritual aspirant. There have been many examples of how a person who has surrendered feels. Saint Francis said, "Make me an instrument of Thy peace." When Lord Krishna was asked why the flute was his favourite instrument, he said, "Because it is hollow inside, I can play different tunes on it." Surrender is becoming hollow. These are the qualities of a disciple and only to such a person should instructions for enlightenment be given.

Such instructions may also be given to the offspring. Our physical child is considered to be our offspring because we identify with the physical. But the offspring is also known as *manas putra*, a child born of will, an avatar, a divine and gifted being with a nature that is induced as a result of *shaktipat*, or transmission. Offspring is not just genetic. A disciple can become an offspring. Here spiritual genetics have to be considered.

A guru can give shaktipat in order to elevate the consciousness, provided there is readiness on behalf of the disciple, either from the previous birth or due to letting go of the barriers in this birth. When the energy of the guru is transmitted, the person who receives the transmission becomes the offspring. The guru may be young and the offspring may be a hundred years old. A transference of energy takes place in the right conditions at the right time for the right person. That is the meaning of *putra*, or offspring, for a paramahamsa. The offspring is one who receives the transmission of spiritual power, and only to such qualified people can this kind of higher knowledge and process be taught.

Mantra 62

इति निर्वाणोपनिषत्समाप्ता: ॥ 62 ॥

Iti Nirvaana Upanishat Samaaptaah. (62)

Translation

Thus ends the Nirvanopanishad.

Commentary

With this, we end the commentary on this unique and valuable Nirvanopanishad.

31

कुण्डिकोपनिषत्
Kundikopanishad

This Upanishad is the seventy-fourth among the one hundred and eight Upanishads and forms part of the *Sama Veda*. It gives the duties prior to renunciation, the importance of renunciation to prevent rebirth, its rules, the necessity of yoga for self-realization and finally the attainment of liberation by those who realize the unconditioned Brahman.

कुण्डिकोपनिषत्ख्यातपरिव्राजक संततिः ।
यत्र विश्रान्तिमगमत्तद्रामपदमाश्रये ॥

Kundikopanishatkhyaataparivraajaka Samtatih;
Yatra Vishraantimagamattadraamapadamaashraye.

The famous Kundikopanishad is meant for the mendicant ascetics where they attain eternal peace (Brahmapada). I seek the shelter of that Brahmapada.

शान्ति पाठ
SHANTI PATH

ॐ आप्यायन्तु ममाङ्गनि, वाक् प्राणश्चक्षुः श्रोत्रमथो बलमिन्द्रियाणि च सर्वाणि ।
सर्वं ब्रह्मोपनिषदं मोह ब्रह्म निराकुर्याँ मा मा ब्रह्म निराकरोत्,
अनिराकरणमस्त्वनिराकरणमेऽस्तु। तदात्मनि निरते य उपनिषत्सु धर्मास्ते मयि सन्तु,
ते मयि सन्तु ॥

ॐ शान्ति: शान्ति: शान्ति:

Aum Aapyaayantu Mamaangaani Vaak Praanashchakshuh
Shrotramatho Balamindriyaani Cha Sarvaani; Sarvam
Brahmopanishadam Maaham Brahma Niraakuryaam Maa Maa
Brahma Niraakarot, Aniraakaranamastvaniraakaranam Meastu;
Tadaatmani Nirate Ya Upanishatsu Dharmaaste Mayi Santu, Te
Mayi Santu.

Aum Shaantih, Shaantih, Shaantih

Aum! May all my limbs, speech, eyes, strength and all other
organs and faculties become vigilant, keenly active and well-
developed. Everything is Brahman described in the
Upanishads. May I surely not be neglectful of Brahman nor
Brahman of me. Let there be no rejection of me by Brahman
and of Brahman by me. May all the virtues revealed in the
Upanishads be evident in me giving great joy to Atman. May
they be evident in me.

Aum peace, peace, peace

Mantra 1

हरि: ॐ ब्रह्मचर्याश्रमे क्षीणे गुरुशुश्रूषणे रत: ।
वेदानधीत्यानुज्ञात   उच्यते   गुरुणाश्रमी ॥ 1 ॥

Harih Aum Brahmacharyaashrame Ksheene Gurushushrooshane Ratah; Vedaanadheetyaanujnaata Uchyate Gurunaashramee. (1)

Translation

After completing brahmacharya life, being involved in the service of the guru and having studied the Vedas with diligence, (and after being called) one who has gained knowledge.

Mantra 2

दारानहृत्य सदृशमग्निमाधाय शक्तित: ।
ब्राह्मीमिष्टिं यजेत्तासामहोरात्रेण निर्वपेत् ॥ 2 ॥

Daaraanahritya Sadrishamagnimaadhaaya Shaktitah; Braahmeem-ishtim Yajettaasaamahoraatrena Nirvapet. (2)

Translation

(The student) takes a wife (considering her) as the sacred fire, (and) with effort he should do the Brahmi yajna (for progeny) and by that impregnate her.

Mantra 3

संविभज्य सुतानर्थे ग्राम्यकामान्विसृज्य च ।
संचरन्वनमार्गेण शुचौ देशे परिभ्रमन् ॥ 3 ॥

Samvibhajya Sutaanarthe Graamyakaamaanvisrijya Cha; Sam-charanvanamaargena Shuchau Deshe Paribhraman. (3)

Translation

For the sake of the offspring he should divide (the wealth) and do away with lower duties and go to the tirthas (sacred places) by the forest paths.

Mantra 4

वायुभक्षोऽम्बुभक्षो वा विहितैः कन्दमूलकैः ।
स्वशरीरे समाप्याथ पृथिव्यां नाश्रु पातयेत् ॥ 4 ॥

Vaayubhaksho Ambubhaksho Vaa Vihitaih Kandamoolakaih;
Svashareere Samaapyaatha Prithivyaam Naashru Paatayet. (4)

Translation

(There) he should subsist on air, water or prescribed roots
and bulbs, and assimilate only those in his body, his tears
should not fall on the earth.

Mantra 5

सह तेनैव पुरुषः कथं संन्यस्त उच्यते ।
सनामधेयो यस्मिंस्तु कथं संन्यस्त उच्यते ॥ 5 ॥

Saha Tenaiva Purushah Katham Samnyasta Uchyate; Sanaama-
dheyo Yasmimstu Katham Samnyasta Uchyate. (5)

Translation

(In other circumstances) how can the man be called a
renunciate? If he is to be worthy of the name, how can he be
called a renunciate?

Mantra 6

तस्मात्फलविशुद्धाङ्गी संन्यासं संहितात्मनाम् ।
अग्निवर्णं विनिष्क्रम्य वानप्रस्थं प्रपद्यते ॥ 6 ॥

Tasmaatphalavishuddhaangee Samnyaasam Samhitaatmanaam;
Agnivarnam Vinishkramya Vaanaprastham Prapadyate. (6)

Translation

As a result (of all this) the pure-bodied man, by his own
intuition, should come out of the fire (household life) and
resort to vanaprastha.

Mantra 7

लोकवद्द्रार्ययासक्तो वनं गच्छति संयत: ।
संत्यक्त्वा संसृतिसुखमनुतिष्ठति किं मुधा ॥ 7 ॥

Lokavadbhaaryayaasakto Vanam Gachchhati Samyatah; Samtyak-
tvaa Samsritisukhamanutishthati Kim Mudhaa. (7)

Translation

A worldly person, attached to his life companion, after
achieving self-control goes to the forest and stays there,
leaving worldly pleasures. Is it in vain?

Mantra 8

किंवा दु:खमनुस्मृत्य भोगांस्त्यजति चेच्छृतान् ।
गर्भवासभयाद्भीत: शीतोष्णाभ्यां तथैव च ॥ 8 ॥

Kimvaa Duhkhamanusmritya Bhogaamstyajati Chechchhritaan;
Garbhavaasabhayaadbheetah Sheetoshnaabhyaam Tathaiva Cha.
(8)

Translation

Or is it due to remembering the sufferings (of life that man)
leaves the great pleasures, due to the fear of again living in
the womb (rebirth), and of (dealing with) opposites.

Mantra 9

गुह्यं   प्रवेष्टुमिच्छामि   परं   पदमनामयमिति ।
संन्यस्याग्निमपुनरावर्तनं   यन्मृत्युर्जाय   मावहमिति ।
अथाध्यात्ममन्त्राञ्जपेत् ।   दीक्षामुपेयात्काषायवासा: ।
कक्षोपस्थलोमानि वर्जयेत् । उर्ध्वबाहुविमुक्तमार्गो भवति ।
अनिकेतश्चरेद्दिक्षाशी   ।   निदिध्यासनं दध्यात् ।
पवित्रं धारयेज्जन्तुसंरक्षणार्थम् । तदपि श्लोका भवन्ति ।
कुण्डिकां   चमसं   शिक्यं   त्रिविष्टपमुपानहौ ।
शीतोपघातिनीं   कन्थां   कौपीनाच्छादनं   तथा ॥ 9 ॥

Guhyam Praveshtumichchhaami Param Padamanaamayamiti;
Samnyasyaagnimapunaraavartanam Yanmrityurjaaya Maavahamiti;
Athaadhyaatmamantraanjapet; Deekshaamupeyaatkaashaaya
Vaasaah; Kakshopasthalomaani Varjayet; Oordhvabaahurvi-
muktamaargo Bhavati; Aniketashcharedbhikshaashee; Nididhya-
asanam Dadhyaat; Pavitram Dhaarayejjantusamrakshanaartham.
Tadapi Shlokaa Bhavanti; Kundikaam Chamasam Shikyam
Trivishtapamupaanahau; Sheetopaghaatineem Kanthaam
Kaupeenaachchhaadanam Tathaa. (9)

Translation

"In order not to come back after renouncing the sacred fire
(household responsibilities), I want to enter into the sacred
Supreme state which conquers death and does not allow
return." After this, one should repeat the spiritual mantras
and after securing initiation, wear the geru cloth (and)
remove the hair, excluding that in the armpits and private
parts. (That saint with) one hand raised becomes free of
(any set) path. He should be homeless, always moving,
living on alms, practising unbroken meditation. For
protection of creatures he should maintain pavitra (sanctity).
There are also the slokas (verses of instruction): (He should
have) a water container, spoon, string bag, three-fold staff,
sandals, blanket, patched cloth, undergarment and clothing.

Mantra 10

पवित्रं स्नानशाटीं च उत्तरासङ्गमेव च ।
अतोऽतिरिक्तं यत्किंचित्सर्वं तद्व्रजयेद्यतिः ॥ 10 ॥

Pavitram Snaanashaateem Cha Uttaraasangameva Cha; Ato
Atiriktam Yatkimchitsarvam Tadvarjayedyatih. (10)

Translation

Also a clean bathing towel along with an upper cloth,
whatever is other than this is to be given up.

Mantra 11

नदीपुलिनशायी स्याद्देवागारेषु बाह्यतः ।
नात्यर्थे सुखदुःखाभ्यां शरीरमुपतापयेत् ॥ 11 ॥

Nadeepulinashaayee Syaaddevaagaareshu Baahyatah; Naatyarthe Sukhaduhkhaabhyaam Shareeramupataapayet. (11)

Translation

He should sleep on the bank of a river or outside a temple. He should not trouble his body for the sake of pleasure or pain (heat or cold).

Mantra 12

स्नानं पानं तथा शौचमद्भिःपूताभिराचरेत् ।
स्तूयमानो न तुष्येत निन्दितो न शपेत्परान् ॥ 12 ॥

Snaanam Paanam Tathaa Shauchamadbhih Pootaabhiraacharet; Stooyamaano Na Tushyeta Nindito Na Shapetparaan. (12)

Translation

He should use pure water for bathing, drinking and washing, etc. He should not try to satisfy (praise) a good man nor curse a bad man.

Mantra 13

भिक्षादिवैदलं पात्रं स्नानद्रव्यमवारितम् ।
एवं वृत्तिमुपासीनो यतेन्द्रियो जपेत्सदा ॥ 13 ॥

Bhikshaadivaidalam Paatram Snaanadravyamavaaritam; Evam Vrittimupaaseeno Yatendriyo Japetsadaa. (13)

Translation

He should accept alms (in) a vessel made of halves of any fruit (e.g. coconut shell) and (for sleep use) bedding materials which are not prohibited. A man practising upasana with an attitude of self-control should do japa all the time.

Mantra 14

विश्वाय मनुसंयोगं मनसा भावयेत्सुधी: ।
आकाशाद्वायुर्वायोज्योतिर्ज्योतिष आपोऽदभ्य: पृथिवी ।
एषांभूतानां ब्रह्म प्रपद्ये । अजरममरमक्षरमव्ययं प्रपद्ये ।
मय्यखण्डसुखाम्भोधौ बहुधा विश्ववीचय: ।
उत्पद्यन्ते विलीयन्ते मायामारुतविभ्रमात् ॥ 14 ॥

Vishvaaya Manusamyogam Manasaa Bhaavayetsudheeh;
Aakaashaad Vaayur Vaayor Jyotir Jyotisha Aapoadbhyah Prithivee;
Eshaam Bhootaanaam Brahma Prapadye; Ajaramamaramak-
sharamavyayam Prapadye; Mayyakhanda Sukhaambhodhau
Bahudhaa Vishvaveechayah; Utpadyante Vileeyante Maayaa-
maarutavibhramaat. (14)

Translation

The learned person should think in his mind, this body
which I got by chance is for the good of the world. From
space (comes) air, from air, fire (light), from fire, water,
from water, earth. I resort to (bow to) that Brahman who is
the cause of the five elements, who is ageless, deathless,
undecaying and as it is (with nothing left out of it). This
world is like a wave which comes and goes, created on the
ocean of uninterrupted pleasure by the wind of illusion.

Mantra 15

न मे देहेन संबन्धो मेघेनेव विहायस: ।
अत: कुतो मे तद्धर्मा जाग्रत्स्वप्नसुषुप्तिषु ॥ 15 ॥

Na Me Dehena Sambandho Meghanaiva Vihaayasah; Atah Kuto
Me Taddharmaa Jaagratsvapna Sushuptishu. (15)

Translation

As the cloud is (not part) of the sky, so I am not related to
the body. Then how can I be of that (gross) nature in my
waking, dreaming and sleeping states?

Mantra 16

आकाशवत्कल्पविदूरगोऽहमादित्यवद्भस्यविलक्षणोऽहम् ।
अहार्यवन्नित्यविनिश्चलोऽहमम्भोधिवत्पारविवर्जितोऽहम् ॥ 16 ॥

*Aakaashavat Kalpa Vidoorago Aham Aadityavad Bhaasya
Vilakshano Aham; Ahaaryavannityavinishchalo Aham Ambhodhivat
Paaravivarjito Aham.* (16)

Translation

In my imagination (thought) I am just like space. In
knowledge I am just like a mountain. I am brilliant like the
sun and unique. I am always stable like a mountain. I am
always like the boundless ocean.

Mantra 17

नारायणोऽहं नरकान्तकोऽहं पुरान्तकोऽहं पुरुषोऽहमीश: ।
अखण्डबोधोऽहमशेषसाक्षी निरीश्वरोऽहं निरहं च निर्मम: ॥ 17 ॥

*Naaraayano Aham Narakaantako Aham Puraantako Aham
Purushoahameeshah; Akhandabodhoahamasheshasaakshee Nireesh-
varoaham Niraham Cha Nirmamah.* (17)

Translation

I am Narayana (Vishnu). I am (Krishna) the slayer of the
demon Naraka. I am (Shiva) the slayer of the demon Pura. I
am that Purusha (dweller in the body) and I am that Isha
(Lord). I am uninterrupted knowledge. I am the complete
witness. I am without a master, without ego and free from
attachment.

Mantra 18

तदभ्यासेन प्राणापानौ संयम्य तत्र श्लोका भवन्ति ।
वृषणापानयोर्मध्ये पाणी आस्थाय संश्रयेत् ।
संदश्य शनकैर्जिह्वां यवमात्रे विनिर्गताम् ॥ 18 ॥

Tadabhyaasena Praanaapaanau Samyamya Tatra Shlokaa Bhavanti;
Vrishanaapaanayormadhye Paanee Aasthaaya Samshrayet;
Samdashya Shanakairjihvaam Yavamaatre Vinirgataam. (18)

Translation

For the practice of balancing prana and apana, there are the
following slokas (instructions): (with the teeth) slowly biting
the tongue, which protrudes (from the mouth) the distance
of a grain of barley, place both hands beside each other,
between the anus and the scrotum.

Mantra 19

माषमात्रां तथा दृष्टिं श्रोत्रे स्थाप्य तथा भुवि ।
श्रवणे नासिके गन्धा यत: स्वं न च संश्रयेत् ॥ 19 ॥

Maashamaatraam Tathaa Drishtim Shrotre Sthaapya Tathaa
Bhuvi; Shravane Naasike Gandhaa Yatah Svam Na Cha
Samshrayet. (19)

Translation

Direct the partially open eyes (to the extent of a blackgram
seed) and gaze while being firmly seated (in a posture) and
control the ears (hearing), nose (smell, i.e., the senses from
distraction).

Mantra 20

अथ शैवपदं यत्र तद्ब्रह्म ब्रह्म तत्परम् ।
तदभ्यासेन लभ्येत पूर्वजन्मार्जितात्मनाम् ॥ 20 ॥

Atha Shaivapadam Yatra Tadbrahma Brahma Tatparam;
Tadabhyaasena Labhyeta Poorvajanmaarjitaatmanaam. (20)

Translation

After that (contemplate) where the place of Shiva is; that is
Brahman and that Brahman is Supreme. Those souls who

407

have acquired (knowledge through yoga) in the previous life, attain that Brahman by practice.

Mantra 21

संभूतैर्वायुसंश्रावैर्हृदयं तप उच्यते ।
उर्ध्वं प्रपद्यते देहाद्भित्त्वा मूर्धानमव्ययम् ॥ 21 ॥

Sambhootairvaayusamshraavairhridayam Tapa Uchyate. Oordhvam Prapadyate Dehaadbhittvaa Moordhaanamavyayam. (21)

Translation

To hear attentively the vibration of the heart produced by vayu (pranayama) is called tapa (transformation). By piercing the crown of the head, the undecayable soul goes up from the body.

Mantra 22

स्वदेहस्य तु मूर्धानं यं प्राप्य परमां गतिम् ।
भूयस्ते न निवर्तन्ते परावरविदो जना: ॥ 22 ॥

Svadehasya Tu Moordhaanam Ye Praapya Paramaam Gatim; Bhooyaste Na Nivartante Paraavaravido Janaah. (22)

Translation

Those persons who know the opposites do not come back again after reaching the crown of the head (sahasrara or the Supreme State).

Mantra 23

न साक्षिणं साक्ष्यधर्मा: संस्पृशन्ति विलक्षणम् ।
अविकारमुदासीनं   गृहधर्मा:   प्रदीपवत् ॥ 23 ॥

Na Saakshinam Saakshyadharmaah Samsprishanti Vilakshanam; Avikaaramudaaseenam Grihadharmaah Pradeepavat. (23)

Translation

Those (practitioners) should behave in a unique way as they are neither witnesses, nor having the nature of witnessing, they are changeless (without modification) and detached, like a lamp (not affected by the things it illumines).

Mantra 24

जले वापि स्थले वापि लुठत्वेष जडात्मक: ।
नाहं विलिप्ये तद्धर्मैर्घटधर्मैर्नभोयथा ॥ 24 ॥

Jale Vaapi Sthale Vaapi Luthatvesha Jadaatmakah; Naaham Vilipye Taddharmairghatadharmairnabhoyathaa. (24)

Translation

As an earthen pot is not affected by the nature of the space (in which it exists), similarly I am not affected by the water or earth on which I rest (like an inanimate object).

Mantra 25

निष्क्रियोऽस्म्यविकारोऽस्मि निष्कलोऽस्मि निराकृति: ।
निर्विकल्पोऽस्मि नित्योऽस्मि निरालम्बोऽस्मि निर्द्वय: ॥ 25 ॥

Nishkriyo Asmyavikaaro Asmi Nishkalo Asmi Niraakritih; Nirvikalpo Asmi Nityo Asmi Niraalambo Asmi Nirdvayah. (25)

Translation

I am without action. I am indivisible. I am formless. I am without substitute. I am eternal, without support and without a second.

Mantra 26

सर्वात्मकोऽहं सर्वोऽहं सर्वातीतोऽहमद्वय: ।
केवलाखण्डबोधोऽहं स्वानन्दोऽहं निरन्तर: ॥ 26 ॥

Sarvaatmako Aham Sarvo Aham Sarvaateeto Ahamadvayah;
Kevalaakhandabodho Aham Svaanando Aham Nirantarah. (26)

Translation

I am in everything and I am everything and I am beyond everything. I am without a second. I am only uninterrupted knowledge (perception). I am Self-bliss always.

Mantra 27

स्वमेव सर्वतः पश्यन्मन्यमानः स्वमद्वयम् ।
स्वानन्दमनुभुञ्जानो निर्विकल्पो भवाम्यहम ॥ 27 ॥

Svameva Sarvatah Pashyan Manyamaanah Svamadvayam;
Svaanandamanubhunjaano Nirvikalpo Bhavaamyaham. (27)

Translation

I see myself everywhere and I consider myself to be without a second. I become the enjoyer of Self-bliss, without any substitute.

Mantra 28

गच्छंस्तिष्ठन्नुपविश्ञ्छयानो वान्यथापि वा ।
यथेच्छया वसेद्विद्वानात्माराम: सदा मुनि: ॥ 28 ॥

Gachchhamstishthannupavishanchhayaano Vaanyathaapi Vaa;
Yathechchhayaa Vasedvidvaanaatmaaraamah Sadaa Munih. (28)

॥ इत्युपनिषत् ॥
Ityupanishad.

Translation

The Muni who is always happy (Self-joyful) should, in moving, stopping, sitting, sleeping or in any other condition, live according to his own will.

Thus ends the Upanishad.

32

भिक्षुकोपनिषत्

Bhikshukopanishad

This Upanishad is the sixtieth among the one hundred and eight Upanishads and forms part of the *Shuklayajurveda*. It classifies ascetics into four categories as kutichaka, bahudaka, hamsa and paramahamsa and explains their distinctive characteristics.

भिक्षूणां पटलं यत्र विश्रान्तिमगमत्सदा ।
तत्रैपदं ब्रह्मतत्त्वं ब्रह्ममात्रं करोतु माम् ॥

Bhikshoonaam Patalam Yatra Vishraantimagamatsadaa;
Tattraipadam Brahmattvam Brahmamaatram Karotu Maam.

Where the mendicants always attain (enjoy) absolute peace, may that Brahma – pranava (Aum) make me Brahman itself.

शान्ति पाठ
SHANTI PATH

ॐ पूर्णमद: पूर्णमिदं पूर्णात् पूर्णमुदच्यते ।
पूर्णस्य पूर्णमादाय पूर्णमेवावशिष्यते ॥

ॐ शान्ति: शान्ति: शान्ति:

Aum Poornamadah Poornamidam Poornaat Poornamucachyate;
Poornasya Poornamaadaaya Poornameva Avashishyate.

Aum Shaantih, Shaantih, Shaantih

That is full, this is full. From the full, the full is taken, the
full has come. If you take out the full from the full, the full
alone remains.

Aum peace, peace, peace

Mantra

ॐ अथ भिक्षूणां मोक्षार्थिनां कुटीचकबहूदकहंसपरमहंसाश्चेति चत्वार: । कुटीचका
नाम गौतमभरद्वाजयाज्ञवल्क्यवसिष्ठप्रभृतयोऽष्टौ ग्रासांश्चरन्तो योगमार्गे मोक्षमेव
प्रार्थयन्ते । अथ बहूदका नाम त्रिदण्डकमण्डलुशिखायज्ञोपवीतकाषायवस्त्रधारिणो
ब्रह्मर्षिगृहे मधुमांसं वर्जयित्वाष्टौ ग्रासान्भैक्षाचरणं कृत्वा योगमार्गे मोक्षमेव प्रार्थयन्ते ।
अथ हंसा नाम ग्राम एकरात्रं नगरे पंचरात्रं क्षेत्रे सप्तरात्रं तदुपरि न वसेयु: ।
गोमूत्रगोमयाहारिणो नित्यं चान्द्रायणपरायणा योगमार्गे मोक्षमेव प्रार्थयन्ते। अथ परमहंसा
नाम संवर्तकारुणिश्वेतकेतुजडभरतदत्तात्रेयशुकवामदेवहारीतक प्रभृतयोऽष्टौ
ग्रासांश्चरन्तो योगमार्गे मोक्षमेव प्रार्थयन्ते। वृक्षमूले शून्यगृहे श्मशानवासिनो वा
साम्बरा वा दिगम्बरा वा । न तेषां धर्माधर्मौ लाभालाभौ शुद्धाशुद्धौ द्वैतवर्जिता
समलोष्टाश्मकाञ्चना: सर्ववर्णेषु भैक्षाचरणं कृत्वा सर्वत्रात्मैवेति पश्यन्ति। अथ
जातरूपधरा निर्द्वन्द्वा निष्परिग्रहा: शुक्लध्यानपरायणा आत्मनिष्ठा: प्राणसंधारणार्थं
यथोक्तकाले भैक्षमाचरन्त: शून्यागारदेवगृहतृणकूटवल्मीक वृक्षमूलकुलालशालाग्निहोत्र
शालानदी पुलिनगिरिकन्दर कुहरकोटरनिर्झर स्थण्डिले तत्र ब्रह्ममार्गे सम्यक्संपन्न:
शुद्धमानसा: परमहंसाचरणेन संन्यासेन देहत्यागं कुर्वन्ति ते परमहंसा नामेत्युपनिषत् ॥

इति भिक्षुकोपनिषत्समाप्ता: ॥

412

Aum Atha Bhikshoonaam Mokshaarthinaam Kuteechaka-
bahoodakahamsaparamahamsaashcheti Chatvaarah; Kuteechakaa
Naama Gautamabharadvaajayaajnavalkyavasishthaprabhritayo
Ashtau Graasaamshcharanto Yogamaarge Mokshameva
Praarthayante; Atha Bahoodakaa Naama Tridandakamandal-
ushikhaayajnopaveetakaashaayavastradhaarino Brahmarshigrihe
Madhumaamsam Varjayitvaashtau Graasaanbhaikshaacharanam
Kritvaa Yogamaarge Mokshameva Praarthayante; Atha Hamsaa
Naama Graama Ekaraatram Nagare Pancharaatram Kshetre
Saptaraatram Tadupari Na Vaseyuh; Gomootragomayaahaarino
Nityam Chaandraayanaparaayanaa Yogamaarge Mokshameva
Praarthayante; Atha Paramahamsaa Naama Samvartakaaruni-
shvetaketujadbharatadattaatreyashukavaamadevahaareetaka Pra-
bhritayo Ashtau Graasaamshcharanto Yogamaarge Mokshameva
Praarthayante; Vrikshamoole Shoonyagrihe Shmashaanavaasino
Vaa Saambaraa Vaa Digambaraa Vaa; Na Teshaam Dharma-
adharmau Laabhaalaabhau Shuddhaashuddhau Dvaitavarjitaa
Samaloshtaashmakaanchanaah Sarvavarneshu Bhaikshaacharanam
Kritvaa Sarvatraatmaiveti Pashyanti; Atha Jaataroopadharaa
Nirdvandvaa Nishparigrahaah Shukladhyaanaparaayanaa
Aatmanishthaah Praanasamdhaaranaartham Yathoktakaale
Bhaikshamaacharantah Shoonyaagaaradevagrihatrinakoota-
valmeeka Vrikshamoolakulaalashaalaagnihotra Shaalaanadeepulina
girikandara Kuharakotaranirjhara Sthandile Tatra Brahmamaarge
Samyaksampannaah Shuddhamaanasaah Paramahamsaacharanena
Samnyaasena Dehatyaagam Kurvanti Te Paramahamsaa
Naametyupanishat.

Iti Bhikshukopanishatsamaaptaah.

Translation

Where the bhikshus (sadhus) are, peace always exists. That
state is the threefold Aum and that (realization) makes me
Brahman.

Among the liberation-seeking bhikshus there are four
categories: kutichak, bahudak, hamsa and paramahamsa.

Kutichaks such as Gautam, Bharadwaj, Yajnavalkya
and Vashishtha, etc. eat eight morsels (of food) (the eight-

413

fold path of yoga) and following that, they pray for liberation.

The bahudaks, having a threefold staff, a water-pot, a tuft, a sacred thread and geru cloth, eating eight morsels of food (eight disciplines) as alms in the house of brahma rishis, barring meat and wine, pray for liberation and remain in the path of yoga.

The hamsa bhikshus stay in a village for one night, in a city for five nights and in a particular area for seven nights and no more. They subsist on the urine and dung of cows and observe chandrayanvrat (taking between one and fifteen mouthfuls of food daily according to the lunar cycle). In the path of yoga they pray for liberation.

Now (about) paramahamsa; Samvartaka, Aruni, Shveta-ketu, Jadabharata, Dattatreya, Shuka, Vaamadeva, Haritaka, etc. eat eight morsels and pray only for moksha (liberation) in the path of yoga. They live under trees, in empty houses, in cemeteries, maybe clothed or naked. For them there is no prohibition (restrictions of duality) of dharma or adharma, loss or gain, purity or impurity. For them stone and gold are equal and they take alms from people of any caste, and perceive everywhere as their own Self.

Clothed as at birth, without conflict, without collections (possessions), engrossed in shukla dhyana (white, light, pure lifelong meditation), true to themselves (established in the Self), they eat at the proper time only sufficient to keep themselves alive.

Becoming accomplished in the path of Brahman, pure-minded, through the conduct of being a paramahamsa sannyasin, they leave their body (die) in a vacant house, temple, in a room made of grass, in an anthill, beneath trees, in a kiln of a potter, in the place where agnihotra is done, on the bank of a river, in a mountain cave, in a hollow tree, by a waterfall or on bare ground. They are the paramahamsas in whose name this Upanishad is (written).

Thus ends the Bhikshukopanishad.

33

अवधूतोपनिषत्
Avadhootopanishad

This Upanishad is the seventy-ninth of the one hundred and eight Upanishads and forms part of the *Krishna-yajurveda*. It describes the nature of the avadhoota ascetic and his conduct. It concludes with the enunciation of Self-realization.

गौणमुख्यावधूतालिहृदयाम्बुजवर्ति यत् ।
तत्रैपदं ब्रह्मतत्त्वं स्वमात्रमवशिष्यते ॥

Gaunamukhyaavadhootaalihridayaambujavarti Yat;
Tattraipadam Brahmatattvam Svamaatramavashishyate.

In the lotus heart of the avadhoota, the three-syllable Brahman element, Aum, primary or secondary (manifest or unmanifest) remains itself.

शान्ति पाठ
SHANTI PATH

ॐ सहनाववतु । सह नौ भुनक्तु । सह वीर्यं करवावहै । तेजस्वि नावधीतमस्तु ।
मा विद्विषावहै ॥

ॐ शान्ति: शान्ति: शान्ति:

*Aum Saha Naavavatu; Saha Nau Bhunakt;. Saha Veeryam
Karavaavahai; Tejasvi Naavadheetamastu; Maa Vidvishaavahai.*

Aum Shaantih Shaantih Shaantih

Aum. May the Lord protect both teacher and disciple and
may He cherish us both. May we be strong together that our
study be bright (so as to brighten the path of others). May
we never feel ill will towards each other.

Aum peace, peace, peace

Mantra 1

हरि ॐ अथ ह सांकृतिर्भगवन्तमवधूतं दत्तात्रेयं परिसमेत्य प्रपच्छ भगवन्कोऽवधूतस्तस्य
का स्थिति: किं लक्ष्म किं संसरणमिति । तं होवाच भगवो दत्तात्रेय: परमकारुणिक: ॥
अक्षरत्वाद्वरेण्यत्वाद्धू तसंसारवन्धनात् । तत्त्वमस्यादिलक्ष्यत्वादवधूत इतीर्यते
॥ 1 ॥

*Harih Aum Atha Ha Saamkritirbhagavantamavadhootam Datta-
atreyam Parisametya Paprachchha Bhagavanko Avadhootastasya
Kaa Sthitih Kim Lakshanam Kim Samsaranamiti; Tam Hovaacha
Bhagavo Dattaatreyah Paramakaarunikah.
Aksharatvaadvarenyatvaaddhootasamsaarabandhanaat; Tattvam-
asyaadilakshyatvaadavadhoota Iteeryate.* (1)

Translation

Hari Aum. The rishi named Samkriti approached the
venerable avadhoota, Dattatreya, and asked, "Bhagavan (O
Illustrious One), who is an avadhoota, what is his state, what
are his signs and how does he move?" Bhagavan Dattatreya,

who was full of compassion, replied to him. "Because he is undecayable, excellent (the chosen one), because he has shaken off worldly bondage and has Tattvamasi (You are That) as the goal, he is called avadhoota."

Mantra 2

यो विलङ्घयाश्रमान्वर्णानात्मन्येव स्थित: सदा ।
अतिवर्णाश्रमी योगी अवधूत:स कथ्यते ॥ 2 ॥

Yo Vilanghyaashramaanvarnaanaatmanyeva Sthitah Sadaa;
Ativarnaashramee Yogee Avadhootah Sa Kathyate. (2)

Translation

One who had crossed (gone beyond) the varnashrama system (caste system or division of people by profession of brahmin, kshatriya, vaishnava and shudra), and one who is always established in himself, that yogi (one who is in union with the Supreme) who is above the varnashrama divisions, is called an avadhoota.

Mantra 3

तस्य प्रियं शिर: कृत्वा मोदी दक्षिणपक्षक: ।
प्रमोद उत्तर: पक्ष आनन्दो गोष्पदायते ॥ 3 ॥

Tasya Priyam Shirah Kritvaa Modo Dakshinapakshakah; Pramoda Uttarah Paksha Aanando Goshpadaayate. (3)

Translation

The conditions under which an avadhoota spends his life are four-fold. Joy represents his head, delight represents his right wing, ecstasy represents his left wing and bliss represents his very self. (Goshpadaayate likens these conditions to the four footprints of a cow, and also the avadhoot's bliss to the unlimited pasture in which cows graze.)

Mantra 4

गोपालसदृशं शीर्षे नापि मध्ये न चाप्यध: ।
ब्रह्मपुच्छं प्रतिष्ठेति पुच्छाकारेण कारयेत् ॥ 4 ॥

Gopaalasadrisham Sheershe Naapi Madhye Na Chaapyadhah;
Brahmapuchchham Pratishtheti Puchchhaakaarena Kaarayet. (4)

Translation

Gopal (the protector) is not in the middle, head or bottom (of that which he protects), so the spiritual energy of Brahman is to be worked upon beginning with the tail (i.e. mooladhara).

Mantra 5

एवं चतुष्पथं कृत्वा से यान्ति परमां गतिम् ।
न कर्मणा न प्रजया धनेन त्यागेनैके अमृतत्वभानशु: ॥ 5 ॥

Evam Chatushpatham Kritvaa Te Yaanti Paramaam Gatim; Na
Karmanaa Na Prajayaa Dhanena Tyaagenaike Amritatvamaa-
nashuh. (5)

Translation

Like this, making four paths, they go to the Supreme State; it is neither by karmas nor by progeny, nor property, but by tyaga (renunciation) only (that) they can glimpse immortality.

Mantra 6

स्वेरं स्वैरविहरणं तत्संसरणम् । साम्बरा वा दिगम्बरा वा । न तेषां धर्माधर्मौ न
मेध्यामेध्यौ । कृत्स्नमेतच्चित्रं कर्म । स्वैरं न विगायेत्तन्महाव्रतम् । न स मूध्वल्लिप्यते ।
यथा रवि: सर्वरसान्त्रभुड्क्ते हुताशनश्चापि हि सर्वभक्ष: । तथैव योगी विषयान्त्रभुड्क्ते
न लिप्यते पुण्यपापंश्च शुद्ध ॥ 6 ॥

Svairam Svairaviharanam Tatsamsaranam; Saambaraa Vaa
Digambaraa Vaa; Na Teshaam Dharmaadharmau Na Medhyaa-
medhyau; Sadaa Saamgrahanyeshtyaashvamedhamantaryaagam

418

Yajate; Sa Mahaamakho Mahaayogah; Kritsnametachchitram
Karma; Svairam Na Vigaayettanmahaavratam; Na Sa Moodha-
vallipyate; Yathaa Ravih Sarvarasaanprabhunkte Hutaashanash-
chaapi Hi Sarvabhakshah; Tathaiva Yogee Vishayaanprabhunkte
Na Lipyate Punyapaapaishcha Shuddhah. (6)

Translation
Their movements should be according to their own will
(slow, spontaneous) either with or without clothes. For them
dharma and adharma, and work (sacrifice) or no sacrifice is
nothing. Accepting inner sacrifice with their full will, they
always do the asvamedha sacrifice. That is the greatest
sacrifice and the greatest yoga. This whole karma (performance) is wonderful (bright). He does not involve himself
foolishly. As the sun consumes all the essence and agni (fire)
consumes everything, like that the yogi enjoys the objects of
the senses but he is not smeared by virtue and vice, he is
pure.

Mantra 7

आपूर्यमाणचलप्रतिष्ठं समुद्रमापः प्रविशन्ति यद्वत् ।
तद्वत्कामा यं प्रविशन्ति सर्वे स शान्तिमाप्नोति न कामकामी ॥ 7 ॥

Aapooryamaanamachalapratishtham Samudramaapah Pravishanti
Yadvat; Tadvatkaamaa Yam Pravishanti Sarve Sa Shaantimaapnoti
Na Kaamakaamee. (7)

Translation
He attains peace into whom all desires enter as waters enter
the ocean which, filled from all sides, remains unmoved;
but not the man who is full of desires.

Mantra 8

न निरोधो न चोत्पत्तिर्न बद्धो न च साधक: ।
न मुमुक्षुर्न वै मुक्त इत्येषा परमार्थता ॥ 8 ॥

*Na Nirodho Na Chotpattirna Baddho Na Cha Saadhakah; Na
Mumukshurna Vai Mukta Ityeshaa Paramaarthataa.* (8)

Translation

According to the highest truth or reality, for him there is
neither birth nor death, neither is he in bondage nor is he
an aspirant, neither is he a seeker of liberation nor liberated.

Mantra 9

ऐहिकामुष्मिकव्रातसिध्यै मुक्तेश्च सिद्धये ।
बहुकृत्यं पुरा स्यान्मे तत्सर्वमधुना कृतम् ॥ 9 ॥

*Aihikaamushmikavraatasidhaih Mukteshcha Siddhaye; Bahukrityam
Puraa Syaanme Tatsarvamadhunaa Kritam.* (9)

Translation

Perhaps there are many works which have been done by me
till now for achieving mundane or higher accomplishments,
or for achieving liberation; (these) are now things of the
past.

Mantra 10

तदेव कृतकृत्यत्वं प्रतियोगिपुर:सरम् ।
अनुसंदधदेवायमेवं तृप्यति नित्यश: ॥ 10 ॥

*Tadeva Kritakrityatvam Pratiyogipurahsaram; Anusamda-
dhadevaayamevam Tripyati Nityashah.* (10)

Translation

He is satisfied everyday by discovering that those successes
are forerunners of opposites effects (enemies).

Mantra 11

दु:खिनोऽज्ञाः संसरन्तु कामं पुत्राद्यपेक्षया ।
परमानन्दपूर्णोऽहं संसरामि किमिच्छया ॥ 11 ॥

Duhkhino Ajnaah Samsarantu Kaamam Putraadyapekshayaa;
Paramaanandapoorno Aham Samsaraami Kimichchhayaa. (11)

Translation

The sufferers and the ignorant move in expectation of desire and progeny, etc. I, who am full of Supreme bliss, should move with what desire?

Mantra 12

अनुतिष्ठन्तु कर्माणि परलोकयियासवः ।
सर्वलोकात्मकः कस्मादनुतिष्ठामि किं कथम् ॥ 12 ॥

Anutishthantu Karmaani Paralokayiyaasavah; Sarvalokaatmakah
Kasmaadanatishthaami Kim Katham. (12)

Translation

Those who yearn for the other world may sit for rituals. I, who am omnipresent by nature, should sit for what?

Mantra 13

व्याचक्षतां ते शास्त्राणि वेदानध्यापयन्तु वा ।
येऽत्रधिकारिणो मे तु नाधिकारोऽक्रियत्वतः ॥ 13 ॥

Vyachakshataam Te Shaastraani Vedaanadhyaapayantu Vaa; Ye
Atraadhikaarino Me Tu Naadhikaaro Akriyatvatah. (13)

Translation

Those who are qualified may interpret the shastras or teach the Vedas. Since I am free from actions, I am not qualified.

Mantra 14

निद्राभिक्षे स्नानशौचेनेच्छामि न करोमि च ।
द्रष्टारश्चेत्कल्पयन्तु किं मे स्यादन्यकल्पनात् ॥ 14 ॥

Nidraabhikshe Snaanashauche Nechchhaami Na Karomi Cha;
Drashtaarashchetkalpayantu Kim Me Syaadanyakalpanaat. (14)

Translation

I neither do, nor desire, sleep, begging, bathing nor cleaning.
Those who observe may contemplate this, what have I to do
with these contemplations?

Mantra 15

गुञ्जापुञ्जादि दह्येत नान्यारोपितवह्निना ।
नान्यारोपितसंसारधर्मा नैवमहं भजे ॥ 15 ॥

Gunjaapunjaadi Dahyeta Naanyaaropitavahninaa; Naanyaaro-
pitasamsaaradharmaa Naivamaham Bhaje. (15)

Translation

Other people do not arrange the fire to burn the red-black
berries. Similarly, I am not bound by rituals which have
been prescribed by others.

Mantra 16

श्रृणवन्त्वज्ञाततत्त्वास्ते जानन्कस्माच्छृणोम्यहम् ।
मन्यन्तां संशयापन्ना न मन्येऽहमसंशयः ॥ 16 ॥

Shrinvantvajnaatatattvaaste Jaanankasmaachchhrinomyaham;
Manyantaam Samshayaapannaa Na Manye Ahamasamshayah. (16)

Translation

They should hear the unknown facts. Why should I hear
that which I know? Those who are doubtful should consider;
I, who am free from doubts, do not consider.

Mantra 17

विपर्यस्तो निदिध्यासे किं ध्यानमविपर्यये ।
देहात्मत्वविपर्यासं न कदाचिद्भजाम्यहम् ॥ 17 ॥

Viparyasto Nididhyaase Kim Dhyaanamaviparyaye; Dehaatmatva-viparyaasam Na Kadaachidbhajaamyaham. (17)

Translation

You, who are in illusion (a contrary or reverse state, mistaking what is real) should meditate repeatedly. Why should I, who am not in illusion, mediatate? I do not share in this illusion related to the quality of material things.

Mantra 18

अहं मनुष्य इत्यादिव्यवहारो विनाप्यमुम् ।
विपर्यासं चिराभ्यस्तवासनातोऽवकल्पते ॥ 18 ॥

Aham Manushya Ityaadivyavahaaro Vinaapyamum; Viparyaasam Chiraabhyastavaasanaato Avakalpate. (18)

Translation

These actions or utterances (such as) 'I am a man', etc. come out even without illusion (mistaking what is real), because of long (acquired) habitual vasanas (unconscious impressions).

Mantra 19

आरब्धकर्मणि क्षीणे व्यवहारो निवर्तते ।
कर्मक्षये त्वसौ नंव शाम्येद्ध्यानसहस्रतः ॥ 19 ॥

Aarabdhakarmaniksheene Vyavahaaro Nivartate; Karmakshaye Tvasau Naiva Shaamyeddhyaanasahasratah. (19)

Translation

Such actions come back even after the exhaustion of prarabdha karma (the karmas which have already been

423

performed by us, like arrows already shot from the bow). Because even after thousands of meditations such actions do not stop after exhaustion of karma.

Mantra 20

विरलत्वं व्यवह्तेरिष्टं चेद्ध्य यानमस्तु ते ।
बाधिकर्मव्यवह्तिं पश्यन्ध्यायाम्यहं कुत: ॥ 20 ॥

Viralatvam Vyavahriterishtam Cheddhyaanam Astu Te; Baadhi-karmavyavahritim Pashyandhyaayaamyaham Kutah. (20)

Translation

They (people in general) meditate because they want their desires to be fulfilled, which they rarely achieve. Why should I meditate, having seen the disturbance of the process of karmas?

Mantra 21

विक्षेपो नास्ति यस्मान्मे न समाधिस्ततो मम ।
विक्षेपो वा समाधिर्वा मनस: स्याद्विकारिण: ।
नित्यानुभवरूपस्य को मेऽत्रानुभव: पृथक् ॥ 21 ॥

Vikshepo Naasti Yasmaanme Na Samaadhistato Mama; Vikshepo Vaa Samaadhirvaa Manasah Syaadvikaarinah; Nityaanubh-avaroopasya Ko Me Atraanubhavah Prithak. (21)

Translation

Due to this, there is no distraction and there is no samadhi for me. Distraction and samadhi are possibly modifications of mind. I am eternal experience itself, what should (could) be a separate experience for me here?

Mantra 22

कृतं कृत्यं प्रापणीयं प्राप्तमित्येव नित्यश:।
व्यवहारो लौकिको वा शास्त्रीयो वान्यथापि वा।
ममाकर्तुरलेपस्य   यथारब्धं   प्रवर्तताम् ॥ 22 ॥

Kritam Krityam Praapaneeyam Praaptamityeva Nityashah;
Vyavahaaro Laukiko Vaa Shaastreeyo Vaanyathaapi Vaa;
Mamaakarturalepasya Yathaarabdham Pravartataam. (22)

Translation
Doing what should be done and gaining what should be gained, such worldly, scriptural or any other kind of actions are done like arabdha (pregnant karma which must give a result, like the arrow already in flight from the bow) by me, who is a non-doer and uninvolved (with action).

Mantra 23

अथवा कृतकृत्येऽपि लोकानुग्रह काम्यया।
शास्त्रीयेणैव मार्गेण वर्तेऽहं मम का क्षति: ॥ 23 ॥

Athavaa Kritakritye Api Lokaanugraha Kaamyayaa; Shaa-
streeyenaiva Maargena Varte Aham Mama Kaa Kshatih. (23)

Translation
After having done what should be done, what do I lose if, with a wish for the well-being of the world, I behave in the way prescribed by the scriptures?

Mantra 24

देवार्चनस्नानशौचभिक्षादौ   वर्ततां   वपु:।
तारं जपतु वाक्तद्वत्पठत्वाम्नायमस्तकम् ॥ 24 ॥

Devaarchanasnaanashauchabhikshaadau Vartataam Vapuh;
Taaram Japatu Vaaktadvatpathatvaamnaayamastakam. (24)

Translation

Let the body be engaged in the worship of gods, bathing, cleaning and begging, etc. The voice should repeat the tara (Aum mantra) or read the Vedas which are the highest knowledge.

Mantra 25

विष्णुं ध्यायतु धीर्यद्वा ब्रह्मानन्दे विलीयताम् ।
साक्ष्यहं किंचिदप्यत्र न कुर्वे नापि कारये ॥ 25 ॥

Vishnum Dhyaayatu Dheeryadvaa Brahmaanande Vileeyataam;
Saakshyaham Kinchidapyatra Na Kurve Naapi Kaaraye. (25)

Translation

Meditate upon Vishnu or merge your intellect in the bliss of Brahman. I am a witness, so I neither act nor cause any action at all.

Mantra 26

कृतकृत्यतया तृप्त: प्राप्तप्राप्यतया पुन: ।
तृप्यन्नेवं स्वमनसा मन्यतेसौ निरन्तरम् ॥ 26 ॥

Kritakrityatayaa Triptah Praaptapraapyatayaa Punah; Tripyan-
nevam Svamanasaa Manyatesau Nirantaram. (26)

Translation

He is contented with the action done or fit-to-be-done, and with achievement or that worth achieving. Therefore he considers himself always mentally blessed.

Mantra 27

धन्योऽहं धन्योऽहं नित्यं स्वात्मानमञ्जसा बेझि ।
धन्योऽहं धन्योऽहं ब्रह्मानन्दो विभाति मे स्पष्टम् ॥ 27 ॥

Dhanyo Aham Dhanyo Aham Nityam Svaatmaanamanjasaa Vedmi;
Dhanyo Aham Dhanyo Aham Brahmaanando Vibhaati Me
Spashtam. (27)

Translation

I am blessed, I am blessed, as I always know my atman (Self)
immediately. I am blessed, I am blessed, the bliss of Brahman
flashes before me clearly.

Mantra 28

धन्योऽहं धन्योऽहं दुःखं सांसारिकं न वीक्षेऽद्य ।
धन्योऽहं धन्योऽहं स्वस्याज्ञानं पलानितं पलायितं क्वापि ॥ 28 ॥

Dhanyo Aham Dhanyo Aham Duhkham Saamsaarikam Na Veekshe
Adya; Dhanyo Aham Dhanyo Aham Svasyaajnaanam Palaayitam
Kvaapi. (28)

Translation

I am blessed, I am blessed, that today I am not seeing the
worldly pains. I am blessed, I am blessed that my ignorance
has escaped somewhere (away from me).

Mantra 29

धन्योऽहं धन्योऽहं कर्त्तव्यं मे न विद्यते किंचित् ।
धन्योऽहं धन्योऽहं प्राप्तव्यं सर्वमत्र संपन्नम् ॥ 29 ॥

Dhanyo Aham Dhanyo Aham Kartavyam Me Na Vidyate Kinchit;
Dhanyo Aham Dhanyo Aham Praaptavyam Sarvamatra Sampa-
nnam. (29)

Translation

I am blessed, I am blessed that I have no duty to perform at
all. I am blessed, I am blessed that I have achieved all that is
worth achieving.

Mantra 30

धन्योऽहं धन्योऽहं तृप्तेर्मे कोपमा भवेल्लोके ।
धन्योऽहं धन्योऽहं धन्यो धन्य: पुन: पुनर्धन्य: ॥ ३० ॥

Dhanyo Aham Dhanyo Aham Tripterme Kopamaa Bhavelloke;
Dhanyo Aham Dhanyo Aham Dhanyo Dhanyah Punah Punar-
dhanyah. (30)

Translation

I am blessed, I am blessed, in this world there is no
comparison to one who is contented like me. I am blessed, I
am blessed, blessed, blessed, again and again blessed.

Mantra 31

अहो पुण्यमहो पुण्यं फलितं फलितं दृढम् ।
अस्य पुण्यस्य संपत्तेरहो वयमहो वयम् ॥ ३१ ॥

Aho Punyamaho Punyam Phalitam Phalitam Dridham; Asya
Punyasya Sampatteraho Vayamaho Vayam. (31)

Translation

Aho! (exclaiming with joy – Wonderful!) Virtue Aho! Virtue
has yielded fruit and indeed it has yielded fruit. By the
treasures of this virtue Aho! We are blessed, we are blessed.

Mantra 32

अहो ज्ञानमहो ज्ञानमहो सुखमहो सुखम् ।
अहो शास्त्रमहो शास्त्रमहो गुरुरहो गुरु: ॥ ३२ ॥

Aho Jnaanamaho Jnaanamaho Sukhamaho Sukham; Aho
Shaastramaho Shaastramaho Gururaho Guruh. (32)

Translation

Aho! Wisdom Aho! Wisdom Aho! Pleasure Aho! Pleasure.
Aho! Scriptures Aho! Scriptures Aho! Guru Aho! Guru.

इति य इदमधीते सोऽपि कृतकृत्यो भवति ।
सुरापानात्पूतो भवति । स्वर्णस्तेयात्पूतो भवति ।
ब्रह्महत्यात्पूतो भवति । कृत्याकृत्यात्पूतो भवति ।
एवं विदित्वा स्वेच्छाचारपरो भूयादोंसत्यमित्युपनिषत् ॥

Iti Ya Idamadheete So Api Kritakrityo Bhavati; Suraapaanaatpoo-
to Bhavati; Svarnasteyaatpooto Bhavati; Brahmahatyaatpooto
Bhavati; Krityaakrityaatpooto Bhavati Evam Viditvaa Svechchha-
achaaraparo Bhooyaadomsatyamityupanishat.

Translation
One who studies this also becomes pure of the sin of taking
wine. He becomes pure of the sin of stealing gold. He
becomes pure of the sin of killing a brahman. He becomes
pure (from the sins of) actions fit to be done and not fit-to-
be-done. Knowing this let him behave according to his will.
Aum truth.

Thus ends the Upanishad.

34

परमहंसपरिव्राजकोपनिषत्
Paramahamsa Parivraajaka Upanishad

This Upanishad is the sixty-sixth among the hundred and eight Upanishads and forms part of the *Atharva Veda*. It states the qualifications of the paramahamsa parivrajaka, the characteristics of the pranava that is Brahman, and establishes the Brahmanhood of the ascetics who do not wear the sacred thread and tuft.

परिव्राज्यधर्मवन्तो यज्ञानाद्ब्रह्मतां ययुः ।
तद्ब्रह्म प्रणवैकार्थं तुर्यतुर्यं हरिं भजे ॥

Paarivraajyadharmavanto Yajjnaanaadbrahmataam Yayuh;
Tadbrahma Pranavaikaartham Turyaturyam Harim Bhaje.

(I) meditate on that Brahman-pranava (which is my) only goal (and is) Turyaatita Brahman (itself). With its knowledge, the ascetics become mendicants and attain Brahman.

शान्ति पाठ
SHANTI PATH

ॐ भद्रं कणेभि: शृणुयाम देवा भद्रं पश्येमाक्षभिर्यजत्रा: । स्थिरैरंगैस्तुष्टुवाँ
सस्तनूभिर्व्यशेम देवहितं यदायु:।। स्वस्ति न इन्द्रो वृद्धश्रवा: स्वस्ति न: पूषा
विश्ववेदा: । स्वस्ति नस्ताक्ष्यों अरिष्टनेमि: स्वस्ति नो बृहस्पतिर्दधातु ।।

ॐ शान्ति: शान्ति: शान्ति:

Aum Bhadram Karnebhih Shrinuyaama Devaa Bhadram
Pashyemaakshabhiryajatraah. Sthirairangaistushtuvaam Sastanoo-
bhirvyashema Devahitam Yadaayuh. Svasti Na Indro Vriddha-
shravaah Svasti Nah Pooshaa Vishvavedaah. Svasti Nastaarkshyo
Arishtanemih Svasti No Brihaspatirdadhaatu.

Aum Shaantih, Shaantih, Shaantih

Aum. O ye Gods. May we hear auspicious words and see
auspicious sights while worshipping you. May we be blessed
in life with perfect health and vigour while singing your
praise. May the Lord Indra, the loved one of old, be well
inclined towards us. May he in his kindness, be watchful for
our prosperity. May he the nourisher and the possessor of
all wealth, give us what is good for us. May the Lord, the
destroyer of evil and the protector of the great ones, protect
us too.

Aum peace, peace, peace

Mantra 1

हरि: ॐ अथ पितामह: स्वपितरमादिनारायणमुपसमेत्य प्रणम्य प्रपच्छ
भगवंस्त्वन्मुखाद्वर्णाश्रमधर्मक्रमं सर्वं विदितमवगतम् । इदानीं परमहंसपरिव्राजकलक्षणं
वेदितुमिच्छामि क: परिव्रजनाधिकारी कीदृशं परिव्राजकलक्षणं वेदितुमिच्छामि क:
परिव्रजनाधिकारी कीदृशं परिव्राजकलक्षणं क: परमहंस: परिव्राजकत्वं कथं तत्सर्व मे
ब्रूहीति। स होवाच भगवानादिनारायण: ॥ 1 ॥

431

Harih Aum Atha Pitaamahah Svapitaramaadinaaraayanam-
upasametya Pranamya Paprachchha Bhagavanstvanmukhaadvarna-
ashramadharmakramam Sarvam Shrutam Viditamavagatam.
Idaaneem Paramahamsaparivraajakalakshanam Veditumichchaami
Kah Parivrajanaadhikaaree Keedrisham Parivraajakalakshanam
Kah Paramahamsah Parivraajakatvam Katham Tatsarvam Me
Broohiti. Sa Hovaacha Bhagavaanaadinaaraayanah. (1)

Translation

Hari Om. Brahma approached his procreator, Adi Narayana
and, after bowing to him asked, "O Bhagavan (Illustrious
One) I have heard from your mouth, known and understood
the sequence of all varnashrama dharma (the four ashramas
or stages of life through which one moves). Now I want to
know the characteristics of that paramahamsa parivrajaka.
Who is authorized to become a wandering mendicant? What
are the attributes of a parivrajaka? Who is a paramahamsa?
And what is meant by being parivrajaka? Tell me all that."
Bhagavan Adi Narayana spoke to him.

Mantra 2

सद्गुरुसमीपे सकलविद्यापरिश्रमज्ञो भूत्वा विद्वान्सर्वमैहिकामुष्मिकसुखश्रमं
ज्ञात्वैषणात्रयवासनात्रयममत्वाहंकारादिकं वमनान्नमिव हेयमधिगम्य मोक्षमार्गैकसाधनो
ब्रह्मचर्यं समाप्य गृही भवेत् । गृहाद्वनी भूत्वा प्रव्रजेत् । यदि वेतरथा ब्रह्मचर्यादेव
प्रव्रजेद्गृहाद्वा वनाद्वा। अथ पुनरव्रती वा व्रती वा स्नातको वाऽस्नातको
वोत्सन्नाग्निरनग्निको वा यदहरेव विजेत्तदहरेव प्रव्रजेदिति बुद्धा सर्वसंसारेषु विरक्तो
ब्रह्मचारी गृही वानप्रस्थो वा पितरं मातरं कलत्रपुत्रमाप्तबन्धुवर्गं तदभावे शिष्यं सहवासिनं
वानुमोदयित्वा तद्धैके प्राजापत्यामेविष्टि कुर्वन्ति तदु तथा न कुर्यात् । आग्नेय्यामेव
कुर्यात् । अग्निर्हि प्राण: प्राणमेवैतया करोति त्रैधातवीयामेव कुर्यात् । एतयैव त्रयो
धातवो यदुत सत्वं रजस्तम इति । अयं ते योनिर्ऋत्वियो यतो जातो आरोचथा: । तं
जानन्नग्न आरोहाथानो वर्धया रयिमित्यनेन मन्त्रेणाग्निभाजिघ्रेत् । एष वा अग्नेर्योनिर्य:
प्राणं गच्छ स्वां योनिं गच्छस्वाहेत्येवमेवैतदाहो ग्रामाच्छोत्रियागारादग्निमाहत्य
स्वविध्युक्तक्रमेण पूर्ववदग्निमाजिघ्रेत् । यद्यातुरो वाग्नि न विन्देदप्सु जुहुयात् । आपो
वै सर्वा देवता: सर्वाभ्यो देवताभ्यो जुहोमि स्वाहेति हुत्वोद्धृ त्य प्राश्नीयात् साज्यं

432

हविरनामयम् । एष विधिर्वीराध्वाने वाऽनाशके वा संप्रवेशे वाग्निप्रवेशे वा महाप्रस्थाने वा । यद्यातुर: स्यान्मनसा वाचा वा संन्यसेदेष पन्था: ॥ 2 ॥

Sadgurusameepe Sakalavidyaaparishramajno Bhootvaa Vidvaan-sarvamaihikaamushmikasukhashramam Jnaatvaishanaatrayava-asanaatrayamamatvaahamkaaraadikam Vamanaannamiva Heyamadhigamya Mokshamaargaikasaadhano brahmacharyam Samaapya Grihee Bhavet. Grihaadvanee Bhootvaa Pravrajet. Yadi Vetarathaa Brahmacharyaadeva Pravrajedgrihaadvaa Vanaadvaa. Atha Punaravratee Vaa Vratee Vaa Snaatako Vaa Snaatako Votsannaagniranagniko Vaa Yadahareva Virajettadahareva Pravrajediti Buddhvaa Sarvasamsaareshu Virakto Brahmachaaree Grihee Vaanaprastho Vaa Pitaram Maataram Kalatraputra-maaptabandhuvargam Tadabhaave Shishyam Sahavaasinam Vaanumodayitvaa Taddhaike Praajaapatyaameveshtim Kurvanti Tadu Tathaa Na Kuryaat. Aagneyyaameva Kuryaat. Agnirhi Praanah Praanamevaitayaa Karoti Traidhaataveeyaameva Kuryaat. Etayaiva Trayo Dhaatavo Yaduta Sattvam Rajastama Iti. Ayam Te Yonirritviyo Yato Jaato Aarochathaah. Tam Jaanannagna Aarohaathaano Vardhayaa Rayimityanena Mantrenaagnimaajighret Esha Vaa Agneryoniryah Praanam Gachchha Svaam Yonim Gachchhasvaahetyevamevaitadaaha. Graamaachcchrotriyaagaaraadagnimaahritya Svavidhyukta-kramena Poorvavadagnimaajighret. Yadyaaturo Vaagnim Na Vindedapsu Juhuyaat. Aapo Vai Sarvaa Devataah Sarvaabhyo Devataabhyo Juhomi Svaaheti Hutvoddhritya Praashneeyaat Saajyam Haviranaamayam. Esha Vidhirveeraadhvaane Vaa Anaashake Vaa Sampraveshe Vaagnipraveshe Vaa Mahaa-prasthaane Vaa. Yadyaaturah Syaanmanasaa Vaachaa Vaa Samnyasedesha Panthaah. (2)

Translation

After acquiring all the knowledge by intense effort from the true guru, the learned (disciple), treating all the worldly and higher pleasures as illusion, and treating the three desires (for wealth, children and fame) and three vasanas (possessiveness, egotism, etc.) as being worth discarding, and after completing brahmacharya ashrama, which is a means on the path of liberation, should become a householder. After being a householder he should be a vanaprasthi (one who lives in the jungle), and after that a parivrajaka. He may become a parivrajaka directly from brahmacharya, or from the householder stage, or from vanaprastha.

After that, either a non-brahmachari or brahmachari, graduate (one who has completed the brahmachari stage) or non-graduate, one who has left the fire or one who has not established the fire, the day he is free from attachment, knowing this, from that very day he should become a parivrajaka, so say the sages.

Detached from the whole world, the brahmachari or householder or forest dweller performs the Prajapati sacrifice to obtain the support of the father, mother, wife, son, near relatives or, in their absence, disciples or those who live with him. After that he should not perform that (sacrifice again). He should (instead) perform the Agneyi sacrifice (whose presiding deity is Fire) only. And as Agni is the prana he should do this through prana. He may perform the Traidhataviya ceremony concerning the three dhatus (root ingredients) sattwa, rajas and tamas.

"This is your generating cause (source), which is doing sacrifice regularly. From here it (the flame) rises and shines. Knowing that, O Fire, please ascend to increase my (spiritual) prosperity." (While reciting) this mantra the fire should be smelled. That should be uttered or this should be uttered. "Go to the prana which is the generating cause of fire. Go to your own generating place. Svaha." (Place the offering on the fire.)

After bringing fire from the house of the village vedic scholar, fire should be smelt as described earlier, in the order which is prescribed in the rules. If the anxious one (due to illness) cannot smell the fire, he should drop the oblation in water. Water itself represents all the gods. "I am offering the oblation for all the gods. Svaha." Offering the oblation thus, he should take it from the water and should eat the oblation which is mixed with ghee and good for health.

This is the ritual before proceeding on the warrior's path, before fasting, before entering fully, before entering fire, or before death. Sick people can do the same mentally, or by speech, this is the method.

Mantra 3

स्वस्थक्रमेणैव चेदात्मश्राद्धं विरजाहोमं कृत्वाग्निमात्मन्यारोप्य लौकिकवैदिकसामर्थ्यं स्वचतुर्दशकरणप्रवृत्तिं च पुत्रे समारोप्य तदभावे शिष्येवात‌द्‌द्वे स्वात्मन्येव वा ब्रह्मा त्वं यज्ञस्त्वमित्यभिमंत्र्य ब्रह्मभावनया ध्यात्वासावित्रीप्रवेशपूर्वकमप्सु सर्वविद्यार्थस्वरूपां ब्राह्मणाधारां वेदमातरं क्रमाद्व्याहृतिषु त्रिषु प्रविलाप्य व्याहृतित्रयमकारोकारमकारेषु प्रविलाप्य तत्सावधानेनाप: प्राश्य प्रणवेन शिखामुत्कृष्य यज्ञोपवीतं छित्वा वस्त्रमपि भूमौ वाप्सु वा विसृज्य ॐ भू: स्वाहा ॐ भुव: स्वाहा ॐ सुव: स्वाहेत्यनेन जातरूपधरो भूत्वा स्वं रूपं ध्यायन्पुन: पृथक् प्रणवव्याहृतिपूर्वकं मनसा वचसापि संन्यस्तं मया संन्यस्तं मयासंन्यस्तं मयेति मन्द्रमध्यमतारध्वनिभिस्त्रिवारं त्रिगुणीकृतप्रेषोच्चारणं कृत्वा प्रणवैकध्यानपरायण: सन्नभयं सर्वभूतेभ्यो मत्त: स्वाहेत्यूर्ध्वबाहुर्भूत्वा ब्रह्माहमस्मीति तत्त्वमस्यादिवाक्यार्थस्वरूपानुसंधानं कुर्वन्नुदीचीं दिशं गच्छेत् । जातरूपधरश्चरेत् । एष संन्यास: । तदधिकारी न भवेद्यदि गृहस्थप्रार्थनापूर्वकमभयं सर्वभूतेभ्यो मत्त: सर्व प्रवर्त्तते सखा मा गोपायौज: सखा योऽसीन्द्रस्य वज्रोऽसि वार्त्रघ्न: मे भव यत्पापं तन्निवारयेत्यनेन मन्त्रेण प्रणवपूर्वकं सलक्षणं वैनवं दण्डं कटिसूत्रं कौपीनं कमण्डलुं विवर्णवस्त्रमेकं परिगृह्य सद्गुरुमुपगम्य नत्वा गुरुमुखात्तत्त्वमसीति महावाक्यं प्रणवपूर्वकमुपलभ्याथ जीर्णवल्कलाजिनं धृत्वाथ जलावतरणमूर्ध्वगमनमेकभिक्षां परित्यज्य त्रिकालस्नानमाचरन्वेदान्तश्रवणपूर्वकं प्रणानुष्ठानं कुर्वन्ब्रह्मार्गे सम्यक् सम्पन्न: स्वाभिमतमात्मनि गोपयित्वा निर्ममोऽध्यात्मनिष्ठ: कामक्रोधलोभमोहमदमात्सर्यदम्भदर्पाहंकारासूया- गर्वेच्छाद्वेषहर्षामर्षममत्वादींश्च हित्वा ज्ञानवैराग्ययुक्तो वित्तस्त्रीपराङ्मुख: शुद्धमानस: सर्वोपनिषदर्थमालोच्य ब्रह्मचर्यापरिग्रहाहिंसासत्यं यत्नेन रक्षञ्जितेन्द्रियो बहिरन्त: स्नेहवर्जित: शरीरसंधारणार्थं वा त्रिषु वर्णेष्वभिशस्तपतितवर्जितेषु पशुरुद्रोही भैक्षमाणो ब्रह्मभूयाय भवति । सर्वेषु कालेषु लाभालाभौ समौ कृत्वा करपात्रमाधुकरेणान्नमशनन्मेदो- वृद्धिमकुर्वन्कृशीभूत्वा ब्रह्माहमस्मीति भावयन्नुर्वर्थं ग्रामुपेत्य ध्रुवशीलोऽष्टौ मास्येकाकी चरेद्‌द्वावेवनवनचरेत् । यदालंबुद्धिर्भवेत्तदा कुटीचको वा बहूदको वा हंसो वा परमहंसो वा तत्तन्मन्त्रपूर्वकं कटिसूत्रं कौपीनं दण्डं कमण्डलुं सर्वमप्सु विसृज्याथ जातरूपधरश्चरेत् ।

ग्राम एकरात्रं तीर्थे त्रिरात्रं पत्तने पञ्चरात्रं क्षेत्रे सप्तरात्रमनिकेत: स्थिरमतिरनग्निसेवी निर्विकारो नियमानियमुत्सृज्य प्राणसंधारणार्थमयमेव लाभालाभौ समौ कृत्वा गोवृत्या भैक्षमाचरन्नुदकस्थलकमण्डलुरबाधकरहस्यस्थलवासो न पुनर्लोभालाभरत: शुभाशुभकर्मनिर्मूलपर: सर्वत्र भूतलशयन: क्षौरकर्मपरित्यक्तो युक्तचातुर्मास्त्रतनियम: शुक्लध्यानपरायणोऽर्थस्त्रीपुरपराङ्मुखोऽनुन्मत्तोऽप्युन्मत्तवदाचरन्नव्यक्तलिङ्गोऽ व्यक्ताचारी दिवानक्तसमत्वेनास्वप्न: स्वरूपानुसंधानब्रह्मप्रणवध्यानमार्गेणावहित: संन्यासेन देहत्यागं करोति स परमहंसपरिव्राजको भवति ॥ ३ ॥

Svasthakramenaiva Chedaatmashraaddham Virajaahomam Kritvaagnimaatmanyaaropya Laukikavaidikasaamarthyam Svachaturdashakaranapravrittim Cha Putre Samaaropya Tadabhaave Shishye Vaa Tadbhaave Svaatmanyeva Vaa Brahmaa Tvam Yajnastvamityabhimantrya Brahmabhaavanayaa Dhyaatvaa Saavitreepravesha Poorvakam Apsu Sarvavidyaartha Svaroopaam Braahmanya Aadhaaraam Vedamaataram Kramaadvyaahritishu Trishu Pravilaapya Vyaahrititrayamakaarokaaramakaareshu Pravilaapya Tatsaavadhaanenaapah Praashya Pranavena Shikhaamutkrishya Yajnopaveetam Chhittvaa Vastramapi Bhoomau Vaapsu Vaa Visrijya Aum Bhooh Svaahaa Aum Bhuvah Svaahaa Aum Suvah Svaahetyanena Jaataroopadharo Bhootvaa Svam Roopam Dhyaayanpunah Prithak Pranavavyaahritipoorvakam Manasaa Vachasaapi Samnyastam Mayaa Samnyastam Mayaa Samnyastam Mayeti. Mandramadhyamataaradhvanibhistrivaaram. Triguneekritapreshochchaaranam Kritvaa Pranavaikadhyaanaparaayanah Sannabhayam Sarvabhootebhyo Mattah Svaahetyoordhvabaahurbhootvaa Brahmaahamasmeeti Tattvamasyaadivaakyaartha Svaroopa Anusamdhaanam Kurvannudeecheem Disham Gachchhet. Jaataroopadharashcharet. Esha Samnyaasah. Tadadhikaaree Na Bhavedyadi Grihasthapraarthanaapoorvakamabhayam Sarvabhootebhyo Mattah Sarvam Pravartate Sakhaa Maa Gopaayaujah Sakhaa Yo'seendrasya. Vajro'si Vaartraghnah Sharga Me Bhava Yatpaapam Tannivaarayetyanena Mantrena Pranavapoorvakam Salakshanam Vainavam Dandam Katisootram Kaupeenam Kamandalum Vivarnavasramekam Parigrihya Sadgurumupagamya Natvaa Gurumukhaattatvamaseeti Mahaavaakyam Pranavapoorvakamupalabhyaatha Jeernavalkalaajinam

Dhritvaatha Jalaavataranamoordhvagamanamekabhikshaam Parit-
yajya Trikaalasnaanamaacharanvedaantashravanapoorvakam
Pranavaanushthaanam Kurvanbrahmamaarge Samyak Sampannah
Svaabhimatamaatmani Gopayitvaa Nirmamo'dhyaatmanishthah
Kaamakrodhalobhamohamadamaatsaryadambhadarpaaham-
kaaraasooyaagarvechchhaadveshaharshamamatvaadeemshcha
Hitvaa Jnaanavairaagyayukto Vittastreeparaanmukhah Shuddha-
maanasah Sarvopanishadarthamaalochya Brahmacharya-
aparigrahaahimsaasatyam Yatnena Rakshanjitendriyo Bahirantah
Snehavarjitah Shareerasamdhaaranaartham Vaa Trishu Vernesh-
vabhishastapatitavarjiteshu Pashuradrohee Bhaikshamaargo
Brahmabhooyaaya Bhavati. Sarveshu Kaaleshu Laabhaalaabhau
Samau Kritvaa Karapaatramaadhookarenaannamashnanmedo-
vriddhimakurvankrisheebhootvaa Brahmaahamasmeeti Bhaavay-
angurvartham Graamamupetya Dhruvasheelo Ashtau
Maasyekaakee Charetadvaavevanacharet. Yadaalambuddhir-
bhavettadaa Kuteechako Vaa Bahoodako Vaa Hamso Vaa
Paramahamso Vaa Tattanmantrapoorvakam Katisootram
Kaupeenam Dandam Kamandalum Sarvamapsu Visrijyaatha
Jaataroopadharashcharet. Graama Ekaraatram Teerthe
Triraatram Pattane Pancharaatram Kshetre Saptaraatramaniketah
Sthiramatiranagnisevee Nirvikaaro Niyamaaniyamutsrijya
Praanasamdhaaranaarthamayameva Laabhaalaabhau Samau
Kritvaa Govrittyaa Bhaikshamaacharannudakasthalakamandalura-
baadhakarahasyasthalavaaso Na Punarlaabhaalaabharatah
Shubhaashubhakarmanir moolaparah Sarvatra Bhootalashayanah
Kshaurakarmaparityakto Yuktachaaturmaasyavrataniyamah
Shukladhyaanaparaayan Aarthastreepuraparaanmukho Anun-
mattoapyunmatte Avadaacharannavyaktalingo Avyaktaachaaro
Divaanaktasamatvenaa Svapnah Svaroopaanusamdhaanbrahma-
pranavadhyaanamaargenaavahitah Samnyaasena Dehatyaagam
Karoti Sa Paramahamsa parivraajako Bhavati. (3)

Translation

A healthy person proceeding through the sequence of the
prescribed method should perform the ceremony which is
done after death and also the viraja homa (fire ceremony for

getting rid of passions). Establishing fire (prana) in his self, he should entrust the worldly vedic duties and the fourteen attitudes of activities of active worldly life (pravritti and karana) to his offspring, in his absence to his disciple, or in the absence of all, to himself.

He should do the invocation with the mantra 'You are Brahman, you are yajna (sacrifice)' and meditating upon the Sun or Gayatri with Brahman bhavana (the feeling that Gayatri is Brahman), by uttering the three vyahrittis (Aum Bhu, Aum Bhuvah, Aum Svaha) he should consign to the water all the forms of knowledge, the prop of Brahmanhood and the scriptures, in the same order. While uttering the three vyahrittis in the pranava A-U-M, he should sip water.

After that, with the pranava mantra (Aum) he should remove the tuft, break the sacred thread and (dispose of) clothing also on the ground or in water. After that with 'Aum bhu svaha', 'Aum bhuvah svaha' and 'Aum svah svaha', and while being naked, he should again meditate on his own form. Then he should pronounce separately with pranava and vyahritti (Aum bhu, Aum bhuvah, Aum svah) "I am a renunciate, I am mentally and vocally also a renunciate, I am a renunciate, I am a renunciate."

After pronouncing it three times in a soft voice, three times in a medium voice and three times in a loud voice, and being fully absorbed in only one pranava, and being free from fear of any creature, and being full of joy, raising his hands up, he should proceed in a northerly direction, discovering the meaning and form of the phrases 'Aham Brahmasmi' (I am Brahman), 'Tattvamasi' (Thou are That), etc.

He should move in the form he was born in (naked). This is sannyasa. If he is not fit for that, that householder should remain full of prayer and free from the fear of any creature, and remain joyous.

"My friend, guard me; you are strength, you are the *vajra* (thunderbolt) of Indra which killed Vritra, the demon. Be a blessing to me and prevent me from doing anything which is sinful."

Reciting the above mantra along with the pranava, he should approach the true guru wearing a white cloth and having a water-pot, loincloth, a thread tied round the waist and a bamboo staff as prescribed. After bowing down before the guru, he should receive the maha vakya 'Tattwamasi' along with pranava from the mouth of the guru.

After that, wearing old bark from trees and deer skins, and abandoning (refraining from) going into water (of rivers, etc.) or climbing up (trees etc.) and (missing) one meal, he should wash three times a day. Listening to Vedanta, doing pranava sadhana, and enriched in the proper path of Brahman, and keeping his desires sacred in himself, he should leave attachment, (being) absorbed in spirituality, leaving passion, anger, greed, infatuation, conceit, jealousy, deceit, arrogance, ego, intolerance, pride, desire, envy, hilarity, non-endurance, affectionate regard, etc.

Enriched with wisdom and non-attachment, and becoming uninterested in wealth and females, being pure in mind and reflecting on all the Upanishads, protecting with effort brahmacharya, non-possessiveness towards things, ahimsa (non-violence) and truth, being master of the senses, being without affection internally or externally, in order to maintain his body he should accept alms from the three prescribed varnas (castes) who are not against any creature, but avoid wicked people. By doing so he merges with Brahman.

All the time treating loss and gain as equal he should eat food using his hands as a vessel, by begging in such a measure that it should not increase (his) fat, (rather he) should become thin. Meditating on 'Aham Brahmasmi', firm in character, he should go to villages in the interest of his guru, not with anyone (alone), travelling for eight months.

When the intellect becomes sufficient, then the kutichak or bahudak or hamsa or paramahamsa, by the above quoted mantra, abandons his waist-thread, loin cloth, staff, water-pot, everything, in water and moves in the form in which he was born. (Staying) in a village one night, in a holy place three nights, in a city five nights and in any area seven nights, without any house.

He should be firm-minded, not maintaining fire, free from all kinds of impurities, leaving (both) restraints and non-restraints. Just for maintaining life, treating loss or gain equally, he should move, eating like a cow (food he comes across) by begging. He should stay near a place where water is available so that even the water-pot is not a distraction while living in a lonely place. He is again neither concerned with loss nor gain. He should be serious in destroying good and bad karmas. Everywhere, he should sleep on the earth. He should leave shaving. With all these, he should observe the rules of chaturmas. Absorbed in shukla dhyana, he should be away from wealth, women and dwelling places. He should behave normally or abnormally. He should be without identity and expressed behaviour, without dreaming day or night, by meditating on the Self and by the path of pranava meditation and adwaita (non-duality) and by meditating on sannyasa he leaves his body. One who acts in this way becomes a paramahamsa parivrajaka."

Mantra 4

भगवन् ब्रह्मप्रणवः कीदृश् इति ब्रह्मा पृच्छति। स होवाच नारायणः। ब्रह्मप्रणवः षोडशमात्रात्मकः सोऽवस्थाचतुष्टयचतुष्टयगोचरः। जाग्रदवस्थायां जाग्रदादिचतस्रोऽवस्थाः स्वप्ने स्वप्नादिचतस्रोऽवस्थाः सुषुप्तौ सुषुप्त्यादिचतस्रो-ऽवस्थास्तुरीये तुरीयादिचतस्रोऽवस्था भवन्तीति। जाग्रदवस्थायां विश्वस्य चातुर्विध्यं विश्वविश्वो विश्वतैजसो विश्वप्राज्ञो विश्वतुरीय इति। स्वप्नावस्थायां तेजसस्य चातुर्विध्यं तैजसविश्वस्तैजसतैजसस्तैजसप्राज्ञस्तैजसतुरीय इति। सुषुप्त्यवस्थायां प्राज्ञस्य चातुर्विध्यं प्राज्ञविश्वः प्राज्ञविश्वः प्राज्ञतैजसः प्राज्ञप्राज्ञः प्राज्ञतुरीय इति। तुरीयावस्थायां तुरीयस्य चातुर्विध्यं तुरीयविश्वस्तुरीयतैजसस्तुरीयप्राज्ञस्तुरीयतुरीय इति। ते क्रमेण षोडशमात्रारूढः अकारे जाग्रद्विश्व उकारे जाग्रत्तैजसो मकारे जाग्रत्प्राज्ञ अर्धमात्रायां जाग्रत्प्राज्ञ अर्धमात्रायां जाग्रत्तुरीयो बिन्दौ स्वप्नविश्वोनादे स्वप्नतेजसः कलायां स्वप्नप्राज्ञः कलातीते स्वप्नतुरीयः शान्ती सुषुप्तविश्वः शान्त्यतीते सुषुप्ततैजस उन्मन्यां सुषुप्तप्राज्ञो मनोन्मन्यां सुषुप्ततुरीयः पुर्यां तुरीयविश्वो मध्यमायां तुरीयतैजसः पश्यन्त्यां

तुरीयप्राज्ञ: परायां तुरीयतुरीय: । जाग्रन्मात्राचतुष्टयमकारांशं स्वप्नमात्राचतुष्टयमुकारांशं
सुषुप्तिमात्राचतुष्टयं मकारांशं तुरीयमात्राचतुष्टयमर्ध -मात्रांशम् । अयमेव ब्रह्मप्रणव: ।
स परमहंसतुरीयातीतावधूतैरुपास्य: । तैनैव ब्रह्म प्रकाशते तेन विदेहमुक्ति: ॥ 4 ॥

Bhagavan Brahmapranavah Keedrisha Iti Brahmaa Prichchhati.
Sa Hovaacha Naaraayanah. Brahmapranavah Shodasha-
maatraatmakah So Avasthaachatushtayachatushtaya Gocharah
Jaagradavasthaayaam Jaagradaadichatasro'vasthaah Svapne
Svapnaadichatasro'vasthaah Sushuptau Sushuptyaadichatasro'-
vasthaastureeye Tureeyaadichatasro'vasthaa Bhavanteeti.
Jaagradavasthaayaam Vishvasya Chaaturvidhyam Vishvavishvo
Vishvataijaso Vishvapraajno Vishvatureeya Iti. Svapnaavasthaayam
Taijasasya Chaaturvidhyam Taijasavishvastaijasataija-
sastaijasapraajnastaijasatureeya Iti. Sushuptyavasthaayaam
Praajnasya Chaaturvidhyam Praajnavishvah Praajnataijasah
Praajnapraajnah Praajnatureeya Iti. Tureeyaavasthaayaam
Tureeyasya Chaaturvidhyam Tureeyavishvastureeyataijasastureeya-
yapraajnastureeyatureeya Iti. Te Kramena Shodasha-
maatraaroodhaah Akaare Jaagradvishva Ukaare Jaagrattaijaso
Makaare Jaagratpraajna Ardhamaatraayaam Jaagrattureeyo
Bindau Svapnavishvonaade Svapnataijasah Kalaayaam
Svapnapraajnah Kalaateete Svapnatureeyah Shaantau
Sushuptavishvah Shaantyateete Sushuptataijasa Unmanyaam
Sushuptapraajno Manonmanyaam Sushuptatureeyah Puryaam
Tureeyavishvo Madhyamaayaam Tureeyataijasah Pashyantyaam
Tureeyapraajnah Paraayaam Tureeyatureeyah. Jaagranmaatra-
achatushtayamakaaraamsham Svapnamaatraachatushtaya-
mukaaraamsham Sushuptimaatraachatushtayam Makaaraamsham
Tureeyamaatraachatushtayamardhamaatraamsham. Ayameva
Brahmapranavah. Sa Paramahamsatureeyaateetaavadhootairoo-
paasyah. Tenaiva Brahma Prakaashate Tena Videhamuktih. (4)

Translation

Brahma again asks (Adi Narayana), "O Bhagavan, what is
Brahma pranava?"

Narayana answered, "Brahma pranava is of sixteen
matras. (Ordinarily this means the time required to pro-

441

nounce a short vowel, in this context it means sixteen stages of the mental processes.) His four states can be known in four ways. The awakened state is that in which there are four stages – jagrat (awakened) etc. In the dream state there are four stages – svapna (dream), etc. In the sleep state there are four stages – sushupti (sleep), etc. In the fourth state there are four stages – turiya (beyond or fourth), etc.

"In jagrat (the awakened state) there are four forms of the world: vishva-vishva (worldly world), vishva-tejas (bright world), vishva-prajna (world of knowledge), vishva-turiya (the world beyond). In svapna (the dream state) the tejas is of four types: tejas-vishva (bright world), tejas-tejas (bright brightness), tejas-prajna (bright knowledge), tejas-turiya (the bright fourth state beyond). In the sleep state prajna (knowledge) is of four types: prajna-vishva (world knowledge), prajna-tejas (bright knowledge), prajna-turiya (knowledge of the fourth state). In turiya also there are four types of turiya: turiya-vishva (fourth stage of the world or the world beyond), turiya-tejas (fourth stage of brightness), turiya-prajna (fourth state of knowledge), turiya-turiya (fourth state of the fourth state).

"In that order, riding on the sixteen matras (are) jagrat vishnu in A, jagrat tejas in U, jagrat prajna in M, and jagrat turiya in the half matra. In bindu (the seed point of the universe) svapna vishva (the dream world), in nada (the original vibration represented by Aum) svapna tejas (bright dream), in kala (the visual manifestation of prakriti or maya) svapna prajna (knowledge of dream), and in beyond kala, svapna turiya (beyond dream). In shanti (peace), sushupta vishva (the sleep world); in beyond shanti, sushupta tejas (bright sleep); in unmani (the threshold state), sushupta prajna (knowledge of sleep); in mental unmani, sushupta turiya (the fourth state of sleep). In puri (city or body), turiya vishva; in the middle, turiya-tejas; in the end, turiya-prajna and beyond that, turiya-turiya.

"The four matras of jagrat are part of A and the four matras of svapna are part of U and the four matras of

442

sushupti are part of M and the four matras of turiya are part of the half matra. This is the brahma pranava that is worth worship for the paramahamsa, turyateertha and avadhoota. By that the Brahman brightens and in turn one gets liberated beyond as if one is without the body."

Mantra 5

भगवन् कथमयज्ञोपवीत्यशिखी सर्वकर्मपरित्यक्त: कथं ब्रह्मनिष्ठापर: कथं ब्राह्मण इति ब्रह्मा पृच्छति। स होवाच विष्णुर्भोभोऽर्भक यस्यास्त्यद्वैतमात्मज्ञानं तदेव यज्ञोपवीतम्। तस्य ध्याननिष्ठैव शिखा। तत्कर्म से पवित्रम् । स सर्वकर्मकृत् । स ब्राह्मण:। स ब्रह्मनिष्ठापर:। स देव:। स ऋषि:। स तपस्वती। स श्रेष्ठ:। स एव सर्वज्येष्ठ:। स एव जगतद्गुरु:। स एवाहं विद्धि। लोके परमहंसपरिव्राजको दुर्लभतरो यद्येकोऽस्ति। स एव नित्यपूत:। स एव वेदपुरुषो महापुरुषो यस्तच्चित्तं मय्येवावतिष्ठते। अहं च तस्मिन्नेवावस्थित:। स एव नित्यतृप्त:। सशीतोष्णसुखदु:ख मानावमानवर्जित:। स निन्दामर्षसहिष्णु:। स षड्मूर्मिवर्जित:। षड्भावविकारशून्य:। स ज्येष्ठाज्येष्ठव्यवधानरहित:। स स्वव्यतिरेकेण नान्य द्रष्टा। आशाम्बरो न नमस्कारो नस्वाहाकारो नस्वधाकारश्च नविसर्जनपरो निन्दास्तुतिव्यतिरिक्तो नमन्त्रतन्त्रोपासको देवान्तरध्यानशून्यो लक्ष्यालक्ष्यनिवर्तक: सर्वोपरत: ससच्चिदानन्दाद्वयचिद्घन: संपूर्णादैनन्दैकबोधो ब्रह्मैवाहमस्मीत्यनवरतं ब्रह्मप्रणवानुसंधानेन य: कृतकृत्यो भवति स ह परमहंसपरिव्राडित्युपनिषत् ॥ 5 ॥

हरि ॐ तत्सत् ।

इति परमहंस परिव्राजकोपनिषत्समाप्ता: ॥

Bhagavan Kathamayajnopaveetyashikhee Sarvakarmaparityaktah Katham Brahmanishthaaparah Katham Braahmana Iti Brahmaa Prichchhati. Sa Hovaacha Vishnurbhobhoarbhaka Yasyaasty-advaitamaatmajnaanam Tadeva Yajnopaveetam. Tasya Dhyaananishthaiva Shikhaa. Tatkarma Sa Pavitram. Sa Sarvakarmakrit. Sa Braahmanah. Sa Brahmanishthaaparah. Sa Devah. Sa Rishih. Sa Tapasvee. Sa Shreshthah. Sa Eva Sarvajyeshthah. Sa Eva Jagadguruh. Sa Evaaham Viddhi. Loke Paramahamsaparivraajako Durlabhataro Yadyekoasti. Sa Eva Nityapootah. Sa Eva Vedapurusho Mahaapurusho Yastachchittam

443

Mayyevaavatishthate. Aham Cha Tasminnevaavasthitah. Sa Eva Nitya Triptah. Sa Sheetoshnasukhaduhkhamaanaava- maanavarjitah. Sa Nindaamarshasahishnuh Sa Shadoormivarjitah. Shadbhaavavikaarashoonyah. Sa Jyeshthaajyeshthavyavadhaana- rahitah. Sa Svavyatirekena Naanya Drashtaa. Aashaam Baro Na Namaskaaro Na Svaahaakaaro Na Svadhaakaarashcha Navisar- janaparo Nindaastutivyatirikto Namantratantropaasako Devaantaradhyaanashoonyo Lakshyaalakshyanivartakah Sarvoparatah Sasachchidaanandaadvayachidghanah Sampoornaa- nandaikabodho Brahmaivaahamasmeetyanavaratam Brahma- pranavaanusamdhaanena Yah Kritakrityo Bhavati Brahmai- vaahamasmeetyanavaratam Brahmapranavaanusamdhaanena Yah Kritakrityo Bhavati Brahmaivaahamasmeetyanavaratam Brahmapranavaanusamdhaanena Yah Kritakrityo Bhavati Sa Ha Paramahamsaparivradityupanishat. (5)

Hari Aum Tat Sat.

Iti Paramahamsa Parivraajakopanishatsamaaptah.

Translation

Brahma again asked, "O Bhagavan! How does one abandon the sacred thread, tuft and all karmas (duties), become totally situated (engrossed) in Brahman, and become a Brahmin?"

(Adi Narayana) replied to Brahma, addressing him as a small child. "His non-dual Self-knowledge is the sacred thread, his complete faith in meditation is the tuft, his karmas are pure, he has performed all the karmas. He is Brahman. He is completely situated in Brahman. He is a deva (shining one). He is a rishi (seer), a tapasvi (ascetic). He is superior. He is superior to all. He is the teacher of the world. Know that he is I.

"In the world the paramahamsa parivrajaka is most rare. If there is one, he is ever pure. He is the vedapurusha (knowledgeable man), the great man who is established in me alone and I am established in him. He is ever contented. He is without cold and heat, pleasure and pain, respect and

444

disrespect. He tolerates abuse, censure and anger. He is without the six waves (desires). He is free from six emotional modifications. He is free from the obstruction of being superior or inferior. He, by his distinction, is not a seer of others. His clothes are the directions. He does not bow to anybody. He neither offers oblation to the fire nor to ancestors. He is not interested in visarjanam (sending away the invoked deity). He is totally unconcerned with insult and praise. He is not a worshipper of mantra or tantra. He is free from (the need of) meditation on other than God.

"He is away from goal or no-goal. He is detached from all. He is satchidananda (truth, consciousness, bliss) without a second and chidghada (Supreme spirit or Brahman). He is knowledge of total bliss. One who becomes contented by discovery of Brahman pranava, continuously remembering 'I am Brahman', he is a paramahamsa parivrajaka."

Hari Aum Tat Sat.

Thus ends the Paramahamsa Parivraajaka Upanishad.

Glossary

Abhanga – devotional song, expressing longing for God
Abhiman – conceit; pride; vanity; arrogance
Abhishek – ceremonial bath
Achamanam – sipping water from the palm of the hand
Acharya – preceptor; teacher; spiritual guide
Achintyabhedabheda – philosophy of inconceivable unity in diversity
Adharma – disharmony; not fulfilling one's natural role in life
Adiguru – first guru
Adivasi – tribal people
Adwaita – monistic vision of reality, philosophy of absolute non-dualism
Agama – sacred tantric literature
Agni – fire; the god of fire; digestive faculty
Agnihotra – fire ritual
Aham Brahmasmi – one of the great vedic mantras used by a meditator as an aid in reaching the supreme state of Existence, "I am Brahman"
Ahamkara – ego principle
Ajna chakra – the third eye; command centre; located at the mid-brain behind the eyebrow centre
Akhara – place for training in arms; headquarters of the Naga sect
Akshara – imperishable
Aksharatvat – imperishability

Alakh bara – 'invisible boundary'; the place where paramahamsa sannyasins live in seclusion

Amma – mother

Amsha – part; fragment

Anagha – sinless; innocent; free from dirt

Anala – ever hungry; never satisfied

Ananda – bliss; happiness; joy; delight

Ananda vrata – worship of Vishnu performed in Bhadrapad, the ninth month of the Hindu year

Ani – companies

Anugraha – divine grace

Anushthana – a resolve to perform mantra sadhana with absolute discipline for a requisite period of time

Apana – one of the five sub-pranas located in the lower abdominal region, responsible for elimination and reproduction

Aparokshanubhuti – direct experience of the Self

Aranya – jungle or forest

Aranyaka – 'situated in the forest'; ancient scripture containing subtle, mystical interpretations of Vedic rituals; transition from ritual to philosophy

Aranyakula ashrama – another word for vanaprastha ashrama

Ardhamatra – half syllable

Arghya – offering of water to the gods or to guests

Artha – accomplishment; attainment in all spheres of life

Asana – steady, comfortable position of the body, a seat or mat on which one sits for meditation

Ashada – impure; unreal

Ashrama – hermitage; stage of life; the abode of a guru or saint; community where spiritual discipline is practised

Astradhari – weapon holder

Ashtami – star constellation; eighth day of the dark and bright fortnight on the lunar calendar

Ashtashraddha – funeral rites done for all worldly relations, including one's previous self, performed when taking initiation into sannyasa

Ashtasiddhis – eight yogic powers

Asura – demon; evil spirit
Atharva Veda – fourth Vedic text containing the tantric concepts
Atithi – guest
Atma – individual soul; spirit; self beyond mind and body
Atma chintan – introspection
Atma priya – beloved
Atma vidya – knowledge of the inner self
Aupasana – sacred fire for pooja or ritual worship
Avadhoota – one whose ego is destroyed; final stage of sannyasa when a sannyasin has attained total transcendence of the body; one whose behaviour is no longer bound by ordinary social conventions
Avatara – incarnation of the divine
Avidya – ignorance; wrong knowledge; failure to realize the unity behind all manifestations of nature
Avimuktam – eyebrow centre
Avyakta – unmanifest; unseen
Avyakta prakriti – unmanifest nature
Ayam Atma Brahma – one of the four great statements of Vedanta meaning 'The Soul is Brahma'
Bahudak – 'supported by many'; stage of sannyasa
Baliyajna – serving the creatures of the Lord
Beejakshara – seed syllable containing the latent power of a mantra
Bhagavan – illustrious one; one who is glorious and venerable; literally, 'the Lord'
Bhajan – devotional song in praise of God
Bhakta – devotee
Bhakti – devotion
Bhalla – spear
Bharat – original name of India; 'land which is engulfed by light'
Bharati – without bondage; adept in brahmavidya; wife of Mandan Mishra whom Shankaracharya defeated in debate
Bhasma – sacred ash
Bhasma nishta – one who loves bhasma
Bhiksha – begging, alms

448

Bhikshu – one who receives alms; mendicant
Bhoga – experience and craving of pleasure
Bhojanam – food which is offered to a guest
Bhoktritva – the desire for enjoyment
Bhramara keelaka – wasp; twenty-fourth guru of Dattatreya
Bhuradi sannyasa – the sadhaka is choiceless (detached) in all
    dimensions of his consciousness; stage of sannyasa
Bindu – point or dot
Brahma – creator in the Hindu pantheon; presides over
    mooladhara chakra; manifest force of life and creation
Brahma vidya – science of the self
Brahmachari – one who practices brahmacharya
Brahmacharya – to move, learn and live in the higher reality;
    redirection of sexual energy towards spiritual or meditative
    experience sexual abstinence
Brahmacharya ashrama – first stage of life; childhood and
    student life up to 25 years
Brahmamuhurta – 4–6 a.m.; most appropriate time for sadhana
Brahman – expanding consciousness; vedantic term for the
    absolute reality
Brahmana – one who belongs to the Brahmin caste; one who
    constantly endeavours to realize Brahman
Brahmanas – integral part of the Vedas which elucidate the
    path of ritual to be followed by householders
Brahmayajna – study of scriptures; one of the five maha yajnas
Brahmin – priest caste; one of the four varna or divisions of
    the caste system of India
Brihaspati – guru of the devas or gods
Bruhmadhya – eyebrow centre
Chadar – upper cloth
Chakra – major psychic centre or nerve plexus; literally, 'wheel'
Chandala – untouchable
Chappal – sandals
Chatuh sampradaya – four schools of Vaishnavism
Chaturmas – four months of the rainy season
Chetana – consciousness
Chidagni – flame of consciousness

Chimta – tongs
Chinamasta – divine energy of the supreme
Chinmaya – supreme intelligence
Chitabhoomi – cremation ground
Chitta – individual consciousness, including the subconscious and unconscious layers of mind; memory, thinking, concentration, attention, enquiry
Chitta shuddhi – purification of chitta
Dacoit – bandit
Dama – one of the six-fold virtues; sensory restraint
Damaru – drum of Shiva
Danda – stick or staff
Dargha – Moslem grave
Darshan – glimpse; vision; being in the presence of a holy being; seeing God or an image of God
Darshanarthi – one desirous of darshan
Dashnami sampradaya – ten orders of sannyasa; the vedic Shaiva tradition established by Adi Shankaracharya
Dehadhyasa – identification with the body
Devadvishah – haters of light
Devakulya – another name of Ganga
Devendra – king of the gods
Devi – goddess; female deity
Dharana – concentration; sixth stage of raja yoga
Dharitri – 'she who holds'; name for the earth
Dharma – fulfilling one's role in life; duty; righteousness; the highest dharma is to recognize the truth in one's own heart
Dhuni – sadhana fire
Dhyana – meditation; seventh stage of raja yoga
Digvijay – victory (over all directions)
Diksha – initiation
Divya drishti – divine sight
Dukha – suffering, pain
Dwaitadwaita – dualistic monism
Ekagrata – one-pointedness
Ekavira – single, invincible force
Gada – mace

450

Gandharva – celestials who engage in musical arts, dancing and singing

Garbha – womb

Garbha griha – most sacred room; sanctum sanctorum

Gaushala – cowshed

Gayatri – Vedic goddess; female counterpart of the sun

Gayatri mantra – Vedic mantra of 24 syllables; a sacred mantra suitable for everyone

Gayatri pravesha – entering into the spirit of the Gayatri mantra

Ghat – riverbank for bathing, washing, cremation

Giri – hill

Gokul – birthplace of Krishna near Vrindavan

Gopi chandan – clay brought from sacred places

Gotra – spiritual lineage

Grihastha – second stage of life; householder, married life from 25 to 50 years

Grihasthi – householder

Grihini – housewife

Guna – quality or attribute of nature

Guru – 'dispeller of darkness'; a spiritual teacher or master who has attained oneness with God

Guru bhai – disciples of the same guru; guru brother

Guru bhakta – devotee of the guru

Gurukul – educational system of ancient India where children lived in the ashram or family of the guru and were taught by the guru

Guruseva – service to the guru

Gurutwam – quality of the guru

Hamsa – swan; stage of sannyasa; the natural vibration of the self, which occurs spontaneously with each outgoing and incoming breath

Hamsa vidya – the ability to discriminate between real and unreal

Homa – sacrificial fire which symbolizes the divine light on earth

Homa dhenus – sacred cows owned by rishis whose milk was used to make the ghee for the sacrificial offerings

Homa dhuni – sacrificial fire

Iccha bhojanam – food requested by a guest

Ida nadi – a major pranic channel in the body; conductor of the passive aspect of prana manifesting as mental force; lunar force or chitta shakti; governs the manifest subtle dimension

Indra nila – sapphire

Ishta devata – personal deity

Jagrat – waking consciousness

Jambha – eating; biting; a portion

Jambhaka – one who kills; destroys; power presiding over sensory activities, lower consciousness

Japa – repetition of mantra

Jata mandala – matted locks coiled on top of the head

Jhola – shoulder bag

Jignasu sannyasa – aspirant; spiritual seeker; preliminary stage of sannyasa

Jivanmukta – soul who is liberated while living

Jivatma – individual soul

Jnana – knowledge; wisdom

Jnana chakshu – eye of wisdom

Jnanakanda – section of the Vedas comprised of Upanishadic texts which elucidate the path and the experience of absolute knowledge

Jyoti mandir – temple of light

Kaivalya – final liberation

Kala – time; period; age; era

Kalagni – eternal fire

Kalash – copper vessel

Kama – emotional fulfilment

Kamandalam – water-pot carried by wandering sannyasins

Kapalika – tantric sect whose practices involve the use of skulls

Karma – cause and effect; action and result; destiny, which is caused by past actions

Karmakanda – Vedic text on ritual

Karma sannyasa – householder sannyasa; renunciation combined with duty

Karma yoga – yogic path of selfless service
Karobari – administrator or director of the akhara or alakh bara
Kartritva – doership
Karya samiti – working committee for selection of initiates for Naga sannyasa
Katisutra – waist thread
Kaupeen – loin cloth
Kaya kalpa – intensive purification practice
Kharau – wooden sandals
Khechari mudra – 'drinking the nectar'; tongue lock
Kirtan – singing of God's name
Klesha – afflictions of worldly life; the source of all suffering
Krodha – anger
Kshatriya – one of the four divisions of the caste system in India; warrior; one who protects others from injury
Kshetra – place; region; area; sacred spot; place of pilgrimage; field
Kumaras – the mental sons of Brahma, the creator
Kumbha mela – huge bathing festivals held at certain auspicious places on the Ganga river every few years
Kundala kesha – curly-haired
Kurta – shirt
Kutichak – hut dweller; stage of sannyasa
Kutir, kutiya – small hut; simple dwelling
Lobha – greed, avarice; covetousness
Lokeshana – attachment to one's place or to one's past, attachment to anything expected from people or this world
Mada – arrogance; passion; intoxication
Madhukari – alms in the form of cooked food
Maha – great; mighty; powerful; noble
Mahabharata – epic poem of ancient India in Sanskrit, composed by Sage Vyasa recounting the great war between the Pandava and Kaurava princes
Mahant – head of a math
Mahatma – great soul; saint; sage
Mahavakyas – four great saying of Vedanta: (i) Prajnanam Brahma (consciousness is Brahman), (ii) Aham Brahma Asmi

(I am Brahma), (iii) Tat Twam Asi (Thou are That), (iv) Ayam Brahma Asmi (I am Brahma)

Manas putra – mentally conceived

Manes – souls of departed ancestors

Manu – the first law-giver; the primogenitor of the human race

Marga Shirsha – ninth month of Hindu year

Marhi – recruiting centre for Naga sect

Marjara nyaya – kitten theory

Markat nyaya – monkey theory

Math – monastery; temple

Maya – illusion; cause of the phenomenal world; term used in Vedanta for the power which veils the true nature of the Self and projects the experience of multiplicity and separation from God

Mimamsa – one of the six darshana or systems of Vedic philosophy, elucidating the path of karma or ritual; divided into two sections: Poorva Mimamsa (questions) and Uttar Mimamsa (answers)

Moha – infatuation, attachment

Moksha – liberation from the cycle of birth, death and rebirth

Mouna – silence

Mudra – literally means 'gesture'; physical, mental and psychic attitude expressing and channelling cosmic energy; psychophysiological posture, movement or attitude; a movement or position made or taken by the fingers or limbs in meditation

Mumukshutva – intense desire for liberation

Mundan – shaving of the head

Muni – one who contemplates or who has conquered the mind ascetic; hermit

Nada – subtle sound vibration which is heard in the meditative state

Nada prakasha – light which emanates from the primordial sound vibration

Nag Nath – emanation of Shiva in the form of a serpent

Naga – militant sannyasa sect

Nandini – sacred cow of Sage Vashishtha

454

Narasimha – man/lion; an incarnation of Vishnu

Narayana – name of Vishnu

Nath – Lord, master

Navaratri anushthana – special sadhana done during the nine day festival of Durga

Niranjana – stainless; one who is beyond maya or worldly defects

Nirguna – without attributes

Nishkam – selfless; without desire

Nishkama sevak – selfless servant

Nitya karma – daily rituals; eternal actions

Nivritti marga – path of introversion, renunciation, without vrittis

Niyamas – five observances or rules of personal discipline, laid down by Patanjali to help render the mind tranquil in preparation for meditation

Nriyajna – service and care of a guest

Nyaya – one of the six darshana or systems of Indian philosophy; logic; recognition of real spiritual experience by the omniscient mind, that is all-encompassing and all-pervading

Padma – lotus

Padmasana – lotus posture

Paduka – sandals worn by the guru; pooja is performed to them and they are objects of the highest veneration

Padya – water offered for washing the feet

Pakhand – hypocrisy, false behaviour

Pancha bhoota – five elements

Pancha prana – five pranas located in the physical body

Panchagni vidya – knowledge of the five fires

Pania pagar – plentiful water

Paramahamsa – 'supreme swan'; the highest class of sannyasins; one who controls or subdues the passions

Paramahamsa sannyasa – having completed their work, paramahamsa sannyasins live in the Alakh bara where they are able to devote themselves totally to sadhana, and thus approach the final goal of moksha or self-liberation

Paramarthika – spiritual aspects
Paramatma – cosmic soul; supreme self
Parameshwara – supreme being
Paramguru – supreme guru
Parampara – tradition
Paravairagya – absence of attachment in any form
Parikrama – circumambulation
Parivrajaka – wandering religious mendicant; ascetic
Parivrajna – wandering
Parvata – mountain
Parvati – 'daughter of the mountains' consort of Shiva and daughter of the king of the Himalayas; a name for the Universal Mother or Shakti
Patanjali – great sage and compiler of the famous Yoga Sutras, the exposition of one of the six orthodox philosophies of India, and the authoritative text of the path of raja yoga
Pativratya – devotion of wife towards her husband
Pavitra – sanctity
Pindadan – riceballs
Pingala nadi – a major pranic channel in the body which conducts the dynamic pranic force manifesting as prana shakti
Pitriyajna – offering made to the ancestors
Pooja – rites; worship
Poojari – officiating priest at religious ceremony
Poornahuti – final oblation or offering; consummation
Prajapatya – four penances performed by an aspirant before sannyasa initiation
Prajnanam Brahma – one of the four great statements of Vedanta meaning, 'Knowledge is Brahman'
Prakriti – manifest and unmanifest nature; cosmic energy
Prana – energy; the vital life-sustaining force of both the individual body and the universe
Pranam – reverential salutation; bowing respectfully
Pranava – the mantra Om; (Aum)
Pranayama – expansion of the range of vital energy
Prapanchika – worldly aspects

Prarabdha karma – actions already performed which, like arrows shot from the bow, cannot be retrieved; fixed, unalterable

Prasadam – blessed or divine gift; often refers to food that has first been offered to God and is thus blessed; full of grace

Pravritti marga – path of extroversion

Prayaschitta – atonement for one's acts of unawareness during all births

Punyakshetram – holy place

Puranas – 'ancient legends'; eighteen sacred books by Sage Vyasa containing stories, legends and hymns about the creation of the universe, the incarnations of God, the teachings of various deities, and the spiritual legacies of ancient sages and kings

Purashcharana – an observance consisting of the repetition of mantras

Puri – town; city

Purusha – consciousness

Purusha Sukta – hymn of the Rig Veda

Purushartha – human attainment; the four goals to be fulfilled in life: artha (wealth), kama (love), dharma (duty), and moksha (liberation)

Putramohan – blind affection for one's children

Putreshana – one's children; one's future

Raga – attraction

Raja – royal; king

Raja rishi – royal sage, king who renounced his kingdom to become a rishi

Raja yoga – the yoga of awakening psychic awareness and faculties through meditation; according to Patanjali's Yoga Sutras it includes concentration and meditation

Rajoguna – one of the three gunas; quality of rajas; mode of activity, creativity, dynamism

Raksha – protection

Rakshasha – demon

Ramanuja – reformer of Vaishnavism

Ramayana – epic Sanskrit poem of ancient India by Sage

Valmiki which recounts the life and exploits of Rama, the seventh incarnation of Vishnu

Ramta panch – wandering committee of sannyasins; part of the akhara structure

Rig Veda – oldest of the four Vedic texts

Rishi – seer; realized sage; one who meditates on the self

Rishi patni – wife of a rishi

Rukmini – consort of Krishna

Sadhaka – aspirant

Sadhana – spiritual practice done regularly for attainment of inner experience and self-realization

Sadhu – holy man; monk or ascetic

Sagara – sea; ocean

Saguna – with form or attribute; the personal aspect of God

Sahasrara chakra – abode of Shiva or superconsciousness; 'the thousand petal lotus'; highest chakra or psychic centre, which symbolizes the threshold between the psychic and spiritual realms, located at the crown of the head

Sai – mother

Sakshatkara – direct experience of the absolute

Sakshi – eternal witness or observer

Sakshi bhava – awareness; attitude of witness

Sakyamuni – one of Buddha's names

Sama Veda – second of four Vedic texts

Samadhana – one of the six-fold virtues; mental equilibrium; constant concentration on reality

Samadhi – culmination of meditation; state of unity with the object of meditation and universal consciousness

Samatwam – equipoise

Samhita – collection of hymns, prayers and mantras; oldest part of the Vedas

Samkhya – one of the six darshana or systems of Vedic philosophy; 'numbers'; spiritual science dealing with the twenty-four attributes of human nature

Sampradaya – tradition

Samsara – illusory world; manifest gross world; cycle of birth, death and rebirth; the world of becoming

Samskara – mental impressions of past actions or thoughts which remain in the unconscious

Sanatan – eternal

Sanatan dharma – system of eternal values

Sanatani – follower of sanatan dharma

Sanchit – stored, collected karma

Sandhya – rite performed by rishis; early morning or evening twilight

Sankalpa – resolve; resolution

Sankirtan – singing of God's name

Sannyasa – complete renunciation; fourth stage of life in which, after fulfilling one's worldly obligations, one is free to pursue the goal of self-realization

Sannyasa ashrama – fourth stage of life from 75 years onwards; total renunciation

Sannyasin – renunciate

Santan – children

Santosha – contentment

Saptapadi – 'seven steps'; ritual of the marriage ceremony

Saptodharini – 'seven stories' narrated by Dattatreya to Kartaveerya to explain yoga

Saraswati – goddess of knowledge; name of one of the ten orders of sannyasa formed by Shankaracharya

Sarva sakshin – eternal witness; witness of everything

Satguru – true guru; inner guru

Satisutra – thread worn around the waist

Satsang – spiritual gathering for discussion pertaining to truth

Sattoguna – one of the three gunas; quality of harmony, equilibrium, purity and luminosity

Saundarya Lahari – devotional Sanskrit hymn to Shakti by Adi Shankaracharya

Seva – service; work performed with attitude of non-doership

Shad sampatti – the six-fold virtues: sama (equanimity), dama (self-control), uparati (sensory withdrawal), titiksha (endurance), shraddha (faith), and samadhana (the constant concentration on reality)

Shaivism – sect where Shiva is worshipped as the supreme reality

Shakti pitha – place where Shakti is worshipped

Shankaracharya – an enlightened sage who lived from 788–820 AD and established the Dashnami Order of Sannyasa

Shankha – conch

Shanti – peace; tranquillity; silence; calm

Shasti – force behind Parashurama, sixth avatar of Vishnu

Shastra – scripture

Shastradhari – scripture holder

Shikha sutra sannyasa – the sadhaka shaves the tuft of hair and removes the sacred thread, symbols of caste, showing his readiness to go beyond all barriers towards consciousness that is unlimited and unconditioned

Shiva – 'auspicious'; the first yogi; supreme deity of the Hindu trinity representing God as the destroyer of ignorance; cosmic consciousness

Shiva priya – lover of Shiva, the auspicious

Shivoham – 'I am Shiva'

Shmashan bhoomi – burial ground

Shodashi pooja – tantric ritual

Shoonya – void

Shraaddha – commemorative religious rites

Shraddha – faith; one of the six-fold virtues

Shrotriya – one who guides the performance of a yajna

Shrutis – 'what has been heard'; Indian scriptures

Shuddhadwaita – philosophy of pure monism

Shudra – one of the four varna or divisions of the caste system in India; one whose consciousness is least developed, due to which he remains in ignorance, causing him to weep and mourn

Shukla dhyana – meditation on pure, white light

Siddha – perfected yogi; one who has attained enlightenment

Siddhi – paranormal or supernormal power

Sloka – verse; hymn of praise

Smriti – 'memory'; Vedic texts transmitted by memory; one of the five vrittis

Soma – amrit; nectar; the moon; creeper yielding an intoxicating juice which was drunk at sacrifices

460

Sri Panch – governing body in the akhara system; consisting of five persons, representing Brahma, Vishnu, Shiva, Shakti, and Ganesha

Sthal – place; location; site; region

Sufi – mystic of the Islam religion

Sushumna nadi – central nadi or channel in the spine which conducts the kundalini or spiritual force

Sushupti – deep sleep or unconscious state

Swadhyaya – self-study

Swami – master of the self; term of a respectful address for a sannyasin

Swapna – dreaming or subconscious state

Swayamvara – selection of husband in public ceremony

Tamoguna – one of the three gunas; quality of inertia, stability, stillness

Tantra – most ancient universal culture which deals with transcendence of human nature from the present level of evolution and understanding to transcendental knowledge, experience and awareness; esoteric spiritual discipline in which, Shakti, the creative power of the universe, is worshipped as the Divine Mother

Tapasvin – one who practises tapasya; an ascetic

Tapasya – austerity; the experience of heat which occurs during the process of practising yoga; it is said that this heat or 'fire of yoga' burns up all the impurities that lie between the seeker and the experience of the truth

Tapovan – forest suitable for tapas

Tarpana – rite performed by rishis; libation of water to deceased ancestors

Tat Twam Asi – 'Thou art That'; one of the four mahavakyas; 'great statements' from the Upanishads; it expresses the identity of the individual self with the Supreme Self

Tattwa – element

Tattwa jnana – knowledge of the elements

Thanapati – supervisor

Theri – female renunciate

Tirtha – sacred place

Tirthasthana – holy places
Titiksha – endurance; one of the six-fold virtues
Traipada – mantra Aum
Tribanda – three bamboo sticks tied together
Tripura rahasyam – secrets of the three lokas or tripura sundari
Tripura sundari – highest truth; goddess
Trishna – internal craving
Turiya – fourth dimension of consciousness; superconsciousness; the state of samadhi
Turiyatita – 'beyond the fetters of nature'; stage of sannyasa
Tyaga – renunciation; leaving; abandonment; relinquishment
Tyaga abhimana – pride of renunciation
Tyagi – one who has renounced
Upadesh – spiritual advice
Upanayana – sacred thread ritual
Upanishads – 'sitting close to'; ancient Vedic texts containing intimate dialogues and discussions between guru and disciple on the nature of the absolute and the path leading towards it
Uparati – one of six-fold virtues; desisting from worldliness
Upasana – personalized form of worship
Vairagi – sannyasins of the Vaishnava Ramananda sampradaya
Vairagya – non-attachment; dispassion
Vairagya sannyasa – one of the stages of sannyasa where one is detached and indifferent to worldly pleasures from an early age
Vaishnavism – sect that reveres incarnations of Vishnu as the supreme reality
Vaishya – one of the four varna or divisions of the caste system in India; one who undertakes the responsibility to care for society
Vanam – forest
Vanaprastha ashrama – third stage of life from 50–75 years; retirement from worldly life
Varenyatvat – devout
Varna – colour; caste

Varnashrama – caste system in India; the four ashramas or stages of life through which one moves

Vasanas – desires that are the driving force behind every thought and action in life

Vashishtha – celebrated sage or seer, family priest of the solar race of kings and the author of several Vedic hymns

Vastra – garment; cloth; textile; apparel

Vayu – god of the wind

Vedanta – 'end of perceivable knowledge'; philosophy of realization of Brahman; the mind experiencing its outer limits; one of the six orthodox schools of Indian philosophy

Vedas – oldest literature revealed to sages and seers in India, expressing the knowledge of the whole universe; the four ancient Hindu scriptures, Rig Veda, Yajur Veda, Sama Veda and Atharva Veda

Vedi – altar; platform

Vibhooti – sacred ash; spiritual power

Vibhu – glorious; gracious

Videhamukti – state beyond body consciousness

Vidya – higher knowledge; discipline; skill

Vihara – monastic centre; wandering; roaming

Viraja – renunciation; detachment

Virajahoma – offering oblations to the fire; symbolic death rite

Vishishtadwaita – philosophy of qualified monism which refutes Shankaracharya's philosophy of Adwaita or monism; an offshoot of Adwaita Vedanta

Vishnu – Vedic deity; preserver of the universe in the Hindu trinity; supreme consciousness; it is said that during times of wickedness, Lord Vishnu incarnates to protect human beings and re-establish righteousness

Vishwadevas – gods of the universe

Vishwaguru – guru of the universe

Vitteshana – desire for material possessions; security

Viveka – discrimination; judgement

Vrat – vow; pledge; religious observance

Vyakta – manifest; seen

Vyakta prakriti – manifest nature
Yajamana – chief performer of the yajna
Yajna – sacrifice
Yajur Veda – third of the four Vedas; 'knowledge of sacrifice'
Yama – five self-restraints or rules of conduct designed to remove emotional disorders in preparation for higher yoga practices
Yama – god of death
Yantra – geometric symbol designed for concentration to unleash the hidden potential within the consciousness
Yati – Dravidian ascetics; earliest sannyasins
Yatra – pilgrimage; journey; trip; tour
Yoga mitra mandal – yoga fellowship
Yoga patta – name given to aspirant when initiated; identity
Yogin – one who practises yoga

Index

Akhara 60–62
Alakh Bara 63–65
Anger 143
Ashrama system 13–16, 130–131
Atura sannyasa 31
Avadhootopanishad 415–429

Bhikshukopanishad 411–414
Brahmacharya 129–134

Caste system 22–26
Code of conduct 91–102

Dashnami Sampradaya 48–50, 56–59
Dattatreya 169; life of 180–209; lineage 210–226; murtis 227; twenty-four gurus 196–204
Dedication 109–110
Desire 123–124, 128
Diet 121–127
Discipleship 204–205

Earth 197–198

Gunas 26, 124–125
Guru 112–120
Gurukul sannyasa 87

Honesty 104
Humility 104

Independence 106–107

Jignasu sannyasa 86, 92, 103–105

Jnana sannyasa 30
Jnana-vairagya sannyasa 30, 87

Karma sannyasa 86–87, 94–98, 105–107
Karma yoga 93–94, 96–97, 143
Kleshas 9
Kundikopanishad 398–410

Maths established by Shankara 251
Moon 199
Munis 21
Murtis of Dattatreya 227

Nirvanopanishad and commentary 345–397

Obedience 109, 295–296

Paramahamsa sannyasa 87–88
Paramahamsaparivrajaka Upanishad 430–445
Patience 105
Perseverance 104
Poorna sannyasa 98–102

Qualities needed for sannyasa 88–90, 103–111, 253–254, 273–274, 276–277

Renunciation 276–277, 296, 398–410
Rishis 10–11, 17–21
Rites 33–37, 78, 228

465

Sannyasa, atura sannyasa 31;
gurukul sannyasa 87; jignasu
sannyasa 86, 92–94, 103–105;
jnana sannyasa 30; jnana-
vairagya sannyasa 30, 87; karma
sannyasa 86–87, 94–98, 105–
107; paramahamsa sannyasa
279–341; poorna sannyasa 98–
102; qualities needed for
sannyasa 88–90, 103–111, 253–
254, 273–274; stages of sannyasa
38–42, 86–88, 411–416; traditional rules 43–46; vairagya
sannyasa 29–30, 108–111;
vidvat sannyasa 31; vividisha
sannyasa 31; women and
sannyasa 145–149
Self-control 103–104, 105, 135–
139
Self-observation 106
Shaivism 47–48
Shankaracharya, life of 2, 48, 51–
55, 231–250; maths established
by 251; views on sannyasa 251–
255
Shaktism 49–50
Spiritual diary 140–144

Sri Panch Dashnam Parama-
hamsa Alakh Bara 64–65
Stages of sannyasa 38–42, 86–88,
411–414
Suppression 135–139
Surrender 110
Swami Satyananda 279–341
Swami Sivananda 256–278

Tirtha kshetram 226–227
Transmission 113–114
Truthfulness 104
Twenty-four gurus of Dattatreya
196–204

Vairagya 28–29, 106–107, 143,
273
Vairagya sannyasa 29–30, 108–
111
Vaishnavism 66–70
Vedanta 277–278
Vidvat sannyasa 31
Viveka 45
Vividisha sannyasa 30

Women and sannyasa 145–149
Women saints 150–165

SYNOPSIS OF THE LIFE OF
SWAMI SATYANANDA SARASWATI

Swami Satyananda Saraswati was born in 1923 at Almora (Uttaranchal) into a family of farmers. His ancestors were warriors and many of his kith and kin down the line, including his father, served in the army and police force.

However, it became evident that Sri Swamiji had a different bent of mind, as he began to have spiritual experiences at the age of six, when his awareness spontaneously left the body and he saw himself lying motionless on the floor. Many saints and sadhus blessed him and reassured his parents that he had a very developed awareness. This experience of disembodied awareness continued, which led him to many saints of that time such as Anandamayi Ma. Sri Swamiji also met a tantric bhairavi, Sukhman Giri, who gave him shaktipat and directed him to find a guru in order to stabilize his spiritual experiences.

In 1943, at the age of 20, he renounced his home and went in search of a guru. This search ultimately led him to Swami Sivananda Saraswati at Rishikesh, who initiated him into the Dashnam Order of Sannyasa on 12th September 1947 on the banks of the Ganges and gave him the name Swami Satyananda Saraswati.

In those early years at Rishikesh, Sri Swamiji immersed himself in guru seva. At that time the ashram was still in its infancy and even the basic amenities such as buildings and toilets were absent. The forests surrounding the small ashram were infested with snakes, scorpions, mosquitoes, monkeys and even tigers. The ashram work too was heavy and hard, requiring Sri Swamiji to toil like a labourer carrying bucket loads of water from the Ganga up to the ashram and digging canals from the high mountain streams down to the ashram many kilometres away in order to store water for constructing the ashram.

Rishikesh was then a small town and all the ashram requirements had to be brought by foot from far away. In addition there were varied duties, including the daily pooja at Vishwanath

Mandir, for which Sri Swamiji would go into the dense forests to collect bael leaves. If anyone fell sick there was no medical care and no one to attend to them. All the sannyasins had to go out for bhiksha or alms as the ashram did not have a mess or kitchen.

Of that glorious time when he lived and served his guru, Sri Swamiji says that it was a period of total communion and surrender to the guru tattwa, whereby he felt that just to hear, speak or see Swami Sivananda was yoga. But most of all his guru's words rang true, for through this dedication and spirit of nishkama seva he gained an enlightened understanding of the secrets of spiritual life and became an authority on Yoga, Tantra, Vedanta, Samkhya and kundalini yoga. Swami Sivananda said of Swami Satyananda, "Few would exhibit such intense vairagya at such an early age. Swami Satyananda is full of Nachiketa vairagya."

Although he had a photographic memory and a keen intellect, and his guru described him as a versatile genius, Swami Satyananda's learning did not come from books and study in the ashram. His knowledge unfolded from within through his untiring seva as well as his abiding faith and love for Swami Sivananda, who told him, "Work hard and you will be purified. You do not have to search for the light, the light will unfold from within you."

In 1956, after spending twelve years in guru seva, Swami Satyananda set out as a wanderer (parivrajaka). Before his departure Swami Sivananda taught him kriya yoga and gave him the mission to "spread yoga from door to door and shore to shore".

As a wandering sannyasin, Swami Satyananda travelled extensively by foot, car, train and sometimes even by camel throughout India, Afghanistan, Burma, Nepal, Tibet, Ceylon and the entire Asian subcontinent. During his sojourns, he met people from all stratas of society and began formulating his ideas on how to spread the yogic techniques. Although his formal education and spiritual tradition was that of Vedanta, the task of disseminating yoga became his movement.

His mission unfolded before him in 1956 when he founded the International Yoga Fellowship Movement with the aim of creating a global fraternity of yoga. Because his mission was revealed to him at Munger, Bihar, he established the Bihar School of Yoga in Munger. Before long his teachings were rapidly spreading throughout the world. From 1963 to 1983, Swami Satyananda took yoga to each and every corner of the world, to people of every caste, creed, religion and nationality. He guided millions of seekers in all continents and established centres and ashrams in different countries.

His frequent travels took him to Australia, New Zealand, Japan, China, the Philippines, Hong Kong, Malaysia, Thailand, Singapore, USA, England, Ireland, France, Italy, Germany, Switzerland, Denmark, Sweden, Yugoslavia, Poland, Hungary, Bulgaria, Slovenia, Russia, Czechoslovakia, Greece, Saudi Arabia, Kuwait, Bahrain, Dubai, Iraq, Iran, Pakistan, Afghanistan, Colombia, Brazil, Uruguay, Chile, Argentina, Santo Domingo, Puerto Rico, Sudan, Egypt, Nairobi, Ghana, Mauritius, Alaska and Iceland. One can easily say that Sri Swamiji hoisted the flag of yoga in every nook and cranny of the world.

Nowhere did he face opposition, resistance or criticism. His way was unique. Well-versed in all religions and scriptures, he incorporated their wisdom with such a natural flair that people of all faiths were drawn to him. His teaching was not just confined to yoga but covered the wisdom of many millenniums.

Sri Swamiji brought to light the knowledge of Tantra, the mother of all philosophies, the sublime truths of Vedanta, the Upanishads and Puranas, Buddhism, Jainism, Sikhism, Zoroastrianism, Islam and Christianity, including modern scientific analysis of matter and creation. He interpreted, explained and gave precise, accurate and systematic explanations of the ancient systems of Tantra and Yoga, revealing practices hitherto unknown.

It can be said that Sri Swamiji was a pioneer in the field of yoga because his presentation had a novelty and freshness. Ajapa japa, antar mouna, pawanmuktasana, kriya yoga and prana vidya are just some of the practices which he introduced in such a methodical and simple manner that it became possible for everyone to delve into this valuable and hitherto inaccessible science for their physical, mental, emotional and spiritual development.

Yoga nidra was Sri Swamiji's interpretation of the tantric system of nyasa. With his deep insight into this knowledge, he was able to realize the potential of this practice of nyasa in a manner which gave it a practical utility for each and every individual, rather than just remaining a prerequisite for worship. Yoga nidra is but one example of his acumen and penetrating insight into the ancient systems.

Sri Swamiji's outlook was inspiring, uplifting as well as in-depth and penetrating. Yet his language and explanations were always simple and easy to comprehend. During this period he authored over eighty books on yoga and tantra which, due to their authenticity, are accepted as textbooks in schools and universities throughout the world. These books have been translated into Italian, German, Spanish, Russian, Yugoslavian, Chinese, French, Greek, Iranian and most other prominent languages of the world.

People took to his ideas and spiritual seekers of all faiths and nationalities flocked to him. He initiated thousands into mantra and sannyasa, sowing in them the seed to live the divine life. He exhibited tremendous zeal and energy in spreading the light of yoga, and in the short span of twenty years Sri Swamiji fulfilled the mandate of his guru.

By 1983, Bihar School of Yoga was well established and recognized throughout the world as a reputed and authentic centre for learning yoga and the spiritual sciences. More than that, yoga had moved out of the caves of hermits and ascetics into the mainstream of society. Whether in hospitals, jails, schools, colleges, business houses, the sporting and fashion arenas, the army or navy, yoga was in demand. Professionals such as lawyers, engineers, doctors, business magnates and professors were incorporating yoga into their lives. So too were the masses. Yoga had become a household word.

Now, at the peak of his accomplishment, having fulfilled his guru's wish, Swami Satyananda renounced all that he created and appointed his successor, Swami Niranjanananda, to continue the work.

In 1988 Sri Swamiji renounced disciples, establishments and institutions, and departed from Munger, never to return again, on a pilgrimage through the siddha teerthas of India, as a mendicant, without any personal belongings or assistance from the ashrams or institutions he had founded.

At Trayambakeshwar, the jyotir linga of Lord Mrityunjaya, his ishta devata, he renounced his garb and lived as an avadhoota, during which time his future place of abode and sadhana were revealed to him.

According to the mandate of his ishta devata, which was revealed to him at the source of the Godavari river near Neel Parbat at Trayambakeshwar (Maharashtra), Swami Satyananda came to the cremation ground of Sati in 1989, and took up residence in Rikhia, on the outskirts of Baba Baidyanath Dham in Deoghar (Jharkhand).

Swami Satyananda has been residing at Rikhia since September 1989. During this period he has undertaken long and arduous sadhanas such as Panchagni and Ashtottar-shat-laksh (108 lakh) mantra purascharana. Here he entered the lifestyle of the Paramahamsas who do not work for their flock and mission alone but have a universal vision. He does not associate with any institutions, nor does he give diksha, upadesh or receive dakshina, but remains in seclusion and sadhana, only on rare occasions coming out to give darshan to devotees who are always yearning for a glimpse of him.

INTERNATIONAL YOGA FELLOWSHIP MOVEMENT (IYFM)

The IYFM is a charitable and philosophical movement founded by Swami Satyananda at Rajnandgaon in 1956 to disseminate the yogic tradition throughout the world. It forms the medium to convey the teachings of Swami Satyananda through its affiliated centres around the world. Swami Niranjanananda is the first Paramacharya of the International Yoga Fellowship Movement.

The IYFM provides guidance, systematized yoga training programs and sets teaching standards for all the affiliated yoga teachers, centres and ashrams. A Yoga Charter to consolidate and unify the humanitarian efforts of all sannyasin disciples, yoga teachers, spiritual seekers and well-wishers was introduced during the World Yoga Convention in 1993. Affiliation to this Yoga Charter enables the person to become a messenger of goodwill and peace in the world, through active involvement in various far-reaching yoga-related projects.

BIHAR SCHOOL OF YOGA (BSY)

The Bihar School of Yoga is a charitable and educational institution founded by Swami Satyananda at Munger in 1963, with the aim of imparting yogic training to all nationalities and to provide a focal point for a mass return to the ancient science of yoga. The Chief Patron of Bihar School of Yoga is Swami Niranjanananda. The original school, Sivanandashram, is the centre for the Munger locality. Ganga Darshan, the new school established in 1981, is situated on a historic hill with panoramic views of the river Ganges.

Yoga Health Management, Teacher Training, Sadhana, Kriya Yoga and other specialized courses are held throughout the year. BSY is also renowned for its sannyasa training and the initiation of female and foreign sannyasins.

BSY provides trained sannyasins and teachers for conducting yoga conventions, seminars and lectures tours around the world. It also contains a comprehensive research library and scientific research centre.

SIVANANDA MATH (SM)

Sivananda Math is a social and charitable institution founded by Swami Satyananda at Munger in 1984, in memory of his guru, Swami Sivananda Saraswati of Rishikesh. The Head Office is now situated at Rikhia in Deoghar district, Jharkhand. Swami Niranjanananda is the Chief Patron.

Sivananda Math aims to facilitate the growth of the weaker and underprivileged sections of society, especially rural communities. Its activities include: distribution of free scholarships, clothing, farm animals and food, the digging of tube-wells and construction of houses for the needy, assistance to farmers in ploughing and watering their fields. The Rikhia complex also houses a satellite dish system for providing global information to the villagers.

A medical clinic has been established for the provision of medical treatment, advice and education. Veterinary services are also provided. All services are provided free and universally to everyone, regardless of caste and creed.

YOGA RESEARCH FOUNDATION (YRF)

The Yoga Research Foundation is a scientific, research-oriented institution founded by Swami Satyananda at Munger in 1984. Swami Niranjanananda is the Chief Patron of the foundation.

YRF aims to provide an accurate assessment of the practices of different branches of yoga within a scientific framework, and to establish yoga as an essential science for the development of mankind. At present the foundation is working on projects in the areas of fundamental research and clinical research. It is also studying the effects of yoga on proficiency improvement in various social projects, e.g. army, prisoners, children. These projects are being carried out in affiliated centres worldwide.

YRF's future plans include literary, scriptural, medical and scientific investigations into other little-known aspects of yoga for physical health, mental well-being and spiritual upliftment.

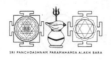

SRI PANCHDASHNAM PARAMAHAMSA ALAKH BARA (PPAB)

Sri Panchdashnam Paramahamsa Alakh Bara was established in 1990 by Swami Satyananda at Rikhia, Deoghar, Jharkhand. It is a charitable, educational and non-profit making institution aiming to uphold and propagate the highest tradition of sannyasa, namely vairagya (dispassion), tyaga (renunciation) and tapasya (austerity). It propounds the tapovan style of living adopted by the rishis and munis of the vedic era and is intended only for sannyasins, renunciates, ascetics, tapasvis and paramahamsas. The Alakh Bara does not conduct any activities such as yoga teaching or preaching of any religion or religious concepts. The guidelines set down for the Alakh Bara are based on the classical vedic tradition of sadhana, tapasya and swadhyaya, or atma chintan.

Swami Satyananda, who resides permanently at the Alakh Bara, has performed the Panchagni Vidya and other vedic sadhanas, thus paving the way for future paramahamsas to uphold their tradition.

BIHAR YOGA BHARATI (BYB)

Bihar Yoga Bharati was founded by Swami Niranjanananda in 1994 as an educational and charitable institution for advanced studies in yogic sciences. It is the culmination of the vision of Swami Sivananda and Swami Satyananda. BYB is the world's first accredited institution wholly devoted to teaching yoga. A comprehensive yogic education is imparted with provision to grant certificates and diplomas in yogic studies. It offers a complete scientific and yogic education according to the needs of today, through the areas of Yoga Philosophy, Yoga Psychology, Applied Yogic Science and Yogic Ecology.

Residential courses of four months to one year are conducted in a gurukul environment, so that along with yoga education, the spirit of seva (selfless service), samarpan (dedication) and karuna (compassion) for humankind is also imbibed by the students.

YOGA PUBLICATIONS TRUST (YPT)

Yoga Publications Trust (YPT) was established by Swami Niranjanananda in 2000. It is an organization devoted to the dissemination and promotion of yogic and allied knowledge – psychology (ancient and modern), ecology, medicine, vedic, upanishadic, tantric darshanas, philosophies (Eastern and Western), mysticism and spirituality – nationally and internationally through the distribution of books, magazines, audio and video cassettes and multimedia.

YPT is primarily concerned with publishing textbooks in the areas of yoga philosophy, psychology and applied yogic science, research materials, practice texts and the inspiring talks of eminent spiritual personalities and authors aimed at the upliftment of humanity by means of the eternal yogic knowledge, lifestyle and practice.